MW00489365

THE TEMPLE OF SOLOMON

"Wasserman's lavishly illustrated narrative places the Temple of Solomon, with all its rich cultural and metaphorical meanings, in its proper literary context by returning to the original source of everything we know about it: The Bible. *The Temple of Solomon* is more than just the literary biography of a building, however; it is the anatomy of an icon that has shaped humanity's faith, history, art, literature, archaeology, fraternity, and so much more."

RICHARD KACZYNSKI, PH.D., author of *Perdurabo: The Life of Aleister Crowley*

"James Wasserman provides a great service by keeping the story of the Holy Temple firmly fixed in the narrative of the Scriptures. From the Books of Moses to the vision of the New Jerusalem in the Revelation of St. John the Divine, from the Crusades of the Knights Templar to the esoteric interpretations of Freemasonry, the evolution and meaning of the Temple is revealed in a rich matrix of history, hope, faith and personal spiritual experience. It is this latter component that gives this book such immediacy. With genuine passion, the author demonstrates that historicity—while vital to our knowledge of the subject—is far less important than coming to understand that the Holy of Holies lies within the human heart and that the Temple of God is the body of the flesh that beareth it."

J. DANIEL GUNTHER, author of *Initiation in the Aeon of the Child*

"In *The Temple of Solomon*, James Wasserman has delivered an inspired work on one of the most important subjects in the history of the spiritual tradition. This book is unique and timely, serving to bring the Judeo-Christian foundations of Western civilization into focus. *The Temple of Solomon* explores the spiritual and cultural origin of the threats to life and liberty we face in our lives today. The author brings clarity, wisdom, and personal experience to this work, which sets it apart from all other books on the subject."

DANIEL PINEDA, author of *The Book of Secrets*

"James Wasserman has done it again! In *The Temple of Solomon* he brings dusty, biblical history to life in an exciting but scholarly way and then fully meets the challenge of making it relevant to the modern reader. He shows that when the law of God is written in our hearts and flowing in our blood, our physical body temple becomes our spiritual temple. Well done!"

DR. BOB HIERONIMUS, author of *Founding Fathers, Secret Societies*
and host of 21st Century Radio

"While the Holy Ground of the Temple Mount has long been mentioned in esoteric literature, for far too long those who would claim to be its modern heirs have ignored and even been hostile to their Abrahamic origins. In the Holy of Holies it is said that God spoke to Israel; in these pages, it may be said that God is speaking to us, making it essential reading for students of the Western esoteric traditions."

MARK STAVISH, author of *Between the Gates* and
Freemasonry: Rituals, Symbols & History of the Secret Society

THE TEMPLE OF SOLOMON

From ANCIENT ISRAEL to SECRET SOCIETIES

JAMES WASSERMAN

Foreword by

PETER LEVENDA

*With contemporary photos of the Holy Land by
the author, Steven Brooke, and Vere Chappell*

INNER TRADITIONS
Rochester, Vermont • Toronto, Canada

Inner Traditions
One Park Street
Rochester, Vermont 05767
www.InnerTraditions.com

Copyright © 2011 by James Wasserman

All rights reserved. No part of this book may be reproduced or utilized,
in any form or by any means, electronic or mechanical, including photocopying, recording, or by
any information storage and retrieval system, without permission
in writing from the publisher.

Library of Congress Cataloging in Publication Data
Wasserman, James, 1948–
   The Temple of Solomon : from ancient Israel to secret societies / James Wasserman ;
foreword by Peter Levenda ; with contemporary photos of the Holy Land by the author, Steven
Brooke, and Vere Chappell.
     p. cm.
   Summary: "A fully illustrated history of the Temple of Solomon"—Provided by publisher.
   Includes bibliographical references and index.
   ISBN 978-1-59477-483-6 (cloth)
  1. Temple of Jerusalem (Jerusalem)—History. 2. Temple of Jerusalem (Jerusalem)—
In the Bible. 3. Temple of Jerusalem (Jerusalem)—Miscellanea. 4. Templars.
5. Freemasonry. I. Title.
   DS109.3.W37 2011
   296.4'91—dc23   2011027486

Printed and bound in India by Replika Press Pvt. Ltd.

10 9 8 7 6 5 4 3 2 1

Book design and typography by Studio 31 (www.studio31.com)
This book was typeset in Palatino

Permissions to reproduce the many works of art that appear in this volume
and their provenance are either given in the text of the captions or may be found
on pages 377–78.

The images on pages 39, 50, 115, 119, 122–23, 152–53, 218, and 304–5 are courtesy of Wikimedia
Commons, GNU Free Document License. For a copy of the GNUFDL,
go to http://en.wikipedia.org/wiki/GNU_Free_Documentation_license.

Photographs and illustrations not credited in the captions or in the permissions section on
pages 377–78 are by the author. All rights reserved.

Frontispiece: *Solomon Dedicates the Temple at Jerusalem*, by James Jacques Joseph Tissot,
ca. 1896–1902.

I<small>T CAME EVEN TO PASS</small>, as the trumpeters and singers were as one, to make

one sound to be heard in praising and thanking the L<small>ORD</small>; and when they lifted

up their voice with the trumpets and cymbals and instruments of musick, and

praised the L<small>ORD</small>, saying, "For He is good; for His mercy endureth for ever":

that then the house was filled with a cloud, even the house of the L<small>ORD</small>; So that

the priests could not stand to minister by reason of the cloud: for the glory of the

L<small>ORD</small> had filled the house of God.

II Chronicles 5:13–14

A <small>CAREFUL READING OF THE BIBLICAL TEXT</small> discloses a myriad of archival

and other details that can be correlated with the archaeological record and are

consistent with the framework of events presupposed by the narrative. Thus,

the skepticism of some modern historians, who argue that the biblical accounts

of the United Monarchy are fictional retroversions from a later time, seems

unwarranted.

The New Oxford Annotated Bible
Page 512, Essays

Medieval representation of the Temple of Solomon from a fifteenth-century French manuscript. The Ark of the Covenant may be seen through the open doorway.

This book is dedicated

to

DONALD WEISER

*Keeper of the Keys
to God's Library*

ACKNOWLEDGMENTS

My profound thanks to the many people who have helped with this book. First to Nancy Wasserman, whose artistic sensitivity and biblical research helped to bring alive the historical line drawings in accurate and elegant color. Her painting of the Queen of Sheba is exquisite. Most especially, I am grateful for her acceptance, assistance, encouragement, and cheerfulness as her husband's biblical obsession lasted far longer than either of us anticipated. Rachel Wasserman obviously inherited a portion of her mother's talent as her artwork shows. Rachel's transcriptions of the audio recordings of my conversations in Israel with Elie Ben-Meir were invaluable. My son, Satra, was the first person in our nuclear family to travel to Israel. His unexpected enthusiasm, and the depth of the spiritual experience he underwent there, opened my eyes to its importance in my own life.

Emma Gonzales again contributed her photographic expertise, helping me to learn how to record some of the most beautiful and interesting sites in the world. She also generously loaned me her camera and two lenses to accomplish this more professionally.

Steven Brooke, photographer par excellence whose magnificent images grace our second collaborative effort after *An Illustrated History of the Knights Templar,* freely shared his extensive knowledge of Jerusalem and introduced me to Walter Zanger. Steven's two brilliant biblical books, *Views of Jerusalem* and *Sacred Journey,* have been invaluable resources, both for their meticulous history of the region and their inspiring and exquisite imagery. Once again, Steven's technical expertise with retouching is the most advanced I have encountered in my career. As he did with *The Secrets of Masonic Washington,* he has redeemed many images that would otherwise have been lost, and improved the rest.

Vere Chappell shared his extensive image collection as he did for *An Illustrated History of the Knights Templar.* His tales of his own travels in the region were informative, and he introduced me to Herschel Shanks' exceptional book *Jerusalem's Temple Mount.*

Peter Levenda's writings and conversations were especially helpful in the process of formulating my ideas. His editorial comments were much appreciated as was his generosity in contributing the foreword.

Dr. Michael Aquino's penetrating critique of what I thought was a nearly finished draft of my History of Jerusalem improved this book enormously.

Stella Grey, as ever, gave me the benefit of her critical eye, wide learning, and exceptional mind as I progressed.

My conversations with Daniel Pineda were illuminating, inspiring, and confirming. He remained a close and tireless ally throughout this project.

Keith Stump, friend and cowriter of *Divine Warriors,* provided assistance on biblical archaeology, Temple sacrifice, and other aspects of this effort. He was an excellent sounding board for the early development of my thought and contributed much insight. J. P. Lund's appreciation for the esoteric aspects of this subject is extraordinary. He helped guide me to insights of which I was previously unaware. J. Daniel Gunther's biblical erudition and friendship were most appreciated, as were those of Sean Konecky. Brandon Flynn's expertise in Bible studies was helpful, and he generously shared his excellent reference library. Stuart Weinberg of Seven Stars Bookstore provided help with translation and stimulating conversation throughout this process. Ana Lonngi de Vagi made important contributions to my understanding of the nuances of the New Testament. Her insights improved this book, as did her skillful proofreading. Timothy Linn's review of a complex puzzle within the manuscript was particularly helpful. Yvonne Weiser offered significant insights into European religious practices and allowed me to test my thoughts with her. Michael Antinori and I shared many helpful discussions. Harry Widoff of Bookateria.com helped locate rare references. Genevieve and William Breeze provided research assistance as well.

John Wesley Chisholm, Jessica Brown, and Andrew Killawee of Trail of the Templars Productions Inc. brought me to Israel for an interview for their documentary *Templars Last Stand* for the National Geographic Network and Vision TV in Canada. Their role in this book is beyond my power of words to describe, other than to say, "Thank you."

Bernard Friedrich and Jerry and Doris Kaplan introduced me to Elie Ben-Meir. Elie guided me through Jerusalem and the surrounding areas, becoming a friend in the process. His encyclopedic knowledge, humanitarianism, and sense of humor were as invaluable as his guiding skills and education. His personal extension of kindness to a lonely traveler will be forever appreciated.

Abu Isa was my guide through the Palestinian territories and drove me back and forth to the Temple Mount area for the rest of my time in Jerusalem. We shared the common language of men of goodwill—love of family, children, country, and peace. He provided more insight with his quiet good nature than any number of opinion pieces by "experts" ever could.

Walter Zanger gave me the benefit of his expert's eye on my initial proposed itinerary, allowing me to avoid complete chaos. Thanks for persuading me in advance that Israel is not a Mideast version of New Jersey! And for introducing me to Yael Petretti, who kindly provided assistance.

Thanks to Cami Byerly of Timna Park near Eilat. Her graciousness and goodwill in allowing me to photograph the exquisite model of the Tabernacle, with no advance notice, was most generous. The work of the Timna Park Tabernacle Restoration is a true contribution to preserving and celebrating human history.

Nader Yunes of the Alcazar Hotel in Jerusalem made the planning stages of my photo trip an unexpected pleasure. He and his staff turned my eight-day stay in Jerusalem into a visit with new friends.

Colonel Jeff Cooper opened my eyes to an important and unexpected spiritual reality of the Holy Land. His daughter and my dear friend Lindy Cooper Wisdom helped make my trip to Israel, and therefore this book, possible. My friend and mentor Randy Cain provided critical logistical support for my travels.

Nicole Laliberte helped in transcription and the organization of the photos. Shelley Marmor rode in on her white horse just in time. Teresa Norris' expressions of support were most welcome, as was her review of the manuscript.

Martin P. Starr introduced me to data regarding genetic similarities between Israelies and Palestinians, which may yet hold answers to vexing problems. Peter Conte sent along a series of articles on Temple Mount excavations that were most timely, as was his eagle eye during the final proofing cycle.

The enthusiasm and open-hearted embrace of the Bible by Kathy and Doug Jager, Lori Reardon, and Linda Friedrich are inspiring.

The dedicated research of two somewhat obscure biblical scholars of the late-nineteenth and early-twentieth centuries provided images that have made this book more instructive and attractive. Timothy Otis Paine, in his two-volume opus *Solomon's Temple and Capitol*, and Clarence Larkin, in his *Dispensational Truth*, both made careful renderings of the Tabernacle and Temple. I hope their efforts may here receive a wider audience.

I am honored to again be able to highlight an exquisite painting by Linda Gardner. Fred Mayer generously allowed me the use of his unique photo of the Foundation Stone of the World in the Dome of the Rock, the best one I have ever seen. Thanks once again to George Seghers of the George Washington National Masonic Memorial for his generosity in allowing me to use the phenomenal images of the Temple and especially to Art Pierson for his brilliant photos of same. I appreciate the help of my friend, author, numismatist, and publisher David Hendin for providing the image of the rare first-century Bar Kochba coin from his encyclopedic *Guide to Biblical Coins*. Jennifer Belt of Art Resource extended a helping hand once again. I thank Bella Gershovich of the Israel Museum and Efrat Turgeman of Albatross Aerial Images for their help. Thanks to Laura McCormick and Jeff Julius of XNR Productions for their assistance with the maps. Illia Tulloch's photo of Nancy's painting of the Queen of Sheba shows guys like me how it's done.

* * * *

Jeanie Levitan of Inner Traditions International was the guardian of reality and my sanity throughout this process. My most difficult book became my most important. Without Jeanie's expert guidance, and my faith in her wisdom and friendship, it could never have been completed. Her editorial skills are simply awesome. The reader will never know how much her critical eye improved this work, but I do and thank her for it. Janet Jesso reminded me how much better a great copyeditor can make a text when she did her final reading.

Jon Graham, gatekeeper of Infinity, originally suggested this life-changing project and made important editorial contributions that dramatically improved it.

My special thanks to my friend and publisher, Ehud Sperling, for offering me this opportunity and for his incredible patience as year by year (after my deadline passed) it took shape.

* * * *

It is characteristic for authors to free their contributors of responsibility for the mistakes that inevitably accompany human endeavor. Consider that done.

I ask forgiveness for any errors in my understanding of the profundity of the subject matter of this book. Despite what may appear to be my presumption in tackling the Bible, I have done my utmost to approach these Mysteries with respect—removing my shoes—understanding that the ground whereon I would tread is holy.

CONTENTS

FOREWORD

PETER LEVENDA

There is a secret at the heart of Western esotericism. It is an open secret, a secret that hides in the plain sight of every Freemason, every Templar, every Rosicrucian. It is the pulsing center of Kabbalah and of Jewish mysticism since the time of Ezekiel and the Exile. Its creator is as famous and renowned among Muslims as among Christians. It was the backdrop to the agony of Jesus, and the focus of the mysterious Essenes.

It is nothing less than the Temple of Solomon, the King.

The idea of the Temple is one that many of us take for granted. We think we know what it was, and what it represented. The Temple is duplicated in the degree rituals of Blue Lodge Freemasonry. It appears in the names of several modern secret societies, such as the Ordo Templi Orientis, or "Order of the Temple of the East," which takes as its inspiration those French noblemen who bivouaced at the site of Solomon's Temple in Jerusalem in the eleventh century and who returned to Europe with something unimaginably precious. Just about everything you need to know about the Temple is in the Tanakh—the Hebrew Scriptures—as well as the New Testament.

But how many of us have actually read the Bible cover-to-cover? Even more important, how many modern initiates of secret societies and lovers of esoteric literature have studied the references to the Temple and subjected those texts to the kind of rigorous analysis they demand? When a Freemason experiences the ritual of the third degree and the murder of Hiram Abiff, does he really have a context for it? When members of the modern Templar societies experience initiations that take as their inspiration the fierce beliefs of the Knights Templar do they understand what those knights fought and died for? And why?

Do they realize it was a real place, an actual building, with a secret chamber that gave direct access to God?

What James Wasserman has done in this book is to perform an invaluable service, one long overdue. Working from the basic documents of Judaism and Christianity, he has collected all of the references to the Temple and presented them in one place along with a detailed account of the historical events that surrounded its building and its eventual destruction, first at the hands of the Babylonians and later under the Roman sword: a monument to monotheism, attacked and destroyed —twice—by polytheists. Only in this way can we begin to understand why the

Templars were obsessed with it, and why they named their Order after it. Only in this way can we realize the links that Freemasonry has with the Templars through their common reverence for the Temple. Only in this way can we start to appreciate the importance the Temple has for the Jewish mystics known as the Descenders to the Chariot. How else to understand the poignant rituals of the Qumran sect, as contained in the passionate Song of the Sabbath Sacrifice, which places the Temple in a spiritual realm accessible only to the pure of heart?

Even if one has no affiliation with esotericism or has no mystical ideas or impulses, a knowledge of the history of the Temple is essential to anyone who professes to understand (or be part of) Western culture. Stories and legends about the Temple are part of our shared literature. And yet, as someone who was brought up a Catholic, I can attest that the only time I was ever told anything about Judaism was when it was absolutely necessary to explain something about the life of Jesus. We know that Jesus cast out the moneychangers from the Temple, but we never had any idea what they were doing there in the first place! All we ever knew about Solomon was that he was wise. Something about cutting a baby in half . . .

As a student in Catholic school I saw statues of saints, crucifixes, and the Stations of the Cross. I was taught how to pray and sing in Latin, not Hebrew. Somehow we all thought that Latin was the language of Jesus. Certainly Saint Peter spoke Latin. He's buried beneath the Basilica that bears his name—in Rome, not Jerusalem.

Thus, we were robbed of the opportunity to gain a deeper and richer understanding of the Temple and all it represents: for Jews, for Freemasons, and for that enigmatic organization known as the Knights Templar. This is a glaring defect that James Wasserman repairs for us.

The urge to re-create the Temple through visualization, meditation, ritual, and prayer is only comprehensible when we remember how it was built, why it was built, and what its destruction meant for Jews and Christians alike. This the author has done in a remarkable accomplishment, at once scholarly and enlightened. What was destroyed by soldiers and buried under the rubble of centuries has been excavated and reborn in this masterful re-creation that takes us from Genesis to the present day. It is an essential volume for the Western magician and mystic, to be sure, for it provides all the basic information about the real Temple that one needs in order to unpack the rituals of modern ceremonial magic. But it is also an invaluable resource for anyone with a desire to understand not only the roots of Western culture and history—and especially of the rise of monotheism, which gave us the great Abrahamic religions of Judaism, Christianity, and Islam—but also a context for appreciating the ramifications of the conflicts in the Middle East and the precarious situation that is created by the hotly contested Temple Mount: for things have not changed much since the days of the Knights Templar and the struggle over control of Jerusalem. We cannot understand the news unless we understand history.

Solomon is a name to conjure with in modern esotericism. Literally. There are grimoires that bear his name, such as the famous Keys of Solomon. There is an Arab tradition that Solomon built the Temple with the aid of the *jinn:* the spiritual forces that were kept in a bottle bearing the famous Seal of Solomon. Of Solomon in the Qur'an it is written:

And We made the wind subservient to Solomon . . . We made a fountain of molten brass to flow for him. And of the jinn there were those who worked before him by the command of his Lord. (34:12)

Is it any wonder, then, that the building of his Temple would be considered a kind of miracle in itself, something to be commemorated in the Masonic degrees? Solomon controlled the forces of nature and the forces of the spiritual realms. The reference to the molten brass is a reference to 1 Kings 7:23–26 and the sea of brass that was part of the Temple. Most important, the Temple contained the Holy of Holies, the secret chamber that housed the Ark of the Covenant: the tangible, physical evidence of God's covenant with the Jews and, by extension, with humanity itself. While we have all seen *Raiders of the Lost Ark*, we have yet to see a film based on the Lost Temple. Yet it is there, like an insistent shadow, a magnetic force, a subliminal drumbeat to the magic and mysticism of the past three thousand years of spiritual longing for that lost connection, that pipeline to the Divine. Magicians of the Middle Ages called upon the same jinn as did Solomon, they believed. Steeped in the Bible, they thought they knew what he knew. They reached out blindly into the ether to tear the veil away that hangs before the Holy of Holies.

They still do so, today.

Did the Templars find the Ark during their sojourn at the Temple? There are many who think so. Did they find the Rod of Aaron? The tablets on which were written the Ten Commandments in letters of flame and the blood and tears of Moses? What was the secret of Rennes-le-Château that forms the heart of not only *The Da Vinci Code* but also of *Holy Blood, Holy Grail:* the nonfiction source and inspiration for the former? Don't we need a framework for understanding the question, something more than pop history and speculative fiction, before we can hope to come up with an answer?

Wasserman gives us the tools we need. By examining each of the books of the Bible in turn he walks us through the thousand years of the Temple's history. We come away confident that we have not only what facts are available but also a sense of the importance of this building and its relevance to us today, an excitement that is contagious. The yearning of the Jews, the passion of the Templars, the anger of Jesus, the quiet confidence of the Masons, the awe of the Muslims—all of this is wrapped up in the tale of an impossible dream: a house built for God, where God could meet His people. An intersection in time and space, a tangent point between this world and the next.

This book is your guide through that tangent point. You will find yourself internalizing the Temple, making it part of who you are and a part of what you do. This is not a book for a specialist or an academic only; it is for all of us who need to reconnect with some of the basic information of our culture. It allows us to reconsider our values in light of that magnificent achievement: a building, a thing of stone, of stairways and corridors, of altars and sacrifices that still hold us in thrall two thousand years after its disappearance from the face of the earth.

The Temple lives on, and Wasserman shows us how, and why.

PETER LEVENDA is the author of numerous books including *Stairway to Heaven: Chinese Alchemists, Jewish Kabbalists, and the Art of Spiritual Transformation,* and *The Secret Temple: Masons, Mysteries, and the Founding of America.* His most recent book is *Tantric Temples: Eros and Magic in Java.*

Knights Templar seal depicting the al-Aqsa Mosque as the Temple of Solomon, twelfth century. The mosque was the headquarters of the Templar order in Jerusalem.

The Dome of the Rock on Mount Moriah, looking west from the Mount of Olives.

PROLOGUE

The Presence of the Lord

Untold aeons ago, a spark of light shot forth from the heavens to become the first speck of matter in that region of space now known as Earth. From that minute particle—the Foundation Stone (*even shetiyya*)—grew our world. Three thousand years ago, that stone served as the base for the Temple of Solomon, later the Temple of Zerubbabel, and later still Herod's Temple. Today it is enclosed by the Muslim shrine the Dome of the Rock.

The plans and materials for Solomon's Temple were collected by his father David, warrior king of the Jews. The Temple housed the golden Ark of the Covenant, the powerful home of the two Tablets of the Law carved directly by the hand of God when He met with Moses on Mount Sinai. The Ark had remained in the Tabernacle, an elaborately constructed ritual tent, for some four hundred years before it found its resting place in the Holy of Holies of the Temple.

The Temple Mount, Mount Moriah, in Jerusalem is regarded as sacred by the three great monotheistic faiths of the descendants of Abraham—Judaism, Christianity, and Islam. The first century CE Jewish Roman general and historian Josephus, in speaking of Abraham's revelation, said this:

> He began to have higher notions of virtues than others had … for he was the first that ventured to publish this notion: That there was but one God, the Creator of the universe; and that, as to other [gods], if they contributed anything to the happiness of men, that each of them afforded it only according to his appointment, and not by their own power.[1]

It was on Mount Moriah that God tested Abraham's faith by commanding him to sacrifice his beloved son Isaac, and which He repeatedly sanctified throughout the Old Testament as His dwelling place on earth; here where Jesus spoke with the Rabbis as a child, later ejected the moneychangers, then preached his reformation of the severity of the monotheism of his forebears; and here, where six centuries later, Muhammad met with Moses and Jesus in a vision before ascending on his fiery steed through the heavens. There are traditions that identify the Temple Mount as the location of the Garden of Eden.[2]

---

1 Josephus, *The Antiquities of the Jews*, 1, 7, 155.

2 "And he knew that the Garden of Eden is the holy of holies, and the dwelling of the Lord." The Book of Jubilees, 8:19, a second century BCE Hebrew text, translated by R. H. Charles in *The Apocrypha and Pseudepigrapha of the Old Testament*.

The site of Solomon's Temple became the headquarters of the divine warriors of the Crusades, the Knights Templar, sworn to protect the Holy City of their faith. Countless legends and rumors have come down through the centuries about the Order's relation to the site and the secrets they may have uncovered there. Whatever truth such legends may or may not have, what is absolutely true is that the Bible and the Temple were the beating heart that animated the Knights Templar as they risked their lives to defend the Holy Land. Saint Bernard, the spiritual guide of the Order, lived and breathed the words of the Bible.

The building of the Temple of Solomon is the founding myth of Freemasonry. The craftsmen directed by Master Mason Hiram Abiff labored to erect the perfectly proportioned mystical edifice that would house and celebrate the presence of the Lord.[3] Who else but the most skilled and spiritual artisan/adepts could be entrusted with such a task? Each and every Freemason has walked between the pillars of Solomon's Temple on his path to Truth.

This book should be considered a source work for any person who seeks to understand the Knights Templar or the Freemasons. Everything you read about them will have been based on the Bible.

The Temple of Solomon remains as important today as the day it was completed in 957 BCE. It is a fundamental component of the spiritual and religious yearnings of millions of people and has been the symbolic focus of the teachings of esoteric societies for three thousand years.

* * * *

---

3 For more on Hiram Abiff, see pages 330–31.

And let them make me a sanctuary; that
I may dwell among them. (Exodus 25:8)

The act of creation proceeds as unity manifests itself in duality. In the beginning God created the heaven and the earth. The Temple exists because of this division. It is the separation of sacred and profane, the sacrifice of space, effort, and resources to a greater yet invisible purpose. It signifies the distillation of the spiritual aspiration from the realm of the physical body. It is the manifestation of faith, the materialization of intention, the dedication of oneself and one's community to the service and celebration of the divine. It is the Word made Flesh.

The story of the Temple of Solomon begins in the Garden of Eden. For within the enclosed sacred space of the Garden, the first couple walked with God in a state of undivided unity. That period of bliss came to an end at the Fall, when Adam and Eve were expelled from the Garden and prevented from returning by armed cherubim guarding the entrance. Since the Fall, the reestablishment of the unity between God and man may be called the central theme of human existence. It is the underlying goal of the entire biblical narrative that follows Eden. It was pursued each time an Altar was built, the Tabernacle moved, the Temple completed. When, like Eden, the Temple was taken away, the balance of the Old Testament became a lament over its absence and a quest for its renewal. This motif continued uninterrupted in the New Testament, established within its own symbol set.

The integration of heaven and earth that remains to be achieved enjoys this most glorious and profound distinction from that of the Garden. This time we enter the Lord's presence as fully conscious beings—having eaten of the fruit of the Tree of the Knowledge of Good and Evil and become as gods—free to choose acceptance of, and surrender to, the Infinite.

Freemasons at work in the tenth century

* * * *

Long after the closing of Eden and the destruction of the Flood, the Tabernacle was built in the book of Exodus on the plan communicated to Moses by God. It was designed as the central place of worship for the nomadic tribes of Israel as they walked through the desert for forty years.

What more fitting symbol of the interaction between humanity and the divine than these final verses of Exodus, when the Lord inhabited and surrounded the Tabernacle and guided His chosen people in their daily wanderings?

Then a cloud covered the tent of the congregation, and the glory of the LORD filled the tabernacle. And Moses was not able to enter into the tent of the congregation, because the cloud abode thereon, and the glory of the LORD filled the tabernacle. And when the cloud was taken up from over the tabernacle, the children of Israel went onward in all their journeys: But if the cloud were not taken up, then they journeyed not till the day that it was taken up. For the cloud of the

OVERLEAF: *The Foundation Stone of the World. A view from above in the Dome of the Rock. The Holy of Holies in the Temples of Solomon, Zerubbabel and Herod are each believed to have stood upon the* even shetiyya. *Photo by Fred Mayer.*

*The Tabernacle of Israel built by Moses during the Exodus on instructions received
from God on Mount Sinai. From a drawing by Clarence Larkin.*

LORD was upon the tabernacle by day, and fire was on it by night, in the sight of all the house of Israel, throughout all their journeys. (Exodus 40:34–38)

The portable Tabernacle, or Tent of Meeting, was the precedent of the Temple of Solomon, built after the land of Israel was settled and Jerusalem conquered and established as David's capital. Appropriately, the story of Solomon's Temple ends at the conclusion of the Bible with a description of the New Jerusalem in Revelation. The perfection of Eden is reestablished. John tells us first, "And I saw a new heaven and a new earth: for the first heaven and the first earth were passed away; and there was no more sea. And I John saw the holy city, new Jerusalem, coming down from God out of heaven, prepared as a bride adorned for her husband" (Revelation 21:1–2).

After describing some of the marvelous characteristics of the heavenly Jerusalem, John comments on the Temple, saying, "I saw no temple therein: for the Lord God Almighty and the Lamb are the temple of it" (Revelation 21:22).

We have at last returned to the Garden of Eden and the immanence of God on earth.

INTRODUCTION
The Key to Solomon's Temple

King Solomon, the greatest monarch of biblical times, reigned in Jerusalem, the ancient and eternal capital of Israel, from 968 to 928 BCE.[4] Renowned for his wisdom and piety, Solomon was the son and chosen successor of King David (r. 1005–965 BCE), the shepherd boy hero who had slain the giant Goliath in individual combat, thereby ending the Philistine threat for a time. During his forty-year reign, David had established and spread the boundaries of the nation of Israel. He moved the Ark of the Covenant to Jerusalem.

David yearned to construct a permanent Temple space to properly house the Ark but was prevented by the Lord because of the amount of blood he had shed in the various wars with which his reign was characterized. Instead, God gave him the design and plans for the Temple, which David drew up and passed to Solomon along with much store of accumulated treasure and building supplies. David's military and diplomatic efforts had brought an extended period of peace to Israel that allowed Solomon to focus on constructing the House of the Lord.

In 957 BCE, Solomon completed the magnificent edifice to honor the one God of the Hebrew people. It remained the permanent meeting place of heaven and earth for nearly four hundred years until its destruction by the Babylonian invasion of Nebuchadnezzar in 586 BCE.

After a hiatus of seventy years, a second Temple was completed on Mount Moriah in 515 BCE. It lasted another six hundred years. The Second Temple, as restored by King Herod, would become a central location in the story of Jesus and the activities of the Apostles upon his death. It was destroyed by the Romans in 70 CE.

Thus for one thousand years, with the exception of seventy years, the First and Second Temples stood on the Temple Mount as the central place of worship for Israel. Since that time, many Jews have prophesied and longed for a Third Temple to be built on the site—either by the messiah or as a predicate to his coming.

Solomon's Temple was unique, however, because of the presence of the Ark of the Covenant and the two tablets of the Law from Mount Sinai. The Ark was kept in an inner chamber known as the Holy of Holies—guarded by two cherubim whose wings were spread across it as a symbolic re-creation of the perfection of Eden. Two smaller cherubim sat atop the Ark itself, protecting the Treasure within, and acting

---

4 Ancient dates are, of course, approximations and will vary with different sources. I have used the dates given in *The New Oxford Annotated Bible* and *The Jewish Study Bible.*

The Ark holding the Torah in the Safed Synagogue in Israel. Photo by Vere Chappell.

as the resting place of the Lord, forming what was known as the Mercy Seat with their wings. On only one day each year, *Yom Kippur,* the Day of Atonement, the high priest of the Jews would enter the Holy of Holies, re-creating the primal experience of the parents of the human race by standing in the presence of God.

The Ark was the talismanic treasure of the Jewish people, their three-dimensional symbolic identity, the physical representation of God's seal on their status as His Chosen People. Once the destruction of the Temple of Solomon occurred and the Babylonian Exile began, the Ark was never referred to again in the canonical Old Testament. In the afterword to this book, I present the all-important apocryphal account of the prophet Jeremiah hiding the Ark before the destruction of Jerusalem.[5]

---

5 As written in 2 Maccabees sometime between 124 and 63 BCE.

In synagogues throughout the world today, the Torah, the sacred scroll of the Law, is housed in a cabinet known as the *aron ha'kodesh,* the Holy Ark, oriented to face the Temple Mount in Jerusalem. The Law within the Ark thus remains the focal point of Jewish religious life, a reminder of God's continuing presence in Jewish affairs. Ironically, as Steven Brooke noted in conversation, the destruction of the Temple as Israel's central place of worship may have contributed to the survival of the Jewish people by offering the strategic gift of decentralization.

An even earlier form of what might be called spiritual decentralization was practiced by the Essenes, a sect of mystic Jews who flourished in Qumran near the Dead Sea from the second century BCE through the first century CE. They worked with a series of meditation and visualization exercises centered around the inner Temple. They sought to create a sacred space in their personal spiritual lives that was not vulnerable to the decadence of rulers, priests, and people. For they understood what will become painfully clear in the pages that follow: the Bible ascribes the problems faced by the Jews to their own intransigence in denying the authority and prescriptions of God.

* * * *

The goal of this book is to understand the Temple of Solomon by placing it in context. The legend, the image, the archetype, all derive from one and only one source—the Bible. Whether one looks at the founding myth of Freemasonry, the myriad legends of the Knights Templar, or even Muhammad's visionary night journey through the heavens—all are rooted in the Bible.

We will, therefore, tour the historical books of the Bible to explore the concept of sacred space: the building of altars; the creation of the Tabernacle, its rituals and requirements; the receiving of the Ten Commandments and their

The caves of Qumran where the Dead Sea Scrolls were first discovered by Bedouin shepherds in 1947 and brought to the attention of scholars. Photo by Steven Brooke.

protective storage in the Ark of the Covenant; and the Ark's placement—first within the Tabernacle and later in the Temple of Solomon. The journey is complex. The battles, bloodshed, and betrayals reveal a painful history interspersed with some of the most inspiring and elevating ideals in all religious literature.

We will meet myriad people—both famous and lesser known—all of whom figure in this remarkable story of the building of God's House on Earth.

The Bible will be our guide because it is the single document of record describing the period from the birth of humanity in the Garden of Eden until Solomon laid the first stone of the Temple on Mount Moriah. The Bible is the single most influential book in Western culture. It has defined our legal and moral codes for millennia; shaped our political principles, concepts of history, philosophy, religion, science, economic activity, and war-making criteria; it

has defined our conventions of marriage, child-rearing, education, and charity. It has been a source of unlimited literary references and allusions and given birth to the vast field of biblical scholarship.

Yet in the past half century, the Bible has suffered a certain neglect. Political correctness, advancing secularism, multiculturalism, moral relativism, along with declining educational standards, have made it less a part of our common cultural dialog than in previous generations. Some may celebrate this as a step beyond the rigidity and superstition of earlier times. This may be true on one level. But there has been a great deal more lost than gained in the process. Knowledge of the Bible is an essential prerequisite to becoming an educated participant in Western culture.

This book draws nearly exclusively on the Bible in exploring the tradition of Solomon's Temple and its history. It is hoped that the powerful and riveting stories that follow will encourage readers to revisit the Bible in their personal intellectual and spiritual curriculums. It is a source of ever fresh understanding.

I have taken some liberties by grouping the books of the Bible in a manner that I hope will help the reader. The first five books of Moses, the *Torah* (the Law), are Genesis through Deuteronomy. I have divided these into two parts, telling the story of Creation and the origins of the Hebrew people, relative to the Temple, beginning with Genesis as part 1. Part 2 is the story of Moses from his birth in Exodus to his death in Deuteronomy.

The books of Joshua, Judges, Ruth, and the first section of 1 Samuel are included together as part 3, the Pre-Monarchical Leadership of Israel. Here we experience the righteousness of Joshua followed by the lawlessness characteristic of Judges. The vignette from Ruth introduces David's great grandmother. Samuel was the last of the Judges, the prophet who anointed the first two kings of Israel. I treat the United Monarchy of Saul, David, and Solomon as part 4, exploring the biblical books of 1 Samuel, 2 Samuel, 1 Kings, 1 Chronicles, and 2 Chronicles.

Part 5, the Divided Monarchy draws on 1 Kings, 2 Kings, and 2 Chronicles. The history of the northern and southern kingdoms follows the biblical pattern of presenting synchronous histories, first one then the other. The dates of the reigns of the kings are taken from the chronological tables in *The New Oxford Annotated Bible* and *The Jewish Study Bible* of the Jewish Publication Society and are, as mentioned, approximations. Two Chronicles focuses exclusively on the southern kingdom during the Divided Monarchy, while 1 and 2 Kings include histories of the North and South. I have pointed out several instances of variations in the history of a ruler as given in Chronicles and Kings. I have also added the prophetic books of Isaiah

and Jeremiah to part 5. While I have little to say about Isaiah, Jeremiah's story is replete with the history of the Jerusalem community both before and soon after the destruction of Solomon's Temple.[6] Part 5 ends with 2 Kings and 2 Chronicles discussing the seventy-year exile in Babylon and the proclamation of Cyrus II allowing for the return to Jerusalem and building of the Second Temple.

Part 6 begins with Ezekiel's vision of the mystical Temple received soon after Nebuchadnezzar's destruction of Jerusalem. Ezekiel set the stage for the idea of renewal. I follow with the books of Ezra and Nehemiah and their somewhat lackluster accounts of the Second Temple. As such, I have added the extra-biblical story of the Maccabean revolt and the origin of the Festival of Hanukkah in order to convey a sense of Jewish enthusiasm for the Second Temple. The later grandeur of Herod's Temple is described as well using Josephus as the primary source.

Part 7 discusses the New Testament story of Jesus and the important part played by the Second Temple in his life and teaching. The Book of Revelation ends the Bible where it began—with God and His creation walking together.

Part 8 specifically explores the Temple in the Western Mystery Tradition by examining its role in the two most important repositories of esoteric thought. The relationship between the Knights Templar, the Freemasons, and the Temple of Solomon forms the foundation of all Western secret societies in operation today.

I have spent more time on the First Temple than the Second. There are several reasons for this. The First Temple celebrated both the religious and political ascension of Israel. David and Solomon are both characters who may be described as larger than life. Their interaction

---

6 Jeremiah's hiding of the Ark is described in the afterword.

with the Ruler of the Universe was direct and personal. They were unique: David the warrior poet, Solomon the man of wisdom. Their building of the Temple was intended to be an eternal shrine to the Lord their God. Had their descendants lived up to their obligations, the Temple of Solomon would stand on Mount Moriah today as a center of pilgrimage and a testament of faith to the entire world.

The Second Temple, by contrast, was built at the pleasure of a good and sympathetic Persian king. The absence of the Ark of the Covenant insured that it remain a mere shadow of its former self. Israel was under the political domination of a medley of foreign powers throughout most of the life of the Second Temple. While, after Herod's restoration and expansion at the end of the first century BCE, the Second Temple was larger than the First, it never achieved the spiritual grandeur of its predecessor.

The criteria for including the biblical stories presented here are their relevance to the Temple of Solomon. This book is by no means intended as a "condensed version" of the Bible. I do hope that it will provide the reader with a firm grounding in the primary source material of the Temple as a basis for any further study of the derivative wisdom teachings associated with this religious, spiritual, and cultural symbol.

The King James translation (KJV) is the one primarily quoted here, as it is 1) a beautiful rendering of the text, 2) the most often quoted and familiar in English literature, and 3) far more accurate than many modern readers may realize. The New Revised Standard Version (NRSV) has been widely consulted for clarity, and quoted where helpful. It is highly recommended as a modern translation. I have also made extensive use of the Tanakh translation by the Jewish Publication Society. *The Septuagint Bible,* the Greek translation of the Old Testament, has been consulted when the translated Hebrew text was ambiguous. *The New Oxford Annotated Bible* (NOAB) has been an invaluable resource as a résumé of the universe of Biblical Commentary as has *The Jewish Study Bible* (JSB). I have capitalized the pronouns *He* and *Him* when referring to God to avoid confusion. Despite all attempts to understand the complexity of biblical texts, there is much that remains mysterious.

I made my first trip to Israel and Mount Sinai in late 2009 as part of the research and photography for this book. Some of my experiences and thoughts are presented in the afterword.

The appendices contain a brief history of Jerusalem and its ever-changing political fortunes, along with observations of the modern situation in the Middle East. Appendix 2 presents an overall chronology. Appendix 3 briefly summarizes the Jewish liturgical calendar. A series of maps are also included to help the reader make sense of the geography involved in the story.

* * * *

I began this research, frankly, with a limited appreciation of the importance of the Temple of Solomon. Almost at once, I understood the Temple as the symbolic affirmation of the presence of God in human affairs. Over the years of meditation, research, travel, and writing, the story of the Temple has become a central focus of my consciousness and spiritual life. Thus the archetype has grown in my heart exactly as intended by the Lord three thousand years ago. The Temple of Solomon is a bridge between our ancient selves and future glory. May this book help the reader walk that path.

PART ONE

IN THE BEGINNING

(GENESIS)

God, the Grand Architect, creating the
world with the principles of Geometry.
From Bible Moralisée, *1220–1230.*

CHAPTER ONE

CREATION AND DESTRUCTION

THE GARDEN TO THE FLOOD

In the beginning God created the heaven and the earth. (Genesis 1:1)

Thus begins the quintessential account of creation for the West. The construction of the world took place over a seven-day period. "And the Spirit of God moved upon the face of the waters. And God said, Let there be light: and there was light" (Genesis 1:2–3). And He separated the light from the darkness on the first day. On the second day, He created the dome of the sky and separated the waters that were above from those that were below. The third day witnessed the appearance of dry land from the midst of the waters and the coming into being of plants yielding seed and trees bearing fruit. The fourth day gave birth to the stars and planets and the great lights of the Sun and Moon—to illuminate the day and night and mark the seasons of the year. On the fifth day were brought forth the birds of the sky and creatures of the sea. And God blessed them. On the sixth day, He created all the animals that move upon the earth. And He created man, male/female, in his own image, giving them dominion over all that moved: the fish in the sea, the birds in the sky, and the animals that walked on the earth.

> And God said, "Behold, I have given you every herb bearing seed, which is upon the face of all the earth, and every tree, in the which is the fruit of a tree yielding seed; to you it shall be for meat." (Genesis 1:29)

> And God saw every thing that He had made, and, behold, it was very good. (Genesis 1:31)

On the seventh day, He rested. This is known as the First Creation and represents the undivided unity of God.

OPPOSITE: The Tree of Good and Evil, *by Berthold Furtmeyr, ca. 1478–1489. Mary, at left, nourishes the righteous with the host of the crucified Christ, while the Serpent passes the Bread of Sorrow to Eve who feeds the wicked.*

31

The Creation of Adam, *by Michelangelo in the Sistine Chapel, 1508–1512*

THE GARDEN OF EDEN

A second creation takes place beginning in Genesis 2:4. Here a new order is given to the creation and a different methodology employed. The Second Creation is administered by an apparently less powerful and universal deity who makes errors and is forced to reconsider certain actions. Biblical scholars and symbolists have addressed such issues for centuries, if not millennia. In the Second Creation, God formed man, Adam, from the dust of the ground, breathing life into his nostrils. God planted a garden in Eden (the meaning of Eden is "delight"), and this became man's home. The Garden contained all trees pleasing to the sight and good for fruit. Among these were two special trees—the tree of life and the tree of the knowledge of good and evil. Adam was given access to all the fruit-bearing trees but forbidden to eat from the tree of the knowledge of good and evil on pain of death.

Then God took pity on Adam's loneliness. In this second creation story, He created the animals of the field and the birds of the air as Adam's companions (reversing the order of the first creation which had brought forth the animals earlier than humans). While Adam named all the animals, he did not find a helper or partner among them. So God placed him in a deep sleep and took one of his ribs and created Eve. "Therefore shall a man leave his father and his mother, and shall cleave unto his wife: and they shall be one flesh"[1] (Genesis 2:24).

Eve was tempted by the Serpent (more crafty than any other animal) to eat of the tree of the knowledge of good and evil. The Serpent convinced her that God would not really kill them for eating of the tree, "For God doth know that in the day ye eat thereof, then your eyes shall be opened, and ye shall be as gods, knowing good and evil" (Genesis 3:5). And she looked at the tree and it appeared beautiful to

---

1 In Genesis 5:2, again it is written "Male and female created He them; and blessed them, and called their name Adam, in the day when they were created." The NRSV translates the verse as, "Male and female He created them, and He blessed them and named them 'Humankind' when they were created." "Humankind" is "Adam" in Hebrew.

Eve Tempted by the Serpent, *by William Blake, late eighteenth century*

her, filled with desirable fruit, and she took of the fruit and shared it with Adam. "And the eyes of them both were opened" (Genesis 3:7). Then they heard the sound of God walking in the Garden and hid from Him. He was not pleased by their disobedience. Adam blamed Eve and Eve blamed the Serpent. God cursed the serpent so it would crawl on its belly henceforth and be despised of men; made childbirth painful for women and placed them under the dominion of men; and bequeathed to Adam toil and trouble, work and struggle all the days of his life.

After clothing them, God realized that since they now knew the difference between good and evil, they might further challenge Him by consuming the fruit of the tree of life and live forever. Thus He sent them forth from the Garden, placing cherubim at the entrance and a flaming sword that turned about in every way to block their return.

After their banishment from Eden, Eve gave birth to Cain and then Abel. Cain slew Abel, and was forced to wander as a fugitive and vagabond. However, he was marked by God in such a way that he would not be attacked by those who resented his murder of Abel. Cain was the first builder. He constructed the first city, which he named for his son Enoch. Generations later, Cain's descendant Tubal-Cain was known as an instructor in the arts of brass and iron. Adam and Eve had a third son named Seth. It was in

The Creation of the World and the Expulsion from Paradise, *by Giovanni di Paolo, ca. 1445*

the time of Seth's son Enosh that people began to call upon the name of the Lord.[2]

THE FLOOD

As the earth became populated, the "sons of God" saw that the women were fair and took them as wives. God was angry at this and limited the human lifespan to one hundred and twenty years rather than endure competition from His creation. The children of this angelic/

human intercourse became the heroes and warriors of renown.[3]

God saw that the wickedness and corruption of men were great and decided to destroy

---

2 Genesis 4:26.

3 For more on Genesis 6:2 and 6:4, see, among others, Ida Craddock, *Heavenly Bridegrooms* reprinted in Vere Chappell, *Sexual Outlaw and Erotic Mystic*, and *Comte de Gabalis*, by the Abbe N. de Montfaucon de Villars, particularly Discourse IV. In both cases, these unions are regarded as positive. The apocryphal Book of Tobit presents a problematic, if humorous, account of one such interaction. In the Book of Enoch, a second century BCE text, the angels involved are sinister. See chapters VI–XI, *The Book of Enoch the Prophet*, translated by R. H. Charles.

Adam and Eve mourn the discovery of Cain's murder of Abel, by William Blake, ca. 1826

all life upon earth. Yet Noah, a descendant of Cain, found grace in His eyes, for he walked with the Lord. So God commanded Noah to build an ark. The construction of the Ark anticipates the Tabernacle of Exodus and the Temple of Solomon. It is the first container of the worthy, the sacred space distinguished from all other existence on earth (which here perished), and the first edifice built on measurements and principles divinely revealed directly to Noah.

The Ark was three stories high. Described in Genesis 6:14–16, it was built of cypress wood and covered with pitch. Its length was three hundred cubits, its width fifty cubits, and its height thirty cubits.[4]

God explained that destruction would soon rain down upon the earth and offered to save Noah and his wife, their three sons and their wives, and two of every animal, bird, and creeping thing, male and female. He also provided for extra sacrificial animals to allow for ritual obligations after Noah was safe.

---

4 One cubit equals approximately eighteen inches. Thus the Ark was 450 feet long by 75 feet wide, by 45 feet high. This structure is considerably larger than the Temple of Solomon which was 60 cubits long by 20 cubits wide by 30 cubits high, i.e., 90 feet by 30 feet by 45 feet. See 1 Kings 6:2–3.

Noah's Ark on Mount Ararat, *by Timothy Otis Paine, colored by Nancy Wasserman*

God caused it to rain for forty days and nights and all life on earth was destroyed, save for Noah's family and the wildlife in the ark. The waters remained for one hundred fifty days until God made the winds to blow and the earth to dry. And the ark rested upon Mount Ararat (now also known as Mount Buyuk Agri Dagi in Armenia).

NOAH BUILDS THE FIRST ALTAR

When Noah's testing revealed it was safe to leave the ark after some two more months, they went forth to repopulate the earth. Noah built the first altar mentioned in the Bible, making sacrifices of the clean animals as burnt offerings. Their sweet savor was pleasing to the Lord. God promised Himself never again to curse the ground nor to destroy mankind, understanding and accepting that "the imagination of man's heart is evil from his youth" (Genesis 8:21).

Then God blessed Noah and his sons, telling them, "Be fruitful, and multiply, and replenish the earth" (Genesis 9:1). He gave them dominion over all creatures of the earth, air, and sea, and gave man the flesh of every moving thing for meat, as previously He had given all green herbs and fruit in the First Creation. But eating living animals was forbidden, as was consuming blood. And "whoso sheddeth man's blood, by man shall his blood be shed; for in the image of God made He man" (Genesis 9:6). God promised Noah and his family never again to destroy the human race, and announced that the rainbow would be the token of the covenant between Himself and the earth.

Noah began to cultivate the earth and planted a vineyard. One day he became drunk and lay naked in his tent. His youngest son, Ham, saw him in this condition. Ham should have shielded his eyes in modesty. He further erred by telling his two brothers, Shem and

The Tower of Babel, *by the Bedford Master, ca. 1423–1430*

Japheth. They properly covered their father, walking backward so as not to see his nakedness. When Noah awoke and realized what had occurred, he cursed Ham and his descendants, the tribes of Canaan, declaring them to be the servants of the elder two sons.

As the descendants of Noah increased through the generations, all people spoke one language. Some traveled east and decided to build a city, Babel, with a tower so high it would reach to heaven. God was irritated by their effrontery. "And the LORD said, 'Behold, the people is one, and they have all one language; and this they begin to do: and now nothing will be restrained from them, which they have imagined to do'" (Genesis 11:6). So He caused them to speak a multitude of languages to confound them, rending them incapable of accomplishing any task in unison, then scattering them upon the earth.

CHAPTER TWO

THE PATRIARCHS AND MATRIARCHS

And in thy seed shall all the nations of the earth be blessed; because thou hast obeyed my voice. (Genesis 22:18)

ABRAHAM, SARAH, AND MONOTHEISM

Many generations later, Abram was born. He was descended from Noah's son Shem. His wife was named Sarai. They lived in the Chaldean city of Ur (near Basra in modern Iraq) and traveled with other members of their family to Haran (in modern Turkey near the Syrian border). After the death of Abram's father, God instructed him and Sarai to leave their relatives and travel to the land of Canaan (modern Israel) with Abram's nephew Lot and all their household. And God promised to make of Abram a great nation (though Sarai was barren), to bless and prosper them, and to make them and their descendants a blessing to all mankind. "And I will bless them that bless thee, and curse him that curseth thee: and in thee shall all families of the earth be blessed" (Genesis 12:3).

When they crossed the Jordan River and traveled to Shechem (modern Nablus) in Canaan, the Lord appeared to Abram and promised him and his seed the land. Abram built an altar to the Lord. He then traveled on to Bethel (north of Jerusalem)

Hilltop in Shechem, the ancient city where Abraham built his first altar

Abraham and his family begin the journey to the Land of Canaan, by József Molnár, 1850

where he built a second altar and invoked the name of the Lord.

A famine caused them to travel to Egypt, where, in a bizarre scene, Abram pretended Sarai was his sister so the Egyptians would not kill him and seize her because of her beauty. Pharaoh was distraught when he learned of Abram's deception and scolded him for causing Pharaoh to commit adultery and bring bad for-tune upon his house. Then Pharaoh sent them away and they returned to Bethel.

Their herds had grown so numerous that Lot went on to Sodom (probably near the south end of the Dead Sea) to seek more grazing land. God promised to Abram a great multi-tude of descendants and all the land he could see. Abram journeyed on to Hebron where he erected a third altar.

Abram learned that Lot had been captured in a raid on Sodom. He launched a daring and successful guerilla-style night operation with a force of three hundred eighteen of his men and rescued Lot. After this, he was introduced to Melchizedek, king of Salem (Jerusalem), described as "the priest of the most high God" (Genesis 14:18), who blessed him.

When Abram lamented that he and Sarai were childless, the Lord promised him descendants as numerous as the stars in heaven. And Abram believed Him. Making a sacrifice, he fell into a deep sleep and saw a vision of his descendants under the yoke of Egypt for four hundred years. Then he was promised the greatest expanse of land of all the boundaries of Israel mentioned in the Bible.

Soon after, the barren Sarai invited Abram to lay with her Egyptian maid Hagar that they might have children. After Hagar conceived, she looked at Sarai with contempt. Sarai became angry and punished Hagar who fled. But an angel of the Lord came upon Hagar and commanded her to return to Abram's household and submit herself to Sarai and promised her that her descendants would be multiplied exceedingly. He told her she was carrying a male child whom she should call Ishmael. "And he will be a wild man; his hand will be against every man, and every man's hand against him; and he shall dwell in the presence of all his brethren" (Genesis 16:12). Ishmael was born when Abram was eighty-six.

When Abram was ninety-nine years-old, the Lord appeared to him again and promised to multiply his seed. Abram fell to his face in prayer and awe. The Lord changed his name from Abram ("exalted father") to Abraham ("father of a multitude"). He established an everlasting covenant with the generations of Abraham, and the sign was to be the circumcision of all male children on the eighth day of birth. Sarai's name ("my princess") was changed to Sarah ("princess"), indicating her more impersonal status as queen of the race. The Lord promised Abraham that Sarah would bear him a son and she would become the mother of nations. Then Abraham expressed

Hagar and Ishmael being told by an angel to return to the home of Abram and Sarai, by Giovanni Battista Tiepolo, ca. 1732

his gratitude and laughed in his heart that he would become a father at a hundred years old and Sarah a mother at ninety. And he asked God's blessing on Ishmael. God repeated that Sarah would indeed have a son whose name would be Isaac ("he will laugh"), with whom God would continue His everlasting covenant. Ishmael was blessed as well and would also become a great nation. Abraham and Ishmael (who was then thirteen), and all the male servants, workers, and slaves in his household, were circumcised that day.

The Lord appeared to Abraham again at Mamre (Hebron) in the form of three visiting men to whom Abraham and Sarah extended hospitality. The men asked about Sarah and said they would return after a child was born to her. Sarah laughed at the thought but the divine forms asked, "Is any thing too hard for the LORD" (Genesis 18:14)? In addition to this announcement, the visit of the three beings was the prelude to the story of the destruction of Sodom and Gomorrah in Genesis 18–19. While somewhat afield from the Temple theme, it does make clear the power of the judgment of the Lord and His intolerance of communal sin. This has already been demonstrated in the story of Noah and the Flood, and will certainly be revisited in the history to follow.

THE BIRTH OF ISAAC

Isaac was born and circumcised on the eighth day, and Sarah laughed with God. But she saw Ishmael mocking the baby and demanded that he and Hagar be cast out of the house. Abraham was greatly distressed, but God told him to obey Sarah's request, for Isaac would be the primary holder of Abraham's legacy. Yet He promised to care for Hagar and Ishmael and reaffirmed that Ishmael would found a great nation. Abraham led them away and they reached the wilderness

of Beer-sheba. Hagar despaired, but an angel preserved them. As Ishmael grew, he became expert with the bow. Hagar found him a wife from the land of Egypt.

The Temple Mount and the Near-Sacrifice of Isaac

God decided to test Abraham. He commanded him to sacrifice, "thine only son Isaac, whom thou lovest" (Genesis 22:2). He was to make of his body a burnt offering in "the land of Moriah," on the mountain traditionally identified as Mount Moriah in Jerusalem, the site of the future Temple of Solomon. Abraham answered the Lord's command and made the three-day journey with Isaac and two servants. Arrived on the third day, father and son left the others and went to build the sacrificial altar. As Abraham gathered the wood, Isaac asked where was the lamb for the offering. Abraham replied that God would provide it. He then bound Isaac to the altar and stretched forth his knife. At this point, an angel called out and commanded him to stay his hand, announcing that Abraham had been found worthy. He saw a ram caught in a thicket and offered it as a burnt offering instead. And God said to Abraham, "And in thy seed shall all the nations of the earth be blessed; because thou hast obeyed my voice" (Genesis 22:18).

The Death of Sarah and the Wedding of Isaac and Rebecca

Sometime later, Sarah died. She was buried in Hebron in a cave in the field of Machpelah that Abraham purchased from the Hittites as his family's burial plot. He then sent his servant to find a wife for Isaac from among his kindred in the region of Haran. He made the servant swear that he would help Abraham maintain the purity of tribal blood by not looking among

The angel stops Abraham from sacrificing Isaac on Mount Moriah, by Linda Gardner, 1989

The shrine of Machpelah was built by King Herod on the site of the cave where the Patriarchs and Matriarchs of Western Civilization were laid to rest during Genesis. My guide Abu Isa is standing in foreground.

the daughters of Canaan whom he might meet on his journey. Abraham also forbade him from bringing Isaac to meet his potential bride in Haran. He reasoned that the Lord had taken him from that land and promised him that he and his descendants would dwell in Israel thereafter.

Upon arriving at Haran, Abraham's servant prayed for the success of his mission. He watered his camels at the town well where he met Rebecca. Her grandfather was Abraham's brother. Her generosity and kindness touched the servant's heart, and he noted she was fair of form. After he explained his mission to Rebecca's family, she traveled to meet Isaac with their

blessing. "May you, our sister, become thousands of myriads; may your offspring gain possession of the gates of their foes" (Genesis 24:60 NRSV). When Rebecca arrived in Canaan, she and Isaac were married.

Abraham died and was buried in the cave of Machpelah alongside Sarah by Ishmael and Isaac. After a period of infertility, the Lord answered Isaac's prayer and Rebecca gave birth to the twins Esau and Jacob. They were said to have contested even in the womb. Esau became a hunter, Jacob, a dweller in tents, that is, a shepherd. Esau was favored by Isaac, Jacob by Rebecca. Jacob was cunning and took advantage of Esau, demanding his birthright in

This altar was assembled from pieces found in a storage chamber during the excavations at Tel Beer-sheba. It is currently in the Israel Museum. Reproduced by permission.

exchange for feeding the famished hunter. Esau agreed and thereby lost his considerable privilege as the firstborn of the twins. Esau married a woman of the neighboring tribes which disturbed his mother and Jacob. Esau is characterized as having despised his birthright, both by selling it to Jacob and by marrying outside the Hebrew community.[5]

A famine came upon the land and God commanded Isaac to move east to Gerar (southwest of Gaza). The Lord promised him protection and pledged the land to him and his descendants. Isaac settled in Gerar. Here he resorted to the same tactic as Abraham. He lied that Rebecca was his sister, putting her at risk and angering the Philistine king who reprimanded him. If someone had unwittingly lain with Rebecca, thinking she was a single woman, they would have sinned against the Lord and brought retribution to Gerar.

---

5 Genesis 25:34 and 26:34.

Isaac prospered in Gerar, arousing the envy of the Philistines. He was asked to leave. He went further south into the valley. At first he argued with local Philistines, but these disputes were eventually resolved. He proclaimed in gratitude, "Now the LORD hath made room for us, and we shall be fruitful in the land" (Genesis 26:22). He again grew wealthy in flocks and cultivated land.

Isaac then traveled to Beer-sheba, where God visited him and confirmed the covenant He had made with Abraham. Isaac built an altar to the Lord at this place. A delegation of Philistines visited him and acknowledged that Isaac was blessed of the Lord. They formed a covenant of peace between them and feasted together.

When Isaac was advanced in age and weak in eyesight he prepared to bestow his paternal blessing on the elder Esau. Rebecca schemed with Jacob and tricked Isaac into passing on this crucial blessing to Jacob instead. Esau hated Jacob for his treachery. Rebecca, learning of Esau's intention to kill him, arranged to send Jacob to her brother Laban's household in Haran that Jacob might be safe until Esau's anger had cooled. Rebecca asked Isaac to encourage Jacob to travel to Haran that he might find a wife of his own people, rather than among the Canaanites as had Esau.

JACOB AND RACHEL

On his journey to Haran, Jacob came to Bethel where Abraham had built an altar. Here Jacob dreamed of a ladder to heaven with angels ascending and descending and beheld the Lord. God promised Jacob the land on which he lay for his generations and extended the patriarchal blessing to him and his seed as He had done before to Abraham and Isaac. And Jacob built an altar of the stones he had used as pillows and

Jacob's Ladder, *by William Blake, ca. 1800*

*Jacob wrestling with the Angel, from an
engraving by Gustave Doré, 1865*

poured oil upon it. And he swore allegiance to the Lord.

Jacob continued on to Haran and met Rachel, the daughter of Laban, and loved her. He worked seven years to earn Rachel. But Laban gave him his elder daughter, Leah, instead—veiling her—thus tricking the trickster Jacob. Laban explained that the eldest daughter must be married before the youngest is allowed to do so; that in return for another seven years labor, Jacob could wed Rachel. Jacob and Leah had six sons and a daughter. Because Rachel was barren, she gave her maid to Jacob who bore him two sons. Then Leah's maid gave birth to two more sons. At last, God opened Rachel's womb and Joseph was born.[6]

The names of the twelve sons of Jacob (with his two wives and two concubines), heads of the twelve tribes of Israel, in order of birth were: Reuben, Simeon, Levi, Judah, Dan, Napthali, Gad, Asher, Issacher, Zebulun, Joseph, and Benjamin. A daughter named Dinah was born between Zebulun and Joseph.

After twenty years, Jacob returned to the land of Canaan. On the eve of his reconciliation with Esau, Jacob spent the night wrestling with an angel. The angel sought to leave at daybreak, but Jacob demanded a blessing before releasing him. The angel blessed him and told him

---

6 Rachel later died during the birth of her youngest boy,

Benjamin. Her tomb in Bethlehem is venerated to this day as a site of pilgrimage. As the mother of Joseph, she is broadly viewed as the mother of the Jewish people, and by some, as the embodiment of the archetypal divine feminine.

Bethel was the site of several altars erected by the Patriarchs in Genesis.

he would no longer be called Jacob, but Israel ("the one who strives with God"), "for you have striven with God and with humans, and you have prevailed" (Genesis 32:28 NRSV). In naming the site of the wrestling match, Jacob proclaimed, "I have seen God face to face, and my life is preserved" (Genesis 32:30).

Pitching his tent in Shechem, Jacob (now Israel) erected another altar. After a time, the Israelites were directed to continue on to Bethel where Jacob again erected an altar to the Lord. God spoke to him directly, confirmed his change of name to Israel, blessed him and his descendants, and renewed His promise concerning the land of Israel as the Jewish homeland. Jacob/

Israel continued on to Hebron to see his father Isaac before he passed away. After the death of Isaac, Esau and Israel buried their father. Then Esau traveled on to Edom, west of the Dead Sea, where he and his descendants would remain.

JOSEPH AND PHARAOH

Jacob/Israel loved Rachel's son Joseph more than all his sons and made him a coat of many colors.[7] But his brothers were jealous and hated Joseph. When Joseph related two dreams in

---

7 Genesis 37:3.

which he described himself as reigning over his brothers, their anger grew. They conspired to kill him but instead sold him to merchants traveling to Egypt. They tricked their aging father into believing he was dead.

The merchants sold Joseph to an Egyptian official in whose household he rose to prominence as a capable manager. But falsely accused by his master's wife, Joseph was thrown into prison. Here he interpreted dreams for two members of Pharaoh's court who had suffered temporary incarceration. Two years later, Pharaoh had a disturbing dream that his court magicians and wisemen were unable to interpret. His butler (one of the courtiers formerly incarcerated with Joseph) told Pharaoh of Joseph's skills with dream interpretation. Pharaoh sent for him. Joseph first explained to Pharaoh, "It is not I; God will give Pharaoh a favorable answer" (Genesis, 41:16 NRSV). Pharaoh then related his dream and Joseph explained its meaning. He offered a plan to save Egypt from the prophesied famine and was given the highest office in the land. His organizational skills allowed the Egyptians to survive the famine and remain well-fed during the seven years of hardship. Joseph married the daughter of the priest of On, and they had two children, Manasseh and Ephraim.

The famine reached far and wide and all nations came to Egypt to purchase food. In the land of Canaan, Joseph's family suffered the famine's effects. Jacob/Israel sent the ten brothers to buy food in Egypt, keeping his youngest son Benjamin with him. When the brothers arrived, they were brought to Joseph but did not recognize him. He set them a number of tasks and trials, sending them home and exposing them to danger and anxiety. He finally disclosed his identity in a scene of great emotional depth. He forgave his brothers their treachery and welcomed the Hebrew tribe to Egypt. As Joseph

explained, their evil behavior in betraying him had been God's will. "God sent me before you to preserve you a posterity in the earth, and to save your lives by a great deliverance"[8] (Genesis 45:7).

Joseph's brothers were showered with hospitality by Pharaoh. "Take your father and your households, and come unto me: and I will give you the good of the land of Egypt, and ye shall eat of the fat of the land" (Genesis 45:18). They traveled to Canaan to retrieve their father and his household. On the journey to Egypt, Jacob/Israel stopped to offer sacrifice at Beer-sheba, where the Lord told him not to fear. "I will go down with thee into Egypt; and I will surely bring thee up again" (Genesis 46:4). Seventy people traveled with Jacob/Israel to Egypt. He blessed Pharaoh upon their meeting and lived in Egypt seventeen years. He charged his family to bury him in the cave of Machpelah with Abraham, Sarah, Isaac, Rebecca, and Leah.

As Jacob/Israel lay dying, he called for Joseph who brought his two sons with him. Jacob/Israel blessed Manasseh and Ephraim with the intention of passing his lineage blessing from Abraham and Isaac to his grandsons. He then called before him his twelve sons and blessed them, making observations and prophesies of their futures. Reuben, the eldest, had violated a tribal precept by sleeping with one of his father's concubines, so he was excluded from the honor of his position as firstborn. Neither Simeon nor Levi were given the honor of next eldest because they had created a situation of political vulnerability for the family. Their sister Dinah had been raped in Shechem,

---

8 Throughout the trials and tribulations of their two journeys to Egypt, particularly the second, Judah repeatedly proved himself to be the natural leader of the brothers in courage and morality. This will later be significant as we note his lineage will include David and Solomon, and eventually Jesus.

and they avenged her honor by killing many Canaanites, despite the fact that the Israelites were not strong enough to survive a major military confrontation. Judah was singled out as the leader of the Israelites and his was the lineage designated to receive the mantle of kingship. Joseph was accorded the strongest blessing as he who was set apart from his brothers.

When Jacob/Israel died he was embalmed with the Egyptian rites for forty days and mourned for seventy days more. His body was then taken in a grand procession from Egypt to Hebron, where he was buried at Machpelah.

Joseph and his family lived the rest of their days in Egypt. Joseph made the Israelites swear an oath that when the people of Israel should be removed from Egypt, as God had promised, they would not fail to take his bones and lay them with his kindred. And so he too was embalmed with the sacred rites and buried in Egypt. Some four centuries later, his remains would be carried back to join his ancestors in the land of Israel, accompanying the Ark across the Jordan River at the end of the Exodus.

The Egyptian burial rites were strictly controlled. Jacob and later Joseph would have been mourned in a procession similar to this from The Papyrus of Ani, *ca. 1250* BCE.

PART TWO

MOSES, THE TABERNACLE, AND THE LAW

(Exodus, Leviticus, Numbers, Deuteronomy)

Statue of Moses by Michelangelo in the Church of San Pietro in Vincoli, Rome (1513–1515). Photo by Jean-Christophe Benoist.

Moses rescued from the waters by the daughter of Pharaoh as she was bathing.
Fresco from the Dura Europas synaogue in Syria, ca 239.

CHAPTER THREE

Exodus

THE FREEDOM TO WORSHIP

Now there arose up a new king over Egypt, which knew not Joseph. (Exodus 1:8)

Four hundred years later, the children of Israel had grown strong and become an established presence in Egypt. Memories of Joseph's contribution to the salvation of the nation were old and forgotten. The present Pharaoh was uneasy about the independent power of the Hebrews, fearing they could form alliances with his enemies or fight directly against Egypt. "Therefore they did set over them taskmasters to afflict them with their burdens" (Exodus 1:11). But the Israelites still multiplied, even under conditions of slavery. Next, the Pharaoh turned to genocide. He ordered that all male children born to the Israelites be thrown in the Nile.

Moses ("drawn from the water"), a child of the tribe of Levites, was three months old when he was set afloat in an ark of bulrushes. His sister Miriam observed him from her concealed position on the shore. The daughter of Pharaoh was bathing when she saw the infant. She had compassion toward him and took him as her son. Miriam approached her and arranged for Moses' mother to serve as his wet nurse.

Moses grew strong within the court of Egypt. But one day he came upon an Egyptian beating a Hebrew. Moses slew him. Fearing discovery, he fled to the Midianite desert region in the northern Arabian Peninsula. He was welcomed there after rescuing seven sisters at a well. These were the daughters of Jethro (or Reuel), the priest of the tribe. He offered Moses his daughter Zipporah in marriage. They had a son whom Moses named Gershom ("exile"), for he said, "I have been a stranger in a strange land" (Exodus 2:22).

At length, Pharaoh died and the Israelites continued to suffer and cry out to the Lord. He remembered His covenant with Abraham, Isaac, and Jacob, and His promise to bring forth the children of Israel from out of the land of Egypt.

MOSES MEETS THE LORD AT MOUNT SINAI

While Moses grazed the flock of his father-in-law, he wandered onto the sacred Mount Sinai (also known as Mount Horeb). An angel appeared in a flame in the midst of a bush that was not consumed by the fire. As Moses turned to look at the bush, God warned him not to approach, saying, "Put off thy shoes from off thy

53

feet, for the place whereon thou standest is holy ground … And Moses hid his face; for he was afraid to look upon God" (Exodus 3:5–6). God commanded Moses to lead the children of Israel from out of the land of Egypt, to a land "flowing with milk and honey" (Exodus 3:8), the land of Canaan promised of old. He further stated that He would give a sign to Moses of the truth of His identity: when Moses brought the people out of Egypt, they would return to worship the Lord here at Mount Sinai.

The strategy that God communicated to Moses was to begin with a request to Pharaoh to allow the Israelites to make a three-day journey to the wilderness that they might make a sacrifice to the Lord. However, God noted He would purposely harden Pharaoh's heart so he would not allow the Hebrews to do this unless compelled by a more mighty hand. "I will stretch out my hand, and smite Egypt with all my wonders which I will do in the midst thereof: and after that he will let you go" (Exodus 3:20).

Moses was unsure of himself and hesitated. God promised him that he would be able to accomplish the task. When Moses asked what name he should give the people when they asked who had sent him, God replied, "I Am That I Am" (Exodus 3:14). He gave Moses further instruction to declare to the Israelites that "The Lord God of your fathers, the God of Abraham, the God of Isaac, and the God of Jacob, hath sent me unto you: this is my name for ever, and this is my memorial unto all generations" (Exodus 3:15).

Moses continued to vacilate, hesitant about accepting the mission. God gave him miraculous signs that he might use to convince the people and Pharaoh of his power. These included changing his staff into a snake and then back to a staff; turning his hand leprous white and then healing it; and pouring Nile water on the ground where it would turn to blood. Moses

argued that he was not eloquent enough and begged the Lord to send someone else. His hesitation began to anger the Lord. God suggested that Aaron, Moses' more eloquent elder brother, could help him in communicating to both the Pharaoh and the Israelites.

Moses finally accepted his destiny and traveled with his family to Egypt. Along the way, a scene occurred that reflects the recurring sense of high personal drama in the story of Moses. God told Moses he should threaten Pharaoh with the death of his firstborn son because of Pharaoh's unwillingness to free God's firstborn, the Hebrew people, from bondage. In the meantime we learn that the conditions of ritual purity for the household of Moses had not been met. God sought to kill Moses while he stayed with his family at an inn. The quick work of Zipporah in circumcising Gershom, Moses' firstborn, then touching Moses with the blood, saved Moses' life.[1]

Moses and Aaron greeted each other after many years of separation. Moses explained their mission; then they explained it to the elders of Israel. Moses demonstrated the miraculous signs God had given him. The people bowed their heads and worshipped the Lord.

MOSES AND AARON IN THE COURT OF PHARAOH

Moses and Aaron visited Pharaoh and informed him of the Lord's commandment, "Thus saith the Lord God of Israel, let my people go that they may hold a feast unto me in the wilderness" (Exodus 5:1). Pharaoh replied that he knew not this God and refused, for the Lord had hardened Pharaoh's heart. Pharaoh made more oppressive the lot of the Hebrew slaves,

---

1 Exodus 4:22–26.

forcing them to fetch their own straw to mix for bricks, yet demanding the same output. If they had time to worship their God, they could obviously work harder.

As their hardships escalated, the people reproached Moses for making their situation even worse. Moses asked the Lord why He had increased the suffering of the people. God answered that He had heard their groans and would free them, that He remembered the covenant formed in time past with Abraham, Isaac, and Jacob. The Lord announced His name JEHOVAH to Moses for the first time in Exodus 6:3. He renewed His pledge to bring them forth from Egypt to the Promised Land. He also made the soon-to-be familiar proclamation: "I will take you to me for a people, and I will be to you a God: and ye shall know that I am the LORD your God, which bringeth you out from under the burdens of the Egyptians" (Exodus 6:7).

The people would not listen to Moses because their spirits had been broken. God again ordered Moses to Pharaoh but Moses demurred. If the Israelites would not listen to him, how could he convince Pharaoh of God's word? God prepared Moses and Aaron with a powerful statement of the events that would follow:

> I have made thee a god to Pharaoh: and Aaron thy brother shall be thy prophet. Thou shalt speak all that I command thee … And I will harden Pharaoh's heart … that I may lay my hand upon Egypt, and bring forth mine armies, and my people the children of Israel, out of the land of Egypt…. And the Egyptians shall know that I am the LORD. (Exodus 7:1–5)

THE TEN PLAGUES

And so it was. Moses and Aaron entered the court. Moses directed Aaron to throw down his staff and it became a serpent. The Egyptian magicians did the same, but Aaron's serpent consumed them all. Next, a cruel series of ten plagues of increasing severity came upon the land. The first nine included the waters turning to blood, followed by infestations of frogs, gnats, flies, pestilence, boils, hail, locusts, then darkness covering the land for three days. At first, the Egyptian magicians duplicated the plagues, leaving Pharaoh unmoved at this contest between the God of Israel and the gods of Egypt. But as the plagues increased in severity, the Egyptian magicians were unable to replicate them, telling Pharaoh, "This is the finger of God" (Exodus 8:19). But God had hardened Pharaoh's heart and he refused to move. After the extreme misery caused by the first nine plagues, Moses was sent to warn Pharaoh that the firstborn of all that lived in Egypt would be slain. "And there shall be a great cry throughout all the land of Egypt, such as there was none like it, nor shall be like it any more" (Exodus 11:6).

Moses summoned the Hebrew elders and told them to instruct the people to sacrifice a lamb for each household (or to share with those whose households were too small to consume an entire lamb). They were to paint the doorposts of their homes with lamb's blood as a sign of their identity, then roast the meat and consume it entirely. At midnight, the Lord went through the land and slew the firstborn of

OVERLEAF: *Mount Sinai. This mountain, near the fourth-century Saint Katherine's Monastery in the south of the Sinai Peninsula, has been identified for at least two thousand years as the mountain where Moses met the Lord.*

Egypt, passing over the homes of the Israelites because of the lamb's blood.

Pharaoh, whose eldest son had been slain, summoned Moses and Aaron and said, "Rise up, and get you forth from among my people, both ye and the children of Israel; and go, serve the Lord, as ye have said…. and bless me also" (Exodus 12:31–32). The Jews left so quickly they had no time to let the dough rise in the kneading bowls, thus their bread was unleavened.

Moses informed the Hebrews that God had henceforth established the middle of the Spring month of *Nisan* as the beginning of the Jewish year.[2] He commanded them to celebrate a remembrance festival, the Passover, that would extend through the generations and include eating unleavened bread for eight days. And they were to tell this story to their children in the land to which the Lord would lead them. An interesting aspect of the annual Passover celebration is that Judaism is the only religion to celebrate political freedom as a gift of God, a concept later incorporated into America's Declaration of Independence.

The story of the ten plagues expresses a motif that we find throughout the Bible. God has a plan for human behavior. He designates human representatives to communicate it to others who refuse to change their behavior and follow the proper course. What is noteworthy in the story of the Passover is the part the Lord is repeatedly acknowledged to have played in hardening Pharaoh's heart. The Egyptian ruler was forced to capitulate to God's will by an ever-increasing assault against his refusal to cooperate—caused by God stiffening his resistance to comply. The Temple of Solomon will be destroyed because the people chose disobedience rather than following the command-

ments of the Lord. The difference however will be that the evils of the Jewish people and their leaders are not ascribed to God's purposeful incitement. Rather, God will be characterized as saddened, angered, or disappointed by their unwillingness to follow His law. On the other hand, in the Book of Isaiah, God states though the mouth of the prophet, "I form the light, and create darkness: I make peace and create evil: I the Lord do all these things."[3]

The Exodus

The Jews left Egypt 430 years after Joseph's arrival. They had grown from the 70 souls who accompanied Jacob and his sons to some 600,000 men, besides women and children. The people were given laws and ordinances through Moses to consecrate all the firstborn of Israel to the Lord, and additional ordinances regarding celebrating the festival of Passover when they reached the land of Canaan.

Rather than travel to Canaan by the shorter coastal route through the land of the Philistines, the Lord sent them into the wilderness of Sinai. God's reasoning is explained by noting that if the Israelites faced war at this stage of their development, they might just retreat back to Egypt. Moses took the bones of Joseph with him.

> And the Lord went before them by day
> in a pillar of a cloud, to lead them the
> way; and by night in a pillar of fire, to
> give them light; to go by day and night.
> (Exodus 13:21)

God again turned the heart of Pharaoh to anger, "that I will gain glory for myself over Pharaoh and all his army; and the Egyptians shall know

---

2 The New Year was later moved to the Fall. See appendix 3 for the holiday calendar.

3 Isaiah, 45:7.

that I am the LORD" (Exodus 14:4 NRSV). The Israelites were camped along the banks of the Red Sea when the Egyptian army came after them. The Israelites rebelled in fear against Moses, crying out that it would have been better to remain slaves rather than die in the wilderness. But Moses promised divine intervention in their tribulation. And the Red Sea parted. The angel of the Lord and the pillar of cloud moved behind the Israelites, shielding them from the view of Pharaoh's army as they walked across dry land throughout the night. When the Egyptian army finally saw and pursued them in the early dawn, the waters closed upon them and the Egyptians were drowned. "And Israel saw that great work which the LORD did upon the Egyptians: and the people feared the LORD, and believed the LORD, and His servant Moses" (Exodus 14:31).

Moses and the people sang a song praising the Lord's victory over the Egyptian enemy, then prophesying their arrival and victory in the Promised Land. The Temple of Solomon set atop Mount Moriah is presaged near the end of the song: "Thou shalt bring them in, and plant them in the mountain of thine inheritance, in the place, O LORD, which thou hast made for thee to dwell in, in the Sanctuary, O LORD, which thy hands have established" (Exodus 15:17). Miriam, sister of Moses and Aaron, here called a prophetess, played on a tambourine and led the women in song and dance, praising the Lord.

Thus began what would become the forty years of wandering imposed on the Israelites after their departure from the land of Egypt. They are reported to have continually disappointed and angered the Lord with their incessant whining, repeated instances of disobedience, and general lack of faith. Yet, Exodus recounts that in each case of want and privation, danger and distress, God saved them with miraculous power—bringing water in the

Pharaoh's reluctance to accept and obey the commands of the Hebrew God as conveyed by Moses and Aaron was, in part, due to the Egyptian tradition that the Pharaoh was himself regarded as divine. He, or more rarely she, was considered the human representative of Osiris (or Isis), pictured together in The Paprus of Ani, *ca 1250* BCE.

desert to quench their thirst, daily raining manna (or bread) from heaven to assuage their hunger, and defeating the attacks of their enemies. In Exodus 17, we learn that Moses brought forth water from a rock in answer to the unfaithfulness of the people. At the Lord's command, he struck it with his staff and the water flowed. (Not until later do we learn that Moses sinned here by not fully crediting the Lord with the miracle. We shall learn the dire personal consequences for him in the chapters on Numbers and Deuteronomy.)

At one point, the Israelites were attacked by the Amalekites. Moses raised his staff and the Israelites prevailed. Moses built an altar in thanksgiving and called it "the Lord is my banner" (Exodus 17:15).

Moses' father-in-law, Jethro, came to visit him, bringing Zipporah and their now two sons. After hearing Moses' account of all that happened, Jethro acknowledged the supremacy of the Lord, offered sacrifice, and feasted with Moses, Aaron, and the elders. On the advice of Jethro, Moses established the governmental system that would serve Israel for generations thereafter. He appointed judges to hear cases, establishing a legal bureaucracy to allow for efficient disposition of disputes and the teaching of the Law of God.

Moses Returns to Mount Sinai and Receives the Law

After a three-month journey, the Israelites arrived back at Mount Sinai, where Moses had experienced his initial calling. The Lord expressed His vision and promise for an obedient Israel, "And ye shall be unto me a kingdom of priests and an holy nation" (Exodus 19:6). Then He commanded Moses that the people consecrate themselves by bathing, washing their clothes, and maintaining sexual absti-

nence for three days in preparation for His presence. He set limits declaring that none should approach the mountain on pain of death. The people remained at the foot of the mountain; the tribal elders and priests were allowed at a higher elevation; Moses alone was allowed at the top with God.

Then the sky was filled with the thunder and lightning of the presence of the Lord, and the blast of a trumpet filled the air, and the people trembled and stood far off. Moses assured them that God was making this demonstration so they would believe, having seen Him with their own eyes. The mountain was wrapped in a thick cloud of fire and quaked. The voice of the Lord came forth from the cloud in thunder. He summoned Moses to the top of the mountain, leaving the people below.

Then God delivered the Ten Commandments to mankind—the basis of the legal, moral, and ethical systems of Western civilization ever since. In their short form, summarized from Exodus 20:2–17, they are the following:

1. I am the Lord thy God. Thou shalt have no other gods before me.
2. Thou shalt not make unto thee any graven image.
3. Thou shalt not take the name of the Lord thy God in vain.
4. Remember the Sabbath day, to keep it holy.
5. Honor thy father and thy mother.
6. Thou shalt not commit murder.
7. Thou shalt not commit adultery.
8. Thou shalt not steal.
9. Thou shalt not bear false witness against thy neighbor.
10. Thou shalt not covet anything that is thy neighbor's.

The Crossing of the Red Sea, *by Belbello da Pavia, fifteenth century*

The Lord further commanded Moses that the Israelites make no gods of silver or gold, but they should worship Him with an altar of earth or unhewn stone. The latter provision would be a key in the building of the Temple of Solomon, as the stones were fitted at the quarry rather than at the construction site, and no hammer was heard in the House of the Lord.

In Exodus chapters 21 through 23, God listed many of the specifics of the Mosaic Law govern-ing religious practice, social behavior, and legis-lation. These formed a firm organizational skel-eton for the tribal survival of the Hebrews that is still followed by observant Jews worldwide. Many of these tenets also remain the foundation of Western civil and criminal legal codes and social ethics, while others reflect ancient cus-toms no longer deemed acceptable. Among the first category are laws regarding property and criminal procedure. For example, manslaughter and negligent homicide are distinguished from murder; laws establishing civil liability and compensation for property damage are spelled out; conduct during civil lawsuits, rules for witness testimony, and the prohibition of bribery of public officials are explained; tolerance toward immigrants and protection of widows, orphans, and the poor are enumerated. Among the second category are statutes dealing with slavery (remarkably humane for the time), and the application of the death penalty for non-capital offenses including religious apostasy and sexual behavior. Within the legal codes of this section of Exodus is to be found the well-known biblical prescription for an ordered society built on the equivalence between offense and punishment: "And if any mischief follow, then thou shalt give life for life, eye for eye, tooth for tooth, hand for hand, foot for foot, burning for burning, wound for wound, stripe for stripe" (Exodus 21:23–25).

God promised to lead the people in their future travels to the Promised Land and to be at their side in battle. He also put forth a recurrent biblical theme: divine guidance and protection offered to those who follow in the paths charted by the Lord, divine punishment for those who do not.

> Behold, I send an Angel before thee, to keep thee in the way, and to bring thee into the place which I have prepared. Beware of him, and obey his voice, provoke him not; for he will not pardon your transgressions: for my name is in him. But if thou shalt indeed obey his voice, and do all that I speak; then I will be an enemy unto thine enemies, and an adversary unto thine adversaries. (Exodus 23:20–22)

God repeatedly stressed the unique nature of the Hebrew tribe—segregated from all others by the mark of circumcision and the specifics of diet, and forbidden to engage with regional neighbors in intermarriage, shared worship, or diplomatic alliances. "Thou shalt make no covenant with them, nor any of their gods" (Exodus 23:32). Multiculturalism was considered anathema and a snare to the unique position God had ordained for the children of Israel. Again and again the ethnic/spiritual exceptionalism of the Jewish people is repeated as a central theme of the Bible. It remained a major issue of contention during and after the mission of Jesus.

God summoned Moses and the seventy elders for further consultation, but first all the people proclaimed their allegiance to the Lord and His commandments. Moses wrote down the instructions of God in a book. He built an altar at the foot of Mount Sinai encircled by twelve pillars for the twelve tribes and offered sacrifices. He took half the sacrificial blood and threw it against the altar and poured the other half in a basin. He then read the book to the gathered Israelites and sprinkled them with the blood of the covenant—a scene later referred to by Jesus at the Last Supper: "For this is my blood of the new testament" (Matthew 26:28). Then Moses approached the mountain with the elders, "and they saw the God of Israel. Under His feet was something like a pavement of sapphire stone, like the very heaven for clearness" (Exodus 24:10). God summoned Moses further up the mountain alone. "And the sight of the glory of the LORD was like a devouring fire on the top of the mount …" (Exodus 24:17). The glory of the Lord covered the mountain for six days, then Moses ascended into the cloud and remained forty days and forty nights.

This full-size model of the Tabernacle has been erected in Timna Park in southern Israel near the port city of Eilat. It is a meticulously crafted masterpiece of biblical research, scholarship, and cultural preservation. It is open to the public.

THE INSTRUCTIONS FOR THE TABERNACLE AND THE WORSHIP

WHILE MOSES WAS UPON MOUNT SINAI, God laid out a long and elaborate series of instructions for the design of the Tabernacle and the Ark of the Covenant, the ceremonial garments of the Priesthood, and the consecration ceremony establishing the worship service.[4] These would remain critical attributes of the worship at the Temple of Solomon some four centuries later. To begin with, Moses was to receive free will offerings from the congregation of Israel. Since they had endured long years of slavery, and therefore poverty, the offerings would consist primarily of the gold and silver they had been given by their Egyptian neighbors.[5] In addition, colored threads, yarns, animal skins, incense, and stones and gems for the breastplate, oil, and spices would be required.

---

4 Exodus 25–31.

5 Just before leaving Egypt, God instructed the Israelites to ask their Egyptian neighbors for gold and silver objects. He explained that He would cause them to be looked upon with favor so that the Egyptians would be generous. In 2003, a group of Egyptian jurists, led by the Dean of the Faculty of Law at the University of Al-Zaqaziq, announced their intention to file a lawsuit against Jews worldwide, seeking reparations, with interest, based on the Exodus account. (The story was reported August 9, 2003, by the Egyptian weekly *Al-Alhram Al-Arabi* and in English August 22, 2003, by Middle East Media Research Institute. The lawsuit does not appear to have progressed since.)

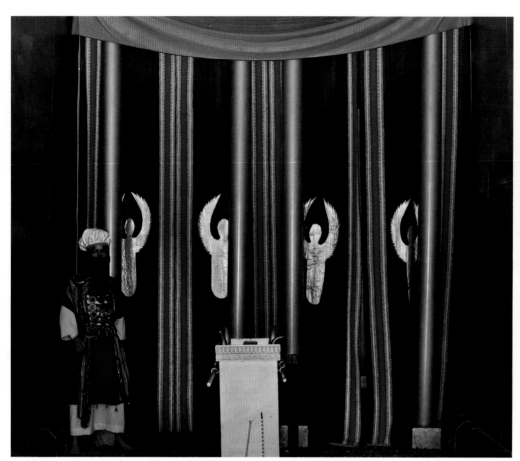

AT LEFT: *Inside the Tabernacle, approaching the Holy of Holies, before which stands the Altar of Incense.*
ABOVE: *The Lampstand*

The Tabernacle

The Tabernacle was a tent, a portable sanctuary to house the Ark, where the Lord might dwell among the children of Israel as they traveled. It was also referred to as the Tent of Meeting, Tent of the Presence, and the Tent of the Congregation. It would be erected when the Israelites were directed by the column of fire and smoke to stop and set up camp and dismantled as they were directed to leave and continue their journey. This sacred tent would later be replaced by the Temple of Solomon, a permanent habitation for the Lord (assuming His alliance with the children of Israel had been reciprocated).

The Ark of the Covenant

The purpose of the Ark of the Covenant was to provide a habitation for the two tablets of the Law (to be received by Moses at the end of chapter 31 of Exodus). The Ark was built of acacia wood, rectangular in shape, 2½ cubits long (45 inches) by 1½ cubits wide (27 inches) by 1½ cubits high. It was overlaid in gold inside and out with gold molding all around. Two gold rings were attached on either side (total four) to allow it to be carried by two poles of acacia wood, also overlaid with gold, slipped through them. The poles remained with the Ark when it was at rest.

The Mercy Seat

God would be present above the golden Mercy Seat on top of the Ark when He communed with the High Priest of Israel. The Mercy Seat was 2½ cubits long and 1½ cubits wide, thus filling the entire top of the Ark. Two golden cherubim, facing each other, were placed at either end. The outspread wings of the cherubim overshadowed the Mercy Seat.

The Table of Offering

A Table of Offering was placed inside the Tabernacle, also of acacia wood covered with gold, 2 cubits long (36 inches) by 1 cubit wide (18 inches), and 1½ cubits high. It had a rim and molding all around it of gold, and golden rings through which golden poles could be slipped to carry it. Upon the Table would be plates and dishes for incense and flagons and bowls for drink offerings, all of pure gold. The Table would be set with the "bread of the Presence" (NRSV) or "shewbread" (KJV). These twelve loaves of holy bread were to be continually offered before the Lord.

CLOCKWISE FROM TOP LEFT: *The Table of Offering with the Bread of the Presence; the Altar of Incense; the Ark of the Covenant and the Mercy Seat within the Holy of Holies; the colored Tabernacle curtains*

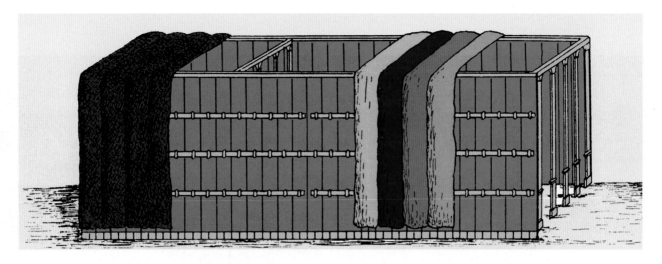

*The framework of the Tabernacle according to the research of
Clarence Larkin, colored by Rachel Wasserman*

The Altar of Incense

An altar for burning incense, constructed of acacia wood covered in gold, with integral horns at the four corners, measured 1 cubit in width and length and stood 2 cubits high. Golden rings allowed it to be carried with golden poles slipped through. It was set inside the Tabernacle before the veil of the Holy of Holies. The high priest was to offer incense on it every day, morning and evening.

The Lampstand

A beautiful golden candlestick with seven lamps or cups filled with oil, three on either side of the center bowl, was decorated with almond petal and leaf designs. The candlestick, its snuffers, trays, and utensils were to be made from a talent of gold, that is, 75 pounds, giving a sense of its enormous size. The lamp before the curtain of the Sanctuary was to burn continually with olive oil, tended by Aaron and his sons. "It shall be a perpetual ordinance to be observed through the generations by the Israelites" (Exodus 27:21 NRSV).

The Curtains

The Tabernacle itself was draped with ten curtains of fine twined linen: blue, purple, and crimson in color, embroidered with cherubim. Each curtain was 28 cubits in length (42 feet) and 4 cubits wide (6 feet). Joined together, the curtains were to have blue loops on their edges, and be held by golden clasps.

A single curtain of blue, crimson, and purple fine twisted linen, embroidered with cherubim, separated the two sections of the Tabernacle. The Ark of the Covenant was placed by itself within the Holy of Holies in the west. Without the veil at the south was the Lampstand. The Table of Offering was in the north. A screen was set at the entrance in the east, crafted of blue, purple, and crimson yarns of fine twisted linen, embroidered with needlework, and held by five pillars of acacia wood overlaid with gold.

The Roof

The roof was covered with eleven curtains of goat hair, 30 cubits long (45 feet) by 4 cubits wide (6 feet). These were held by bronze clasps. An additional covering of ram skins and fine leather was laid on top.

*The Courtyard showing the Sacrificial Altar and the Laver
in front of the Tabernacle at Timna Park*

The Frames

The frames of the tent were acacia wood, 10 cubits in length (15 feet) and 1½ cubits in width (2 feet 3 inches). They were pegged so they could be easily joined together or separated. The north and south sides of the structure had twenty frames, while the rear in the west was six frames wide, with an additional frame at either corner. The frames were reinforced with multiple bars passed through rings attached to them. The frames, bars, and rings were overlaid with gold.

The Courtyard

The Tabernacle was enclosed by a courtyard that contained a sacrificial altar and a large laver. The courtyard was draped with curtains of fine linen. Its length was 100 cubits on each side (150 feet) held by twenty pillars whose bases were bronze, with silver hooks and bands. The width of the courtyards was 50 cubits (75 feet). At the rear were ten curtains with ten pillars and bases. At the east entrance were hangings of 15 cubits (22½ feet) on either side, each held by three pillars and bases. At the entrance was a screen of 20 cubits (30 feet) of blue, crimson, and crimson yarn and fine twisted linen, embroidered with needlework and held by four pillars, all made

The Altar of Burnt Offering (at left) stood outside the Tent. The Laver (at right) was intended for the ritual ablutions of Priests prior to entering the Presence of the Lord.

of bronze and banded in silver with silver rings. The height of the hangings of the outer courtyard was 5 cubits (7½ feet). All the pegs were of bronze.

The Sacrificial Altar

In front of the Tent was a large sacrificial altar of acacia wood, 5 cubits long and 5 cubits wide (7½ feet) and 3 cubits high (4½ feet). Horns were carved at the four corners and the entire altar was overlaid with bronze. The pots, shovels, basins, forks, and fire pans used to collect the ashes of the burnt offerings were also of bronze, as was the grating. Four bronze rings were set at the corners into which two bronze poles were inserted to move it.

The Laver

A bronze laver for the priests to bathe was set between the tent and the sacrificial altar. The high priest and his assistants were to wash their hands and feet each time they entered the tent or made burnt offerings upon the sacrificial altar. "When they go into the tent of meeting, or when they come near the altar to minister, to make an offering by fire to the Lord, they shall wash with water, so that they may not die" (Exodus 30:20 NRSV).

The Oil

The Lord instructed Moses on the formula for the holy anointing oil, composed of myrrh, cinnamon, aromatic cane, cassia, and olive oil. Moses was to use it to anoint the Tabernacle and the Ark, the Table of Offering and the candlestick, the altar of incense, and all objects within the Tabernacle. Outside the tent, the laver and altar of burnt offerings were to be anointed, as were the High Priest and his sons. This specific formula for making oil was not to be used for any other purpose, and the people were instructed that anyone who made such a mixture was to be cut off from the community.

The Incense

The incense was composed of sweet spices, stacte, onycha, galbanum, and frankincense, seasoned with salt. This mixture too was regarded as exclusive to the Lord and not to be used for perfume by anyone else, also on penalty of expulsion from the community.

The Garments of the High Priest

God established a priest caste consisting of Aaron and his sons. The garments of the high priest were carefully described. They consisted of a breastplate, an ephod (a garment similar to a full-length apron), a robe, a checkered tunic, a turban, and sash. The colors were gold, blue, purple, and crimson, and the materials of yarns and fine linen. Upon the shoulders of the ephod were set two onyx stones engraved with the names of the twelve tribes, six names on each stone, set in gold filigree with chains of twisted gold attached.

Under the ephod was a robe of blue, with an opening so that it could be slipped over the head. It was decorated along the hem with alternate embroidered pomegranates of blue, purple, and crimson and bells of gold. "Aaron shall wear it when he ministers, and its sound shall be heard when he goes into the holy place before the LORD, and when he comes out, so that he may not die" (Exodus 28:35). This statement conveys the sense of awe, holiness, and danger attendant upon the priestly function. One has the impression that the sound of the bells would be a signal to the assistants that the priest had survived his time within the Holy of Holies. It is likely that this verse is the source of those traditions that believe the high priest had a rope attached to his ankle, that he might be pulled out should he either encounter difficulty

The high priest shown with the incense thurible, wearing the robe, ephod, breastplate, crown, and mitre as described in Exodus. Drawing by Clarence Larkin, colored by Nancy Wasserman.

or die—without his assistant priests violating the sanctity of the Holy of Holies.

The Breastplate, and of the Urim and Thummin

The breastplate was of gold, with blue, purple, and crimson yarns and fine twisted linen. It was a square of one span (a span measured approximately nine inches). Four rows of three stones each were set in place. The first three stones were carnelian, chrysolite, and emerald. The second row was of turquoise, sapphire, and moonstone. The third row had stones of jacinth, agate, and amethyst. The fourth row was of beryl, onyx, and jasper. These twelve stones, set in gold filigree, corresponded to the twelve tribes. The breastplate hung from two golden chains held by two golden rings. Attached to the ephod at the shoulders, it covered the high priest's heart when he went before the Lord.

The breastplate also held the mysterious Urim and Thummim that were used for oracular consultations.[6]

> And thou shalt put in the breastplate of judgment the Urim and the Thummim; and they shall be upon Aaron's heart, when he goeth in before the LORD: and Aaron shall bear the judgment of the children of Israel upon his heart before the LORD continually. (Exodus 28:30)

The Mitre

Upon the front of Aaron's turban or mitre was a plate of pure gold, fastened with a blue cord, engraved with the words "Holiness to the LORD." Set upon his forehead, it indicated that Aaron took upon himself any guilt incurred in the offering presented by the Israelites.

The Vestments of the Assistants

Moses was also given instruction for the vestments of the sons of Aaron, the assistant priests. These consisted of a checkered tunic, a turban of fine linen, and an embroidered sash. Both Aaron and his sons were to wear undergarments when officiating.

The Consecration of the Priests

The high priest and his sons were to be anointed and consecrated by Moses in an elaborate ritual lasting seven days, as described in Exodus 29. The entire ceremony was to be held at the Tabernacle. Aaron's male descendants were to be members of the priesthood by a perpetual ordinance.

The ceremony began with a set of sacrifices including a young bull, two rams, unleavened bread, cakes, and wafers made of wheat mixed with oil. The meticulous instructions for the consecration ritual included dabbing the earlobes, thumbs, and big toes of the candidates with the blood of the rams, then mixing blood with anointing oil and sprinkling it upon them and their vestments. Aaron and his sons would make a wave offering, or elevation offering, by raising their palms while holding all elements of the sacrifice together.[7] Next they were to place the elements on the altar and burn them; for the offering by fire sent a pleasing odor to the Lord.

Aaron and his sons were to cook and eat one of the rams and the bread while sitting at the entrance of the Tabernacle. No one else was permitted to eat this food. If any flesh remained after they ate, it was to be burned in sacrifice the next morning but not eaten. During the seven-

6 While the NOAB suggests the Urim and Thummim were two sacred lots held in a pouch hanging from the shoulder pieces of the breastplate, there is simply no description in the Bible. The commentary in the JSB also suggests they may have been two or more lots but is perhaps even more tentative in trying to define the terms. They are mentioned in this verse for the first time as if we knew what they were. Alternate interpretations are certainly conceivable.

7 See chapter 4, Leviticus, page 78 for more on these specific techniques of offering.

day ritual, a bull was to be offered each day as a sin offering.[8] The altar itself would be consecrated during this period by the repeated sin offerings. "Seven days you shall make atonement for the altar, and consecrate it, and the altar shall be most holy; whatever touches the altar shall become holy" (Exodus 29:37 NRSV).

When one of his sons would be chosen as successor high priest, he would be given Aaron's vestments and anointed while wearing them. He would wear them for seven days while ministering in the Holy of Holies.

More on the Sacrifices

God gave Moses a set of instructions for the regular sacrifices that were to take place at the Tabernacle. These included a lamb in the morning and another in the evening. Choice flour and beaten oil were added. Wine was to be used as a drink offering.

> This shall be a continual burnt offering throughout your generations at the door of the tabernacle of the congregation before the LORD: where I will meet you, to speak there unto thee. And there I will meet with the children of Israel, and the tabernacle shall be sanctified by my glory. (Exodus 29:42–43)

Once a year, on the Day of Atonement, the high priest was to perform the rite of atonement on the horns of the altar of incense with the blood of the sin offering. Expenses for maintenance of the service were to be met by the people making a ransom donation. God decreed that Moses take a census of the children of Israel. All persons over the age of twenty were to give a monetary atonement offering of half a shekel. The sum was the same for rich and poor; each member of the community thus shared equal responsibility and benefit.

Then the Lord instructed Moses on the sanctity of the Sabbath and the importance of observing it as a sign of the covenant between Himself and the Israelites. Six days were to be dedicated to work but on the seventh, everyone must rest. The penalty for violation of the Sabbath was death. The importance of the Sabbath remembrance was traced back to the fact that God created the heavens and earth and all that were upon it in six days, and on the seventh He rested.[9]

Bezaleel, the Craftsman

The Lord explained to Moses that He had chosen Bezaleel as His designated craftsman to build all that was required of the Tabernacle. This included the Tent itself, the Ark and Mercy Seat, all the ritual implements as described, as well as the vestments for the high priest and his sons. Bezaleel was given the understanding to compound the incense and anointing oil. "And I have filled him with the spirit of God, in wisdom, and in understanding, and in knowledge, and in all manner of workmanship" (Exodus 31:3). God appointed Aholiab as his assistant.

The Tablets of the Law

"When God finished speaking with Moses on Mount Sinai, he gave him the two tablets of the covenant, tablets of stone, written with the finger of God" (Exodus 31:18 NRSV).

---

8 For more on the various categories of offering, see chapter 4, Leviticus.

9 Exodus 31:12–17.

THE EPISODE OF THE GOLDEN CALF

While Moses remained on the mountain to receive his instructions from the Lord, the Israelites had become impatient that he had not returned. They feared he had died. They demanded of Aaron that he make gods for them. Demonstrating his own spiritual weakness, Aaron called upon them to give up their golden jewelry, which he then fashioned into a molten calf. And the people proclaimed, "These be thy gods O Israel ..." (Exodus 32:5). Then Aaron built an altar to it and the people offered sacrifices.

God ordered Moses to go down from the mountain at once. He warned him that the people had become corrupt, that His anger was kindled, and He swore to consume them. Moses pleaded with the Lord not to destroy the people; not to give the Egyptians the opportunity to cast slander on Him for freeing and then killing the Israelites. He implored God to remember His pledge to Abraham, Isaac, and Jacob. Then the Lord repented of His plan and Moses went down the mountain carrying the two tablets of the covenant. "And the tables were the work of God, and the writing was the writing of God, graven upon the tables" (Exodus 32:16).

The people were naked and running wild. When Moses saw for himself what was going on, he grew angry and cast the tablets out of his hands and broke them. He destroyed the golden calf, burnt it, ground it to powder, and placed the powder in the water and made the Israelites drink it. He expressed his anger to Aaron. Then Moses called for the people to divide themselves between those who were on the Lord's side and those who were not. The Levites gathered with Moses, who sent them out to kill those who refused allegiance. Three thousand were slain.

THE COVENANT RENEWED

The next day Moses told the survivors he would plead their case before the Lord. And he begged God to forgive the remaining Israelites. The Lord agreed to honor His commitment to bring the people to the Promised Land but sent a plague against those who had sinned. Then God stated that He would lead the people to the Land of Milk and Honey with an angel rather than go among them Himself, because they were a stiff-necked people. Moses pitched the Tabernacle outside the camp, and those who wished to commune would have to leave the camp to do so. When Moses went out into the Tabernacle, a cloud came over it, signaling that the Lord was in communion with Moses. "Thus the LORD used to speak with Moses face to face, as one speaks to a friend" (Exodus 33:11). Joshua, the trusted ally of Moses, would remain to stand guard at the Tabernacle after Moses had left.[10]

Moses pleaded with the Lord to continue to guide the Israelites to the Promised Land or to abandon the journey altogether, because there was no value to the journey without His presence. They were a unique people, set apart as the Lord's own. God relented and told Moses He would remain with His people. Then Moses asked to see the glory the Lord. "And he said, Thou canst not see my face: for there shall no man see me, and live"[11] (Exodus 33:20).

God commanded Moses to hew two tablets of stone like the ones he had broken, and

---

10 This series of passages (Exodus 33:7–11) is problematic because the actual Tabernacle is not yet built. It may refer to an earlier version of the tent or be out of sequence. The JSB suggests the Tent of Meeting may have been an oracle site for communication with the Lord, rather than the later habitation of the Lord as represented by the Tabernacle.
11 This seems to contradict Exodus 33:11, quoted above.

Moses in sacred rage breaks the Tablets of the Law upon finding the Israelites worshipping the Golden Calf in this dramatic engraving by Gustave Doré, 1865.

to ascend the mountain alone. Moses remained fasting on the mountain for another forty days and nights, neither eating bread nor drinking water. The Lord explained the series of rules by which the people would live in exchange for His alliance with them. He would defeat the inhabitants of Canaan and pass the land to the Israelites. But they must make no alliance with indigenous survivors, destroying their altars and sacred places lest they tempt the Israelites to worship strange gods. There must be no intermarriage with survivors as this would be a likely point of ingress for religious treason. "For thou shalt worship no other god: for the LORD, whose name is 'Jealous,' is a jealous God" (Exodus 34:14).

After forty days had passed and Moses had written the Ten Commandments on two new tablets,[12] he descended the mountain and returned to the people. His skin shone with such brilliance that they were afraid to come near him. Thus he wore a veil as he relayed all that God had said to him of the special relationship with the Israelites. But when he entered the Tabernacle to commune with the Lord, he would remove the veil.

Moses then passed along the extensive instructions for the Tabernacle that God had communicated, as delineated earlier. The Tabernacle was erected and properly consecrated on the first day of the first month. Aaron and his sons were brought to the Tabernacle and anointed and consecrated to serve as the priesthood of Israel.

Then a cloud covered the tent of the congregation, and the glory of the LORD filled the tabernacle. And Moses was not able to enter into the tent of the congregation, because the cloud abode thereon, and the glory of the LORD filled the tabernacle. And when the cloud was taken up from over the tabernacle, the children of Israel went onward in all their journeys. But if the cloud were not taken up, then they journeyed not till the day that it was taken up. For the cloud of the LORD was upon the tabernacle by day, and fire was on it by night, in the sight of all the house of Israel, throughout all their journeys. (Exodus 40:36–38)

And this was true for the remaining thirty-nine years of their journey to the Promised Land.

---

12 Exodus 34:27–28.

CHAPTER FOUR

LEVITICUS

THE LAWS OF SACRIFICE

*And there came a fire out from before the LORD, and consumed upon the altar
the burnt offering and the fat, which, when all the people saw, they
shouted and fell on their faces. (Leviticus 9:24)*

Leviticus explains the conventions for worship that God passed on to Moses at their meetings in the Tabernacle mentioned in Exodus. Leviticus devotes a great deal of attention to the specifics rules and methods for offering sacrifices; the dietary and medicinal laws of the Jews; the behavior of the priest class of Kohathites (*Kohenim*); and the moral values by which the people of Israel were to live. All these details of sacrifice and Tabernacle management were later carried over to the worship in the Temple of Solomon.

It may help the reader contextualize some of what will follow, especially regarding animal sacrifice, by remembering that the Hebrews were among the first people of the ancient world (if not the first) to prohibit human sacrifice. The story of Isaac and Abraham is the telling indicator—the Patriarch of the Israelites was instructed to substitute an animal for a human sacrifice. The Bible stories are also replete with commandments and warnings against the child sacrifice practices associated with the Canaanite worship of Moloch. Another point to consider is that animal sacrifices were not wasted. When the fat and blood were offered to the Lord, the flesh became the food of the priests and the people. The ecology of ritual sacrifice among the Hebrews was respectful both to the life of the animal (whose killing was treated with mercy) and to the well-being of the tribe. Admittedly, what follows from Leviticus is not the description of a trip to the supermarket.

RULES AND TYPES OF OFFERINGS

There were different purposes for various categories of offering and sacrifice. Some were made for maintenance of the community; some for specific holidays during the year; others for atonement, sin, or the violation of specific rules; some for the cures of illness; others for cleansing; those for celebrations and dedications; and some for anointing and consecrating priests.

Timothy Otis Paine's depiction of the Tabernacle as seen from the East. The front curtain has been removed so that we may see the nave and entrance to the Holy of Holies.

The priest or an assistant tending to the sacrifical fires at the Altar of Burnt Offering.
Illustration by Clarence Larkin, colored by Rachel and Nancy Wasserman.

Burnt Offerings

We are told that the sweet savor of burning flesh offered in sacrifice is pleasing to the Lord. The people were to bring their offering directly to the door of the Tabernacle. Burnt offering (such as bulls, sheep, goats, or fowl) should be of an unblemished male. The congregant could slay it himself. The priests, the sons of Aaron, took the blood and sprinkled it about the altar in the courtyard of the Tabernacle. The congregant could flay the burnt offering and cut it into pieces. The congregant could wash certain parts of the carcass, but the priests alone were authorized to place the offering upon the altar. The burnt offering was the only type of sacrifice totally consumed by fire (other than certain grain offerings offered in priestly consecrations). None of a burnt offering was to be eaten by anyone but the Lord. The burnt offering was considered the most holy.

Flour and Grain Offerings

Flour and grain offerings, mixed with oil and frankincense, were also acceptable, either with or without animal flesh with which they were sometimes mixed and baked. Any offerings with flour, if they were meant to be burned, were to be of unleavened bread only. Neither honey nor fruit were to be burned as they do not release a sweet savor. Vegetables such as corn might be properly mixed with meat for a burnt offering. Grain offerings were to include the salt of the covenant. The remains of offerings, other than burnt offerings, were for the sustenance of the priests and their families.

Peace Offerings

Peace or thank offerings (KJV) or well-being offerings (NRSV) of gratitude could be made of male or female animals, as long as they were unblemished. They could be spontaneously offered without a specific ritual calendar.

Heave and Wave Offerings

The techniques of heave offerings (KJV) or elevation offerings (NRSV), and wave offerings (KJV), were associated with the peace offering and were used with other forms of offerings as well. The breast of a sacrificial animal was to be waved in the air around the altar. After the fat was consumed in the fire by the Lord, the breast meat was reserved for the priests. The right thigh or shoulder, considered the choicest part of the animal, was to be heaved, or elevated, above the height of the altar. After the fat was consumed by the fire of the Lord, the meat of the shoulder was reserved exclusively for the officiating priest.[13] The techniques of wave and

---

13 See also Exodus 29:26–28.

heave offering were also applied to sheaves of wheat at Passover, and lambs and grains at Pentecost.

Sin Offerings

Sin or trespass offerings alternately specified male or female animals. The first class of sin offering was for unintentional trespasses. If an individual could not afford a livestock or fowl sacrifice, he or she could offer flour or grain unmixed with oil and frankincense.

Variations of sin offerings included those made for the priest, the entire congregation, the ruler, or individuals—each with its own specific set of procedures. For certain classes of sin offering in which bulls were sacrificed, the skin and unused portions of the animal were taken outside the camp and burned.

Intentional trespass offerings for crimes like violating property, lying, or swearing falsely were to be preceded by first making restitution to the injured party. Then one was free to make the ritual guilt or sin offerings to the Lord.

There were different gradations of sin offerings. The less critical were made in the courtyard of the Tabernacle and the leftover food could be eaten by the priests. The more serious sin offerings were to have the flesh consumed entirely by fire. The blood was collected and brought inside the tent and sprinkled on the altar for atonement.

Additional Rules for Sacrifice

The Jews were forbidden by perpetual statute from eating either the blood or fat of any animal, "For the life of the flesh is in the blood" (Leviticus 17:11). Blood and fat were reserved exclusively for the Lord. Some of the sacrificial blood was collected and used to anoint the horns of the altar of incense inside the Tabernacle. The rest would be poured at the bottom of the altar of burnt offerings in the courtyard. It would also be smeared on the horns of that altar. The high priest alone was allowed to sprinkle blood on the Ark behind the Veil.

The rules were specific that the meat offerings to be consumed by the Kohathites and the people be eaten within carefully codified periods of time so there would be no spoilage. No flesh of animals found dead or killed by wild beasts was to ever be either offered or eaten.

The fire of the altar was an eternal offering. "The fire shall ever be burning upon the altar; it shall never go out" (Leviticus 6:13). A series of procedures and rules also governed the behavior of the priests in the removal and disposing of the ashes of the burnt offerings.

Specific procedures were given for the preparation of grain offerings. Instructions were likewise given for the portions of sacrifices to be left for the sustenance of the priests and their families.

Regarding the Priests

In Leviticus 8–10, the consecration of Aaron and his sons by Moses is described as taking place within the Tabernacle in front of the congregation. This included a ritual bathing, clothing, and anointing with oil, along with a series of sacrificial offerings, both of animals and grains, and the sprinkling of blood upon the altar.

After the initial consecration, Aaron and his sons remained within the Tent of Meeting for seven days. On the eighth day, another elaborate series of sin and peace offerings were conducted with numerous animals and grains. Then Aaron and his sons performed sacrifices. And Aaron blessed the people and the glory of the Lord appeared. "And there came a fire out from before the Lord, and consumed upon the altar the burnt offering and the fat, which,

when all the people saw, they shouted and fell on their faces" (Leviticus 9:24).

Immediately after this consecration ceremony, two of Aaron's sons made an unauthorized sacrifice. They were immediately devoured by flame. Aaron and his two remaining sons were forbidden from mourning and remained in the Tent. The role of the Kohathites was to abide by and teach the statutes of the Lord.[14] Unless they scrupulously obeyed such instructions, their teaching would be irrelevant.

The priest class was to be regarded as separate from the community. They and their families could eat of the sacrificial foods as their children and wives were regarded as sanctified. The rules under which they lived were especially strict and carefully codified throughout Leviticus, and at length in Leviticus 21 and 22. The high priest who has been "exalted above his fellows, on whose head the anointing oil has been poured and who has been consecrated to wear the vestments" (Leviticus 21:10 NRSV) was under even stricter laws than his assistants. Specific customs applied to marriages, mourning for relatives, even the behavior of children. Like the animals they sacrificed, no priest with a blemish or physical imperfection was to make burnt offerings to the Lord, or be appointed high priest and allowed to approach the Holy of Holies.

A lamp was to continually burn in the Tabernacle before the Veil of the Holy of Holies, fueled by olive oil, lasting from evening to morning, tended by the high priest, established as a statute forever. The Shewbread (or Bread of the Presence) was to be set before the Lord in two rows of six cakes each, on a table of pure gold. It was designated as the food of the Kohathites.

---

14 Kohath was one of the three sons of Levi, son of Jacob.

Clarence Larkin's drawing of the Ark of the Covenant, colored by Nancy Wasserman

THE DAY OF ATONEMENT

After the death of Aaron's sons for violating proper ritual procedure, God counseled Moses to warn Aaron not to lightly approach the Holy of Holies and the Ark of the Covenant. He set rules for the Lord's annual gathering with Aaron (and his successors) as high priest of Israel. In contrast to the free access Moses enjoyed, the high priest was only able to enter the Holy of Holies one day each year on the Day of Atonement (*Yom Kippur*), in the seventh month on the tenth day.

In preparation, the High Priest was to ritually bathe and dress himself in consecrated white linen. He would begin with a burnt offering of a ram and a sin offering of a bull. He then cast lots over two goats, one of which would be sacrificed as a sin offering for the community; the other was designated as a scapegoat, the property of the demon Azazel, to be ritually invested with the sins of the Israelite community and sent alone into the wilderness. Aaron was to pass through the Veil into the Holy of Holies with incense, and then sprinkle the blood of the bull upon the Ark and the Mercy Seat. He

The garment worn by the high priest on the Day of Atonement was pure white. He is shown standing before the Veil that hung in front of the Holy of Holies. The curtain was embroidered with cherubim. He is holding a bowl of blood to sprinkle on the Ark and Mercy Seat. Drawing by Clarence Larkin, colored by Nancy Wasserman.

was to slay the first goat, bring its blood into the Holy of Holies, and sprinkle it like he had done with the bull's blood. The bull's blood was for his own sins and those of his family; the goat's blood was for the sins of the people. The annual Day of Atonement was to remain a statute forever as a day of rest and fasting for the entire community.

A SERIES OF LAWS FOR BEHAVIOR

Leviticus outlines a series of additional laws regarding diet and hygiene, sexual conduct, the sharing of resources, ethical behavior, when to gather for festivals, and the Jubilee. All of these would later be incorporated, in one form or another, in the regimen of worship at the Temple of Solomon.

The Jews were to remain apart, righteous in the ways of the Lord. "And ye shall not walk in the manners of the nation, which I cast out before you for ... I abhorred them" (Leviticus 20:23).

Laws of Food and Hygiene

The Kosher laws of the Jewish people regarding food and food preparation are described in Leviticus 11. The rules of hygiene and infection control are detailed in Leviticus 12 through 15. Such laws may appear severe and antiquated to the modern reader, especially at first sight. But they served to keep the Jews healthy in their wanderings and later in their communities.[15]

Such detailed and carefully codified rules also speak volumes about the cleanliness and eating habits of neighboring peoples in the latter half of the second millennium BCE. The Jews

of Leviticus were strictly enjoined toward bathing, washing their clothes, and keeping their houses free of environmental pollution.[16]

Biblical laws so focused on diet, health, and hygiene may help explain the high percentage of physicians, scientists, and medical researchers characteristic of Jewish culture. In the Books of Moses, the responsibilities of the priesthood included intimate involvement with medical care. God passed along certain very specific medical knowledge to them. In time, the priest/physicians would share the results of further research among themselves, their families, and the people at large.

More Laws Regarding Sacrifice

In order to legitimately consume the meat of an animal of his flock, an Israelite had to make it into an offering. The blood, fat, kidneys, and liver belonged to the Lord. A portion of the animal was donated to the priests. The citizen left with the majority of the meat that he and his family could enjoy within the bounds of the law. Such individual sacrifices were considered peace or thank offerings. This procedure would change after entry into the Promised Land and the establishment of a central location for worship at the Temple of Solomon.

No blood sacrifices were to be made by individuals outside the precincts of the Tabernacle. "And they shall no more offer their sacrifices unto devils, after whom they have gone a whoring" (Leviticus 17:7).

The Canaanite deity Moloch, whose worship involved child sacrifice, was particularly singled out as anathema to the Israelites. Any-

---

15 A number of these practices were later adopted by Muhammad as sensible prescriptions for the health of Muslims in that region and climate.

16 In *The Templars and the Assassins,* I discuss the epidemic of skin disease and lice that afflicted even the highest classes of Europe as late as the Middle Ages because of medieval Christian prohibitions against bathing.

one who sacrificed children was to be stoned to death.

Sexual Conduct

Laws of sexual conduct included detailed prohibitions against incest. "After the doings of the land of Egypt, wherein ye dwelt, shall ye not do: and after the doings of the land of Canaan, whither I bring you, shall ye not do: neither shall ye walk in their ordinances" (Leviticus 18:3). The full context of the warning suggests incest to have been quite common.[17] Sexual relations during menstruation were also forbidden. Homosexuality and bestiality were classified as abominations.

General Statutes

Further statutes of ethical uprightness repeat several of the Ten Commandments, but other laws were given as well. The edges of fields were not to be harvested, nor vineyards to be stripped bare, so that sustenance would be available for the poor and the sojourner. Kindness must be shown to the infirm; judgment is to be impartial, favoring neither the rich nor the poor; slander is forbidden; "thou shalt love thy neighbor as thyself" (Leviticus 19:18). Respect for the elderly was added to the commandment about reverence for parents. The consulting of wizards and mediums was forbidden. Kindness was to be shown to immigrants; honesty was to be practiced in business transactions. Penalties for various infractions were given in Leviticus 20 and were severe. An incident of blasphemy is recorded in Leviticus 24 that was punished by death by stoning from the assembled community. Further rules of conduct are given along with the consequences for violation of same. We are reminded again of the formula an "eye for an eye and a tooth for a tooth" (Leviticus 24:20).

The planting cycle, which included six years of growth and one year of rest for the land, is described. This was the source of the crop rotation methods of agriculture used ever since.

The Annual Festivals

The major festivals were outlined during which the people were to gather together as a community. The first is the Sabbath, the seventh day, on which no work is to be done. The Passover feast in the spring is a festival during which the first fruits of the harvest are to be offered with animal sacrifice. The Festival of Weeks (Pentecost or *Shavuot*), fifty days later, calls for an offering of new grain along with animal sacrifice. In the seventh month on the ninth day is the Day of Atonement (*Yom Kippur*). The Festival of Booths (Tents or *Sukkot*) follows on the fifteenth day of the seventh month and lasts seven days. It commemorates the people having lived in tents during the Exodus and upon their arrival in the Promised Land.[18]

The Jubilee

The concept of the Jubilee is introduced in Leviticus 25. Every fifty years, a trumpet was to sound throughout the land on the Day of Atonement. It heralded the time in which land would be returned to its original ownership. The idea was that everything belonged to God, therefore ownership was a form of lease from God. It was acceptable to sell the rights to land use to raise money when needed, but it would eventually need to be returned to the owner and his

---

17 See Leviticus 18:1–18.

18 See appendix 3 for more on the Jewish holidays.

MOSES, THE TABERNACLE, AND THE LAW

descendants as designated by God in the Book of Numbers (see chapter 5). Sale prices were to be calculated against the arrival of the Jubilee. Property bought in the beginning would be more expensive than property bought near the end of the cycle. City property was subject to different rules, as were the homes of the Levites in the Levitical cities.[19]

Bound servants were to be freed at the Jubilee. Residents of Israel other than Jews, to whom an Israelite had fallen in debt, could take a Jew as a bound laborer to satisfy his debt. However, the price was subject to the Jubilee provision when the Israelite debtor would have to be released under the law of the nation. Jews were not to be enslaved. If slaves were bought from surrounding tribes, they were to be treated kindly in remembrance of the fact that the Israelites had themselves been slaves.

The Grace of God and the Wrath of God

A series of promises and threats follow in which obedience to the commands of the Lord is endorsed, and disobedience severely rejected. The magnificent promises that inspired St. Bernard of Clairvaux and the Knights Templar are to be found in Leviticus. "And ye shall chase your enemies, and they shall fall before you by the sword. And five of you shall chase an hundred, and an hundred of you shall put ten thousand to flight: and your enemies shall fall before you by the sword" (Leviticus 26:7–8).

On the other hand, the curses that later became the daily bread of the Jews during the many incidents cataloged in this book— including the loss of the Temple of Solomon and the Babylonian exile, as well as the much later persecutions of the Middle Ages, and even the Nazi Holocaust—may be found in this place.

> But if ye will not hearken unto me, and will not do all these commandments; And if ye shall despise my statutes, or if your soul abhor my judgments ... I will even appoint over you terror, consumption, and the burning ague, that shall consume the eyes, and cause sorrow of heart: and ye shall sow your seed in vain. ... And I will set my face against you, and ye shall be slain before your enemies: they that hate you shall reign over you; and ye shall flee when none pursueth you. (Leviticus 26:14–17)

Yet an opportunity for repentance is offered and the possibility of redemption remains.

> If they shall confess their iniquity, and the iniquity of their fathers, with their trespass which they trespassed against me, and that also they have walked contrary unto me ... Then will I remember my covenant with Jacob, and also my covenant with Isaac, and also my covenant with Abraham will I remember; and I will remember the land. (Leviticus 26:40–42)

When the Temple of Solomon was built some four centuries later, it would be considered an especially consecrated space for the offering of such repentence.

---

19 The Levitical cities are discussed in Numbers. See page 95.

CHAPTER FIVE

NUMBERS

THE JOURNEY TO
THE PROMISED LAND CONTINUES

*The LORD bless thee, and keep thee: The LORD make his face shine upon thee,
and be gracious unto thee: The LORD lift up his countenance
upon thee, and give thee peace. (Numbers 6:24–26)*

In Numbers, we will be given more understanding of the dynamics of God's interaction with the Hebrews and the centrality of the physical Tabernacle in that relationship. Numbers also discusses the formation of a council of governance; the direct communication by the Lord to several people in addition to Moses; inheritance laws and tithing, including rights of female inheritance; and the division of the land of Canaan.

God met with Moses in the Tabernacle and commanded him to make a census in the beginning of the second year of the desert wandering. The total number of able-bodied men over the age of twenty and capable of going into battle was 603,550, not including the Levites. The number of male Levites over one-month-old was 22,000.

The campsite was organized by regiment, with each tribe assigned its designated position relative to the Tabernacle. The Levites were placed around the Tabernacle itself. They were tasked with protecting it, and supervising the Ark, altars, vessels, and all the other sacred instruments associated with the ceremonial liturgy. They were responsible for taking the Tabernacle down and setting it up each time the Israelites moved during the forty years of wandering. This was a great and complex task because of its large size and numerous structural components, including the boards of the frame, the coverings of the roof, walls, and courtyard, let alone the ritual implements, altars, and Ark. They were assigned a fleet of carts and oxen for this purpose.

They were to guard the tent against strangers and put to death any who came near. They were furthermore to act as assistants to the priests and were entrusted with the management of the congregation during worship services. The Lord considered the Levites the firstborn of Israel and therefore His own.[20]

---

20 Numbers 3:13.

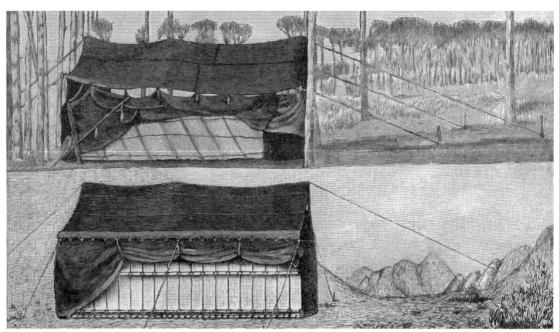

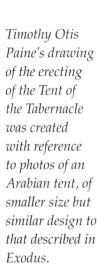

Timothy Otis Paine's drawing of the erecting of the Tent of the Tabernacle was created with reference to photos of an Arabian tent, of smaller size but similar design to that described in Exodus.

The Kohathites, or priests, placed their tents in the east of the Tabernacle. Any stranger who approached too close was to be killed. The priests were charged with taking down the Veil of the Holy of Holies and covering the Ark of the Covenant therewith. They were also to cover the Table of Shewbread and collect the bowls and spoons. Theirs was the responsibility for the candles, incense, vessels of oil, and the golden altar. They were in charge of the sacrificial instruments. No one was allowed to enter the Holy of Holies, nor to watch the covering activities the sons of Aaron performed, "lest they die" (Numbers 4:20). The Kohathites were responsible for moving those ritual objects that were to be carried on the shoulders.[21]

Various communal statutes were given in Numbers. These included additional hygienic laws such as segregating lepers and those with running sores outside the camp boundaries. A ritual for jealousy offering was outlined by which it could be determined if a husband's suspicion of his wife's adultery was proved, and the woman either punished or held innocent. The vow of the Nazarite was explained. We will later encounter two important Nazarites in Samson and Samuel. Nazarites were specially dedicated men and women who served the Lord for the period of their vow. They consumed no alcohol, ate no grapes, let their hair grow unshorn, and avoided all contact with corpses. "All their days as Nazarites, they are holy to the LORD" (Numbers 6:8 NRSV).

When the Tabernacle and altar and all ritual objects were set up for the first time and anointed by Moses, a festival of offerings was performed lasting twelve days. One tribe per day contributed stores of ritual supplies to the communal worship: silver and gold, incense, oil, grain, and sacrificial animals. At its conclusion, Moses entered the Holy of Holies where he heard the voice of the Lord from the Mercy Seat upon the Ark between the two cherubim. He was commanded to make a ritual cleansing and consecration of the Levites with Aaron.

---

21 Numbers 7:9. Properly carrying the Ark on the shoulders of the priests would later be a critical element for King David. See pages 150–51 and 154.

The pathos of the human condition is eloquently allegorized in Numbers, chapter 11. The people started complaining about their conditions and hardships. God's anger was kindled and He sent a fire against them, burning many in the outer fringes of the camp. The people appealed to Moses, who prayed to the Lord and the fires were quenched. Then they began to cry out and weep for the meat, fish, and fresh vegetables they had in Egypt. Forgetting the pain and humiliation of slavery and the oppression they had suffered, they showed a complete lack of appreciation for their liberation and the miraculous manna with which God preserved them.

The anger of the Lord was kindled again, as was that of Moses. He remonstrated against the Lord asking why he had been burdened with such an unruly and ungrateful people. Why should he be responsible for them and be charged with feeding them meat when it was beyond his power? Moses complained the burden was too heavy for him to carry alone. He begged for death rather than the wretchedness of his position of leadership. The Lord commanded him to form a council of seventy elders who would be consecrated at the Tabernacle and help him with his responsibilities. God would share with the elders a portion of the Holy Spirit which till then had been Moses' alone.

He commanded Moses to tell the people to prepare for meat that they would receive the next day, and for the next thirty days, in such abundance that the smell thereof would sicken them. Moses questioned the Lord. How could six hundred thousand people be fed with meat? Were the herds to be depleted? Were there enough fish in the sea to satisfy the needs of so many? The Lord replied to Moses that He was fully capable of fulfilling His promises.

Moses went out from the Tabernacle to tell the people God's words and gathered the seventy elders around the Tabernacle. The Lord came down in a cloud and took of the spirit that He had given to Moses and shared it with the seventy who began prophesying. Two others in the camp also received the Holy Spirit. When Joshua complained and tried to forbid these two from prophesying, Moses told him he wished that all the Israelites had the Spirit of God descend upon them.

Then the heavens opened up with a rain of quails that fell in enormous quantity among the people, as far as the eye could see. And they gathered the quails and feasted upon the meat as they had been promised. And as they did so, the anger of the Lord was kindled and He smote them with a great plague that killed many.

We are forced again to ask some troubling questions. The Bible expresses the belief in an all-powerful Deity rewarding and punishing behavior of which He—by virtue of His omnipotence—is ultimately responsible. If God is so angered by the decisions people make, why has He given us the power of error? If we are prone to lust after things of the flesh—luxury, sensual pleasures, instinctual demands—why are we so programmed? In other words, why does God punish us for behavior the roots of which He has planted in our hearts? This question has preoccupied philosophers, religious leaders, atheists, and others for millennia. I do not pretend to know the answer. However, I do believe there is a practical strategy available for those who strive after spiritual integrity—aspirants may become aware of the "right course of individual action" through prayer, meditation, and diligent self-searching. Do that, and no other shall say nay. The prophet Jeremiah will later offer a promise about God's solution to this problem.[22]

---

22 See page 238.

The Centrality of the Tabernacle and the Priesthood

A number of important scenes take place in which there is direct communication between the Lord and the Israelites. In each case, the exchange takes place at the Tabernacle. For instance, in chapter 12 of Numbers, Aaron and Miriam complained against Moses. The Lord arranged a meeting with the three of them at the Tabernacle and came down in a pillar of the cloud, standing in the doorway before resolving the issue and departing.

Similarly, in chapters 13 and 14 God sent scouts from each of the twelve tribes into the land of Israel. All but two of them returned with terrifying news. While the land was said to be fruitful, "flowing with milk and honey," they fearfully reported that it was occupied by a strong people against whom the Israelites would be powerless. In contrast, the scouts Caleb and Joshua were enthusiastic and confident of Israelite victory. The people bewailed their fate and plotted a return to Egypt. While they would be slaves again, at least they felt they would be protected by their masters.[23] "But the glory of the LORD appeared in the tabernacle of the congregation before all the children of Israel" (Numbers 14:10). Again, God expressed His impatience with the people's ingratitude and lack of faith. He threatened Moses with their destruction. And in one of those delightful biblical scenes, Moses bargained with the Lord and persuaded Him to withhold destruction of the sinners. He argued that the nations of the earth would regard God's slaying of the Jews as indication of His powerlessness in imbuing them

with righteousness, and therefore His prestige would be lessened throughout the world.

The Lord relented and pardoned them. But He announced that all those who had been slaves would be forbidden entrance into the Promised Land. He had brought them forth from bondage in Egypt and had performed countless miracles in their favor, yet still they desisted from placing their faith and trust in Him. Their ingrained servility and slave spirit had no place among the brave and hardy people He would require in the land of Israel. All former slaves would die off during the forty years of wandering to be imposed on them. He told Moses that the courageous and observant Joshua and Caleb would become the leaders of the next generation in the land of Israel. When the people heard these ill tidings, they mourned. Some arose the next morning to ascend a mountain and look on the Promised Land, and they tried to continue their journey thereto despite warning from Moses. These, for their disobedience, were slain by enemy tribes. Those scouts who had brought back the evil reports that swayed the congregation died by a plague visited upon them.

In chapter 16, a rebellion of two hundred fifty Levites is reported. They were resentful of Aaron having been singled out for the lineage of the priesthood; that Moses should have been chosen as their leader; and that they would die in the desert and be denied entrance into the Promised Land. Moses summoned them to the Tabernacle the next day and called for a test before the Lord. The people were warned to move away from the rebels. The two hundred fifty were consumed as the earth opened to swallow them and a fire descended to consume all traces of them and their tents. The leadership of Moses in deference to the Lord was again acknowledged. To further emphasize the lesson, God commanded Eleazar, the son of

---

23 One is reminded of Benjamin Franklin's apothegm that those willing to trade liberty for security deserve neither and will lose both.

Along the path of the Exodus. A view in Timna Park.

Aaron, to gather the brazen censors of the rebels and melt them and form them into a plate to cover the altar. This was done to remind future generations that none shall usurp the power of the priesthood. When some in the congregation raised their voices against Moses and Aaron for the deaths of the two hundred fifty Levites, the cloud of the Lord covered the Tabernacle. Though the Lord was again persuaded by the prayers and sacrifices of Moses and Aaron to desist from the total destruction of the Israelites, a plague was visited upon them that killed 14,700 people.

The Tabernacle was the scene of another demonstration of God's power. In order to quiet remaining murmurings against the priesthood of Aaron and the status of the Levites as keepers of the sacred rites, God commanded that twelve staffs be inscribed with the names of the leaders of the twelve tribes. Moses placed the rods in the Tabernacle. In the morning, it was discovered that Aaron's rod had flowered and blossomed and brought forth almonds. God then warned Aaron that only he and those of his bloodline were safe to enter the Holy of Holies; that even his brethren of the Levite tribe would perish should they attempt to approach the altar.

Numbers then continues with a discussion of the economics of the ecclesiastical classes. The Levites were to receive ten percent (the tithe) of the wealth of Israel for their service, while taking no part in the inheritance of land. The Kohathites (also unable to own or inherit land) shared in the tithe and received all wave and heave offerings, plus redemption fees for the firstborn of men and beasts. The Levites were to offer a tithe of their tithe as their portion to the Lord.[24]

The Red Heifer

Numbers 19 discusses the special sacrifice of an unblemished red heifer upon which no yoke had ever been placed. It was to be brought to Aaron's son Eleazar and sacrificed in his presence outside the camp. Eleazar was to sprinkle the red heifer's blood seven times before the Tabernacle. The entire animal was then to be burned, while spices and incense were added to the fire. The ashes of the red heifer would be collected and used as an essential ingredient for all later purification rituals. "The red heifer serves to atone for the spiritual chaos brought into the world through the golden calf."[25]

APPROACHING THE PROMISED LAND

The Israelites were now coming to the end of their forty-year period in the desert. Miriam, the sister of Moses who helped save him so long ago in Egypt, died and was buried. In Numbers 20:2–12, we revisit the story of the waters of Meribah coming forth from the rock to satisfy the thirst of the Israelites and their herds as told in Exodus 17:1–7 (see page 60). In Numbers, we learn that the rock was struck with Aaron's rod, the one that had flowered as a sign to quiet the rebels. We also learn that Aaron and Moses either doubted the Lord, or did not properly attribute the miracle to Him. Both were punished by being told they would not be allowed to lead the Israelites into the Promised Land.

As the Israelites neared the land of Canaan, they came to the territory of the Edomites,

the descendants of Jacob's brother Esau. The Edomites forbid them from crossing their land. Rather than fight their kinsfolk, they detoured to Mount Hor. This would be the final resting place of Aaron. He, Moses, and Eleazar climbed the mountain, and the Lord instructed Moses to consecrate Eleazar as Aaron's successor. When Eleazar and Moses returned alone, the people mourned for thirty days. Aaron was one hundred twenty years old.

Numbers records several battles as the Israelites continued their approach to the land of Canaan. In spite of their failings, this generation of free-born Israelites was courageous enough to be victorious in war, unlike their slave forebears whom God had directed away from military confrontation.

The Brazen Serpent

The incident of the Brazen Serpent is related in Numbers 21:5–9. The people were complaining again, wallowing in fear, ingratitude, and lack of faith. The Lord was angered and sent fiery serpents against them. Many were killed. Chastised, the people approached Moses, who prayed on their behalf. Moses was commanded to craft a fiery serpent of brass and set it upon a pole. Anyone who was bitten by a serpent and gazed upon the brazen serpent would be healed.

Balaam and the Moabites

The story of Balaam in Numbers 22–24 is a fascinating tale. Balaam's connection with the Temple of Solomon is that he was a non-Jewish prophet in direct communication with the Lord.

OPPOSITE: The Brazen Serpent, *erected in the desert by Moses, has intriguing parallels in the New Testament as discussed in part 7. Painting by James Jacques Joseph Tissot, ca. 1896–1902.*

---

24 Numbers, 18.

25 www.templeinstitute.org/red_heifer/introduction.htm

He followed divine instructions despite the personal risk to which he was thereby exposed. When we meet Solomon, we will be aware of his ecumenical nature. His close friendship with King Hiram of Tyre is one indication. Solomon's interaction with distant lands is spoken of primarily in terms of the women of alien cultures whom he loved, yet his legendary wisdom implies familiarity with the teachers and holy men of other faiths.

The illustration of Balaam's intimacy with the Lord points to the availability of such knowledge across racial and religious barriers. It may also presage the spreading of the Lord's message, outside the Jewish community proper, that would take place during the mission of Jesus and his disciples.

Balaam was approached by representatives of the king of the Moabites, who was fearful of the Israelites as they approached his territory. King Balak asked Balaam to curse the Hebrews. Balaam, in open dialogue with the Lord, was told the Israelites were a blessed people and that he should not involve himself in Balak's efforts. Balaam explained to the king's messengers that the Lord has refused him leave to go with them. The messengers reported all this to Balak. The king sent even higher ranking ministers to Balaam, promising him great riches for his service. Balaam again refused their entreaty. But this time, the Lord gave him permission to go, reminding him to pay attention to His messages as he received them.

Balaam's journey is one of the more colorful biblical tales. The ass upon which he was riding saw an angel blocking the trail and halted. Balaam angrily hit the ass. Proceeding onward, the ass saw the angel again. This time the ass plunged into a wall of rocks in fear, hurting Balaam's foot. Again Balaam beat the ass. The angel blocked the path entirely, leaving the ass no option but to fall down. Balaam was angered and hit the beast a third time. At which point,

God "opened the mouth of the ass" and she asked Balaam why he had hit her. Should he not ask himself instead whether he had ever known her to behave contrary to his wishes? At which point, "the LORD opened the eyes of Balaam, and he saw the angel of the LORD standing in the way, and drawn sword in his hand; and he bowed down his head, and fell flat on his face" (Numbers 22:31).

Balaam, instead of cursing the Jews at the command of Balak, blessed them thrice. Standing up to Balak's anger, he repeated his obedience to the commands of the Lord. He prophesied the defeat of the Moabites and other indigenous tribes at the hands of the Israelites because they were destined for victory.

Phineas, the Warrior Priest

In direct contrast to Baalam's indication of the universal nature of the God of Israel, we have the story of Phineas. The Jews began to engage in a pattern of intermarriage that will become more familiar as we proceed. In fact, here we find the seeds for the destruction of the Temple of Solomon. For in Numbers 25, we read that the Jews lusted after the daughters of the Moabites, and were led by these women into worshipping their god Baal of Peor. In retaliation, God commanded Moses to arrest the chiefs of the Israelites and impale them in the sun. Those of the people who had worshipped Baal were killed. A plague consumed twenty-four thousand. The plague was stayed in its course by Phineas, son of the high priest Eleazar (son of Aaron), when he slew an Israelite and his new Midianite wife with a single thrust of his spear. God blessed Phineas for his zealousness, declaring him and his seed an everlasting priesthood.[26]

---

26 Numbers 25:6–13.

Looking east across the Jordan River

The Division of the Land of Israel

A census was taken of the generation that had been born since the Israelites left Egypt. None but Moses, Joshua, and Caleb remained of the earlier generation. The Israelites numbered 601,730 able-bodied males over twenty fit for battle. There were 23,000 Levite males over the age of one month. The Promised Land was divided among them by lot (as referenced earlier in Leviticus as the original distribution to be reestablished at each Jubilee). Interestingly, the daughters of Zelophehad, an Israelite who had died on the journey, approached Moses. They sought to be included in the land claims although they were women. Moses brought the case before the Lord, who established the principle of the equality of female inheritance among the Israelites.

Approaching the Jordan River, God summoned Moses to climb Mount Abarim (also known as Mount Nebo) that he might see the Promised Land since he was forbidden from entering it. At Moses' request to protect the Israelites with an upright guide, God confirmed Joshua to receive the spirit of leadership, in alliance with the high priest Eleazar. Joshua was to follow the judgment of the mysterious Urim as communicated by Eleazar.[27] Joshua's role was thus different from that of Moses, who had received his instructions directly from God and was in charge of the priesthood of Aaron. Moses laid hands upon Joshua and passed on the charge of the Lord.

An additional series of laws of sacrifice and the divisions of the ritual year are given in Numbers. Moses followed this by instructing the people on the nature of vows made to the Lord, particularly discussing the difference between vows made by males and females. He pointed out that women must be obedient to their fathers and husbands, unless they were either widowed or divorced. This is a remarkable attitude about the equality of unattached

---

27 Numbers 27:21. For Urim and Thummin, see pages 69–70.

Mount Nebo is on the west side of the Jordan River. Photo by Vere Chappell.

women at a period in history when such regard was uncommon.[28]

Then Moses was commanded to fight the Midianites. The seer Balaam was slain in this battle. He is identified in chapter 31 as one who had advised and plotted with the Midianite women to lead the Israelite men into the worship of Baal. The Israelites killed all the Midianites except the virgins, who numbered thirty-two thousand. Extensive plunder resulted from the victory, including much sacrifice and offerings dedicated for use in the Tabernacle.

As the Israelites approached the Jordan River, people from the tribes of Reuben and Gad wanted to colonize the land east of the river because they viewed it as good land for their

cattle. After agreeing to fight with their kinsmen against the inhabitants of Canaan, they erected sheepfolds for their livestock. Moses promised they would be allowed to return to their wives, children, and herds after victory. The half-tribe of Manasseh (the tribe of Joseph was divided into Manasseh and Ephraim) also received land east of the Jordan.

Moses warned the Israelites that they were to drive out and kill all the inhabitants of Canaan and take possession of the land God had promised them. They were to break down the indigenous altars and destroy the high places. Should they allow any of the inhabitants to live, these "shall be pricks in your eyes, and thorns in your sides, and shall vex you in the land wherein ye dwell. Moreover it shall come to pass that I will do unto you, as I thought to do unto them" (Numbers 33:55–56). Then God

---

28 Numbers 30.

Here we see the division of the Land of Israel between the tribes as performed by Joshua (on the right) and Eleazar (at left) at the command of Moses. Painting by Louis Licherie de Beurie, seventeenth century.

laid out the geographical coordinates of the Israeli nation.[29]

Joshua and Eleazar were tasked by Moses with apportioning the inheritance of the twelve tribes. All the Israelites were to donate pasturages and cities for the Levites, as they were not included in the land divisions. Of the forty-eight cities allotted to the Levites, six were to be known as sanctuary cities, where those guilty of involuntary manslaughter could flee and be safe from vengeance until their trials. Murderers on the other hand were to be put to death by a member of the family of the victim. A murderer must die because his crime polluted the commonweal. Rules of evidence were established, and the ordinance was put forth of relying on the testimony of no fewer than two witnesses.

The daughters of Zelophehad agreed to marry within their ancestral clan so as not to confuse the process of land allotment.

---

29 Numbers 34:1–12.

Chapter Six

Deuteronomy

THE BOOK OF THE LAW OF THE TEMPLE

Thou shalt love the Lord *thy God with all thine heart, and all thy soul,
and all thy might. (Deuteronomy 6:5)*

The Book of Deuteronomy ("second law"), or a variant thereof, is referred to throughout the Bible as the "Book of the Law." It includes a series of addresses to the Israelites by Moses just before his death. The children of Israel were assembled on the east bank of the Jordan prior to their entry into the Promised Land. Moses spoke to them of the history of Israel, put forth a series of behavioral laws, and offered religious and moral teachings on the nature of their relationship with the Creator. He described the central place of worship that would be established in the Promised Land—ultimately the Temple of Solomon—and the central supreme court. He led them in a ritual renewal of the covenant. Then he walked off into eternity.

Moses began his address to the Israelites with an account of their wanderings in the desert following their stay at Mount Sinai. Since all the elders had died out on the journey, he was passing on the national history to a new generation. He submitted a catalog of the decisions and actions they took as they traveled under the guidance of the Lord. He described the organization of the tribal hierarchy in the desert, their battles and victories, their sins of disobedience and lack of faith. He made a detailed review of their recent approach to the shores of the Jordan and the Lord's tactical decisions as their ultimate commander in chief. He spoke of his own request that he be forgiven his misdeeds at Meribah and allowed entrance with them into Canaan, and of the Lord's refusal to grant his wish.

He continued with a discussion of the covenant between the Jews and God. He exhorted them to fulfill their destiny and be worthy of their promise. They should strengthen their faith by remembrance of the manifold blessings they had experienced, including receiving the Ten Commandments at Mount Sinai. He reminded the people that "the Lord thy God is a consuming fire, even a jealous God" (Deuteronomy 4:24). He told them it was their duty to teach their own children the ordinances and statutes unique to the Jews, the laws of the God of the nation.

Moses explained that if they violated these precepts and became corrupt after they entered the Promised Land, they would be defeated and scattered among

A view from the top of Mount Sinai

the nations. "And there ye shall serve gods, the work of men's hands, wood and stone, which neither see, nor hear, nor eat, nor smell" (Deuteronomy 4:28). This anticipates much that we shall be exploring in the following pages. But he extended God's promise of mercy should they call upon Him in their distress. He tried to inspire the congregation with an appreciation of the uniqueness of God's choosing of this people, bringing them forth from the power of greater nations, and directly communicating the divine law to them. He urged them to keep the Lord's statutes.

Moses began to list and review these ordinances. He reminded them that while the cov-enant was made with their forebears, he was now passing the teachings to them directly. He reviewed the Ten Commandments and recollected the fear and awe the Mount Sinai revelation inspired in their parents. He makes an interesting use of past and present tense in his speech to confirm the contemporary relevance of the Law throughout all the generations of Israel.[30] He communicated the formula of the *Shema*, the singular affirmation of the Jews ever since, "Hear O Israel: the LORD thy God, the LORD is one. And thou shalt love the LORD thy God with all thine heart, and all thy soul, and all

---

30 Deuteronomy 5.

Along the path of the Exodus. Timna Park.

thy might" (Deuteronomy 6:4–5). Jesus will later call this, "the first and great commandment"[31] (Matthew 22:38).

Moses pointed out that in the Promised Land the Jews would be given cities they had not built, vineyards they had not planted, and fields they had not tilled. To be worthy of these gifts, they must keep intact the central memory of their identity—their deliverance from Egypt. They must diligently keep the commandments of their faith and teach them to their children. They owed their full allegiance and gratitude to the Lord.

Moses ordered the Israelites to slay the inhabitants of Canaan, make no treaty with them, show no mercy in battle—lest they be diverted from their singular destiny. He declared that the peoples of the region were ever enemies to the Jews. Any form of cultural exchange was laced with potential snares. The altars and idols of the pagan tribes were to be smashed and burned in a campaign of religious iconoclasm that was to cleanse the Promised Land of the religions that God hated—most especially those that practiced child sacrifice.[32] He warned against people who divine by dreams and of false proph-

31 See also Mark 12:29–30.

32 Deuteronomy 12:30–31.

ets arising among the Jews, counseling them to adopt the ways of the pagans.[33] These must be killed as religious traitors. He later issued rules of war and siege that were reasonably merciful, however, they applied only to cities which were outside the homeland of Canaan. Of the present residents of the region, "thou shalt save alive nothing that breatheth" (Deuteronomy 20:16), so that "they teach you not to do after all their abominations" (Deuteronomy 20:18).

The Jews were to be given victory over the indigenous tribes because of the wickedness of those tribes, but the Israelites were never to forget their own wickedness. Moses warned them especially against disobedience and ingratitude. He reminded them of the miracles of the desert, how they were hungry and the Lord fed them, "in order to make you understand that one does not live by bread alone, but by every word that comes from the mouth of the LORD"[34] (Deuteronomy 8:3 NRSV). They must not forget the Lord in their new conditions of prosperity and well-being. Moses described the scorning of the Lord by their forebears and his intercession on their behalf. It was critical that the people enter the Promised Land with humility and right perspective.

He reviewed again the whole process of his receiving the Tablets of the Law on Mount Sinai, the blasphemy of the Golden Calf, and his continuous prayers on behalf of the Israelites. The Lord had desisted from destroying them. God replaced the tablets with two new ones and placed them in the Ark. "And He wrote on the tables, according to the first writing, the ten commandments, which the LORD spake unto you in the mount out of the midst of the fire in the day of the assembly: and the LORD gave them unto me"[35] (Deuteronomy 10:4).

Moses asked rhetorically what God required in return for the blessings which He had given to the Israelites. Moses answered himself by saying they must follow in the ways of the Lord, walk in the paths He laid out for them, follow the commandments that have already been communicated—and do so with love, and the spirit of service in their hearts. From the seventy people who went down to Egypt to join Joseph, the Israelites had become as numerous as the stars of the heaven. Moses explained the very real choice to which the Israelites were bound by the covenant. "Behold, I set before you this day a blessing and a curse; A blessing if ye obey the commandments of the Lord your God, which I command you this day: And a curse if you will not obey the commandments of the Lord your God…" (Deuteronomy 11:26–28).

THE STATUTES AND ORDINANCES OF THE BOOK OF THE LAW

In chapters 12 through 26 of the Book of Deuteronomy, Moses delivered a long series of detailed instructions on communal regulations, social customs, and ethical norms that form a coherent résumé of earlier religious laws. These expound the Lord's guidance on many topics: the making of sacrifices and offerings; hygienic and dietary laws; religious observances and festivals; the behavior of priests, Levites, and those who claim to be prophets; the swearing of vows; tithing; charity; marriage; divorce; sexual morality; inheritance; care and education of children, as well as their punishment; sanitation; treatment of immigrants, servants, and slaves; criminal laws, procedures, and

---

33 Deuteronomy 13:1–5.

34 Quoted by Jesus in Matthew 4:4 and Luke 4:4.

35 This varies with the text of Exodus 34:27–28, which says that Moses inscribed the second pair of tablets. See page 74 of this book.

punishment; laws of evidence; conduct of war, treatment of troops, and the disposition of captives; commerce; lending of money and charging of interest; political organization, and more.

The Establishment of the Monarchy

Moses prophesied that when the people settled in the Promised Land they would want to set a king over themselves to be like other nations.[36] This would be acceptable if pursued in cooperation with the Lord, to which end the king should have a copy of this Book of Deuteronomy continually at his side. A short list of rules was set forth for the king, among which were that he was forbidden from owning many horses or acquiring them from Egypt, "forasmuch as the LORD hath said unto you, 'Ye shall henceforth return no more that way'" (Deuteronomy 17:16). The future king was also warned against the acquisition of too many foreign wives and too vast stores of wealth; these would tend to turn him away from the Lord. We will later witness the violation of these statutes in the story of the decline of King Solomon.

THE CENTRAL PLACE OF WORSHIP IN THE PROMISED LAND

The centrality of worship in Israel around a place of the Lord's choosing is discussed in detail throughout Deuteronomy.

> But unto the place which the LORD your God shall choose out of all your tribes to put His name there, even unto His habitation shall ye seek, and thither thou shalt come: And thither ye shall bring your burnt offerings, and your sacri-

fices, and your tithes, and heave offerings of your hand, and your vows, and your freewill offerings, and the firstlings of your herds and of your flocks (Deuteronomy 12:5-6).

Jerusalem (although not yet identified as such) will be the pilgrimage point for the entire nation. The Temple Mount (also not yet identified) would become the new Tabernacle, the place of meeting between the Lord and Israel, the site of the Temple of Solomon.

The Erecting of Altars and Making of Sacrifice

When the Israelites crossed over into the Promised Land, and the place of the Lord's choosing was revealed, random sacrifices and erecting altars—previously part of the landscape of worship—would no longer be acceptable. "Take heed to thyself that thou offer not thy burnt offerings in every place that thou seest: But in the place which the LORD shall choose in one of thy tribes, there thou shalt offer thy burnt offerings, and there thou shalt do all that I command thee" (Deuteronomy 12:13–14). In other words, the nature of the worship ritual would change. After four decades of desert wandering, the Jews would erect a stationary home for the Lord—the Temple of Solomon.

In our discussion of Leviticus (page 82), we noted that the only legitimate way for an Israelite to consume meat from his herd was as part of a sacrificial peace offering. The consumption of flesh was strictly controlled. In Deuteronomy 12:15 this regimen changes because of practical concerns. The distances involved will be too great once the territory of the Israelites is so dramatically expanded. Therefore people will be free to slay their own meat and to hunt, as long as they pour out the blood on the ground.

---

36 Deuteronomy 17:14–20.

The Tithing Journey

The central site of worship was explained to be the place where tithes were to be carried. "And thou shalt eat before the LORD thy God, in the place which He shall choose to place His name there, the tithe of thy corn, of thy wine, and of thine oil, and the firstlings of thy herds and of thy flocks; that thou mayest learn to fear the LORD thy God always" (Deuteronomy 14:23). However, if a person lived so far away that carrying the sacrifice was unrealistic, the tithe could be turned into money and donated to the Temple as part of one's pilgrimage.[37]

The establishment of a central Temple meant that collections of offerings were to be gathered from throughout the land at certain times of the year and brought to the Temple by faithful Jews scattered far and wide. Every third year the tithes normally destined for Jerusalem were to be collected and given to the poor, the alien, widows and orphans, and to be shared with the Levites (who did not own property).

The Annual Communal Festivals

Jerusalem and the Temple Mount were singled out (although not yet by name) as the pilgrimage destination for the great communal gatherings during the annual sacred festivals. "Three times a year shall all thy males appear before the LORD thy God in the place which he shall choose; in the feast of unleavened bread (Passover), and in the feast of weeks (Shavuot), and in the feast of tabernacles (Sukkot)" (Deuteronomy 16:16).

The Levitical Supreme Court

Courts of civil and criminal justice were to be established throughout the land to judge with integrity. However, when a case was too complicated to be decided at the local level, it was to be brought before the Levites at the central place of worship, the court of last resort at the Temple. The judgment of the Levitical court was to be accepted as final.[38]

THE RITUAL ON THE BANKS OF THE JORDAN RIVER

Before the people crossed over the Jordan River and entered the land of Canaan, Moses describes a ritual to take place. They were to erect stones and plaster them, and inscribe them with the Laws of the Torah, and build an altar and offer sacrifice. Six tribes were to stand on one mountain facing six tribes on another. The Levites were to recite a series of curses for violations of the laws of God, to which the people would reply, "Amen." The counterpoint blessings are not recorded. However, the text continues with another series of blessings and an even longer set of curses.[39]

In Deuteronomy 30, the punishments and blessings appear inevitable, but the people are promised that in their misery to come, the Lord will show mercy when they call upon Him. But in verses 16–20, it is as if the people have a choice. God counsels, "therefore choose life, that both thou and thy seed may live" (Deuteronomy 30:19).

---

37 This would later become a matter of grave concern for Jesus. See page 300–301.

38 Deuteronomy 17:8–9.

39 The intensity of these curses will make it easy for the reader to appreciate why King Josiah rent his clothes in despair after reading the Book of the Law, discovered some five centuries later during a restoration of Solomon's Temple. See pages 225–26.

THE PASSING OF THE MANTLE OF LEADERSHIP

Moses, now one hundred twenty years old, publicly acknowledged Joshua as his successor as political and military leader of the Hebrew nation. After completing the writing of the text of Deuteronomy, Moses committed the book to the Levites to act as a spiritual guide. He commanded them to read it aloud every seven years to the assembled multitude at the Feast of Tabernacles, "When all Israel is come to appear before the LORD thy God in the place which He shall choose" (Deuteronomy 31:11).

Then the Lord called Moses and Joshua to enter the Tabernacle so that Joshua might receive the Lord's charge. God appeared in a pillar of cloud at the entrance of the tent. Then He told Moses of the future of the people, and their disobedience and betrayal of the rigors and exclusivity of the Jewish Law, and the punishment and suffering to follow.

> For when I shall have brought them into the land which I sware unto their fathers, that floweth with milk and honey; and they shall have eaten and filled themselves, and waxen fat; then will they turn unto other gods, and serve them, and provoke me, and break my covenant. (Deuteronomy 31:20)

God commanded Moses to write a song for the Jews that they might leave aside their transgressions and remember their obligations and the path of return to grace. Moses instructed the Levites to take the Book of Deuteronomy and place it beside the Ark, that it act as a spiritual anchor and a reminder of the Torah. He recited the words of the song to the people (a terrible song—like so much of the Bible, it is filled with a litany of threats and recriminations offset with declarations of love and promise).

The Death of Moses

Then God commanded Moses to ascend Mount Nebo near Jericho—as Aaron had ascended Mount Hor—that he might behold the Promised Land before he died. Moses blessed the twelve tribes and invoked God's mercy upon them. And he ascended the mountain and was granted a vision of the entire land of Israel; then he died. He was buried in secret by the Lord in the land of Moab near Beth-peor in a hidden tomb. The Israelites mourned him for thirty days. "And there arose not a prophet since in Israel like unto Moses, whom the LORD knew face to face" (Deuteronomy 34:10).

OPPOSITE: *This manificent image from the ninth-century Carolingian Bible of San Paolo shows Moses in the center panel giving his final instructions to the Israelites as they stand along the banks of the Jordan River. The Patriarchs Abraham, Isaac, and Jacob are to his right. Above, Moses is shown experiencing the vision of the Promised Land. At top left he dies on Mount Nebo while his body is guarded by an Angel.*

The king of Arad is mentioned in Joshua 12:14 as one of those conquered by the armies of Israel during the military campaigns throughout the Holy Land. Today Tel Arad is the scene of extensive archaeological explorations of both Jewish and Canaanite remains.

PART THREE

PRE-MONARCHICAL LEADERSHIP

(Joshua, Judges, Ruth, 1 Samuel)

Tel Jericho is the site of an extensive archaeological exploration of the ancient city. These rock forms suggest the once mighty walls of the city conquered by the army of Joshua with reliance on the power generated by the Ark of the Covenant.

CHAPTER SEVEN

JOSHUA

SUBDUING THE LAND OF ISRAEL

Be strong and of a good courage; be not afraid, neither be thou dismayed:
for the LORD thy God is with thee whithersoever thou goest. (Joshua 1:9)

Upon the death of Moses, Joshua became the commander of the Israelites. Under his leadership, the Israelites began the process that would lead them to the conquest of Jerusalem and the establishment of the Temple of Solomon. God ordered Joshua to bring the people across the Jordan River into Canaan and promised, "as I was with Moses, so shall I be with thee: I will not fail thee, nor forsake thee" (Joshua 1:3). Further, He counseled Joshua on the means by which he could best carry out his task.

> This book of the law shall not depart out of thy mouth; but thou shalt meditate therein day and night, that thou mayest observe to do according to all that is written therein: for then thou shalt make thy way prosperous, and then thou shalt have good success. (Joshua 1:8)

Joshua readied the people for an imminent crossing, reminding the tribes of Reuben, Gad, and the half-tribe of Manasseh that they were to help in the conquest west of the Jordan before being free to return to inhabit the Transjordan. They recognized Joshua and renewed the oath of loyalty and military obedience they had sworn to Moses.

Joshua sent two spies to investigate the situation in Jericho. They stayed at the home of a prostitute named Rahab. The king of Jericho learned of their presence and sent officers to Rahab to capture them. She hid the men and deceived the king, telling him the spies had already left. He sent soldiers looking for them. Rahab explained to the Israelites that word of the deeds of the Lord had gripped the people of Canaan with fear of His might, "for the LORD your God, he is God in heaven above, and in earth beneath" (Joshua 2:11). She asked them to spare her and her family when the army invaded, which they promised to do.

Joshua made camp near the Jordan River. On God's signal, he directed the Levites to carry the Ark toward the banks of the river while the people followed at a safe distance. The Jordan parted as soon as the feet of the Levites touched the waters. They carried the Ark to the middle of the river. A pathway of dry land formed and the people walked across it to Jericho, their first destination.

After everyone had crossed, the Lord instructed Joshua to assemble twelve men, one from each of the tribes. They were to gather a stone from the place where the Ark had stood in the middle of the river. These twelve stones formed the first memorial altar in the land of Canaan at Gilgal, just east of Jericho. Joshua also laid twelve stones in the midst of the Jordan where the priests holding the Ark had stood, "and they are there unto this day" (Joshua 4:9). When the people had all passed safely to the other side, the Lord told Joshua to call to the priests carrying the Ark to come to land as well. As soon as their feet touched the other shore, the Jordan flowed normally. One result of this episode was the acknowledgment of Joshua's stature as Moses' true successor.

Among the Israelites were some forty thousand armed warriors ready for battle. Those males who had not been circumcised during the desert wandering became so at Gilgal. They kept the Passover on the plain of Jericho. And they ate of the corn of Canaan. The manna ceased to fall at this time.

Joshua met an armed warrior and asked him which side he was on. The warrior answered that he was an angel, a captain of the host of the Lord. Joshua fell on his face before him. The angel commanded him, "Loose thy shoe from off thy foot; for the place whereon thou standest is holy" (Joshua 5:15). He laid out a series of instructions for Joshua, explaining that Jericho would fall to the Israelites after the following manner: the warriors were to circle the city once each day for six days, with seven priests bearing the Ark of the Covenant and blowing seven trumpets of ram's horns. On the seventh day, they were to circle seven times while blowing their trumpets. When the priests blew a single long blast, the people were to make a great shout and the walls of the city would fall.

The Israelites were further ordered not to take any of the ritual objects of the cult of Jericho lest they bring destruction upon themselves. They were allowed to take any gold, silver, bronze, or iron implements to add to the Temple treasury. They were to kill all the people of the city with the exception of Rahab and her family. And Rahab dwelt with Israel "even unto this day" because of her faithfulness (Joshua 6:25).

Unfortunately, one of the Israelites took some ritual objects, kindling the anger of the Lord. Such an act of faithlessness, even by one person, redounded against the entire community. The Israelite army was defeated in battle by a numerically smaller force of the people of Ai. Joshua cried before the Lord in front of the Ark. He lamented that the Israelites had been encouraged to cross the Jordan only to face defeat. They could have stayed in the Moabite lands they had already conquered. But the Lord explained that a sin had been committed and that unless the perpetrator were caught and killed, and the cult objects destroyed, the Israelites were in trouble. And indeed the perpetrator was discovered by the process of casting lots. He admitted his guilt, confessing that he had coveted what he saw, disobeyed the commands of the Lord, and taken the forbidden materials. The people found the booty, and the miscreant and his family were stoned; their bodies and the unholy objects were burned and buried. Then Joshua defeated the Ai, killing their king and all the inhabitants of the city.

Joshua built an altar of unhewn stones upon Mount Ebal where they sacrificed burnt offerings and peace offerings unto the Lord. He wrote out a copy of the law of Moses upon some other stones. Then he divided the people into two groups on either side of the Ark and read the ritual of the blessings and cursing as described by Moses in Deuteronomy, ceremonially renewing the covenant thereby. "There was not a word of all that Moses commanded that Joshua did not read before all the assembly of Israel" (Joshua 8:35 NRSV).

A number of Canaanite tribes joined in a military alliance against Israel. But the people of the city of Gibeon tricked the Israelites into making a separate peace treaty with them. The Gibeonites pretended to have traveled from a far off land to forge an alliance with the God and people of Israel. Because the Israelites did not first seek the counsel of the Lord, they made vows of peace and protection with the Gibeonites. Upon the ruse being discovered, the Gibeonites explained that they knew the Lord had given the land of Canaan to the Israelites. They wanted to save themselves from being killed. Joshua told them they would henceforth become the servants of the Jews, and that their condition of servitude would extend to the time of the future Temple. "And Joshua made them that day hewers of wood and drawers of water for the congregation, and for the altar of the LORD, even unto this day, in the place which He should choose" (Joshua 9:27).

Five surrounding tribes learned of the Gibeonite treaty and determined to band together under the leadership of the king of Jerusalem and attack them. The people of Gibeon called on Joshua for protection. Joshua's army utterly defeated the five allied kings. At one point the Lord cast down great hailstones upon the fleeing armies, killing more in this manner than died by the sword. Joshua called out to the Lord to prolong the day that the Israelites might not be interrupted from slaying their foe.

And the sun stood still, and the moon stayed, until the people had avenged themselves upon their enemies.... And there was no day like that before it or after it, that the LORD hearkened unto the voice of a man: for the LORD fought for Israel. (Joshua 10:13–14)

Joshua then led the Israelites in a great series of conquests throughout the region. Neighboring kings formed alliances against the Israelites but it was impossible to stop the God-led juggernaut. The allied enemy armies numbered like "the sand on the seashore" (Joshua 11:4 NRSV). In each case, Joshua's army defeated them and killed all the residents of the cities and towns they attacked—following the battle plans outlined by Moses. Joshua eventually conquered much of the territory that had been promised to the Israelites and there was peace.

Meanwhile Joshua had grown old. God advised him that while much territory remained to be taken, the Lord Himself would lead the charge. Joshua could begin to divide the land. He and the high priest Eleazar began to assign the land of Canaan among the tribes of Israel by drawing lots. "And the whole congregation of the children of Israel assembled together at Shiloh, and set up the tabernacle of the congregation there. And the land was subdued before them" (Joshua 18:1).

Joshua next summoned the tribes of Reuben and Gad and the half-tribe of Manasseh and freed them of their oaths and allowed them to return to their lands east of the Jordan. Then he blessed them. A telling episode occurred when the departing tribes built an altar in remembrance of the Lord on the west side of the Jordan just before they crossed over. The Israelites,

OVERLEAF: *Joshua and the army of the Israelites battle throughout the Promised Land in this dramatic painting by Nicolas Poussin, 1624.*

An archaeological excavation at Tel Shiloh, the site that once held the Tabernacle

learning of this, feared that they were either embracing alien gods or countermanding the instructions of Deuteronomy to have a central altar of sacrifice associated with the location of the Tabernacle. The redoubtable Phineas, son of Eleazar, went with an army against them lest they defile the entire congregation again. But the trans-Jordanian tribes explained the altar was not for sacrifice but for a sign of remembrance, a witness that they and their children were part of the nation of Israel though they lived east of the Jordan. All rejoiced that the commandments of the Lord were being honored.

Joshua was now one hundred ten years old and spoke to the people before he died. He reminded them of the victories the Lord had won for them and of His promise to complete the conquest of the land. He counseled that they be steadfast in their observance of the Book of the Law of Moses so that they not be swayed to apostasy by their contact with their neighbors. He raised the specter of intermarriage with the surviving residents of Canaan and the dilution of the tribal purity of the Israelite nation. He warned they would lose the Lord's favor if they chose that path. He pointed out their power when aligned with God's will with words that would inspire the Knights Templar over two millennia later: "One man of you shall chase a thousand: for the LORD your God, he it is that fighteth for you, as he hath promised you" (Joshua 23:10).

Joshua reminded them that the ancestors of Abraham had worshipped strange gods before the Flood but that the Lord had reached out and taken Abraham and established His covenant with him and his descendants. He told the Israelites they faced a choice from among three possibilities: they could serve the gods of the ancients; they could serve the gods of the tribes that had fallen to them; or they could follow Joshua's example and serve the Lord.

The people recoiled in horror at the suggestion that they would serve other gods and swore they too would serve the Lord only. But again, Joshua reminded them of the severity of the law of Israel, "Ye cannot serve the Lord: for He is an holy God; He is a jealous God; He will not forgive your transgressions nor your sins. If ye forsake the Lord, and serve strange gods, then He will turn and do you hurt, and consume you, after that He hath done you good" (Joshua 24:19–20).

And again the people swore eternal allegiance to the Lord. Joshua took their oath and explained that it was a covenant and they agreed to abide by it.

And Joshua wrote these words in the book of the law of God, and took a great stone, and set it up there under an oak, that was by the sanctuary of the Lord. And Joshua said unto all the people, "Behold, this stone shall be a witness unto us; for it hath heard all the words of the Lord which He spake unto us: it shall be therefore a witness unto you, lest ye deny your God." (Joshua 24: 26–27)

Joshua now too passed away and was buried in the region of Mt. Ephraim. Eleazar died as well and Phineas succeeded him as high priest. Joshua's time is remembered as one in which the people of Israel kept the commandments of the Lord. They also fulfilled the promise to Joseph and buried his bones, carried from Egypt, in the tomb he had purchased long ago at Shechem.

The Lord gave unto Israel all the land which He sware to give unto their fathers; and they possessed it, and dwelt therein. (Joshua 21:43)

CHAPTER EIGHT

JUDGES

THE PEOPLE DEPART FROM RIGHTEOUSNESS

*In those days, there was no king in Israel, but every man did
that which was right in his own eyes. (Judges 17:6)*

Upon the death of Joshua, the tribes of Judah and Simeon led the continued military campaign of Canaanite conquest. They mounted the first successful attack against Jerusalem, although the Jebusites were not totally defeated and continued to live among the Israelites. We learn early on in Judges that adherence to the commands of the Lord, especially regarding the conduct of military operations, had become a thing of the past. The observation is repeated over and over that the Israeli victors did not kill their Canaanite foes when they took possession of their towns and villages. Instead they allowed them to live among them as tributaries and forced laborers.

The policies communicated by Moses and Joshua, on instructions from the Lord, were ignored. We will soon witness the profoundly negative influence that the surviving indigenous Pagan cults exerted on the Israelites. Ultimately, of course, they strayed so far from adherence to the ways of the Lord by adopting pagan practices that the Temple of Solomon itself would be destroyed.

An angel came and pointed out their violation of God's instructions. He reminded the people of the Lord's policy. They were to make no league with the inhabitants of the land and they were to throw down their altars. He asked them why they had disobeyed. And he warned of the consequences they would now face as a result. "I will not drive them out from before you; but they shall be as thorns in your sides, and their gods shall be a snare unto you" (Judges 2:3). Upon hearing this the people wept and sacrificed to the Lord.

Yet the degeneration of Israel was well under way. Bereft of leaders who walked with God such as Moses and Joshua, this generation "knew not the LORD, nor yet the works which He had done for Israel" (Judges 2:11). Instead, the Israelites intermarried with the various tribes of Canaan and followed their gods. "And they forsook the LORD, and served Baal and Ashtaroth" (Judges 2:13). The Lord's anger caused the Israelites to suffer a series of military defeats.

However, during this period, God raised up a series of leaders to guide the community for a time. The pattern of the Book of Judges is the following: The people would do wrong and be defeated and enslaved; they would cry out to the Lord; a judge would arise from among them and be touched by the Lord; he or she would lead the people to righteousness and prosperity for a time; then the judge would die and the cycle of disobedience would be repeated. The term "judge" implied not only a leader to whom the people would turn for moral and legal guidance, but also a military commander and religious arbiter.

The generation that followed the death of Joshua had no experience of war. They were surrounded by numerous Canaanite tribes. Because of their pattern of intermarriage and apostasy, they fell under the hand of a local king and served him in bondage for eight years. The first of the judges arose, Othniel, the nephew of Caleb. He brought liberation and peace for forty years before he died.

Then the people reverted to behavior that displeased the Lord. The Moabites defeated and enslaved them for eighteen years until Ehud, a Benjamite, arose to free them. "A man lefthanded" (Judges 3:15), Ehud slew the Moabite king with a hidden dagger. He escaped the palace and assembled an army. The Israelites defeated ten thousand Moabite soldiers. They enjoyed eighty years of freedom under the leadership of Ehud and his successor Shamgar, who led them to victory against the Philistines.

Falling back to their old ways, the Israelites were defeated and enslaved for twenty years by the Canaanites. The prophetess Deborah arose as the next judge. The community's allegiance to the ways of the Lord resulted in victory over their enemies. Deborah led a successful campaign, with her general Barak, against a huge army that included nine hundred iron chariots, commanded by the Canaanite general Sisera. The Israelite troops numbered just ten thousand. They defeated the Canaanite army to a man. Sisera fled the battlefield and attempted to hide himself in the home of an Israelite woman

Jael, an Israeli heroine, as depicted in a mosaic on the floor of the Dormition Church in Jerusalem. She is shown holding the hammer and spike with which she killed Sisera as he slept. Photo by Deror avi.

named Jael, a descendant of Moses' father-in-law, Jethro. Sisera thought he had an alliance with Jael who pretended she would protect him, but when he was at his ease, she killed him. The Israelites flourished forty years under Deborah's leadership.

They fell back into their evil ways after her death and languished under the Midianites for seven years. A prophet came to remind them that they had once been beloved of the Lord. Then an angel appeared to Gideon and promised him victory and salvation. Gideon, in humility, asked how such a thing could be possible given their circumstances of servitude. He asked the angel to await his sacrifice and prepared an offering and laid it on a rock. The angel brought forth fire from the rock and consumed the offering and departed. And Gideon built an altar to the Lord.

 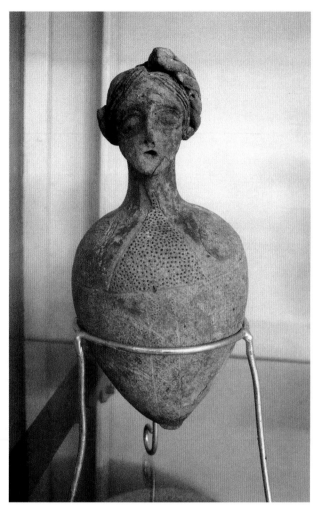

Canaanite fertility goddess at left is dated from Early Bronze Age I (3300–3000 BCE).
Both icons are in the collection of the Archaeological Museum, Amman, Jordan.
Photos by Vere Chappell.

Then God commanded Gideon to tear down his father's altar to Baal and cut down the nearby pagan grove. He should build an altar to the Lord in its place and sacrifice a bullock thereon. Gideon did this at night for fear of the townsfolk. When morning came and the people saw what had happened, they demanded Gideon's father bring him out so they could execute him. But Gideon's father scoffed at them and at Baal. He told them it was Baal's problem to punish Gideon for destroying his altar. The worshippers of Baal encamped for war.

The spirit of the Lord descended upon Gideon and he blew his trumpet, and the first of the soldiers gathered around him. He sent out messengers to the Jewish tribes. He asked the Lord for another sign of his mission and the Lord granted him assurance twice more.

God decided to make it clear to the Israelites exactly who was responsible for their victories. Gideon's army consisted of thirty-two thousand men. The Lord knew that if the Israelites won the upcoming battle, they would take credit for it. So He progressively reduced the size of the Israeli army until it numbered but three hundred soldiers. The Midianites and Amakelites, on the other hand, were "like grasshoppers for multitude; and their camels were without num-

A series of cult deities in the Citadel Museum in Jerusalem. Photo by Vere Chappell.

ber, as the sand by the sea side for multitude" (Judges 7:12).

Gideon was inspired with confidence by the Lord and employed a series of deceptive tactics against the enemy. The Hebrew warriors sowed confusion and fear among their opponents and the Midianites fled the tiny force. Then Gideon called up the reserve troops and they chased after the enemy. One hundred and twenty thousand Midianite soldiers were killed. After the victory was complete, the Israelites came to Gideon and asked that he and his descendants rule over them. But Gideon replied, "I shall not rule over you, neither shall my son rule over you; the LORD shall rule over you" (Judges 8:23).

Next follows a confusing scene, indicative of the endemic corruption that runs throughout the period described in Judges. Gideon asked the people to donate some of the gold they had seized from the defeated enemy. They gave him over forty pounds of the metal from which he fashioned an idol. "And all Israel prostituted themselves to it there and it became a snare to

This altar to Astarte in the Archaeological Museum in Amman, Jordan, is dated to the Iron Age I (1200–100 BCE). Photo by Vere Chappell.

Gideon and his family" (Judges 8:27–28 NRSV). Despite such a blatant violation of the law, the country remained at peace for forty years under Gideon's leadership.

Upon his death, the people reverted to the worship of Baal. Gideon's son Abimelech connived to murder his seventy brothers and proclaim himself king of Israel. Yet he and the conspirators who helped elevate him were all slain after a three-year reign.

A new judge arose named Tola, who led Israel for twenty-three years. He was followed by Jair who judged for twenty-two years. Then the community reverted again to the worship of Baal and Ashtaroth and the gods of Syria, Sidon, Moab, Ammon, and the Philistines. God's anger was kindled and they fell to the Philistines and the Ammonites for the next eighteen years. They cried to God begging his help. He replied, "Go and cry unto the gods which ye have chosen; let them deliver you in the time of your tribulation" (Judges 10:14). Then they put away their strange gods and served the Lord alone, "and His soul was grieved for the misery of Israel" (Judges 10:16).

When the Ammonite army came against the city of Gilead, the town elders sought a leader. The warrior Jephthah may have seemed an unlikely choice. Although a "mighty man of valor" (Judges 11:1), he was the son of a prostitute. Raised by his father and stepmother, along with their legitimate children, Jephthah was banished by his brothers and sisters that he might not inherit any of their father's estate. He became an outlaw chieftain in a neighboring land.

When the elders of Gilead asked him to protect them, Jephthah was suspicious and resentful. He agreed to command the army on condition that if successful, he be acknowledged their leader and commander. They assented.

Jephthah sent messengers to the king of the Ammonites. Their diplomatic exchange smacks of contemporary grievance politics. Jepthah complained, "What hast thou to do with me, that thou are come against me to fight in my land" (Judges 11:12)? The Ammonite king, still chafing from the weight of his three-hundred-year-old resentments, replied, "Because Israel took away my land, when they came up out of Egypt … now therefore restore those lands again peaceably" (Judges 11:13). Not to be outdone in the department of long-simmering animosity, Jepthah recited a centuries-old litany of the acts of cruelty, oppression, aggression, and rudeness shown by the Canaanites to the Israelites during the period of the Exodus. Next, he pointed out that the Ammonites had been defeated in battle; therefore they had lost their land to the victorious Israelites. "Should you not possess what your god Chemosh gives you to possess? And should we not be the ones to possess everything that the LORD our God has conquered for our benefit" (Judges 11:24 NRSV)?

During the ensuing campaign, one of the most distressing scenes of the Bible followed. The spirit of the Lord descended upon Jephthah before a battle. While he might have been assured that the Lord's presence was His promise of victory, Jephthah felt the need to make a vow for extra security. He swore that if he was able to defeat the Ammonites, he would make a burnt offering of the first living thing that came to meet him when he returned home. (Normally, livestock would have been wandering around the yard so he probably assumed a lamb or goat would have been the first to approach him.) He defeated the Ammonites in a brilliantly successful campaign. When he returned home, his daughter, his only child, ran out to greet her father. He tore his clothes when

Jephthah recoils in horror as he realizes that his daughter is the first living being to greet him when he returns home after his victory over the Ammonites, by Antonio Giovanni Pellegrini, ca. 1700–1725.

he saw her. She counseled him to fulfill his vow as the Lord had brought him to victory. She asked for two months of solitude to bewail the fact that she would die childless and after that period returned to her fate. Jephthah sacrificed her according to his vow.

An intra-tribal feud followed. Members of the tribe of Ephraim resented being left out of the Ammonite campaign. While Jephthah carefully justified his actions, a battle ensued in which forty-two thousand Ephraimites were killed. Jephthah judged Israel for six years. He was succeeded by Ibzan, who judged for seven years. Elon followed, judging for ten years. Then came Abdon, who judged for eight years.

THE STORY OF SAMSON

After the death of Abdon, the people again did evil in the sight of the Lord and were enslaved by the Philistines for forty years. Then an angel appeared to the wife of Manoah. She had been barren and the angel told her she would conceive a son. He cautioned her against any strong drink or unclean food. He further instructed her concerning the child. "No razor shall come on his head; for the child shall be a Nazarite unto God from the womb: and he shall begin to deliver Israel out of the hand of the Philistines"[1] (Judges 13:5). When she told her husband of the encounter, he prayed that the Lord would send the angel back to instruct them further in the proper ways to raise the child. The angel returned and spoke with them. Then Manoah prepared an offering for the Lord and placed it on a rock, and when the flame went up the angel ascended to heaven within it. "And Manoah and his wife looked on it, and fell on their faces to the ground" (Judges 13:20).

"And the woman bare a son, and called his name Samson" (Judges 13:24). Samson's adventures began after the Lord began to stir within him. He was attracted to a Philistine woman and told his parents to arrange a marriage for him. They naturally asked why he couldn't find a nice Jewish girl instead. "His father and mother did not know that this was from the LORD, that He was seeking a pretext to act against the Philistines" (Judges 14:4 NRSV). On their way to meet the girl's family, Samson (out of his parents' sight) encountered a young lion who roared at him. "And the Spirit of the LORD came mightily upon him" (Judges 14:6), and he tore the animal apart with his hands, not telling his parents.[2]

The Philistine woman pleased Samson and he returned some time later to claim her. Along the way, he noticed that a swarm of bees had nested inside the carcass of the dead lion and that it was filled with honey. He scooped out some of the honey and ate it and later shared it with his parents, careful not to tell them it came from the carcass of a dead animal. He thereby ritually defiled them as well.

At the wedding Samson proposed a bet to thirty of the guests that they couldn't solve a riddle based on his secret encounter with the lion and the honey, the stakes being thirty garments. When they couldn't solve it, they entreated Samson's new wife to give them the answer, threatening to kill her and her family if she refused. After she nagged him relentlessly for seven days, Samson finally gave her the answer. She passed it on to her fellow Philistines. When they gave him the correct answer,

---

1 Normally the vow of a Nazarite would extend for a fixed period of time. Like Samuel in chapter 10, Samson would be dedicated as a Nazarite before his birth.

2 Such an act of bloodletting by a Nazarite would require an eight-day purification ceremony as described in Numbers 6:9–12.

Samson observed, "If ye had not plowed with my heifer, ye had not found out my riddle" (Judges 14:18).

Again, "the Spirit of the LORD came upon him" (Judges 14:19), and he killed thirty Philistines in Ashkelon so that he could pay his bet with their thirty garments. He was angry with his wife and returned to his parent's home. When his passion cooled, he went back to claim her. But her father told him he had been so certain of Samson's unrelenting anger that he had given her in marriage to one of Samson's friends. In a fury, Samson gathered three hundred foxes, tied their tails together in pairs, lit them on fire, and sent them running through the Philistine fields to burn down the crops and vineyards. The Philistines, learning who was responsible, killed his wife and her father. In retaliation, Samson struck down the murderers in a bloody slaughter and went into hiding.

The Philistines came to find him and threatened members of the tribe of Judah. Three thousand Israelites went to Samson and pointed out that the Philistines ruled over Israel. Samson graciously allowed them to bind him and deliver him to the Philistines on their promise they would not harm him themselves. In the presence of the Philistines he was again seized by the Lord and burst the cords that bound him. Grabbing the jawbone of an ass he found on the ground, Samson slew a thousand Philistines with it. In his first recorded instance of prayer, Samson asked the Lord for water to slack his thirst. The Lord provided it, and Samson's spirit revived.

He journeyed on to Gaza where he was attracted by a prostitute. While spending the night with her, he became known to the Gazaites. They laid in wait to kill him the next morning, but he departed at midnight, outwitting them, and vandalized the doors of the gate of the city as he left.

Then he fell in love with Delilah, another Philistine prostitute. She was approached by Philistine leaders who offered her a bounty to discover the secret of Samson's strength. In a replay of his marriage riddle, Delilah begged him for the answer. He gave her several false answers. Each time he did so, she tested the answer by trying it out against him (while a group of Philistine warriors hid in an adjoining room). But since he had lied, her attempts at betrayal never succeeded. Still she implored him to tell the secret. Despite the fact that he should have known better, he eventually submitted to her persistence and told her the truth. The secret of his strength was that as a Nazarite he had never had a razor taken to his hair. Delilah was delighted, knowing she had finally learned the true answer. She called for her pay from the Philistine lords, then caused Samson to be shaven while asleep on her lap. Upon awakening, he realized he had been betrayed. He thought he could still escape, "But he did not know that the LORD had left him" (Judges 16:20 NRSV).

The Philistines blinded and imprisoned him. They then gathered together for a great sacrifice to their god Dagon in gratitude for the capture of Samson. They decided to mock Samson and set him between two pillars to taunt him. However, they failed to notice that his hair had begun to grow again. There were three thousand men and women in the temple. Samson prayed "that I may be at once avenged of the Philistines for my two eyes" (Judges 16:28). And he pushed over the pillars. He and all those inside were killed as the building collapsed. Samson had judged Israel twenty years.

Samson's story demonstrates that the Lord indeed moves in mysterious ways. One chosen for a sacred task may appear an unlikely candidate to mortal eyes. If God's goal was to wreak havoc upon the Philistine captors of Israel, who

better suited to the task than Samson—a vengeful, violent, passionate, self-indulgent warrior? It is worth noting that as colorful and sympathetic a figure as Samson certainly is, he represented an even further downturn in the religious adherence of Israel to the ways of the Lord.

Yet, while Samson may have been a flawed, if spirited, Nazarite, the stories that follow reek with an awful sense of chaos and degeneration. Rape, lawlessness, heresy, theft, murder, and civil war seem to have become a way of life among the Israelites. A refrain runs through the text that acknowledges this state and sets the tone for the monarchy that will follow, "In those days, there was no king in Israel, but every man did that which was right in his own eyes"[3] (Judges 17:6). From the point of view of

3 This formula is repeated in full in Judges 21:25 and alluded to in 18:1 and 19:1.

Samson, tricked by Delilah, is captured by the Philistines, by Anthony van Dyck, 1628–1630.

returned it. She took back the money and had a graven image fashioned for their household. "Micah had an house of gods, and made an ephod, and teraphim"[4] (Judges 17:5). Micah actually consecrated one of his sons to act as a priest. He next invited a traveling Levite to stay with him and eventually hired him to be his personal priest. "Then said Micah, 'Now I know that the LORD will do me good, seeing I have a Levite to my priest'" (Judges 17:13). (And, we might add, a house full of graven images, at least one of which was made of stolen silver, plus an unauthorized ephod and a heretical teraphim!)

Meanwhile, the tribe of Dan had not yet been able to subdue the region allotted to them in the divinely supervised land distribution of Joshua and Eleazar. They went in search of easier territory to conquer. A delegation of five scouts came to Micah's house. They recognized the Levite and asked him for counsel before continuing on their travels. He consulted the Lord and reported that they would be successful in their mission. The scouts found appropriate land in Laish in the far north of Israel and informed their fellow tribesmen.

Six hundred warriors of the tribe of Dan went north to take Laish. When the army passed Micah's house, the scouts told them of the Levite and the graven images, and the ephod and teraphim. They couldn't resist. Rather than destroy this ill-fated trove—as Moses or Joshua would have insisted—they removed the priest, stole the ritual objects, and threatened Micah with retaliation if he contested the matter. They

the Temple, the stories in the final chapters of Judges are most relevant. While they are painful to tell—and will be so to read—they provide an essential understanding of the moral depths to which the Israelites had fallen and the justification for God's anger.

A man named Micah lived in the hill region of Ephraim (near Bethel and Shiloh where the Ark was then located). He had stolen a sum of money from his mother, confessed to her, then

---

4 A teraphim is a type of household deity used for divination.

The road from Bethel to Shiloh, where the Ark once rested, is lined with olive trees.

continued on to Laish, which they renamed Dan. They built a shrine to the false god. It would be administered by the wayward Levite and his descendants for centuries to come.

The final story of Judges is extremely disturbing. It is an account of the causes and events of a civil war with the tribe of Benjamin. It began with a certain Levite taking a concubine who "played the whore against him" (Judges 19:2). She then left him to stay with her father. She remained at her father's house for four months until the Levite went to get her. Her father was very pleased to see him and insisted he lodge with him for several days. Finally the Levite and his concubine left late in the day with a servant and two asses laden with supplies. They traveled to Jerusalem. It was starting to grow dark, but the Levite chose not to stay in the (then) Canaanite city. He insisted on traveling to nearby Gibeah (Gibeon), the Benjamite

town. Arriving in the town square, they found no lodging until an elderly man, returning from the field, offered his hospitality.

Everyone was quite comfortable and enjoying their visit when "certain sons of [the demon] Belial" (Judges 19:22) pounded at the door and demanded the man be sent out so they could sodomize him. The host begged them to desist, offering his own virgin daughter and the Levite's concubine to slake their lust. But they ignored him until the Levite himself gave his concubine to them. They raped her through the night. The Levite came out the next morning and found her. He beckoned her to rise but she was dead. He placed her body on an ass and carried it to his home. He cut the cadaver into twelve pieces and sent them throughout Israel. "All that saw it said, 'There was no such deed done nor seen from the day that the children of Israel came up out of the land of Egypt unto this

Overlooking Gibeon, modern El Jib, from Nabi Samwil

day: consider of it, take advice, and speak your minds'" (Judges 19:30).

The people of Israel gathered themselves together in an assembly at Mizpeh. They numbered among them four hundred thousand warriors. The tribe of Benjamin did not attend. The people asked what had happened, and the Levite rallied them—neglecting to reveal his part in casting out the woman to save his own skin. The people were horrified and pledged to punish the city of Gibeah. They sent representatives to the tribe of Benjamin, demanding they turn over the villains so "'that we may put them to death, and put away evil from Israel.' But the children of Benjamin would not hearken to the voice of their brethren" (Judges 20:13).

The Benjamites numbered some twenty-six thousand warriors. The Israelites went to the Tabernacle of the Lord to seek counsel, and He confirmed the mission and gave instruc-

tion. There followed a devastating loss in which twenty-two thousand Israelites were slain. They wept at their defeat, but the Lord commanded them to continue. Another eighteen thousand men perished the next day. The people were beside themselves and went again to the Tabernacle seeking guidance in the midst of their confusion and uncertainty. They prayed and fasted and made burnt offerings and peace offerings. Phineas asked whether they should continue with or desist from their battle against Benjamin. The Lord promised them victory the following day.

The third day's battle was a rout against the Benjamites. The city of Gibeah was burned and twenty-five thousand warriors of Benjamin were slain. Survivors were pursued and slain as they fled. All the Benjamites in their territories were killed, their cities burned, their women, children, and flocks destroyed. Only six hundred

Benjamite warriors survived and escaped into the wilderness.

When the men of Israel had assembled earlier at Mizpeh, they made an oath. On hearing the Levite's self-serving story, they swore that they would never give their daughters to marry any Benjamite. After the battle, they lamented the destruction of the entire tribe of Benjamin. They came to Bethel and stayed there till evening trying to understand the loss of one of the twelve tribes of Israel. The next morning they built an altar and made burnt offerings and peace offerings.

They arrived at a plan that is as idiosyncratic as any in the Bible. They remembered that the inhabitants of Jabesh-gilead had not been present during the oath-taking against giving their daughters to the Benjamites. So they sent twelve thousand warriors against the town. They commanded the warriors, "Ye shall utterly destroy every male, and every woman that hath lain by man" (Judges 21:11). They found four hundred virgins remaining and brought them to Shiloh. They called out to the exiled warriors of Benjamin and reconciled with them rather than lose an entire tribe. And they gave them the four hundred virgins of Jabesh-gilead.

But of course there were six hundred men so they needed two hundred more wives. Someone pointed out that there was an annual festival in Shiloh. They counseled the Benjamites to lie in wait in the vineyards until the daughters of Shiloh came out to dance. Then the two hundred warriors without brides should each kidnap a wife and flee to the lands of Benjamin. The Israelites would apologize to the fathers and brothers of the seized women and explain there was no other solution to prevent the loss of a tribe of Israel. They would implore them not to pursue and avenge themselves against the Benjamites in the interest of the survival of the Hebrew nation. And they would emphasize that since the women were carried off by force, the families bore no guilt for violating their oath not to give their daughters to the Benjamites.

> And the children of Israel departed thence at that time, every man to his tribe and to his family, and they went out from thence every man to his inheritance. In those days there was no king in Israel: every man did that which was right in his own eyes. (Judges 21:24–25)

The subsequent leadership of the state under an all-powerful monarch—and the centralized worship at the Temple of Solomon in a controlled manner—might seem a welcome respite from such a period of lawlessness as that chronicled above. Yet it should be noted that those who require imposed external discipline have abdicated their responsibility for self-discipline. The imminent arrival of the period of kings—as the Prophet Samuel will later make clear—is an indication of the failure of the Israelites to live within the laws of God. Their need for a king was a testament to their unwillingness and inability to govern themselves. Regarding the formula that "every man did that which was right in his own eyes"; this is not an accurate characterization. It would be more precise to say, "every man did what he wanted, with little concern for what was right." A free people is a moral people. A free people needs no king.

CHAPTER NINE

RUTH

THE MATRIARCH OF THE KINGS OF ISRAEL

For whither thou goest, I will go; and where thou lodgest, I will lodge:
thy people shall be my people, and thy God my God. (Ruth 1:16)

One of the most tender of the stories of the Bible, in fact of all literature, the Book of Ruth is intimately related to the Temple.

During the time of the Judges, there was a famine in the land. It caused Elimelech of Bethlehem, of the tribe of Judah, and his wife, Naomi, and their two sons to move to the lands of Moab. Elimelech died soon after and Naomi was left a widow. The boys each married non-Jewish Moabite brides, one named Orpah and the other Ruth. Ten years later the young men also died. The three widows, Naomi, Orpah, and Ruth, began a journey back to the land of Judah.

Naomi encouraged the two young women to return to their mothers and find new husbands. She thanked them for their kindness and dutiful behavior. All three wept together but Orpah and Ruth refused to leave their mother-in-law. Naomi tried again to persuade them that returning to Moab and finding new husbands was the best course for them. Eventually Orpah relented and kissed her mother-in-law good-bye and went home. Naomi continued to try to persuade Ruth that leaving was best for her too.

> And she said, "Behold, thy sister in law is gone back unto her people, and unto her gods: return thou after thy sister in law." And Ruth said, "Intreat me not to leave thee, or to return from following after thee: for whither thou goest, I will go; and where thou lodgest, I will lodge: thy people shall be my people, and thy God my God: Where thou diest, will I die, and there will I be buried: the LORD do so to me, and more also, if ought but death part thee and me." (Ruth 1:15–17)

Naomi and Ruth traveled to Bethlehem where Naomi had a kinsman through her husband. His name was Boaz, and he was a wealthy man. Ruth, the Moabitess, went into the fields of Boaz to glean the leavings of the barley harvest.[1] When Boaz saw what Ruth was doing, he invited her to continue gathering food in his fields every

---

1 The gleanings were left in conformity with the communal laws of Leviticus 19:9–10 and 23:22 and Deuteronomy 24:19–22 so that the poor and the alien might find sustenance in the land of Israel.

Naomi with Ruth and Orpah, by William Blake, 1795

day and to be sure to ask refreshment when she was thirsty. Ruth thanked him profusely and humbly asked the reason for his kindness. He explained that he had been informed of her loyalty to Naomi. "The Lord recompense thy work, and a full reward be given thee of the Lord God of Israel, under whose wings thou art come to trust" (Ruth 2:12). And Boaz fed her lunch and instructed his field hands to quietly leave a little extra barley to ease her way.

When Ruth told Naomi about the day's events, Naomi was delighted. She began a little seduction and matchmaking effort that proved quite successful. Boaz fell in love with Ruth.

However, an issue needed to first be sorted out of whether the closer kinsman to Ruth's deceased husband would lay claim to her as discussed in Deuteronomy 25:5–6.[2] Boaz being the relative next in line to her deceased husband

would then be free to marry Ruth. He convened a council of ten elders and the nearer kinsman, and they all gave him leave to buy a piece of land that had belonged to Elimelech (of which we had been unaware) and to marry Ruth.

The elders and townsfolk present blessed the union and said, "The Lord make the woman that is come into thine house like Rachel and Leah, which two did build the house of Israel" (Ruth 4:11). Boaz and Ruth were married, and Ruth bore a son. Naomi was blessed with a family again. The presence of the infant and the love of Ruth renewed and sustained her. "And Naomi took the child and laid it in her bosom, and became nurse unto it" (Ruth 4:16).

The child was named Obed. And Obed begat Jesse, and Jesse was the father of David, king of Israel. And David was the father of Solomon, builder of the Temple.

---

2 Since neither man was the brother of Ruth's deceased husband, the statute did not technically apply. However it is written into the story as if it does. See commentary in NOAB, pages 395 and 396.

CHAPTER TEN

SAMUEL

THE PROPHET ESTABLISHES THE MONARCHY

*And ye shall cry out in that day because of your king which ye shall have chosen
you; and the LORD will not hear you in that day. (1 Samuel 8:18)*

The story of the Prophet Samuel, the last of the Judges, the holy man who anointed
the first two kings of Israel, begins in Shiloh at the Tabernacle. Hannah was barren and prayed with intense devotion, promising the Lord that if He would open her
womb, she would dedicate her child as a Nazarite.[3] Eli, the priest and judge, spoke
to her and told her the Lord would answer her prayer. She named her son Samuel.
After he was weaned, she and her husband, Elkanah, brought Samuel back to Shiloh
and left him in Eli's care. Eli loved Samuel and blessed Hannah and Elkanah when
they came to offer the annual sacrifice and visit their son. And they were given three
more sons and two daughters, while Samuel grew in service to the Lord.

Eli had two wicked sons of his own who blasphemed the sacrifice by demanding the fat (reserved for the Lord), bullying people who came to offer, and seduc-
ing women who assembled at the Tabernacle. Eli warned his sons but they ignored
him. A man of God came to reproach Eli for enabling his sons to violate the sanctity of the Tabernacle, and told him they would be killed and his bloodline cut off.
"And I will raise me up a faithful priest, that shall do according to that which is
in my heart and in my mind: and I will build him a sure house; and he shall walk
before mine anointed for ever" (1 Samuel 2:35).

The faithful Samuel continued his service. And the Lord chose him to hear
His words. Eli helped him to understand his task. "And Samuel grew, and the
LORD was with him … and all Israel … knew that Samuel was established to be a
prophet of the LORD" (1 Samuel 3:19–20).

The Israelites went to war against the Philistines and were defeated. Their
leaders decided to bring the Ark of the Covenant from Shiloh to the scene of the
battle that it might help them against their enemies. The two sons of Eli accompanied the Ark. When the Philistines heard the shout of joy from the Jews, they
knew it meant the Ark had arrived in the Israelite camp. They feared greatly and
despaired of victory. But they fought anyway and defeated the Israelites, slaying

---

3 As in the case of Sampson's mother, Hannah dedicated Samuel as a Nazarite from birth. See note
1 on page 120.

thirty thousand men. Then the Philistines captured the Ark, and the sons of Eli were slain, as prophesied. A messenger came to Shiloh and told Eli and the people of the loss of the battle, the death of Eli's sons, and the taking of the Ark. When Eli heard that the Ark had been lost, he fainted, fell, and broke his neck. He died at the age of ninety-eight, having judged Israel for forty years.

"When the Philistines took the ark of God, they brought it into the house of Dagon, and set it by Dagon. And when they … arose … behold Dagon was fallen upon his face to the earth before the ark of the LORD" (1 Samuel 5:2–3). They set the statue aright, but the next morning, found it again on the earth before the Ark, this time broken in pieces. An outbreak of skin eruptions, or tumors, and a plague of mice smote the Philistines. A council was convened to discuss the matter and they decided to move the Ark out of the city. But each place to which they took the Ark was devastated by the tumors and mice. After seven months they called together priests and diviners for help. They advised the Philistines to return the Ark with trespass offering of five tumors made of gold and five golden mice, one for each of the five kings of the Philistines. "And ye shall give glory unto the God of Israel; peradventure He will lighten His hand from off you, and from off your gods, and from off your land" (1 Samuel 6:5). They suggested the Philistines make a new cart and hook it to two young milk cattle on whom there had never been placed a yoke. They should put the Ark and the golden offerings upon the cart, and send it away at its own direction. If the cart went toward the Jewish lands, the Philistines would understand the hand of God had been responsible for their devastation; if it went in another direction, it had all been merely chance. It went toward the Jewish lands.

The cart came to a field in Beth-shemesh.

The Levites took down the Ark and sacrificed the cattle and the golden jewels as a burnt offering on a fire fueled by the wood of the cart. However, one local family refused to celebrate the bounty of the Lord. "And he smote the men of Beth-shemesh, because they had looked into the ark of the LORD, even he smote of the people fifty thousand and threescore and ten men: and the people lamented, because the LORD had smitten many of the people with a great slaughter"[4] (1 Samuel 6:19–21).

The people of Beth-shemesh were terrified. They sent messengers to Kiriath-jearim, saying, "The Philistines have brought again the ark of the LORD; come ye down, and fetch it up to you" (1 Samuel 6:21). The men of Kiriath-jearim came to retrieve the Ark and brought it to the home of Abinadab. They sanctified his son Eleazar to tend to the Ark, which remained in that place for twenty years.

After the Ark was secured and the immediate crisis resolved, Samuel spoke to the people. He communicated a path to the blessings and protection that awaited them.

> If ye do return unto the LORD with all your hearts, then put away the strange gods and Ashtaroth from among you, and prepare your hearts unto the LORD, and serve Him only: and He will deliver you out of the hand of the Philistines. (1 Samuel 7:3)

---

4 The figure of 50,070 is given in the Hebrew and translated accordingly in the KJV and the Jewish Publication Society's *Holy Scriptures According to the Masoretic Text* and later *Tanakh* translation. The NRSV translation gives the number of those slain as seventy, as does Josephus. This number is taken from the Septuagint or Greek translation, which reads, "He smote among them seventy men, including fifty of the men's thousand" (Septuagint I. Basileon [1 Samuel] 6:19). Seventy makes more sense, as also noted in the commentary in the JSB.

Facing north toward Tel Beth-shemesh

The children of Israel did as Samuel recommended and gathered at Mizpeh and Samuel prayed for them. The Philistines assembled an army against them. Samuel made a burnt offering before the Lord and prayed. The Lord sent a great thunder against the Philistines, and the Israelites pursued and smote them. "And the hand of the LORD was against the Philistines all the days of Samuel" (1 Samuel 7:13). The Philistines restored the cities they had taken from the Israelites and there was peace in the land.

THE ESTABLISHMENT OF THE MONARCHY

When Samuel was very old, he appointed his sons as judges. But they did not follow after his ways and were corrupt. The people approached him and demanded he create a king to rule over and judge them as the other nations had.[5]

5 See Deuteronomy 17:14–20 and page 100 of this book.

Samuel was displeased with this request and prayed to the Lord. "And the LORD said unto Samuel, 'Hearken unto the voice of the people in all that they say unto thee: for they have not rejected thee, but they have rejected me, that I should not reign over them'" (1 Samuel 8:7).

And the Lord called upon Samuel to explain to the people the nature of the king that would reign over them. Samuel warned them of their folly in these words.

He will take your sons, and appoint them for himself, for his chariots, and to be his horsemen; and some shall run before his chariots. And he will appoint him captains over thousands, and captains over fifties; and will set them to ear his ground, and to reap his harvest, and to make his instruments of war, and instruments of his chariots. And he will take your daughters to be confectionaries,

This is the Sorek Valley as photographed from Beth-shemesh. The cart carrying the Ark was drawn by the cattle from the land of the Philistines in the west, shown in the background, across the valley to Beth-shemesh.

and to be cooks, and to be bakers. And he will take your fields, and your vineyards, and your oliveyards, even the best of them, and give them to his servants. And he will take the tenth of your seed, and of your vineyards, and give to his officers, and to his servants. And he will take your menservants, and your maidservants, and your goodliest young men, and your asses, and put them to his work. He will take the tenth of your sheep: and ye shall be his servants. And ye shall cry out in that day because of your king which ye shall have chosen you; and the LORD will not hear you in that day. (1 Samuel 8:11–18)

Yet they were determined to be like other nations with a king to judge them and fight their battles. And God told Samuel to comply with their wishes.

PART FOUR

THE UNITED MONARCHY
AND THE FIRST TEMPLE

(1 Samuel, 2 Samuel, 1 Kings,
1 Chronicles, 2 Chronicles)

The tower atop Nabi Samwil, the Tomb of the Prophet Samuel. In 1192, this was the location from which Richard the Lionhearted viewed Jerusalem, some six miles away.

Chapter Eleven

The Reign of Saul

First King of the Realm

(1025–1005 bce)

And the people shouted, "God save the king." (1 Samuel 10:24)

Among the tribe of Benjamin was a mighty man named Kish who had a son named Saul. (Recall that the tribe of Benjamin had nearly been destroyed at the end of the Book of Judges.) Saul was a young man of good character and great height. Some asses wandered off from the fields of Kish and he sent Saul to retrieve them. After a long and fruitless search, Saul decided to stop at the house of Samuel to seek his guidance in the matter. The Lord had alerted Samuel a day earlier of Saul's impending arrival. He explained that He had designated Saul as the king of Israel whom Samuel was to anoint. When Samuel saw Saul, the Lord confirmed that he was the chosen one. Then Saul approached Samuel and the latter welcomed him with words of comfort and praise. And Saul was humble and righteous.

Samuel fed Saul and took him to the sacrifice. The next day he anointed him with the holy oil. And he made prophecies to Saul of his journey: that he would come to Rachel's sepulcher in Bethlehem and be told the asses were found; that he should meet three men carrying sacrifice to the Lord who would offer him nourishment; that he would come upon a company of prophets and the spirit of the Lord would descend upon him and he would prophesy; and that the Lord would fundamentally change him. After these events, Saul was to wait for Samuel to come to Gilgal and make sacrifice. "And it was so, that when he had turned his back to go from Samuel, God gave him another heart; and all those signs came to pass that day" (1 Samuel 10:9).

Samuel gathered the people together at Mizpeh and announced the word of the Lord. "And ye have this day rejected your God, who himself saved you out of all your adversities and your tribulations; and ye have said unto Him, 'Nay, but set a king over us'" (1 Samuel 10:19). And when all had gathered, Samuel proclaimed Saul, "See ye whom the Lord hath chosen … And the people shouted, 'God save the king'" (1 Samuel 10:24). Samuel wrote out the duties and responsibilities of the kingship of Israel in a book and laid it before the Lord.

Samuel anointing Saul

Saul returned to Gibeah, accompanied by a group of advisors who had their hearts touched by the Lord as well. Yet another group of the children of Belial despised Saul and withheld any gifts.

There is a fundamental tension established here that is worth noting. On the one hand, Saul was chosen by the Lord and described as righteous. His heart was changed. His advisors were similarly touched. There is a sense of consecration and holiness associated with the establishment of the line of kings of Israel. On the other hand, God is disappointed that the people went asking for a king, warned them through Samuel of the corruption and arrogance their kings would manifest, and even expressed His own sense of being rejected. Yet the opponents of Saul and his advisors are characterized as "children of Belial." That is, they were evil by nature and in a state of apostasy and rebellion against the proper order of heaven. It is an interesting dichotomy.

We should remember the theme in Judges of every man doing that which he thought good because there was no king in Israel. The contradiction between a people's responsibility to accept the mantle of self-government and the self-evident fact that most men and women are incapable of this and need to be led, is a painful reality. One can sympathize with God's impatience and disappointment that the Israelites demanded a human leader rather than being willing and able to internalize His divine leadership. Yet one can also appreciate that—faced with such an unruly, unworthy, and dependent class of people—the Lord would wish to see their leaders imbued with righteousness and inspiration.

In the meantime, Nahash, the king of the Ammonites, had been oppressing the tribes of Benjamin and Gad, gouging out the right eye of each male. Seven thousand men had escaped to Jabesh-gilead, where Nahash followed them. He demanded their surrender. He promised not to kill them on condition that they willingly submit to having their right eyes torn out. Thus would Nahash demonstrate his continued superiority over Israel. The Israelites stalled for time while sending messages throughout the land pleading for help. Saul learned of their plight and was moved to righteous anger. He exerted his charisma and leadership and assembled a vast army to defend them. The Hebrews slew the Ammonites, and all Israel celebrated their new king.

Then Samuel spoke to the people and reminded them of his own leadership and integrity these many years. He recounted the mercies the Lord had shown to Israel. Then he reminded them of their ingratitude and sins. And he counseled them toward righteous living and promised to continue to pray for them.

SAUL SINS BEFORE THE LORD

Two years later, Saul was found unworthy of continued leadership. He committed a major ritual error under conditions of extreme stress that overwhelmed his judgment. His son Jonathan had defeated a garrison of Philistines. Saul then called the people together to mount a full-scale campaign. In return, the Philistines assembled thirty thousand chariots and six thousand horsemen and an army of warriors as numerous "as the sand which is on the sea shore" (1 Samuel 13:5). The Israelites hid themselves in fear. Some deserted and fled east of the Jordan. Those who remained with Saul were trembling. Saul awaited a visit from Samuel, but he had not yet arrived. "And Saul said, 'Bring hither a burnt offering to me, and peace offerings.' And he offered the burnt offerings" (1 Samuel 13:9). This was a direct violation of Mosaic Law which assigned such responsibilities solely to the Levites and the priestly sub-class of Kohathites.

As soon as Saul finished making the sacrifice, Samuel appeared and asked what was going on. Saul explained that the people were restless; that Samuel had not shown up in time; and that the Philistines were growing more numerous. Therefore he had made a burnt offering to calm the nerves of his troops.

> And Samuel said to Saul, "Thou has done foolishly: thou has not kept the commandment of the LORD thy God, which He commanded thee: for now would the LORD have established thy kingdom upon Israel for ever. But now thy kingdom shall not continue: the LORD has sought Him a man after His own heart, and the LORD has commanded Him to be captain over His

people, because thou hast not kept that which the LORD commanded thee." (1 Samuel 13:13–14)

Despite Saul's spiritual failure, he won a great military victory over the Philistines. His brave son Jonathan conducted a guerilla operation in the Philistine camp and spread chaos among them. And Saul called to the Levites for the Ark of the Covenant to be brought near the site of the battle. He then committed another of those tragic acts of biblical destiny reminiscent of the sorrow of Jephthah and his daughter in Judges. He declared that any Israelite who ate before evening would be cursed, because it was more important to be avenged than fed. The soldiers grew faint and were inefficient. Jonathan had been absent from the camp and had not heard his father's command. He came upon some honey and ate it with gratitude, enhancing his strength. When informed of his father's curse, Jonathan was dismissive. He characterized enforced fasting for soldiers as a tactically poor strategy.[1] Then the Israelite army fell upon the Philistines and took of their herds. The soldiers were so hungry they slaughtered the beasts on the ground and ate them along with their blood—in stark violation of the dietary commands of Mosaic law. Saul had a large stone rolled to him and directed his warriors to slay the animals on the stone so that their blood might drain properly. Then Saul built an altar to the Lord.

Saul sought guidance from the Lord about continuing his attack but received no answer. Sensing trouble, he looked for the source of sin. Saul arranged for lots to be cast between the army on one side and himself and Jonathan on the other. And the lot fell to Saul and Jonathan. Then he had lots cast between himself and Jonathan, and it fell to Jonathan. "Then Saul said to Jonathan, 'Tell me what thou hast done.' And Jonathan told him, and said, 'I did but taste a little honey ... and, lo, I must die.' And Saul answered, 'God do so and more also: for thou shalt surely die, Jonathan'" (1 Samuel 14:43–44). But the people cried out that Jonathan had saved the day with his bravery and delivered the Philistines to Israel, so they temporarily rescued him from Saul's curse.

Saul continued to be a successful commander winning many victories for Israel. Then Samuel came to Saul and delivered the word of the Lord to him, instructing him to slay the Amalekites, every man, woman, child, ox, sheep, camel, and ass. So Saul went forth and smote them and captured their king. But he did not kill the king nor the flocks as instructed. The Lord repented to Samuel of having made Saul king. Samuel approached Saul the next day and asked him his reason for disobedience. Saul said that the sheep and cattle were allowed to live because he intended to sacrifice them to the Lord.

> And Samuel said, "Hath the LORD as great delight in burnt offerings and sacrifices, as in obeying the voice of the LORD? Behold, to obey is better than sacrifice, and to hearken than the fat of rams. For rebellion is as the sin of witchcraft, and stubbornness is as iniquity and idolatry. Because thou hast rejected the word of the LORD, He hath also rejected thee from being king." (1 Samuel 15: 22–23)

Saul asked for Samuel to forgive him, stating that he had responded to the pressure of the people. Samuel refused, explaining that God

---

1 Fasting was specifically forbidden by the monastic Rule of the Knights Templar for this reason, as discussed in *The Templars and the Assassins*, page 161.

had already chosen a better man to replace him as king. Saul pleaded for Samuel to at least accompany him to worship. Then Samuel called for the king of the Amalekites to be brought to him, and he himself cut him to pieces before the Lord. And in his heart, Samuel mourned for Saul.

THE LORD CHOOSES DAVID

God spoke to Samuel and ordered him to anoint the one He had chosen to succeed Saul as king of Israel. Samuel traveled to Bethelem to the family of Jesse, grandson of Ruth and Boaz. When Jesse introduced him to his ten sons, Samuel was confused because none of them had been chosen by the Lord. He asked if there were not another son, and Jesse told him of David, the youngest, who was herding sheep. Samuel called for him.

> Now he was ruddy, and withal of a beautiful countenance, and goodly to look to. And the LORD said, "Arise, anoint him: for this is he." Then Samuel took the horn of oil, and anointed him in the midst of his brethren: and the Spirit of the LORD came upon David from that day forward. (1 Samuel 16:12–13)

At the same time, the Spirit of the Lord departed from Saul. And an evil spirit was sent to trouble him. His servants suggested that Saul find a skillful player on the harp to comfort him when the evil spirit was upon him. One of them knew that David played the harp and brought him to the palace. Saul immediately liked David and made him his armor-bearer. "And it came to pass, when the evil spirit from God was upon Saul, that David played an harp, and … Saul was refreshed" (1 Samuel 16:23).

David and Goliath

Meanwhile, the Philistines gathered their armies together south of Beth-shemesh. The Israelite armies assembled there as well. The armies were camped on two opposing mountains on either side of the valley of Elah.

The Philistines sent forth a champion, a giant named Goliath who challenged the Israelites to choose a man to come against him in solo combat and decide the outcome of the war. He was a huge man by any standard, described by the Bible as over nine feet tall, wearing an armored coat of mail weighing some 126 pounds, carrying a spear whose head weighed 15 pounds.[2] Goliath made the same challenge each day for forty days.

David had returned from Saul's palace to his father's home to care for the sheep, as three of his elder brothers served in Saul's army. Jesse sent David to the Israelite camp with food for his sons and provisions for many soldiers. When David arrived, he heard Goliath's challenge and observed the fear he inspired among the Israelites. "And David said to Saul, 'Let no man's heart fail because of him; thy servant will go and fight with this Philistine'" (1 Samuel 17:32). David convinced Saul to let him go. They tried to dress him in armor but it was too heavy and clumsy and David was inexperienced in its use.

David took his shepherd's staff and sling with five smooth stones and went to confront Goliath. Goliath mocked him.

> Then said David to the Philistine, "Thou comest to me with a sword, and with a spear, and with a shield; but I come in the name of the LORD of hosts, the God

---

2 Conversions of biblical measurements to modern terms are taken from the NOAB, notes to 1 Samuel 17:4–7.

Elah Valley was the scene of the battle between David and Goliath. Photo by Steven Brooke.

of the armies of Israel, whom thou defiest. This day will the LORD deliver thee into mine hand; and I will smite thee, and take thine head from thee; and I will give the carcases of the host of the Philistines this day unto the fowls of the air, and to the wild beasts of the earth; that all the earth may know that there is a God in Israel. And all this assembly shall know that the LORD saveth not with sword and spear: for the battle is the LORD's, and He will give you into our hands." (1 Samuel 17:45–47)

The giant came after David in anger and David slung a stone into the middle of his forehead and killed him. And he took the sword of Goliath and cut off his head with it. And the Philistines fled. David was brought before Saul carrying the head of Goliath.

SAUL'S JEALOUSY AND DOWNFALL

Jonathan, Saul's son, came to love David and they were friends. David served Saul properly and conducted himself wisely. But Saul became possessed of jealousy and anger toward David. One night, the evil spirit entered Saul and he cast a javelin at David, who narrowly avoided it. "And Saul was afraid of David, because the LORD was with him, and departed from Saul" (1 Samuel 18:12). But all Israel loved David.

The courageous young David is filled with the strength of his faith as he answers the challenge of the Philistine giant, by Jacques Legrand, ca. 1490.

Saul plotted to kill David by the hands of the Philistines. He offered David his daughter Michal in marriage in return for David bringing him one hundred Philistine foreskins to avenge Saul against his enemies. David returned with two hundred. This only increased Saul's fear and hatred of him as he understood that David was protected by the Lord. He tried to plot David's death with Jonathan, but Jonathan warned David and counseled him to hide himself. Jonathan spoke words of wisdom to his father in favor of David, his integrity and loyalty, past service to Saul, and the importance of Saul being a virtuous leader. Saul swore to Jonathan that he would not hurt David.

Jonathan got word to David who returned

LEFT: *David played the harp to calm Saul when the king was tormented by his mental illness. As David's popularity grew, Saul became increasingly jealous. Here he raises a javelin against the young musician, by Heinrich Suso, ca. 1455–1460.*

BELOW: *Saul plotted to kill David by challenging him to bring one hundred foreskins of the Philistine enemy in return for the hand of the king's daughter Michal. David brings two hundred and is rewarded with Michal, at right. From the Morgan Crusader Bible, ca. 1250.*

to Saul's presence. David led troops against the Philistines and was successful for Israel. But Saul was seized by the evil spirit again and attacked David by surprise, throwing another javelin at him. David again fled, and his wife Michal helped him to escape her father's fury.

Saul Hunts David

David went to Samuel and told him of Saul's behavior. When Saul learned of David's location, he sent messengers to seize him. They came upon Samuel with a group of his disciples who were prophesying, that is, they were in active communion with the Lord. Then "the Spirit of God was upon the messengers of Saul, and they also prophesied" (1 Samuel 19:20). This happened two more times, rendering Saul's agents incapable of acting against David. Finally Saul himself went to arrest David and the Spirit of the Lord seized him as well. And Saul stripped off his clothes and lay naked for a day and a night, thus humiliated in submission to the power of God.

David traveled to join Jonathan and they swore a covenant of loyalty between themselves and their descendants before David went back into hiding. Saul was determined to slay David. One evening at dinner, Saul cast a javelin at Jonathan in anger at his son's friendship with David. Jonathan warned David of all this and David went deeper into hiding.

When David arrived at Nob, east of Jerusalem, he approached the priest Ahimelech, great grandson of Eli, the priest and judge who was Samuel's mentor. David asked for food, but there was none there except for the Bread of the Presence.[3] Despite his initial misgivings,

The Bread of the Presence on the golden Table of Offering. From the model of the Tabernacle in Timna Park.

Ahimelech used the sacrament to feed David and his men. When David asked for a weapon, Ahimelech gave him the sword of Goliath that was left there.[4] An Edomite soldier named Doeg observed all this and informed Saul. David then traveled on to the court of the Philistine king Achish. Recognized as "the king of the land" (1 Samuel 21:11) of Israel, David feared for his life and pretended madness. Traveling further on, he was joined by his brothers and gathered an army of four hundred men.

David placed his parents in the care of the king of Moab. He was told by a prophet to journey back to the land of Judah, where he again came to the notice of Saul. When Saul learned that David had been fed by Ahimelech, he summoned the priest to his court to answer for himself. Ahimelech spoke in David's defense, pointing out David's integrity, his loyalty to Saul, and the fact that he was the king's son-in-law. Saul was enraged and pronounced a death sentence on the priest, but his soldiers refused to execute the holy man. The evil soldier Doeg the Edomite did slay Ahimelech and eighty-five Kohathites, then led an attack against the

---

3 Loaves of the Bread of the Presence, shewbread, sat on the Table of Offering for a week before being replaced with fresh bread. The older bread was reserved as the food of the Kohathites.

4 1 Samuel 21:1–10.

The Ein Gedi wilderness where David hid from Saul. Photo by Vere Chappell.

nearby Levitical city, slaying men, women, children, and livestock. Abiathar, a son of Ahimelech, survived and escaped to tell David of the slaughter. David felt guilty for having brought this about by seeking food during his flight and offered his protection to Abiathar.

A series of assaults by the Philistines against the city of Keilah was brought to David's attention. He inquired of the Lord and was told to protect the city and promised victory despite the misgivings of his army. David and his men were victorious. When Saul learned that David was nearby, he misinterpreted this to mean that God had delivered David into his hands. But David asked direction from the Lord through Abiathar the priest, who had brought an ephod when he fled from the slaughter of his kinsmen. David was instructed to flee again.

While in the wilderness, David was visited by Jonathan. In a remarkable statement Jonathan told David that Saul would be unable to find him, "and thou shalt be king over Israel, and I shall be next unto thee; and that also Saul my father knoweth" (1 Samuel 23:17). And they swore a new covenant between them. We learn that prior to the death of Saul, many other mighty men of the tribe of Benjamin came to pledge David their support.[5]

---

5 1 Chronicles 12.

The Tomb of the Prophet Samuel, Nabi Samwil

Saul continued to seek after David. In one dramatic episode, Saul unknowingly fell into his hands. David, however, acknowledged the will of the Lord in anointing Saul the rightful king of Israel and refused the opportunity to kill him. David later confronted Saul with this information, addressed him as his father, and proclaimed, "The LORD judge between me and thee, and the LORD avenge me of thee; but mine hand shall not be upon thee" (1 Samuel 24:12). Saul was clearly conflicted and conscious of David's ethical superiority in not having killed him when he had the chance.

"Is this the voice of my son David?" And Saul lifted up his voice and wept. And he said to David, "Thou art more righteous than I: for thou hast rewarded me good, whereas I have rewarded thee evil.... And now, behold, I know well that thou shalt surely be king, and that the kingdom of Israel shall be established in thine hand." (1 Samuel 24:16–20)

The Death of Samuel

Then Samuel died and all Israel mourned the loss of this pivotal Prophet, Priest, and Judge.

David Continues in Righteousness

We are next introduced to Abigail, a woman beautiful and of great wisdom, who prevented David from soiling himself with innocent blood. Her husband, a man of much wealth and an evil disposition, refused David tribute after he had protected the man's flocks. David was enraged. But Abigail mended the situation with her good manners and intelligence, apologizing for her husband's rudeness and stupidity, and proclaiming that she too knew David was destined to be king of Israel. When her husband died of natural causes some ten days later, she gladly became David's wife, along with Ahinoam of Jezreel. Saul had given his daughter Michal, David's wife, to another man.

Again Saul came after David. An incident took place that is reminiscent of a story recorded two thousand years later of the Assassin leader Hasan-i-Sabah and his adversary Sanjar.[6] David went at night by stealth to Saul's campsite. David and his fellow warrior Abisha came upon Saul sleeping. Abisha begged David to allow him to kill Saul. But David again refused to raise his hand against the Lord's anointed. However, they took Saul's spear and water container and left the camp. They climbed a hill, and proclaimed their deed aloud, waking the army and mocking Abner, the captain of the guard, for failing to protect the king. Saul again proclaimed himself reconciled with David, promising him his love and protection.

David Flees to the Land of the Philistines

But David, aware of Saul's treachery, chose to travel to the land of the Philistines that he might be safe from Saul. He was welcomed again at the court of the Philistine king Achish. Saul was content not to seek after him. David remained in the Philistine territory with his six hundred men for some sixteen months. They launched raids against neighboring pagan tribes. David lied to Achish, pretending he was attacking

Israeli tribes in the border territories. Achish was convinced of David's loyalty and estrangement from the Jews. Choosing to mount a campaign against Israel, he appointed David his bodyguard.

Saul Consults the Witch of Endor

When Saul and the Philistines were gathering for battle, Saul rallied his own troops together. But he was fearful and sought communication from the Lord. This was denied him by the usual methods of either the Urim, dreams, or the word of prophets. Thus he turned to the Witch of Endor, disguising himself to seek her counsel in an attempt to make up for the Lord's neglect of him. Saul had earlier expelled witches from Israel, and the woman told him she feared to engage in witchcraft because of the king's edicts. Saul promised that she would not be punished and asked her to call up the spirit of Samuel to advise him. The spirit of Samuel was harsh to Saul, reminding him of his disobedience, stating that God had become Saul's enemy, and that the kingdom was destined for David. Samuel further predicted that Saul would lose the next day's battle with the Philistines, and that he and his sons would be killed.

Achish's fellow Philistine kings refused to allow David to be part of their army, lest he betray them. David and his men were forced to leave the area of the battle. They traveled deeper into Philistine territory to Ziklag, where David had lived during his time under Achish's protection. Upon their arrival, David learned that the Amalekites had raided the area and taken women and children, including his wives Abigail and Ahinoam. He inquired of Abiathar and the ephod as to his course. The Lord immediately answered him, counseling him to pursue the enemy and promising victory. (Unlike Saul,

---

6 See *The Templars and the Assassins,* page 105.

David and his men at war against the Philistines. David is shown center left thrusting his sword through the enemy's shoulder. From the Morgan Crusader Bible, ca. 1250.

we see the open line of divine communication enjoyed by David.) He destroyed the Amakelite force and recovered his wives and the women and children of the others. His army gathered many spoils from the battle, and David divided them evenly among those who had fought and those who had not, and among all his supporters throughout the land.

The Death of Saul and Jonathan

Meanwhile, the battle between Saul and the Philistines was going badly. Jonathan and two of his brothers were killed, and Saul was badly wounded. Rather than be taken alive by the enemy, Saul fell on his sword and died next to his three sons and armor-bearer. The Philistines defiled his body and widely proclaimed their victory. Certain valiant Israelites from Jabesh-gilead seized the bodies of Saul and his sons from the walls of Beth-shan where they had been hung, and burned them, buried the bones, and fasted seven days.

CHAPTER TWELVE

THE REIGN OF DAVID

THE WARRIOR/POET

(1005–965 BCE)

He that ruleth over men must be just, ruling in the fear of God. (2 Samuel 23:3)

Soon after David returned from his victory over the Amalekites, a young Amalekite soldier approached him in despair and announced that Saul was dead. Saul's army had been defeated, and Jonathan too had been killed. The soldier added that he had slain Saul at the latter's request after his attempt at suicide had been unsuccessful and that he had brought Saul's crown and bracelet to David. David and his soldiers rent their clothes and wept. He ordered the young man executed for he had laid his hand on the Lord's anointed. He lamented, "The beauty of Israel is slain upon thy high places: how are the mighty fallen" (2 Samuel 1:19)! He was especially saddened by the loss of Jonathan whom he loved.

David inquired of the Lord for his next step. He was directed to Hebron where he was crowned king of Judah. He sent a message to the people of Jabesh-gilead to thank them for burying Saul and Jonathan properly, offering them his friendship, and announcing that he had been enthroned. But Abner, Saul's general whom David had earlier mocked for failing to catch him entering Saul's tent, chose Ishbosheth (Ishbaal), the son of Saul, to be king. Ishbosheth reigned for two years over the remaining tribes of Israel.

A battle took place between the supporters of both kings in which Abner's men were beaten. In the aftermath, Abner slew the brother of David's general Joab. While the battle ended in a temporary truce, an ongoing civil war raged between the kingdoms of Judah and Israel in which David was ever victorious and the house of Saul progressively weakened.

Then Ishbosheth insulted Abner by accusing him of sleeping with one of Saul's concubines (tantamount to charging him with staking a claim to the kingship). Abner, while not denying such dalliance, was furious at the implied ingratitude and sent messengers with offers of alliance to David. David set the condition that Abner return David's wife Michal, Saul's daughter, who had been married to another man during the feud. Michal represented the physical link of the legitimacy of his claim to the throne of Saul. Abner arranged this and spoke in David's favor to the tribe of Benjamin, from whom both Abner and Saul were descended.

Modern Hebron looking out from the shrine of Machpelah

So David and Abner were allied, and David made a great feast for Abner and his men.

But Joab, learning of this, slew Abner in requital for Abner's slaying of Joab's brother. David distanced himself from any responsibility for the murder and publicly mourned Abner. The people of Israel were satisfied he was innocent of Abner's death. Ishbosheth was deeply troubled by the news. Two of his captains decided to slay Ishbosheth and bring his head to David, who was not pleased. He had them executed and buried the head of Saul's son in Abner's tomb.

The remaining tribes of Israel then approached David and made him king over all Israel. He was thirty years of age and would reign for forty years, seven as king of Judah and thirty-three of united Israel. (In the Chron-

icles account by contrast, all Israel gathered at Hebron to proclaim David their king without the delay, challenges, or civil strife recounted in 2 Samuel.[7])

DAVID ESTABLISHES HIS CAPITAL AT JERUSALEM

David's first great act as king of united Israel was his victory over the Jebusites and the conquest of Jerusalem. He "took the stronghold of Zion, which is now the city of David" (2 Samuel 5:7 NRSV). This has proved to be the most important and far-reaching act of his reign. Joab's military leadership in the Jerusalem campaign caused David to elevate him to commander of the army of Israel.

---

7 1 Chronicles 11.

Looking out from Nabi Samwil to the Church of Our Lady of the Ark of the Covenant at Kiriath-jearim. It marks the location of the Ark before it was moved to Jerusalem.

"And Hiram king of Tyre sent messengers to David and cedar trees, and carpenters, and masons: and they built David an house" (2 Samuel 5:11). This alliance would prove to be one of the most important for both David and Solomon, as Hiram would be instrumental in the construction of the Temple of Solomon.

David was attacked by the Philistines as soon as they learned of his ascension to the throne. He inquired of the Lord for a strategy and was answered. He followed the Lord's plan and his opponents were sorely defeated at Baal-perazim, their idols crushed and burned by David's men. They attacked again and were again beaten back. David simultaneously earned the respect and fear of allies and enemies in the region.

CARRYING THE ARK TO JERUSALEM

The next task before David was bringing the Ark of the Covenant to Jerusalem. He gathered together thirty thousand warriors. They went to the home of Abinadab in Kiriath-jearim.[8] David's men set the Ark upon a new cart for transport. It was driven by Abinadab's two sons. And there was great rejoicing among David and all the people.

But as they traveled, the Ark was shaken and became unsteady from the movement of

---

8 While 2 Samuel 6:3 says Abinadab lived in nearby Gibeah, 1 Chronicles 13:5 agrees with 1 Samuel 7:1–2 which places Abinadab and the Ark in Kiriath-jearim. See also page 130 in this book.

Carrying the Ark from Kiriath-jearim. David was now aware that the proper way to transport the Ark was for the Kohathites to carry it on their shoulders.

the oxen. A soldier named Uzzah reached out to protect it. However, he was not of the tribe of Levi and was slain on the spot by the Lord for his presumption in touching the Ark. "And David was afraid of the LORD that day, and said, 'How shall the ark of the Lord come to me'" (2 Samuel 6:9)? Rather than continue to Jerusalem, he decided to leave the Ark at the house of Obedom, where it remained for three months. "And the LORD blessed Obedom and all his household" (2 Samuel 6:11).

OVERLEAF: *Aerial view of the Temple Mount, the threshing floor of Araunah, showing the southern wall, the mikvahs of the Second Temple, the al-Aqsa Mosque, and the Dome of the Rock. To the right is the Mount of Olives.*

David concluded it was safe to try again to bring the Ark to Jerusalem. This time he was successful. He remembered the specific instructions of Moses concerning the moving of holy things.[9] "And the children of the Levites bare the ark of God upon their shoulders with the staves thereon, as Moses commanded according to the word of the Lord" (1 Chronicles 15:15). The Chronicles account also points out that David was careful to appoint only Levites (specifically Kohathites) for the task of carrying the Ark. He called the priests Zadok and Abiathar to him and expressed his belief that Israel had erred during the previous attempt. "Ye are

---

9 See Numbers 7:9.

the chief of the fathers of the Levites: sanctify yourselves, both ye and your brethren, that ye may bring up the ark of the Lord God of Israel unto the place that I have prepared for it" (1 Chronicles 15:12).

David sacrificed oxen and fatlings as the Ark traveled. "And David danced before the LORD with all his might; and David was girded with a linen ephod" (2 Samuel 6:14). "And all the Levites that bare the ark, and the singers, and … all Israel brought up the ark of the covenant of the LORD with shouting, and with sound of the cornet, and with trumpets, and with cymbals, making a noise with psalteries and harps" (1 Chronicles 15:27–28).

But, when David's wife Michal looked out at him in his ecstatic frenzy and the near nudity of his spiritual abandonment, she despised him, and criticized him for fraternizing with, and uncovering himself before, the maids and the people. David replied that the Lord had chosen him to replace her father as king, and therefore he would play unto the Lord and be held in honor by those maidens she despised. And Michal remained childless all her days.

> And they brought in the ark of the LORD, and set it in His place, in the midst of the tabernacle that David had pitched for it: and David offered burnt offerings and peace offerings before the LORD. And as soon as David had made an end of offering burnt offerings and peace offerings, he blessed the people in the name of the LORD of hosts. And he dealt among all the people, even among the whole multitude of Israel, as well to the women as men, to every one a cake of bread, and a good piece of flesh, and a flagon of wine. So all the people departed every one to his house. Then David returned to bless his household. (2 Samuel 6:17–20)

While the Ark of the Covenant was on Mount Moriah in Jerusalem in the tent pitched for it by David, the Tabernacle itself was in nearby Gibeon resting on a high place and served by Zadok and his family.[10] Here, too, they offered sacrifice, played music, and sang hymns to the Lord. This is a reminder that before the dedication of the Temple of Solomon as the exclusive site of worship in Israel, it was legitimate and appropriate to have shrines in various locations, such as Nob, where David and his warriors had earlier met Ahimelech.

David established the Levitical choirs that were charged to play music and sing psalms of praise "continually before the Ark of the Covenant of God" (1 Chronicles 16:6). The choirs would be part of the worship service in the Temple of Solomon as well. A designated group of Levites was set over the details of the care of the Ark. Others performed the many duties required for the service of the Tabernacle, "But Aaron and his sons [the Kohathites] offered upon the altar of the burnt offering, and on the altar of incense, and were appointed for all the work of the place most holy, and to make an atonement for Israel, according to all that Moses the servant of God had commanded" (1 Chronicles 6:49).

THE COVENANT WITH THE HOUSE OF DAVID AND HIS PREPARATION FOR THE TEMPLE

David began to question the fact that while he as king lived in a house of cedar, the Ark of the Lord was kept in a tent. He raised his concerns with Nathan the prophet, who encouraged him to do what he thought was right. But that night the Lord spoke to Nathan. He commanded him to approach David and point out that the Lord had ever dwelt in a tent since the days of the

---

10 1 Chronicles 16:39.

Exodus and had never encouraged the Israelites to build Him a house of cedar. He had raised David to great heights from being a sheep herder, had cut off the enemies of the Jews, and would care for Israel and make it strong and independent. The Lord promised that when David had fulfilled his days and died, "I will set up thy seed after thee, which shall proceed out of thy bowels, and I will establish his kingdom. He shall build me an house for my name, I will stablish the throne of his kingdom for ever" (2 Samuel 7:12–13).

The Lord further promised David that He would not remove His mercy despite any failings of the king as He had withdrawn it from Saul. "And thine house and thy kingdom shall be established for ever before thee: thy throne shall be established for ever"[11] (2 Samuel 7:16). And David, in solitude, offered prayers of praise and gratitude.

David continued his regional wars of defense and expansion, dedicating the spoils thereof to the eventual construction of the Temple and its ritual objects. As his power grew, other kings sent gifts and tribute to him and he reserved these as well for the House of the Lord.

David sought out surviving family members of Saul's lineage that he might show them kindness in honor of his friendship with Jonathan. He learned that Jonathan's son Mephibosheth was alive and sent for the young man. David restored his lands and Mephibosheth ate at the king's table thereafter.

DAVID SINS BEFORE THE LORD

David next pursued a series of very successful military campaigns throughout the region. Then he learned of the death of King Nahash of the Ammonites, with whom he had a treaty. He made an overture of friendship to Nahash's son Hanun, which was misinterpreted and rebuffed. A large military campaign against the Ammonites and Syria was the result. As his armies successfully engaged in battle against the enemy, David remained in Jerusalem.

> And it came to pass in an eveningtide, that David arose from off his bed, and walked upon the roof of the king's house: and from the roof he saw a woman washing herself; and the woman was very beautiful to look upon. And David sent and inquired after the woman. And one said, "Is not this Bath-sheba, the daughter of Eliam, the wife of Uriah the Hittite?" (2 Samuel 11:2–3)

Uriah being on campaign, David sent for her and lay with her and she conceived a child with David.

David sent word to Joab to order Uriah to come to Jerusalem. David asked Uriah for news of the battle, then told him to go to his home and rest and enjoy his wife. But Uriah slept on the ground outside the king's house. David asked him why.

> And Uriah said unto David, "The ark, and Israel, and Judah, abide in tents; and my lord Joab, and the servants of my lord, are encamped in the open fields; shall I then go into mine house, to eat and to drink, and to lie with my wife? as thou livest, and as thy soul liveth, I will not do this thing." (2 Samuel 11:11)

Then David wrote to Joab and instructed him to send the loyal Uriah into battle in such a manner that he would be killed. And indeed, Uriah was killed.

---

11 This passage is frequently cited as indicative of the mission of Jesus, descendant of the house of David.

This statue of David stands on the grounds of the Crusader Church of
Our Lady of Mount Zion, where David is said to be buried.
His cenotaph has become a religious shrine.

And when the wife of Uriah heard that Uriah her husband was dead, she mourned for her husband. And when the mourning was past, David sent and fetched her to his house, and she became his wife, and bare him a son. But the thing that David had done displeased the Lord. (2 Samuel 11:26–27)

David Is Cursed

The Lord sent Nathan the prophet to David, and he carefully led David, in conversation, to understand the magnitude of the sin he had committed. Then Nathan explained the curses David had brought upon himself and his house because he had betrayed his duty to serve the people of Israel as a just king. He told David that the sword would never depart from his house; that evil would rise up within his family; that his wives would be given to his neighbors in front of him and before all Israel—unlike David

BELOW: *Bathsheba at her bath. She would become the mother of Solomon. Francsco Hayez, 1859.*

who lay with Uriah's wife secretly. Finally, David's woes would include the death of his child by Bathsheba.

And the child indeed became very sick. David fasted and lay all night upon the earth. On the seventh day the child died. When David learned of it, he bathed and anointed himself and dressed in clean clothes and went into the house of the Lord and prayed and ate. The servants questioned him about this and he explained that while the child lived, he sought the Lord's mercy through penance, but now his child was dead and could not be made to return.

And David comforted Bath-sheba his wife, and went in unto her, and lay with her: and she bare a son, and he called his name Solomon: and the LORD loved him. (2 Samuel 12:24)

DAVID'S SORROWS INCREASE

The Ammonite war next claimed David's attention; it was brought to a successful conclusion. However, the curses continued to mount as prophesied. David's daughter Tamar, the full-sister of Absalom, was raped by her half-brother Amnon, David's eldest son and the crown prince. Amnon had been encouraged to this horrific behavior by his cousin. After the rape, Amnon was filled with loathing for Tamar and cast her away into a state of mourning. David learned of this crime and was enraged. Absalom was filled with hatred, and after waiting two years, took his revenge and killed Amnon. When news of this came to David, he was mistakenly told that all his sons had been killed. "Then the king arose, and tare his garments, and lay on the earth" (2 Samuel 13:31). While Absalom had fled, David's other sons returned and all the family and servants wept together. David mourned every day of the three years that Absalom remained in hiding.

Joab, perceiving the sorrow of the king, created a ruse whereby David was encouraged to allow Absalom to return to Jerusalem. Yet David refused to meet in person with his son for two more years. Finally Absalom implored Joab to again intervene on his behalf, and David received him in person. But Absalom bore treachery in his heart. He worked to supplant David in the hearts and minds of the community, acting as a judge and friend of the people. After four years, Absalom begged leave of David to travel to Hebron, capital of Judah, that he might fulfill a vow.[12] (Remember that David had been crowned in Hebron as king of Judah on his way to kingship of all Israel.) Absalom's conspiracy against David grew as the dire prophecies of Nathan continued to be realized. David's counselor Ahithophel joined Absalom. David was informed of all this and chose to flee the city, that he might divert any attack by Absalom away from the citizens of Jerusalem. He left ten concubines at his house to look after it. A recently allied Philistine commander named Ittai, loyal to David, expressed his love of the king in ironic contrast to the revolt of his son and many of the Jews.

Zadok, Abiathar, and the Levites carried the Ark with them as David departed with the people. Yet David told Zadok, "Carry back the ark of God into the city: if I shall find favour in the eyes of the LORD, He will bring me again, and shew me both it, and His habitation: But if He thus say, 'I have no delight in thee'; behold, here am I, let Him do to me as seemeth good unto Him" (2 Samuel 15:25–26). This act of humility demonstrates David's acceptance of the impersonal nature of the Lord's identification

---

12 The Hebrew text of 2 Samuel 15:7 reads "forty," as translated in the KJV and *The Tanakh*. This number contradicts the information about the length of David's reign. The NRSV and some versions of the Septuagint correct it to "four."

Looking out on the Mount of Olives from Mount Zion. Photo by Steven Brooke.

of Jerusalem as His city and David's own role as a servant of the divine. David made the tactical suggestion that the priests act as information gatherers within the city, letting him know when it is was safe to return.

> And David went up by the ascent of Mount of Olives, and wept as he went up, and had his head covered, and he went barefoot: and all the people that was with him covered every man his head, and they went up, weeping as they went up.[13] (2 Samuel 15:30)

When David learned that Ahithopel was with Absalom, he prayed that the Lord would confuse Ahithopel and make his counsel foolish. Hushai, an anchorite, came to David as if in answer to his prayer. He and David plotted to trick Absalom into believing that Hushai was his ally. Thus Hushai joined with Zadok and Abiathar as part of a sacred intelligence network loyal to David.

But David faced further betrayals and insults as the curses upon him continued to play out—turning him into a tragically persecuted figure from the mighty hero and king he had been earlier. Ziba, a servant of Jonathan's son Mephibosheth brought David rich provisions of food, wine, and asses for transport. Then he told David that Mephibosheth—to whom David had shown such kindness—sought to become

---

13 David's sorrow here anticipates that of Jesus in Luke 19:41, weeping on the Mount of Olives when contemplating the future destruction of Jerusalem and the Temple.

king in his place and reestablish the lineage of the house of Saul. Shimei, another of Saul's relatives, cursed David and flung stones at him. One of David's men begged to be allowed to kill the reprobate, but David replied:

> Behold, my son, which came forth of my bowels, seeketh my life: how much more now may this Benjamite do it? let him alone, and let him curse; for the LORD hath bidden him. It may be that the LORD will look on mine affliction, and that the LORD will requite me good for his cursing this day. (2 Samuel 16:11–12)

In the court of Absalom, further evils were being mounted. Ahithopel advised Absalom to publicly go into the ten concubines David had left behind in Jerusalem. This would be a bold statement asserting his usurpation of the kingship, as well as signaling the final breach with his father. Absalom did so, literally fulfilling that part of the Lord's curse against David. Then Ahithopel counseled Absalom to immediately raise an army and pursue and kill David while he was yet weak and unprepared. But Hushai pretended the wiser course was to wait and raise an army of all Israel that Absalom could lead in person, and thereby increase his reputation as a man of valor. (Such a delay would buy time for David.) Absalom and his men decided they would follow the false counsel of Hushai rather than that of Ahithophel. "For the LORD had appointed to defeat the good counsel of Ahithophel, to the intent that the LORD might bring evil upon Absalom" (2 Samuel 17:14). David was warned by members of his network to cross the Jordan and escape. Meanwhile, Ahithophel returned to his house and hung himself, despairing that he had been ignored.

Absalom came after David with his army. Shobi, another son of the late Ammonite king

Nahash, brought much needed provisions to David and his army. Several other pagan neighbors offered their support. When David sent his warriors against Absalom's army, he bade his three generals (Joab, Abisha, and Ittai) to be gentle with Absalom for his sake. But there was a fierce battle and twenty thousand men were slaughtered. Absalom was discovered and killed by Joab and his soldiers. When David learned of this he wept in despair. Victory had become an occasion for mourning. The people, learning of David's grief, were ashamed and ill at ease.

Joab heard of David's public display of sorrow. He came to the king's side and reprimanded him. He said that David's personal sense of loss had overshadowed his judgment and duty as king. The warriors who had saved his life and the lives of his wives, concubines, sons, and daughters needed encouragement. By his public display of grief, David was essentially telling the people that the day would have been better had his soldiers lost the battle and all of them died at Absalom's hand.

> Now therefore arise, go forth, and speak comfortably unto thy servants: for I swear by the LORD, if thou go not forth, there will not tarry one with thee this night: and that will be worse unto thee than all the evil that befell thee from thy youth until now. (2 Samuel 19:7)

David listened and followed Joab's counsel and showed himself to the people. And they repented their betrayal of David in favor of Absalom. The people of Judah were the first to welcome David back as king. And he was gracious to all. He forgave Shimei the Benjamite who had mocked, cursed, and thrown stones at him. Mephibosheth explained that his servant Ziba had deceived David. He swore that he had

The Tomb of Absalom in the Kidron Valley. Photo by Steven Brooke.

remained all along a loyal ally of the king and a grateful recipient of his generosity.

David appointed Amasa, Absalom's chief general, to replace Joab as commander of the army of Israel—possibly because of Joab's role in killing Absalom and earlier Abner. It was certainly intended as a diplomatic gesture to heal the rift of rebellion. As though a sign that better times were coming, the people of the tribe of Judah argued with the other tribes of Israel for the honor of being the first to welcome David back as king. He returned to his house in Jerusalem and saw to the sustenance of his ten con- cubines, although he no longer had sexual relations with them because of Absalom's crime.

Another smaller rebellion soon threatened David. Sheba, a Benjamite called a "man of Belial," stirred trouble among his own people and as many of the northern tribes as he could. David sent his armies against Sheba. But Amasa delayed carrying out David's orders. Joab led the first group and Amasa followed. When Amasa caught up to Joab soon after, Joab killed him. Then Joab negotiated with a wise woman representing the city where Sheba had fled. He persuaded her to kill Sheba, and the rebellion was ended. David restored Joab to his position as commander of the army.

Further campaigns were necessary against the Philistines, but by now David had grown old and was no longer strong enough to bear up to the rigors of battle. In chapters 22 and 23 of 2 Samuel, David offered praises of thanksgiving unto the Lord, retelling the bounties and victories the Lord had brought to him and the people of Israel. The beauty of the language and sentiments are equal to that of Psalms. Here is a small sample from chapter 22.

> With the merciful thou wilt shew thyself merciful, and with the upright man thou wilt shew thyself upright. With the pure thou wilt shew thyself pure; and with the froward thou wilt shew thyself unsavoury. And the afflicted people thou wilt save: but thine eyes are upon the haughty, that thou mayest bring them down. For thou art my lamp, O Lord: and the Lord will lighten my darkness. (2 Samuel 22:26–29)

Chapter 23 records the last words of David and his remembrance of the deeds of the mighty men who had served Israel with him. It begins with a statement, the truth of which David had learned at the price of great suffering, "He that ruleth over men must be just, ruling in the fear of God." (2 Samuel 23:3)

David Purchases the Temple Mount

Our journey through the history preceding the reign of Solomon and the construction of the Temple is drawing to a close. David will face one more major crisis on the road to the Temple. The anger of the Lord was again kindled against Israel. Satan is identified as the adversary who incited David to count the people of Israel.[14] Although censuses were conducted at the command of God in Exodus and Numbers, David undertook this count on his own. It seems to have implied a lack of faith in the bounteousness of the Lord. Joab strongly warned David against making the census, but David stubbornly prevailed and Joab obeyed his orders. After nine months, Joab returned to Jerusalem with a count of eight hundred thousand warriors in greater Israel and five hundred thousand warriors of the tribe of Judah.

"And David's heart smote him after that he had numbered the people. And David said unto the Lord, 'I have sinned greatly in that I have done: and now, I beseech thee, O Lord, take away the iniquity of thy servant; for I have done very foolishly'" (2 Samuel 24:10). The prophet Gad gave David three choices of punishment in expiation: either seven years of famine, three months of military defeat, or three days of plague. David chose the plague, and seventy thousand men perished.

> And when the angel stretched out his hand upon Jerusalem to destroy it, the Lord repented Him of the evil, and said to the angel that destroyed the people, "It is enough: stay now thine hand." And the angel of the Lord was by the threshingplace of Araunah the Jebusite. And David spake unto the Lord when he saw the angel that smote the people, and said, "Lo, I have sinned, and I have done wickedly: but these sheep, what have they done? let thine hand, I pray thee, be against me, and against my father's house." And Gad came that

---

14 1 Chronicles 21:1.

day to David, and said unto him, "Go up, rear an altar unto the LORD in the threshingfloor of Araunah the Jebusite." And David, according to the saying of Gad, went up as the LORD commanded. (2 Samuel 24:16–19)

The threshing floor of Araunah the Jebusite is the Temple Mount in Jerusalem.

Araunah approached David and bowed to him. David requested that he might purchase the threshing floor to build an altar to the Lord to avert the plague from Israel. Araunah offered to give it freely, along with oxen and other instruments for sacrifice and construction of the altar.

> And the king said unto Araunah, "Nay; but I will surely buy it of thee at a price: neither will I offer burnt offerings unto the LORD my God of that which doth cost me nothing." So David bought the threshingfloor and the oxen for fifty shekels of silver. And David built there an altar unto the LORD, and offered burnt offerings and peace offerings. So the LORD was intreated for the land, and the plague was stayed from Israel. (2 Samuel 24:24–25)

Chronicles adds that God "answered him from heaven by fire upon the altar of burnt offering" (1 Chronicles 21:26). David recognized the sanctity of the Temple Mount and identified it as the site the Lord had chosen in the land of Israel to establish His Temple. "This is the house of the LORD God, and this is the altar of the burnt offering for Israel" (1 Chronicles 22:1). This proclamation fulfilled the conditions of the Lord's words in Deuteronomy. It brought about a new order of worship for Israel that the people might conform to the word of Moses.[15]

Two Chronicles further identifies the Temple Mount in Jerusalem as the mythic Mount Moriah of Genesis. "Then Solomon began to build the house of the LORD at Jerusalem in mount Moriah, where the LORD appeared unto David his father, in the place that David had prepared in the threshingfloor of Ornan [Araunah] the Jebusite" (2 Chronicles 3:1). We recall Mount Moriah as the site of the near-sacrifice of Isaac.[16]

DAVID PREPARES FOR THE TEMPLE

One Chronicles 22 records the extent of David's preparations for the Temple, including his gathering of supplies and skilled workmen for the tasks ahead. He called Solomon to him and explained,

> My son, as for me, it was in my mind to build an house unto the name of the LORD my God: But the word of the LORD came to me, saying, "Thou hast shed blood abundantly, and hast made great wars: thou shalt not build an house unto my name, because thou hast shed much blood upon the earth in my sight. Behold, a son shall be born to thee, who shall be a man of rest; and I will give him rest from all his enemies round about: for his name shall be Solomon, and I will give peace and quietness unto Israel in his days. He shall build an house for my name; and he shall be my son, and

---

15 See pages 100–101 for a discussion of the new order of worship presented in Deuteronomy.

16 Genesis 22:2, and see page 41 of this book.

I will be his father; and I will establish [the] throne of his kingdom over Israel for ever." (1 Chronicles 22:6–10)

David implored the princes of Israel to help Solomon in the work ahead—preparing a permanent place for the Ark and the holy vessels and ritual sacraments of their ancestors. Then David passed on to Solomon the plans that the Lord had given him for the pattern of the Temple and its adjacent structures, including the organization of the clerical functions and even the weight of the various ritual objects and Temple furniture. David spoke of Solomon's youth and vulnerability, and explained the pains he had been at to accumulate the materials his son would need for the massive construction project.

Then David proclaimed he would make a generous personal donation to the Temple and encouraged others to do the same. The people rallied to his call and promised much wealth of gold, silver, jewels, and the other necessary materials for the furnishings and construction of the Temple. Then David offered prayers of thanksgiving and praise to the Lord and invoked His blessing on Solomon and the people of Israel. And the people bowed and prostrated themselves and prayed. On the following day they offered sacrifice to the Lord.

One Chronicles 23–28 goes into detail of the care David took in preparing the way for Solomon's reign, both religiously and politically. He numbered the Levites: appointing twenty-four thousand to work in the Temple, six thousand to be officers and judges, four thousand to be porters, and four thousand others to serve in the choirs. He made many other administrative decisions regarding the unique religious responsibilities of the Israelites. He was also concerned with strengthening the bureaucratic apparatus of the monarchy that he might assist his son in meeting the challenges that would lay ahead.

CHAPTER THIRTEEN

THE REIGN OF SOLOMON

THE BUILDING OF THE TEMPLE

(968–928 BCE)

And the LORD magnified Solomon exceedingly in the sight of all Israel,
and bestowed upon him such royal majesty as had not been on
any king before him in Israel. (1 Chronicles 29:25)

David had grown old and feeble, needing to be comforted and kept warm as he slept by a young virgin named Abishag the Shunammite. Adonijah, David's son by Haggith, decided his father's weakness was his call to usurp the throne. He allied himself with Joab and the priest Abiathar. But the priest Zadok, the prophet Nathan, the chief of David's bodyguards Benaiah, and others supported Solomon as David's successor. As Adonijah began to sacrifice and proclaim himself king, Nathan went to Bath-sheba to inform her of these developments. He encouraged her to lay her son's claim before David, who had sworn that Solomon would reign after him. She appeared before the weakened king with Nathan, imploring David's support.

David called Zadok and others and ordered that Solomon should come to Gihon, riding on David's own mule. Then he proclaimed, "Let Zadok the priest and Nathan the prophet anoint him there king over Israel: and blow ye with the trumpet, and say, 'God save king Solomon'" (1 Kings 1:34). Benaiah affirmed that the Lord supported David's choice and offered a blessing and prayer that the Lord be with Solomon as He had with David. "And Zadok the priest took an horn of oil out of the tabernacle, and anointed Solomon" (1 Kings 1:39).

When Adonijah learned of Solomon being crowned and of the extent of his support, he and his allies were in fear that Solomon would come after them. Adonijah "grabbed hold of the horns of the altar" (1 Kings 1:50) seeking the word of Solomon for his protection. When he presented himself to his half-brother, Solomon sent him to his home in peace, having sworn his protection if Adonijah would show himself worthy.

David's death was approaching and he called Solomon to his side to counsel him to stay close to the ways of the Lord. He reminded him of God's promise that David's descendants would remain on the throne of Israel if they kept to His ways. He made certain strategic suggestions to help Solomon consolidate his reign—among which was to kill Joab, his talented but ruthless general who had murdered Abner and Amasa, killed Absalom, and supported Adonijah. He also proposed killing Shimei the Benjamite, who had mocked and cursed him. While David had sworn not to kill Shimei, his promise evidently did not apply to Solomon.

The story of Solomon's succession as told in 1 Kings 1–2 is filled with intrigue, drama, and dissension as we see above. By contrast, 1 Chronicles 28 records that Solomon was unilaterally proclaimed by David in a great assembly before all Israel. David's final address to the Israelites, as recounted in Chronicles, is reminiscent of the statement of Moses as he prepared for death. David explained his faith and love of the Lord. He affirmed his acceptance of the Lord's choice of Solomon to build the Temple that David was not permitted to build. David outlined the conditions of excellence under which Solomon and his descendants must function to maintain the Lord's blessing. "The LORD searcheth all hearts, and understandeth all the imaginations of the thoughts: if thou seek him, he will be found of thee; but if thou forsake him, he will cast thee off for ever" (1 Chronicles 28:9).

David "slept with his fathers, and was buried in the city of David" (1 Kings 2:10). "Then sat Solomon upon the throne of David his father; and his kingdom was established greatly" (1 Kings 2:12).

Soon after David's death, however, Adonijah approached Bathsheba. He asked her to intercede for him with Solomon that he might have the maiden Abishag the Shunammite, David's servant and concubine during his last days. This represented a challenge to Solomon's kingship as we learned earlier during the revolt of Absalom against David. When Bathsheba made the request to Solomon, he realized at once its treasonous implication and had Adonijah slain by the loyal Benaiah.

Next, Solomon warned Abiathar, who had allied himself with Adonijah, to leave Jerusalem. Although he deserved death, Solomon would pardon him because he had borne the Ark for David and was the son of Ahimelech, who had shown such kindness to David during his flight from Saul.[17] Abiathar's demotion fulfilled the prophecy made to Eli during Samuel's youth.[18] Eli had been told that his descendants would be cut off, and that one especially would be filled with remorse because Eli had ignored the sins of his sons against Israel. Abiathar was Eli's great great grandson.

Joab, fearing Solomon, entered the Tabernacle for protection. Benaiah was sent to kill him but Joab would not leave the altar. When Benaiah reported this to Solomon, he was commanded to slay him anyway.

Solomon called for Shimei, who had cursed David. He ordered him to build a house in Jerusalem where he was to remain on pain of death. After three years, Shimei disobeyed him and traveled outside the city. Benaiah was dispatched to slay him.

Solomon raised Benaiah to commander of the armies replacing Joab. Zadok replaced Abiathar as High Priest. The consolidation of Solomon's power was now complete and the fulfillment of his father's commands discharged. He was at peace with his neighbors. He made an alliance with the Egyptian pharaoh and took his daughter to wife, bringing her to the City of David.

SOLOMON GROWS IN WISDOM AND PROSPERITY

Now begins the story of the initiation of Solomon as the proper ruler of the Jewish state and as the religious leader of the Jewish people. The Bible mentions that the people sacrificed at

---

17 1 Samuel 21:1–10 and page 129 of this book.
18 1 Samuel 2:31–33.

The Royal Tombs in the Old City of Jerusalem, the City of David. Photo by Steven Brooke.

the high places because there was yet no permanent Temple to the Lord.[19] Though Solomon loved the Lord, he too sacrificed and burned incense in the high places, in fact, he traveled to the great high place in Gibeon and there made a thousand burnt offerings unto the Lord.[20] Chronicles reminds us that while the Ark was in Jerusalem the Tabernacle was located in Gibeon at this time.[21]

The Lord appeared to Solomon in a dream at Gibeon and asked what gift he would receive. Solomon praised the Lord's beneficence to David and thanked Him for placing him on the throne, calling himself yet a child in the ways of

rulership. He requested an understanding heart and the ability to judge between good and evil. "And the speech pleased the LORD, that Solomon had asked this thing" (1 Kings 3:10). He praised Solomon for his integrity and promised him length of days if he kept to the statutes and commandments. When Solomon awoke, he traveled to Jerusalem "and stood before the Ark of the Covenant of the LORD" (1 Kings 3:15) and made offerings.

The well-known story follows of Solomon's wisdom in judging between two prostitutes in a dispute over a baby. Each woman had recently given birth to a son. One of the babies died and his mother switched her dead baby for the live child just born to the other. Both claimed the other was lying and that the live baby was hers. Solomon ordered one of his warriors to take a

---

19 1 Kings 3:2.

20 1 Kings 3:3–4.

21 2 Chronicles 1:3.

Gibeon (Gibeah) is the scene of repeated sacred encounters throughout the Bible.

sword and split the babe in two—then to give one half of the child to each mother.[22] The real mother begged Solomon to save the life of her child and just give the live infant to the other woman. The false claimant was satisfied with his proposal. Solomon ordered the child be given to his rightful mother. When all Israel heard of his judgment, they feared the king, "for they saw that the wisdom of God was in him, to do judgment" (1 Kings 3:28).

And Solomon's reign prospered and Israel was at peace, "every man under his vine and under his fig tree from Dan even to Beer-Sheba" (1 Kings 4:25). Solomon's wisdom, understanding, and largeness of heart continued to grow under God's direction. God promised Solomon that if he would walk in the ways of the Lord and keep the commandments, He would dwell among the people of Israel and not forsake them.

---

22 Josephus gives the story an interesting twist, writing that Solomon proposed to cut both the live and dead babies in half, sharing a portion of each child with the women. *Antiquities*, Book 8, 12:36.

Solomon is shown in judgment between the two prostitutes. He reveals the wisdom with which he has been imbued by the Lord in this fresco by Raphael, early sixteenth century.

SOLOMON BUILDS THE HOUSE OF THE LORD

David's friend Hiram, king of Tyre, sent ambassadors to Solomon when he learned that he had assumed the throne. Solomon sent word back that he was prepared to build the great House of the Lord that his father could not because of the wars that had plagued his reign. And because the Lord had brought peace to Solomon, "I purpose to build an house unto the name of the LORD my God, as the LORD spake unto David my father" (1 Kings 5:5).

He asked Hiram to send cedars from Lebanon and provide him with skilled workers from his kingdom, for "there is not among us any that can hew timber like unto the Sidonians" (1 Kings 5:6). Hiram rejoiced greatly that the Lord had given his friend a wise son, and he arranged to ship the timber by boat in exchange for food supplies. And these two great kings were allied in peace.

Solomon raised a levy of thirty thousand men to serve as laborers, and sent them to Lebanon in a schedule of rotation to assist Hiram's

Hiram and his architects creating the plans for the construction of the Temple of Solomon in this painting by Allyn Cox at the George Washington Masonic National Memorial. Photo by Arthur W. Pierson.

more skilled workers cut and trim the cedars of Lebanon for the Temple. Meanwhile Solomon's builders hewed great and costly stones for the foundation of the Temple. He began the project in the four hundred eightieth year after the arrival of the Jews from Egypt after the Exodus, and in the fourth year of his reign. The construction lasted seven years.[23]

The Structure

The Temple of Solomon was oriented on an east-west axis, facing the rising Sun. Its length was 60 cubits (90 feet), its width 20 cubits (30 feet), and its height 30 cubits (45 feet). Two Chronicles 3:3-4 provides measurements for the Temple that are the same as 1 Kings 6:2–3, except that the height of the main hall or nave is given in Chronicles as 120 cubits (180 feet).[24]

23 If Solomon began the Temple in 964 BCE, four hundred eighty years after the Israelites arrived in Canaan, forty years after they left Egypt, it would date the beginning of the Exodus to approximately 1484 BCE, which most scholars consider too early. The JSB commentary suggests that if the figure of four hundred eighty years is considered

symbolic of twelve generations of twenty-five years each, the Exodus would be dated closer to 1300 BCE. See commentary to 1 Kings 6:1 in JSB, page 683.

24 We recall that a cubit is 18 inches. Interestingly enough, the height of the nave recorded in Chronicles is the same

*Bible scholar Timothy Otis Paine scrupulously studied the architectural clues
in the Bible to create this representation of the Temple of Solomon.*

The Porch and Storage Chambers

A porch stood in front of the Temple that measured 20 cubits wide and 10 cubits (15 feet) deep. There were narrow windows for light. Storage chambers of three stories were built against the outside walls of the Temple. The chambers on the first floor were 5 cubits wide (7½ feet), the second story 6 cubits (9 feet) wide, and the third story seven cubits (10½ feet) wide. The outer storage chambers were each 5 cubits high.

interior height as the dome of the U.S. Capitol Rotunda on which is painted *The Apotheosis of Washington* fresco. See *The Secrets of Masonic Washington*, page 84.

The Construction and Decoration

The stones were cut and dressed before they were brought to the Temple "so that was neither hammer nor axe nor any tool of iron heard in the house, while it was building" (1 Kings 22:7). Beams and boards of cedar covered the inside of the house and the floor. Designs of gourds and open flowers were carved into the wood.

The Nave

The interior of the Temple, like the Tabernacle, was divided between an entrance hall or nave and the Holy of Holies. The large hall was 40 cubits (60 feet) long approaching the Holy of Holies.

ABOVE: *A view of the interior of the Temple showing the Great Hall or Nave with the Holy of Holies in the east. The storage chambers, mentioned in the text, rising on either side of the walls, are visible. We can also see the galleries on the front walls of the storage chambers, displaying the shields and arms captured by David and guarded by cherubim. The east wall and entranceway have been removed by artist Timothy Otis Paine.*

OPPOSITE: *The Holy of Holies from the Royal Arch Temple at the George Washington Masonic National Memorial. We see the Lampstand, the Table of Offering with the Bread of the Presence, and the Ark of the Covenant with the two cherubim on top. Photo by Arthur W. Pierson.*

The Holy of Holies and the Ark

The Holy of Holies itself was a perfect cube of 20 cubits (30 feet). It stood at the west of the Temple. It has been suggested that the Sanctuary was approached by a staircase or ramp rising 10 cubits, since the ceiling of the Temple itself was 30 cubits.[25]

Inside the Holy of Holies rested the Ark of the Covenant. A partition of gold chains stood in front of the Sanctuary as described in 1 Kings 6:21. One Kings 6:31–32 mentions that doors of olive wood carved with cherubim, palm trees, and flowers—all overlaid with gold—separated the main hall from the Holy of Holies. In 2 Chronicles 3:14, the Sanctuary is separated

---

25 Hershel Shanks, in *Jerusalem's Temple Mount*, discusses a Temple of similar age and design to Solomon's Temple, uncovered in Syria northwest of Aleppo at a site called

'Ain Dara. The Sanctuary of that Temple was approached by a ramp. See pages 133 *ff*.

The golden ritual tools for incense and offerings within the Temple are shown from Timna Park.

from the main hall by curtains of blue, purple, and crimson fabric—the same colors as the veil decorated with cherubim that separated the Holy of Holies in the Tabernacle described in Exodus 26:31.

The Ritual Vessels

The entire interior of the Temple of Solomon was overlaid in gold, as was the altar before the Sanctuary. All the vessels inside the Temple, including the altar, table of shewbread, candlesticks, flowers, lamps, and tongs, were fashioned of gold, as were the bowls, snuffers, basins, spoons, censors, and even the hinges of the doors for both the Temple entrance and the Most Holy Place. Two Chronicles 4:8 mentions ten tables of offering for the shewbread (Bread of the Presence), while 1 Kings 7:48 describes one.

Hiram, the Master Craftsman

"And King Solomon sent and fetched Hiram out of Tyre. He was a widow's son … and was filled with wisdom and understanding and cunning to work all work in brass. And he came to King Solomon, and wrought all his work" (1 Kings 7:3–14). Thus the archetypal Master Mason is introduced as the eponymous subject of Solomon's chief ally, King Hiram of Tyre. In the Hebrew text of 2 Chronicles 2:13, the Tyrian Master is called "Huram-abi" (חירם אבי).[26] This appellation is approaching very close to the name "Hiram Abiff" of Masonic tradition. The KJV translation of 2 Chronicles calls him "Huram my father's" (earlier in 1 Kings, simply "Hiram").

The Pillars Jachin and Boaz

Hiram fashioned two pillars of brass at either side of the porch at the entrance to the Temple. They stood 18 cubits (27 feet) high. Two Chronicles 3:15 gives the height of the two pillars as 35 cubits (52½ feet). He topped the pillars with two caps of molten brass each 5 cubits high. The pillars were highly decorated with pomegranate designs and wreaths of chainwork. The right hand pillar in the south was called Jachin ("He will establish"); the left hand pillar, Boaz ("Swiftness"), stood in the north.

The Molten Sea

Hiram fashioned a molten sea of brass, 10 cubits in diameter and 5 cubits high, decorated with

---

26 "Abi" may mean either "my father" or "fatherless," i.e., the son of a widow. It may also be a title equivalent to "Master" or "Skilled Craftsman." See www.hebrewoldtestament.com/B14C002.htm#v13 and www.ephesians5-11.org/hiram.htm.

Hiram Abiff at prayer in this beautiful painting by Allyn Cox at the George Washington Masonic National Memorial. Photo by Arthur W. Pierson.

gourds. It stood upon twelve oxen facing outward, three in each of the cardinal directions. Two Chronicles 4:6 adds that the Molten Sea was for the priests to wash.

The Ten Lavers

There were ten lavers or basins, 4 cubits (6 feet) in diameter, on wheels, used for the ritual washing of sacrifices. Each sat on a base of brass 4 cubits in length, 4 in breadth, and 3 cubits high (4½ feet), decorated with lions, oxen, and cherubim. The height of the spoked wheels was 1½ cubits (2 feet, 3 inches). Hiram fashioned all the sacrificial utensils for use outside the Temple of brass. He cast the brass pieces in the plain of Jordan.

The Molten Sea atop the brazen Table of Bulls stood in the Courtyard outside the Temple of Solomon, where the priests could wash before entering the Temple. Drawing by Timothy Otis Paine, colored by Nancy Wasserman.

SOLOMON DEDICATES THE TEMPLE

When the construction was finished, Solomon brought in all the gold and silver implements that his father had prepared. Then he assembled all the elders, heads of tribes, and the leaders of the ancestral houses that they might bring the Ark of the Covenant from the City of David up to the Temple Mount and into the Temple.

The sheep and oxen sacrificed before the Ark were without number. The Ark was placed within the Holy of Holies beneath the outstretched wings of the Cherubim.

> There was nothing in the ark save the two tables of stone, which Moses put there at Horeb, when the LORD made a covenant with the children of Israel, when they came out of the land of Egypt. And it came to pass, when the priests were come out of the holy place, that the cloud filled the house of the LORD, so that the priests could not stand to minister because of the cloud: for the glory of the LORD had filled the house of the LORD. Then spake Solomon, "The LORD said that he would dwell in thick darkness. I have surely built thee an house to dwell in, a settled place for thee to abide in forever." And the king turned his face about, and blessed all the congregation of Israel. (1 Kings 8:9–14)

He prayed that future kings who followed him would walk in the ways of the Lord, that the house of David might remain on the throne and lead the people in righteousness. He humbly observed that the vastness of the Lord made the idea of His dwelling place in the Temple incomprehensible, "But will God indeed dwell on the

The two Pillars of Jachin and Boaz stood outside the Temple. Drawing by Timothy Otis Paine, colored by Nancy Wasserman.

One of the ten wheeled bronze lavers for the washing of sacrifices that stood in the courtyard of the Temple. Drawing by Timothy Otis Paine, colored by Nancy Wasserman.

earth? Behold, the heaven and heaven of heavens cannot contain thee; how much less this house that I have builded" (1 Kings 8:27)?

The Centrality of Jerusalem in Jewish Prayer

As Solomon continued his dedication, he established the custom of Jews praying in the direction of Jerusalem.

> Yet have thou respect unto the prayer of thy servant … That thine eyes may be open toward this house night and day, even toward the place of which thou hast said, "My name shall be there": that thou mayest hearken unto the prayer which thy servant shall make toward this place. And hearken thou to the supplication of thy servant, and of thy people Israel, when they shall pray toward this place: and hear thou in heaven thy

dwelling place: and when thou hearest, forgive. (1 Kings 8:28–30)

> If thy people go out to battle against their enemy, whithersoever thou shalt send them, and shall pray unto the LORD toward the city which thou hast chosen, and toward the house that I have built for thy name: Then hear thou in heaven their prayer and their supplication, and maintain their cause. (1 Kings 8:44–45)

Solomon hoped the presence of the House of the Lord in the Holy City would imbue Israel

Looking east into the Great Hall between the pillars of Jachin and Boaz. The curtain covering the Holy of Holies may be seen in the rear. The eastern wall has been removed in this rendering by Timothy Otis Paine.

with a sense of righteousness and incline God to show mercy toward His people—being willing to forgive even when they sin, so long as they turn toward Him and His Temple. That if they be smitten by their enemies and carried off into strange lands because of their sins, their contrition will bring them again to the land promised to them. That drought, pestilence, and plague be removed by the prayers of those who pray toward the House of the Lord.

In fact, he prayed that non-Jews have their prayers answered as well, that this Temple be a universal center of humanity.

> Moreover concerning a stranger, that is not of thy people Israel, but cometh out of a far country for thy name's sake; (For they shall hear of thy great name, and of thy strong hand, and of thy stretched out arm); when he shall come and pray toward this house; Hear thou in heaven thy dwelling place, and do according to all that the stranger calleth to thee for: that all people of the earth may know thy name, to fear thee, as do thy people Israel: and that they may know that this house, which I have builded, is called by thy name. (1 Kings 8:41–43)

Chronicles includes a familiar formula for rekindling God's favor in the midst of sin, while acknowledging the sanctity of the Temple precinct for the first time.

> If my people, which are called by my name, shall humble themselves, and pray, and seek my face, and turn from their wicked ways; then will I hear from heaven, and will forgive their sin, and will heal their land. *Now mine eyes shall be open, and mine ears attent unto the prayer that is made in this place.* [Emphasis added] (2 Chronicles 7:14)

The Sacrifice and Feast

Solomon capped the dedication of the Temple with a huge peace offering in which "he offered unto the LORD, two and twenty thousand oxen, and an hundred and twenty thousand sheep. So the king and all the children of Israel dedicated the house of the LORD" (1 Kings 8:63).

> Now when Solomon had made an end of praying, the fire came down from heaven, and consumed the burnt offering and the sacrifices; and the glory of the LORD filled the house. (2 Chronicles 7:1)

The immense bounty of sacrifice was shared with the people. All Israel gathered together at the Temple and feasted with their king for fourteen days.

A Prophetic Warning

When the people had departed in happiness, Solomon was again visited by the Lord as he had been in Gibeon. And the Lord promised that if he and his descendants held to the ways of righteousness, they would remain as kings of Israel. But if they failed, and if the kings and the people turned after other gods, the consequences would be most dire:

> Then will I cut off Israel out of the land which I have given them; and this house, which I have hallowed for my name, will I cast out of my sight; and Israel shall be a proverb and a byword among all people: And at this house, which is

high, every one that passeth by it shall be astonished, and shall hiss; and they shall say, "Why hath the LORD done thus unto this land, and to this house?" And they shall answer, "Because they forsook the LORD their God, who brought forth their fathers out of the land of Egypt, and have taken hold upon other gods, and have worshipped them, and served them: therefore hath the LORD brought upon them all this evil." (1 Kings 9:7–9)

This has turned out to be a painfully accurate promise indeed.

SOLOMON BUILDS HIS PALACE

As he was building the Temple, Solomon also built a palace for himself. A foreshadowing of later troubles is subtly intimated in the text. There seems an implied criticism when the Bible tells us the construction of Solomon's house took thirteen years, six years longer than the House of the Lord.[27] Also built from cedars of Lebanon, Solomon's palace was larger than the Temple. Known as the House of the Forest of Lebanon, its length was 100 cubits (150 feet), its width 50 cubits (75 feet), and its height 30 cubits (45 feet). The complex of royal buildings included a Hall of Pillars (called a porch of pillars in the KJV), nearly as large as the Temple. There was a Hall of Judgment where Solomon dispensed justice, a separate palace for Solomon, and another for his Egyptian wife. The royal complex is believed to have been located south of the Temple in what is now the area of the al-Aqsa Mosque.[28]

OPPOSITE: *Artists's conception of the Queen of Sheba, by Nancy Wasserman, 2009*

THE FALL OF SOLOMON

A minor conflict between Solomon and King Hiram is recorded in 1 Kings. Solomon gave Hiram twenty cities, which displeased Hiram. This is mentioned immediately after God's warning of the penalty for disobedience quoted above from 1 Kings 9:7–9. It is cause for concern, in that Hiram, David, and Solomon have been untroubled by any dissonance until this incident. On the other hand, 2 Chronicles tells the story differently. In the Chronicles account, the gift is from Hiram to Solomon, who rebuilds the twenty cities as part of a national campaign of construction undertaken after the completion of the Temple. No dissatisfaction is hinted at.

The Queen of Sheba, hearing of the fame of Solomon and of his wisdom came to visit him. And she unburdened herself to him and he counseled her. And she proclaimed that the Lord had shown His love for Israel by placing Solomon on the throne, and gave him valuable gifts of gold, spices, and precious stones. Solomon gave her of his royal bounty in return.

As we learn of the vast and steady increase of his wealth throughout this period, a sense of unease begins to grow within the reader. Solomon's attachment to the Lord appears to be overshadowed by the text's description of his astronomical wealth and the opulence of his palace. Any royal concern for the well-being of the people is not once mentioned. He bought chariots and horses from Egypt—specifically prohibited in Deuteronomy 17:16. And he loved many women of the surrounding pagan tribes in addition to his Egyptian wife—in direct violation of Deuteronomy 17:17. Solomon's misbehavior is specified in clear language.

---

27 1 Kings 7.
28 See NOAB, page 631.

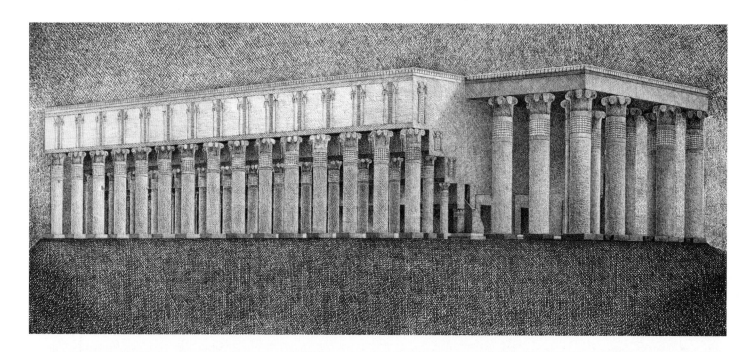

The Palace of Solomon was similar in design to the Temple but larger.
ABOVE: *Here is a view from the northeast.* BELOW: *This is a view facing east from the Porch. The eastern wall has been removed, by Timothy Otis Paine.*

The Hall of Pillars by which the throne of the king would be approached by petitioners,
those who sought royal judgment, and ambassadors and other dignitaries.
Re-created by Timothy Otis Paine.

Of the nations concerning which the LORD said unto the children of Israel, "Ye shall not go in to them, neither shall they come in unto you: for surely they will turn away your heart after their gods": Solomon clave unto these in love. And he had seven hundred wives, princesses, and three hundred concubines: and his wives turned away his heart. (1 Kings 11:2–3)

Solomon began to worship pagan gods, building altars to them on the Mount of Olives, that his wives might burn incense and make sacrifices. All this displeased the Lord. He spoke to Solomon and made clear his failure to live up to the standards expected of him. He told Solomon that because of his betrayal the kingdom would be taken from him, though not while he lived. Instead it would be taken from his son Rehoboam, in deference to the Lord's love for David. All but one tribe would be separated from Rehoboam.[29]

DISSENT AND DIVISION ARISE

The Lord began His punishment of Solomon by raising two military challenges against him, led by commanders who had earlier quarreled with David and fled the kingdom. Thus ended the period of peace that Solomon had enjoyed, and which had allowed him to build the Temple, his palace complex, his other construction projects such as the wall of Jerusalem, and to accumulate his vast wealth and many wives.

Jeroboam, an ally of Solomon, was encouraged by the prophet Ahijah to raise his hand against the king and divide the kingdom of Israel. The Lord spoke to Jeroboam through Ahijah, explaining that after Solomon's death, He would take ten tribes out of the hand of Rehoboam and give them to Jeroboam. Rehoboam would retain Jerusalem, the city in which the Lord had chosen to put His name. The Lord further offered to form a covenant with Jeroboam.

> And it shall be, if thou wilt hearken unto all that I command thee, and wilt walk in my ways, and do that is right in my sight, to keep my statutes and my commandments, as David my servant did; that I will be with thee, and build thee a sure house, as I built for David, and will give Israel unto thee. And I will for this afflict the seed of David, *but not for ever.* [Emphasis added.] (1 Kings 11:38)

When Solomon learned of all this he came after Jeroboam, who fled to Egypt, where he remained until Solomon's death.

After a reign of forty years, Solomon died and was buried in the City of David. It is interesting to note that the story of Solomon in 2 Chronicles makes no mention of his apostasy with either the foreign women or their gods. The conclusion of his reign and his death, as told in Chronicles, indicates unmitigated success with no hint of the civil war and divided kingdom with which his rulership ends in Kings.

---

29 In 1 Kings 12:21 it is clear that the tribe of Benjamin was counted with Judah, thus Rehoboam would actually remain king of two of the twelve tribes of Israel.

PART FIVE

THE DIVIDED MONARCHY
AND THE LOSS OF THE TEMPLE

(1 KINGS, 2 KINGS, 2 CHRONICLES,
ISAIAH, AND JEREMIAH)

A Table of Biblical Rulers*

The United Monarchy

Saul (1025–1005)
David (1005–965)
Solomon (968–928)

The Divided Monarchy

The Kingdom of Judah

Rehoboam (928–911)

Abijam [Abijah] (911–908)

Asa (908–867)

Jehosophat (870–846)

Jehoram [Joram] (851–843)

Ahaziah (843–842)

Athaliah (842–836)

Joash [Jehoash] (836–798)

Amaziah (798–769)

Azariah [Uzziah] (785–733)

Jotham (759–743)

Ahaz (743/735–727/715)

Rulers of Judah after the Fall of the Kingdom of Israel

Hezekiah (727/715–698/687)

Manasseh (698/687–642)

Amon (641–640)

Josiah (640–609)

Jehoaz (609)

Jehoiakim [Eliakim] (608–598)

Jehoiachin (597)

Zedekiah [Mattaniah] (597–586)

The Kingdom of Israel

Jeroboam (928–907)

Nadab (907–906)

Baasha (906–883)

Elah (883–882)

Zimri (882)

Omri (882–871)

Ahab (873–852)

Ahaziah (852–851)

Jehoram [Joram] (851–842)

Jehu (842–814)

Jehoahaz (817–800)

Jehoash (800–784)

Jeroboam II (788–747)

Zachariah (747)

Shalum (747)

Menahem (747–737)

Pekahiah (737–735)

Pekah (735–732)

Hoshea (732–722)

* All dates are BCE. The reigns of some rulers overlap those of others. All dates are historical approximations. The source for the dates is *The New Oxford Annotated Bible* and *The Jewish Study Bible*.

Chapter Fourteen

The Divided Kingdoms of Judah and Israel

For the eyes of the LORD run to and fro throughout the whole earth, to shew himself strong in the behalf of them whose heart is perfect toward Him. (2 Chronicles 16:9)

We are now about to describe a turbulent period lasting some three and a half centuries. It is eerily reminiscent of the wayward era catalogued in the Book of Judges. With few exceptions, the rulers who succeeded Solomon devolved deeper into religious apostasy and political corruption. And their fortunes reflected their parting from the ways of the Lord. The land of Israel was subject first to a civil war that split the country in two (see map on page 373), then a series of invasions by foreign powers and various coup d'états that brought even more chaos and suffering. Yet there were some shining exceptions among the rulers whose fidelity to the Lord was exemplary. Two miracle-working prophets, Elijah and Elisha, demonstrated God's power in the Bible's engaging accounts of their missions. We will observe the Temple of Solomon itself suffering periods of disrepair and desecration at the hands of heretics, while at other times being treated with love and devotion by those who adhered to the laws of Moses.

Reign of Rehoboam (928–911 BCE) and the Division of Israel

Upon the death of Solomon, Rehoboam was crowned in Shechem. Jeroboam, learning of Solomon's death, came to Jerusalem. He spoke to Rehoboam about the burdens on the people caused by the taxes and levies of workers Solomon had instituted to pursue his ambitious projects. "Thy father made our yoke grievous: now therefore make thou the grievous service of thy father, and his heavy yoke which he put upon us, lighter, and we will serve thee" (1 Kings 12:4).

When Rehoboam asked counsel of the elders, they told him to act with mercy. "If thou wilt be a servant unto this people this day, and wilt serve them, and answer them, and speak good words to them, then they will be thy servants for ever" (1 Kings 12:7). However, Rehoboam's heart was misled into seeking the opinions of the young men of his court. They advised him to boldly assert his royal power and assume an unyielding stance in answer to Jeroboam's petition. Rehoboam chose to listen to them. In Chronicles, Rehoboam's bad judgment in accepting such flawed advice is attributed to the Lord's word spoken earlier through Ahijah—Solomon's kingdom was to be condemned to civil war following his death.[1]

Rehoboam proclaimed to Jeroboam, "My father hath chastised you with whips, but I will chastise you with scorpions" (1 Kings 12:11). Ten of the twelve tribes of Israel immediately dissolved their allegiance to the house of David. Rehoboam reigned over those that remained in the cities of Judah. When he sent a tax collector to the outlying regions, the royal official was stoned to death. Rehoboam fled to the safety of Jerusalem.

Chronicles tells us that Rehoboam fortified the Southern Kingdom of Judah and its environs. It also mentions the arrival of the Levites from the Northern Kingdom of Israel. They came to Jerusalem because Jeroboam had prevented them from serving as priests of the Lord. Instead, Jeroboam appointed his own priests for pagan worship, as will be discussed shortly.

Chronicles reports that for three years Rehoboam was strengthened by the presence of the Levites, walking in the ways of David and Solomon, and prospering. However, when he felt he had established his reign and had acquired many wives and children, he abandoned the commands of the Lord and began to worship strange gods and tolerate sodomites in the land.

In the fifth year of Rehoboam's reign, the Egyptian pharaoh Shishak I (r. 945–924 BCE) invaded Jerusalem and carried off much treasure from the Temple of Solomon, along with gold from the Palace of Solomon. In 2 Chronicles 12, the campaign of Shishak is attributed to Rehoboam's abandoning the law. Shishak's victories on his approach to Jerusalem brought the prophet Shemaiah to address Rehoboam and his officers. Shemaiah chastised them for their apostasy. Acknowledging their errors, they humbled themselves before him and thereby

gained the Lord's favor. However, God chose to expose them to defeat at the hands of Shishak so they might know the difference between service to the Lord and service to the king of a foreign land. Yet Rehoboams's repentance had turned away the full wrath of the Lord and he survived to reign seventeen years. The Southern Kingdom of Judah was in a continuous state of war with the Northern Kingdom of Israel throughout those years.

THE REIGN OF JEROBOAM IN ISRAEL (928–907 BCE)

When Rehoboam learned that the majority of Israelites had made Jeroboam their king, he raised an army of 180,000 men to go after them. But the Lord spoke to Rehoboam and the houses of Judah and Benjamin through the prophet Shemaiah. "Thus saith the Lord, Ye shall not go up, nor fight against your brethren the children of Israel: return every man to his house; for this thing is from me" (1 Kings 12:24).

Jeroboam established the capital of the Northern Kingdom in Shechem. He feared that when his subjects would go to the Temple of Solomon in Jerusalem for the three annual pilgrimages, they would embrace Rehoboam, and return to the house of David. He therefore instituted a rival worship in Northern Israel. He explained that because the journey to fulfill their religious duties in Jerusalem was so onerous, he had made two golden calves for them to worship locally. "Behold thy gods, O Israel, which brought thee up out of the land of Egypt" (1 Kings 12:28). He placed one in Bethel, the site of several altars erected earlier by the patriarchs Abraham and Jacob, and the second in the far north in Dan, a center of heretical worship since the days of Micah (see page 123). He also defined a series of competing holidays, invented whole cloth, created his own priesthood, and ordained a spurious regimen of sacrifices.

---

1 See page 184.

The ancient Israelite capital of Shechem is today the modern city of Nablus.

A building in Nablus imaginatively recalls the ancient capital.

A prophet arose out of Judah and traveled to Bethel where Jeroboam stood at the altar. "And he cried against the altar in the word of the LORD, and said, 'O altar, thus saith the LORD; Behold, a child shall be born unto the house of David, Josiah by name; and upon thee shall he offer the priests of the high places that burn incense upon thee, and men's bones shall be burnt upon thee'" (1 Kings 13:2). Jeroboam was enraged.

> And it came to pass, when king Jeroboam heard the saying of the man of God, which had cried against the altar in Bethel, that he put forth his hand from the altar, saying, "Lay hold on him." And his hand, which he put forth against him, dried up, so that he could not pull it in again to him. (1 Kings 13:4)

Jeroboam repented and begged the prophet to ask God to heal his hand, and it was granted. Despite this, he refused to turn away from his evil ways, and his house was cut off from the Lord and destroyed. Jeroboam's eldest child became ill. Jeroboam sent his wife to Ahijah—the prophet who had originally told him he would be king. Ahijah explained that because of Jeroboam's sins, the Lord had cursed him and his family, and the people of Israel whom he had misled. The child died. Jeroboam reigned for twenty-two years, after which the kingdom of Northern Israel passed to his younger son Nadab.

JUDAH: THE REIGN OF ABIJAM [ABIJAH]
(911–908 BCE)

Rehoboam was succeeded in the Southern Kingdom of Judah by his son Abijam. In the account given in 1 Kings, Abijam walked in the evil ways of his father. But out of forbearance and love of David, God allowed him to reign. "Because David did that which was right in the eyes of the Lord, and turned not aside from anything that He commanded him all the days of his life, save only in the matter of Uriah the Hittite" (1 Kings 15:5). Abijam reigned for three years, continuing the war against Jeroboam.

In Chronicles, Abijam is represented quite otherwise. At the scene of a great battle with Jeroboam, Abijam thundered forth his assessment that: 1) the descendants of the house of David were the legitimate rulers of Israel; 2) Jeroboam was in a state of rebellion; and 3) the young men who had counseled Rehoboam were scoundrels, and Rehoboam was so young and inexperienced he was misled. Abijam criticized Jeroboam for making the golden calves and driving the Levites from Northern Israel. He contrasted all these ills with an account of the righteous observance of the people of the Kingdom of Judah.

> But as for us, the LORD is our God, and we have not forsaken Him; and the priests, which minister unto the LORD, are the sons of Aaron, and the Levites wait upon their business: And they burn unto the LORD every morning and every evening burnt sacrifices and sweet incense: the shewbread also set they in order upon the pure table; and the candlestick of gold with the lamps thereof, to burn every evening: for we keep the charge of the LORD our God; but ye have forsaken Him. (2 Chronicles 13:10–11)

Although Jeroboam had used an intelligent set of tactics to surround Abijam's army, the Lord defeated him with a great slaughter of five hundred thousand warriors. "Thus the children of Israel were brought under at that time, and the children of Judah prevailed, because they relied

Detail from the altar to Astarte shown on page 117. The naked goddess stands on an unidentified feline head. Archaeological Museum, Amman, Jordan. Photo by Vere Chappell.

upon the LORD God of their fathers" (2 Chronicles, 13:18). After the battle, the Lord struck Jeroboam and he died, while Abijam grew strong with many wives and children.

JUDAH: THE REIGN OF ASA (908–867 BCE)

Abijam was succeeded by his son Asa, who did that which was right in the eyes of the Lord. He reigned for forty-one years, removing the sodomites and pagan altars from the land. He even removed his mother as queen because she made an idol in a grove that he destroyed.[2] Asa's religious reforms are even more extensively detailed in Chronicles, where he is said to have removed the high places, the sacred poles, and the pagan altars. He also undertook public works of reconstruction and building.

Asa was at war with Baasha, king of Northern Israel, all their days. At some point Zerah the Ethiopian came against Asa with an army of a million men and three hundred chariots. Asa appealed to the Lord for help, noting that whether an army was large or strong did not matter to the Lord. His faith, and the faith of his people, was in the name of the Lord. God protected Judah, smote the Ethiopians and they fled. Asa and his army chased after them and conquered and plundered numerous cities along the way, returning to Jerusalem with many spoils.

Then Azariah, a prophet, came to meet Asa and convey the Lord's words. He stated that the Lord would stand by Asa as long as he stood

---

2 Asa's mother is identified in Chronicles as a devotee of the Canaanite goddess Asherah.

by the Lord, but if Asa abandoned the Lord, he would be abandoned in return. He reminded Asa that in earlier times, Israel was without the Lord's protection and the voice of the prophets, and those were perilous times for the people.

Asa undertook even further reforms, gathering together all the people of Judah and Benjamin, and the many who had fled the idolatrous ways of the Northern Kingdom. He repaired the altar in the Temple of Solomon. The people gathered in the Temple and sacrificed.

> And they entered into a covenant to seek the LORD God of their fathers with all their heart and with all their soul; That whosoever would not seek the LORD God of Israel should be put to death, whether small or great, whether man or woman. (2 Chronicles 15:12–13)

ISRAEL: THE REIGN OF NADAB (907–906 BCE)

In the Kingdom of Israel, Jeroboam was succeeded by his son Nadab. He was the last of Jeroboam's line as prophesied. Nadab reigned for two years before he was slain by Baasha, who continued the war against Judah and King Asa.

ISRAEL: THE REIGN OF BAASHA (906–883 BCE)

Baasha, like Jeroboam and Nadab before him, did evil in the sight of the Lord. A curious story is told in 1 Kings 15:16–22 with modern significance. Baasha built the city of Ramah to prevent people from traveling to Jerusalem. Ramah is probably modern Ramallah, the self-chosen capital of the Israeli-Arabs. I was told by a Palestinian patriot that its symbolic importance as a rival capital for the Palestinians is its proximity to Jerusalem, some eight miles

away. It is the site of the tomb of Yassar Arafat, which has, ironically, become a shrine for some Palestinians.

In response to Baasha's construction of Ramah, Asa allied himself with Benhadad I, the king of Syria. Asa took all the gold and silver that was left in the treasury of the Temple of Solomon and sent it to Benhadad, seeking to persuade him to break his alliance with Baasha and formulate a new alliance with Asa.

Chronicles adds that this caused the Lord to send the seer Hanani to Asa, criticizing him for relying on the Syrian king rather than the Lord. Hanani reminded Asa of his victory over the numerically superior Ethiopians at the Lord's hand.

> For the eyes of the LORD run to and fro throughout the whole earth, to shew himself strong in the behalf of them whose heart is perfect toward him. Herein thou hast done foolishly: therefore from henceforth thou shalt have wars. (2 Chronicles 16:9)

Baasha, under attack from the combined forces of Benhadad I and Asa, was forced to abandon his construction of Ramah. It was destroyed to its foundation and its very stones removed. Then God sent the prophet Jehu to Baasha with His curses.

ISRAEL: THE REIGN OF ELAH (883–882 BCE)

When Baasha died after a twenty-four year reign, his son Elah succeeded him. He also did ill in the sight of the Lord and after two years was slain in a revolt led by Zimri, who killed all the family of Baasha as Jehu had prophesied.

During the reign of King Omri, Samaria replaced Shechem as the capital of the Northern Kingdom of Israel. Photo by Steven Brooke.

ISRAEL: THE REIGN OF ZIMRI (882 BCE)

Zimri reigned for a mere seven days before the people of the Kingdom of Northern Israel learned of his slaying of Elah. They made Omri, the commander of the army, their king. When Zimri learned of this, he went into the king's house, set it on fire, and died in the blaze.

ISRAEL: THE REIGN OF OMRI (882–871 BCE)

Northern Israel was divided for some four years between the followers of Omri and those of Tibni, son of Ginath. But Omri prevailed and Tibni died.[3] Omri reigned for twelve years. He

built the northern city of Samaria as his capital and was a powerful king. But he did evil in the sight of the Lord, leading the children of Israel to sin, and provoking the Lord to anger.

ISRAEL: THE REIGN OF AHAB (873–852 BCE)

Omri was succeeded by his son Ahab, who reigned over the kingdom of Northern Israel for twenty-two years. Married to Jezebel, he worshipped Baal, to whom he built an altar and temple in Samaria. "Ahab did more to provoke the LORD God of Israel to anger than all the

---

3 No further biographical details are given for Tibni.

The civil war between him and Omri extended from the twenty-seventh year of the reign of Asa in Judah to the thirty-first. See 1 Kings 16:15 and 23.

kings of Israel that were before him" (1 Kings 16:33).

The Prophet Elijah in the Northern Kingdom during the Reign of Ahab

In 1 Kings 17, we are introduced to the prophet Elijah, one of the more colorful characters of the Bible. He played a critical role in several episodes that are important to this history.

Elijah was sent to Ahab to announce that neither dew nor rain would fall for a period of years, unless by his word. Then the Lord ordered Elijah to hide himself by a brook near the river Jordan. God informed him that he could drink from the stream and that the ravens would bring him his food. Elijah obeyed and the ravens brought him bread and meat, morning and evening.

Eventually the stream ran dry because of a drought and the Lord sent him to the town of Zarephath. Here he met a widow whom the Lord had appointed to care for him. He asked her for food and drink, but she informed him that her provisions were gone, and that she and her son were preparing to die. But he promised her that her food supply would not fail if she fed him; and indeed it replenished itself daily as he had promised. Then the child fell ill and the woman reprimanded Elijah for coming to her and saving her so that she could watch her son die. Elijah took the child and carried him to a private place and prayed over him with great fervor. "And the Lord heard the voice of Elijah ..." (1 Kings 17:22) and the child was resuscitated and returned to his joyous mother.

Three years had passed. Elijah was commanded to revisit Ahab, in the midst of the drought and famine, and proclaim that the Lord would send rain. Elijah first went to Obadiah who was in charge of the house of the king. Obadiah was a righteous man who had saved the lives of a hundred prophets by hiding them from the murderous fury of Jezebel and her campaign against the Lord's chosen spokesmen. Elijah told Obadiah to announce to Ahab that he had come to speak with him again. Ahab accused Elijah of being responsible for the woes of Israel, to which Elijah replied that instead it was the fault of the faithlessness of Ahab and his father.

Elijah demanded that Ahab assemble all the people of Israel at Mt. Carmel along with the four hundred fifty prophets of Baal and four hundred priests of Asherah—all of whom were associated with Jezebel. Elijah proposed a contest between the Lord and Baal that the Israelites might judge who was the true deity. He suggested two bullocks be prepared for sacrifice: that one be offered to Baal and the other to the Lord. Whichever deity answered by consuming the offering by divine fire would be considered the true god.

The four hundred fifty prophets of Baal prepared their sacrifice and made their invocations, calling forth their god to come and consume the sacrifice. They prayed from morning till noon to no avail. At noon, Elijah mocked them in front of the Israelites. They then began to cut themselves, as was their custom, and blood flowed. They prayed continuously until the evening sacrifice, but again the offering went unconsumed.

Then Elijah summoned the people to watch him rebuild the altar of the Lord that had fallen into disrepair through their negligence. He took twelve stones for the twelve tribes. He made a trench around the altar, and laid the wood, and cut the bullock into pieces. He made the people pour four barrels of water over the wood and the pieces of sacrifice. They did this three times until the trench was filled with water and everything completely soaked. Elijah prayed to the Lord.

Baal was the Canaanite rival of the Jewish God mentioned throughout the Bible.
This ancient personification of Baal wears an Egyptian-style crown.
It dates to the second to first century BCE.

Elijah is fed and nourished by the Angel in this engraving by Gustave Doré, 1865.

*Tel Beer-sheba in southern Israel is an archaeological site in which the ruins
of the ancient biblical city are carefully preserved and studied.*

Then the fire of the LORD fell, and consumed the burnt sacrifice, and the wood, and the stones, and the dust, and licked up the water that was in the trench. And when all the people saw it, they fell on their faces: and they said, "The LORD, He is the God; the LORD, He is the God." (1 Kings 18:38–39)

Elijah ordered them to slay the prophets and priests of Baal. Next, he fulfilled the prophecy made three years earlier by telling Ahab he heard the sound of an abundance of rain coming. He warned Ahab to get up and into his chariot that he be not delayed by the downpour. As the sky darkened and Ahab sped to his court, Elijah ran on foot in front of the speeding horses of the chariot.

When Ahab reached his palace in the city of Jezreel, he informed Jezebel of what had happened. Ever undaunted, she sent a messenger to Elijah. She pledged that if she had not killed Elijah by the next day, she would gladly die as had the priests and prophets of Baal.

Elijah fled to Beer-sheba in Judah and traveled a day's journey further into the wilderness. He begged God that he be allowed to die; but an angel touched him, and fed him, and he rested. The angel came again and he ate and gained strength for the forty-day journey to Mount Horeb.[4] Elijah communed with the Lord on Mount Horeb. God instructed him to return north: to travel to Damascus and anoint Hazael

---

4 Mount Horeb and Mount Sinai are generally considered to be the same mountain in the south of the Sinai Peninsula.

Another view of Samaria. Photo by Steven Brooke.

king of Syria; then to anoint Jehu king of Israel; and finally to anoint Elisha as his successor as prophet.[5] These three were to be established as ferocious bulwarks against apostasy. "Whoever escapes from Hazael, Jehu shall kill; and whoever escapes from the sword of Jehu, Elisha shall kill" (1 Kings 19:17 NRSV). The Lord further explained to Elijah that there remained seven thousand people of Northern Israel who had not bent the knee to Baal.

The Battle of Aphek

Benhadad II had succeeded his father Benhadad I as king of Syria (the region was also known as Aram). He made war against Ahab and the kingdom of Israel. A prophet came to

5 Jehu was actually anointed by an assistant of Elisha, and Elisha announced to Hazael that he would succeed Benhadad II as king of Syria (see page 206).

Ahab and promised him victory, and indeed the Israelites were triumphant. However, the prophet warned that the Syrians would return in the spring. The Syrian king's counselors were meanwhile casting about for a strategy to renew their invasion. They decided that the God of the Israelites was a god of mountains and ascribed their defeat to His power in high elevations. They believed they would be stronger in the plain, so they must choose a low-lying area near the city of Aphek as the site of the next battle. Then they filled the country with their numerically superior troops.

And there came a man of God, and spake unto the king of Israel, and said, "Thus saith the LORD, Because the Syrians have said, 'The LORD is God of the hills, but He is not God of the valleys,' therefore will I deliver all this great multitude into thine hand, and ye shall know that I am the LORD." (1 Kings 20:28)

The Syrians were soundly defeated by the smaller Israelite force. One hundred thousand of the enemy were slain in the battle. When the retreating Syrian troops came to the wall of Aphek, it collapsed upon them, and another 27,000 perished. Benhadad II and his army took counsel together. They decided to ask for mercy, as the Israelites were known to be a merciful people. He came to Ahab and prayed for peace and for his life, and Ahab granted these to him. But Ahab was visited by another prophet and chastened. He was told he had disobeyed the intentions of the Lord. God had appointed that the Syrian king and his remaining court be utterly destroyed. Therefore Ahab would forfeit his own life. Ahab returned to Samaria distraught.

Not to be turned from his wickedness, however, merely by prophecies of his own death, Ahab continued to accumulate sins. He coveted a property bordering his palace that was owned by one of his subjects named Naboth. Ahab asked Naboth to sell the field to him. But Naboth refused, saying he would not sell his patrimony. Jezebel saw her husband's discomfort and asked him the reason. She plotted to murder Naboth in such a manner that his blood would be on the community—arranging for him to be falsely accused of blasphemy by two of her agents, then seeing to it that the Israelites stoned him to death.

The Lord sent Elijah to Ahab to inform him of the doom that would be visited upon him in return for this murder and his other acts of evil, and for causing Israel to sin. Elijah told him the dogs would lick his blood from the ground in the field of Naboth; the blood of Jezebel would be licked by dogs at the walls of Jezreel; and his descendants would be cut off. Ahab tore his

garments and donned sackcloth and ashes and fasted in despair. The Lord then informed Elijah that because of these acts of apparent contrition, He would delay Ahab's promised punishment.

JUDAH: THE REIGN OF JEHOSOPHAT (870–846 BCE)

In the Kingdom of Judah, Asa had died and was succeeded by his son Jehosophat. He strengthened Judah against the Northern Kingdom, outfitting his army as a mighty and well-equipped fighting force. He carried on with his father's religious reforms, continuing to tear down the pagan altars and groves. Further, in the third year of his reign, he sent a series of traveling teachers and missionaries throughout the region to teach the message of the Book of the Law. Neighboring kingdoms feared and respected Jehosophat and he grew wealthy with their tribute.

Jehosphat and Ahab Make an Alliance

One Kings 22 recounts that there was peace between Israel and Syria for three years after the battle of Aphek. Then Jehosophat paid a visit to Ahab and made a marriage alliance—presumably that of his son Jehoram with Ahab's daughter Athaliah. Jehosophat and Ahab also agreed to fight against Syria and retake Ramoth-gilead, east of the Jordan River.

Jehosophat requested they first inquire of the Lord before going to battle. Ahab gathered some four hundred prophets together to inquire of the outcome of the plan. They advised him that victory would be forthcoming. But Jehosophat was uneasy and asked if there was not another prophet in the land. They consulted Micaiah, whom Ahab hated because he so often prophesied evil coming to him. Micaiah indeed prophesied Ahab's death in contrast to the four hundred others. He explained that God had

Along the plains of the Jordan River looking east to Jordan

sent a lying spirit to them so that Ahab could finally be killed. Ahab caused Micaiah to be imprisoned awaiting the successful conclusion of the battle. But Ahab was indeed killed. When his chariot was returned to the field of Naboth to be washed, the dogs licked his blood.[6]

Jehosophat Returns to Jerusalem

Two Chronicles 18:31 adds to the account of the battle above that the Lord helped preserve Jehosophat's life. After the death of Ahab, he returned to Jerusalem. Jehu, the son of the seer Hanani, approached Jehosophat and commented on his ill-fated alliance with Ahab:

Shouldest thou help the ungodly, and love them that hate the LORD? therefore is wrath upon thee from before the LORD. Nevertheless there are good things found in thee, in that thou hast taken away the groves out of the land, and hast prepared thine heart to seek God. (2 Chronicles 19:2–3)

Thus, despite his flawed alliance with Ahab, Jehosophat reigned over the kingdom of Judah for twenty-five years. He continued to walk in the ways of the Lord, although the high places remained where people offered sacrifices and burned incense, "for as yet the people had not prepared their hearts unto the God of their fathers" (2 Chronicles 20:33). Jehosophat did remove the remaining male temple prostitutes who had survived from the days of Asa. He also worked on a series of judicial reforms that included appointing various Levites and

---

6 The NRSV translation adds, "and the prostitutes washed themselves in it," referring to the male and female prostitutes of Ahab's apostasy who were called "dogs." See 1 Kings 22:38.

priests as judges to mediate in disputed cases that reached Jerusalem for resolution.

A massive invasion was launched against Judah by an alliance of neighboring Syrian tribes, including the Moabites and Ammonites. Jehosophat proclaimed a fast throughout the country to seek help from the Lord. The people assembled at the Temple of Solomon and Jehosophat prayed for their deliverance. He specifically invoked the covenant of the centrality of the Temple.

> If, when evil cometh upon us, as the sword, judgment, or pestilence, or famine, we stand before this house, and in thy presence (for thy name is in this house), and cry unto thee in our affliction, then thou wilt hear and help. (2 Chronicles 20:9)

The spirit of the Lord fell upon one of the Levites who comforted the people by explaining that the battle was in the hands of the Lord and He would save them. Then Jehosophat bowed down with his face to the ground and everyone joined him in praising God. The next morning the people assembled and sang hymns of praise to Him and watched their enemies fight against one another in a fury of madness. The people of Judah spent three days collecting the booty and livestock from their fallen opponents. They returned with musical instruments and joy to Jerusalem and the Temple of Solomon.

The Kingdom of Judah entered a period of peace. However, Jehosophat made another mistaken alliance with the Northern Kingdom, this time with King Ahaziah, the son of Ahab and Jezebel. Ahaziah and Jehosophat built a fleet of ships together, which was wrecked upon sailing as prophesied by Eliezer. Later, after Ahaziah's death, Jehosophat formed an alliance with Ahaziah's brother and successor Jehoram. This was a more successful partnership, resulting in the defeat of Moab and giving Jehosophat the opportunity to meet with the prophet Elijah.

ISRAEL: THE REIGN OF AHAZIAH (852–851 BCE) AND MORE ON THE PROPHET ELIJAH

The Northern Kingdom was faced with a revolt by the land of Moab upon Ahab's death. Ahaziah succeeded his father and reigned for two years. He followed in the wickedness of his parents, Ahab and Jezebel, serving Baal, causing Israel to sin, and provoking the Lord to anger.

Ahaziah took a fall in his palace one day and was badly injured. He sent after the priests of Baalzebub to learn whether he would recover. But the Lord gave word to Elijah, who intercepted Ahaziah's messengers, asking why Ahaziah would consult with a deity other than the Lord. He then informed them that the king would die. The messengers returned to Ahaziah and described Elijah as a hairy man dressed in leather. Ahaziah sent fifty soldiers after Elijah as he sat upon a hilltop. When they ordered him to come down, he replied that if he were in fact a man of God, let fire come down from heaven and consume the troops. The fire came down and consumed the troops. Ahaziah sent another fifty soldiers, and the fire again came down. When a third group of soldiers arrived, their captain fell on his knees and begged Elijah to come down and spare him and his soldiers the wrath of the divine fire. An angel counseled Elijah to go with the captain in peace.

When Elijah saw Ahaziah in person, he repeated his message: because of the king's insolence in inquiring after Baalzebub, rather than the God of Israel, he would die. And he died. His brother Jehoram succeeded him as Ahaziah had no son.

Modern Jericho looking west

Elisha Receives the Mantle of Elijah

The Lord had decided to take Elijah into heaven in a whirlwind. Elijah tried repeatedly to slip away from his companion and successor Elisha, who would not leave his master's side. They traveled from Gilgal to Bethel, then back to Jericho and to the Jordan River. At each stop, they were met by a group of prophets who asked Elisha if he were aware that Elijah would be taken up in a whirlwind that day. Each time Elisha answered in the affirmative. Elijah laid his mantle on the Jordan River and the two of them crossed over. "And it came to pass, when they were gone over, that Elijah said unto Elisha, 'Ask what I shall do for thee, before I be taken away from thee.' And Elisha said, 'I pray thee, let a double portion of thy spirit be upon me'" (2 Kings 2:9). And the chariot of the Lord came with His horsemen and Elijah was taken up to heaven and Elisha saw him no more. And he tore his clothes in mourning by the shore of the Jordan. "And he took the mantle of Elijah that fell from him, and smote the waters, and said, 'Where is the LORD God of Elijah?' and when he also had smitten the waters, they parted hither and thither: and Elisha went over" (2 Kings 2:14).

Elisha returned to Jericho where he was acknowledged as Elijah's successor and performed two miracles: a blessing, whereby he healed the water and fructified the barren land; and a curse, whereby a group of children who mocked his baldness were killed by two she-bears. He then traveled to Mount Carmel and on to Samaria. Several stories are recounted in 2 Kings in which the wisdom and uprightness of Elisha are highlighted. The man of God was directed to people in various forms of difficulty, and he rescued and healed them through his own faith and personal surrender to the will of the Lord. On one of these occasions, Elisha performed a miracle such as that later attributed to Jesus. He traveled to Gilgal where a famine was afflicting the land. A man approached him with a plate of scarce food. Elisha commanded that it be given to the hungry. The plate of food multiplied to feed a hundred people.

ISRAEL: THE REIGN OF JEHORAM, ALSO CALLED JORAM (SON OF AHAB) (851–842 BCE) AND MORE ON THE PROPHET ELISHA

Ahaziah's brother Jehoram now reigned in Israel. While he was a sinner, he had at least put away the images of Baal that his father Ahab had made. He negotiated an alliance with Jehosophat of Judah against the king of Moab, who was gearing up for a battle against Edom. The three kings of Judah, Israel, and Edom allied together to fight Moab. They found themselves encamped in a valley with no water. Jehoram despaired, but Jehosophat sought the counsel of a prophet.

The three kings visited Elisha, whose immediate response was disdain for Jehoram. "What have I to do with thee? Get thee to the prophets of thy father, and to the prophets of thy mother" (2 Kings 3:13). However, the presence of Jehosophat inclined Elisha to help. He called for a minstrel to play music and entered a prophetic state of consciousness, during which he told them to dig ditches in the valley. The Lord would fill the ditches with water without sending rain to alert the enemy, and the allies would be victorious. After the morning offering, the valley filled with water. When the Moabites saw the water, it looked red to them. They assumed the kings of Israel, Judah, and Edom had fought amongst themselves and shed much blood. They rode in to reap the spoils and were met by the hidden armies. The allies prevailed and pursued the Moabites to their homeland. There the king of Moab sacrificed his eldest son

as a burnt offering on the walls of the city of Kirharaseth (modern Kerak), magically averting complete devastation.

Elisha helped Jehoram once again in the healing of a Syrian captain named Naaman. Described as a great and honorable man of valor, Naaman was the commander of the Syrian army. He had been stricken with leprosy. A Samaritan woman who had been taken captive and served Naaman's wife told them of the presence of a man of God in Israel who could cure Naaman's affliction. She was referring to Elisha. When word of this came to the Syrian king (not named, but it should be Benhadad II), he sent Naaman with a train of many gifts to the court of Jehoram to seek a cure.

Jehoram misinterpreted this as a taunt. He viewed it as an impossible task. He assumed that when he failed to cure Naaman, the Syrians would use it as the pretext for an invasion. He rent his clothes in anguish. Then Elisha sent word to the court to send Naaman to him. Elisha directed Naaman, through a messenger, to bathe in the Jordan. This angered Naaman as he expected something quite different, however he was persuaded by his servants to do as he was told. He bathed in the Jordan, "and his flesh came again like unto the flesh of a little child, and he was clean" (2 Kings 5:14). Naaman came to Elisha, having experienced a religious conversion. He offered Elisha many gifts in gratitude for his blessing, which Elisha refused. Naaman asked that he be allowed to take earth from the land of Israel that he might build an altar to the Lord when he returned home. Naaman departed with Elisha's good wishes.

In time, the Israelites and Syrians were at war again. Benhadad II made plans to encamp his army in a specific location of which Elisha warned King Jehoram. Such an intelligence leak happened more than once. The king of Syria suspected a spy in his midst. But he was informed

Looking up at the Crusader castle of Kerak in Jordan. Photo by Vere Chappell.

by one of his court that Elisha the prophet was aware of his private conversations. Benhadad sent a great host to Dothan to capture Elisha. Elisha's servant anxiously warned his master of the approaching army. But Elisha told him to remain calm for he had a far greater army at his side than that of Syria. He prayed that the young man's eyes would be opened. "And, behold, the mountain was full of horses and chariots of fire round about Elisha" (2 Kings 6:17). Elisha prayed that the Syrians would be blinded and he led them to Samaria. Then he prayed their sight would return and they perceived that they had been captured. Elisha directed Jehoram to prepare a feast for them and then send them on their way. They returned to Benhadad and the Syrians feared the land of Israel.

But more time passed and Syria mounted yet another invasion. A great famine raged in Israel. Its consequences were so horrible that cannibalism broke out among the populace.

Jehoram was reduced to despair. He blamed Elisha and swore vengeance against him for the horrors that were visiting Israel. He sent a messenger to slay Elisha (who was, of course, aware of Jehoram's intentions). Elisha explained to the assassins that the crisis would be averted the next day. One of Jehoram's captains heard this and scoffed at the promise. Elisha told him that although he would see the Lord's rescue of Israel, his disbelief would bar him from participation in the good fortune of the community.

Then four lepers decided to go down to the camp of the Syrian army and found it empty. The Lord had caused the Syrians to hear a great noise of chariots and horses, and they fled in fear of such a mighty host. The lepers informed the authorities of the city who told Jehoram. After conducting a reconnaissance mission, the Israelites took the vast stores of food and bounty left behind by the fleeing invaders. The scornful captain was trampled in the excitement as he watched the people take their fill of the provisions.

Elisha next traveled to Damascus where King Benhadad II lay ill. The king asked an assistant named Hazael to enquire of Elisha of his prospects for recovery. Elisha stated that the king would die; and then looking deeply at Hazael began to weep, prophesying that Hazael would become king of Syria and bring great evil and cruelty to Israel. Hazael returned to Benhadad and slew him while he slept, usurping the throne of Syria.

JUDAH: THE REIGN OF JEHORAM, ALSO CALLED JORAM (SON OF JEHOSOPHAT) (851–843 BCE)

Returning to the Kingdom of Judah, Jehoram, son of Jehosophat, succeeded his father and would reign for eight years. (The kings of Israel and Judah were now both named Jehoram or Joram.) Jehoram of Judah was married to Athaliah, a daughter of Ahab, late king of Israel.

Jehoram not only intermarried with the Israeli monarchy, he followed its evil ways. His first acts included slaying his brothers who had been given administrative posts in various cities. He then rebuilt the high places in the hill country and led the people in unfaithfulness.

Two Chronicles 21:12–15 discusses a letter sent to Jehoram of Judah by the Prophet Elijah.[7] Elijah's letter spoke of the many sins of Jehoram and his betrayal of his responsibilities as king. Elijah prophesied a plague on the land and a great sickness against Jehoram. Then the Lord aroused the enmity of surrounding tribes who attacked and pillaged the land of Judah. They took the king's possessions and carried away

the members of his family. The land of Edom revolted against Judah and established its own king. Jehoram attacked but was repulsed, and Edom remained in rebellion along with Libnah. Jehoram became ill for two years and died in great agony. He remained unmourned by his people.

JUDAH: THE REIGN OF AHAZIAH (SON OF JEHORAM) (843–842 BCE)

Ahaziah was Jehoram's sole surviving son and became his successor. (He had the same name as Ahab's son, the late king of Northern Israel who had died from injuries sustained in his fall at the palace.) Ahaziah of Judah reigned but one year. Taking the flawed counsel of his mother Athaliah, Ahab's daughter, he walked in the ways of wickedness. Ahaziah of Judah allied himself with Jehoram of Israel and fought against Hazael, king of Syria. During a battle at Ramoth-gilead, Jehoram was wounded. Ahaziah visited him in Jezreel where he was recovering.

The Anointing of Jehu

Elisha sent one of his assistant prophets to Ramoth-gilead to secretly anoint Jehu, a captain of the army, as king of Israel.[8] The young seer commanded Jehu to strike at Jehoram and the house of Ahab in revenge for Jezebel slaying the prophets of the Lord as recounted earlier.[9] He repeated Elijah's augury that the corpse of Jezebel would be eaten by dogs. He foretold the death of all the male line of Ahab.

Jehu went to Jezreel to the field of Naboth. He came upon the armies of Jehoram of Israel and the visiting Ahaziah of Judah. Jehu slew

---

7 Neither Elijah nor Elisha are elsewhere mentioned in Chronicles despite the extensive attention given to both prophets in Kings. The history of the Divided Monarchy as told in Chronicles focuses exclusively on events in the Kingdom of Judah.

---

8 This task was initially given to Elijah in 1 Kings 19:16 as mentioned on page 198.

9 See 1 Kings 18:4 and page 194 of this book.

The murder of Jezebel at the command of Jehu.
Detail from an engraving by Gustave Doré, 1865.

Jehoram and had his body cast into the field of Naboth.[10] Ahaziah fled, but Jehu pursued and killed him too.

Thus both the kings of Israel and Judah perished by the hand of Jehu. The Davidic dynasty in Judah had come to a temporary close for the first time since David's anointing by Samuel over one hundred sixty years earlier. It would await the restoration of Joash.

ISRAEL: THE REIGN OF JEHU (842–814 BCE)

When Jezebel, learned of the death of her son Jehoram and her son-in-law Ahaziah, she attired herself as a harlot and taunted Jehu when he rode into the capital city of Jezreel. He ordered that she be cast out of the palace window and she plunged to her death. Jehu tram-

pled her underfoot. After he ate and drank, he commanded that she be buried as befitted the daughter of a king. But her body had been consumed by dogs while Jehu dined, and there was little left to bury, as had been prophesied by Elijah.[11]

Jehu wrote letters and challenged the elders of the cities where Ahab's seventy sons lived, demanding they prepare for battle. But the elders demurred and swore allegiance to Jehu. He wrote again, commanding them to bring the severed heads of all Ahab's male heirs to him in Jezreel by the next day, which they did.

Then Jehu addressed the people. He pointed out that while some might accuse him of sedition, he was actually fulfilling the command of the Lord and bringing to completion the prophesies of Elijah against the evil of the house of

---

10 2 Kings 9:24–26.

11 1 Kings 21:23.

Jehu destroying the altar of Baal in his campaign with the Recabites is shown on this medallion by Michelangelo in the Sistine Chapel, sixteenth century.

Ahab. After slaying the remaining loyal courtiers of Ahab's dynasty, Jehu went on to Samaria where he met relatives of Ahaziah. They were traveling to Jerusalem to greet Ahaziah and his queen. Jehu ordered them taken and slain.

Soon after, Jehu met Jehonadab son of Recab, the founder of a sect of religious purists called Recabites (later encountered by the Prophet Jeremiah). They became allies. Jehu planned a ruse to bring together all the worshippers of Baal throughout Israel. He announced a great feast in Baal's honor. When the worshippers assembled in the great house of Baal, Jehu had them slain. The image of Baal was destroyed,

and the Temple razed to the ground. Thus did Jehu remove Baal's worship from Israel. However, he did not purge the altars of the golden calves from Bethel and Dan erected earlier by Jeroboam. But the Lord looked favorably upon Jehu and promised his descendants would reign unto the fourth generation.

Yet Jehu's heart turned to wickedness and he mislead the children of Israel into worshiping the golden calves. Hazael, king of Syria, invaded Israel and caused much suffering. After a reign of twenty-eight years, Jehu died and was succeeded by his son Jehoahaz, of whom more will be said.

JUDAH: THE REIGN OF ATHALIAH (842–836 BCE)

After Ahaziah was killed by Jehu, his wicked mother Athaliah learned of her son's death. She killed his royal offspring, her grandchildren, the remaining bloodline of David, and took control as queen of Judah. She reigned for six years.

The Restoration of David's Line by Jehosheba and Jehoiada

However, unbeknownst to Athaliah, Jehosheba, Ahaziah's sister, had saved her nephew Joash, Ahaziah's baby son. She arranged for the infant to be hidden in the Temple of Solomon with his nurse, where they remained for six years. Two Chronicles 22:11 points out that Jehosheba (there called Jehoshabeath) was the wife of the high priest Jehoiada.

After six years had passed, Jehoiada summoned the administrators, governors, military officers, and guards to the Temple. He swore them all to an oath. Then he revealed Joash, the late king's son, his rightful successor, the last living male heir of the royal bloodline of David. Jehoiada crowned and anointed the young prince. Athaliah was alarmed by the noise in the Temple and ran in to see the coronation of her grandson. When she realized what had happened, she rent her clothes, and cried, "Treason." She was removed to the king's house and executed, that she might not be slain in the Temple.

> And Jehoiada made a covenant between the LORD and the king and the people that they should be the LORD's people; between the king also and the people. And all the people of the land went into the house of Baal, and brake it down; his altars and his images brake they in pieces thoroughly, and slew Mattan the

priest of Baal before the altars. And the priest appointed officers over the house of the LORD. (2 Kings 11:17–18)

JUDAH: THE REIGN OF JOASH (JEHOASH) (836–798 BCE)

Joash (now called Jehoash) was seven years old when he took the throne, and ruled for forty years. "And Jehoash did that which was right in the sight of the LORD all his days wherein Jehoiada the priest instructed him" (2 Kings 12:2). But the high places were not taken away and many continued to make sacrifice and burn incense there.

Jehoash Restores the Temple of Solomon

The Temple of Solomon had fallen into disrepair because the people had neglected it when they followed after Baal. Jehoash commanded that all monies that came to the Temple be collected by the priests and used for making repairs. But even by the twenty-third year of his reign, this had not been done. Then Jehoash commanded the priests to no longer take any money. Instead, he himself assumed the responsibility for collecting the funds and supervising the repairs to the Temple.[12]

The high priest Jehoiada set up a collection box at the entrance of the Temple. The money was paid directly to the carpenters and builders for repairs. Although the Temple was cleaned and repaired under the force of Jehoash's

---

12 The discovery of a tablet bearing the royal inscription of Jehoash describing his repairs to the Temple was made public in 2003. It has since been at the center of an academic and legal firestorm regarding its authenticity or lack thereof. Scholars dispute among themselves as do members of the Israel Antiquities Authority and other officials. See Hershel Shanks, *Jerusalem's Temple Mount*, pages 149 *ff*, for a discussion of this yet unresolved controversy.

decree, 2 Kings 12:13 laments that the gold and silver ritual objects that had been lost were not replaced and the Temple of Solomon had not its former glory. However, 2 Chronicles 24:14 reports that the excess money collected for the repairs was used to fashion replacement ritual utensils of silver and gold. "And they offered burnt offerings in the house of the LORD continually all the days of Jehoiada" (2 Chronicles 24:14).

Jehoash Strays from Obedience to the Lord

Upon the death of Jehoiada, Jehoash began to move away from the path of righteousness. The officials of the land of Judah came to the king and together they abandoned the proper worship of the Lord in the Temple of Solomon—renewing instead the pagan worship in groves where they served idols. The Lord sent prophets to Jerusalem to lead the people back to fidelity, but their message was ignored.

Zechariah, the son of the high priest Jehoiada, rose up and conveyed the words of the Lord, "Why transgress ye the commandments of the LORD, that ye cannot prosper? because ye have forsaken the LORD, He hath also forsaken you" (2 Chronicles 24:20). Instead of contemplating his words and correcting their behavior, they rose up and killed him at the command of the king. With his dying breath, Zecharia cursed Jehoash, "May the LORD see and avenge" (2 Chronicles 24:22 NRSV)!

As if in answer to Zecharia's curse, King Hazael of Syria set his sights on Jerusalem. But Jehoash of Judah, collected all the remaining gold and silver treasure from the House of the Lord and gave it to Hazael to avoid war. Within the year, the armies of Syria attacked Judah and Jerusalem anyway. The Syrian army murdered officials and seized the wealth of the kingdom. It is observed that the invaders came with few men but were able to triumph over the larger Judean army because the Kingdom of Judah had been abandoned by the Lord. Jehoash was wounded in the battle. Later, he was murdered by his servants for having shed the blood of Jehoiada's son Zechariah. Jehoash was succeeded by his son Amaziah, of whom more will be said.

ISRAEL: THE REIGN OF JEHOAHAZ (817–800 BCE)

In the Kingdom of Israel, Jehoahaz, son of Jehu, began his reign in Samaria. He would rule for seventeen years. He did what was evil in the sight of the Lord and incurred His wrath. Israel was conquered by the Syrian armies of Hazael and remained under the control of Hazael's son and successor Benhadad III.[13] The army of Israel had been severely reduced by Hazael's forces. Jehoahaz prayed to the Lord for His mercy and Israel was freed from the Syrian yoke. Yet the people continued in their pagan worship.

ISRAEL: THE REIGN OF JEHOASH (SON OF JEHOAHAZ) (800–784 BCE)

Jehoahaz was succeeded by his son, another king named Jehoash, who reigned over Israel sixteen years. Jehoash followed in the ways of wickedness and made war against Amaziah, king of Judah.

The prophet Elisha had fallen ill and Jehoash came to his bed and wept over him. Elisha told him to take up a bow and arrows and placed his own hands around the king's. Elisha told him to open the window and shoot, and he did so. Elisha told him he would thereby smite the Syrians. Then he told him to take the arrows and smite the ground with them. Jehoash did this three times. Elisha was angry and said Jehoash

---

13 2 Kings 13:3.

should have continued at least five or six more times. Now he would not fully conquer the Syrians, but achieve only three victories.

Then Elisha died and was buried. During this period, marauding bands of Moabites periodically invaded Israel. One day, while in the process of conducting a funeral in the cemetery where Elisha had been buried, a group of Israelites spotted a hostile force of Moabites. They hastily threw the dead body into Elisha's tomb. As soon as the corpse touched the bones of the Prophet, the dead man came to life and stood up.[14]

As predicted by Elisha, Jehoash was able to wage three successful victories against Benhadad III. Jehoash also reclaimed several cities lost by his father to Hazael. Before he died, Jehoash would be confronted by the hapless Amaziah, whose story we will now contemplate.

Judah: The Reign of Amaziah (798–769 BCE)

Amaziah, the son of the king of Judah Jehoash (son of Ahaziah), succeeded his father and reigned for twenty-nine years. He was a good king at first, described in 2 Kings as not as upright as David, but one who walked in the ways of the Lord. Chronicles adds the caveat, "He did what was right in the sight of the Lord, yet not with a true heart" (2 Chronicles 25:2 NRSV). Amaziah slew the two servants who had murdered his father, but he did not slay their families, in deference to the teachings of Moses in Deuteronomy 24:16, which prevents vengeance against the children of criminals. The high places of pagan worship remained.

Amaziah made war against Edom. He assembled an army and hired a group of mercenaries from the Northern Kingdom to aid him, paying them a substantial sum for their services. A prophet approached and counseled him to avoid using the mercenaries, even to take a loss of the money he had paid—for the Lord would provide what he needed. Reluctantly, Amaziah obeyed. He sent the angry mercenaries home with their pay. And he was successful in his campaign against the Edomites.

However, after the victory, he took the Edomite idols and began to worship them. The Lord sent another prophet to ask the rather obvious question. "Why have you resorted to a people's gods who could not deliver their own people from your hand" (2 Chronicles 25:15 NRSV)? The king rejected the words of the prophet and threatened him, upon which the prophet announced the Lord's intention to destroy Amaziah.

Amaziah's ego was swelled up by his victory over Edom. He challenged the king of Israel (Jehoash), to do battle. Jehoash congratulated him on the results of his military campaign against Edom and counseled him to enjoy it. Why risk a reversal of fortune by fighting an unnecessary war against Israel? But Amaziah insisted and was sorely defeated at Bethshemesh. Jehoash broke through the walls of Jerusalem and took whatever gold and silver he could find in the Temple of Solomon before returning to Samaria and dying soon after.

Israel: The Reign of Jeroboam II (788–747 BCE)

Jehoash of Israel was succeeded by his son Jeroboam, who reigned for forty-one years. He too did evil in the sight of the Lord. Yet God gave him victory and restored the coastal plains to Israel, as the prophet Jonah foretold.[15] The Lord would not blot out Israel at this time in

---

14 2 Kings 13:20–21.

15 This is the same prophet immortalized in the Book of Jonah.

Looking out on the Sorek Valley from the ruins of Beth-shemesh. Photo by Steven Brooke.

spite of its sins. Jeroboam II was succeeded by his son Zachariah of whom more will be said.

Judah: The Reign of Azariah (Uzziah)

(785–733 BCE)

Though Amaziah lived for fifteen years after the death of his enemy Jehoash of Israel, he was forced to flee Jerusalem after his defeat at Beth-shemesh. The members of the conspiracy ultimately killed him. His son Azariah reigned in his stead in Judah for fifty-two years.[16] Azariah built the port of Elath (modern Eilat) and further consolidated his father's gains in Edom. "He did that which was right in the sight of the

LORD according to all that his father Amaziah had done" (2 Kings 15:3). But again, the high places were not removed, and the people burnt incense and made sacrifices.

Azariah is known as Uzziah in 2 Chronicles. He became king at age sixteen. He applied himself to the teachings of Zechariah (a prophet of the same name as the son of the high priest Jehoiada). The young king prospered under the guidance of his mentor. He battled the Philistines and conquered territory within their borders. He fought and defeated other tribes, fortified Jerusalem, and conducted construction projects throughout the land. He loved agriculture. He commanded a mighty army and developed sophisticated military weapons for the day.

But Azariah (Uzziah) grew proud as he grew stronger. He went so far as to enter the Temple

---

16 Technically, Azariah co-ruled with Amaziah from 785 BCE to the death of his father in 769 BCE. As noted below, he would then co-rule with his son Jotham beginning in 759 BCE.

of Solomon and burn incense on the altar, a task reserved for the priesthood. The high priest of the Temple gathered eighty brave priests and protested to the king.

> It is not for you, Uzziah, to make offerings to the LORD, but for the priests, the descendants of Aaron, who are consecrated to make offering. Go out of the sanctuary; for you have done wrong, and it will bring you no honor from the LORD God. (2 Chronicles 26:18 NRSV)

Uzziah grew angry but was there smitten with leprosy. From that time forward, he dwelt apart. His son Jotham became co-regent. Jotham managed the court, judged the people, and eventually succeeded his father.

JUDAH: THE REIGN OF JOTHAM (759–743 BCE)

Jotham reigned for sixteen years in Judah, doing what was right in the sight of the Lord as his father had done in the earlier part of his reign. While the high places remained, Jotham rebuilt the upper gate of Solomon's Temple (probably because it had been damaged during the invasion of Jehoash). Judah at this time was engaged in defense against campaigns by both Syria and Northern Israel. Jotham undertook additional construction projects throughout Judah and prevailed in battle against the Ammonites. His strength as a ruler was unabated, as he ordered his ways by the word of the Lord.

JUDAH: THE REIGN OF AHAZ (743/735–727/715 BCE)

Jotham was succeeded by his son Ahaz who also reigned for sixteen years. He did not follow in the ways of righteousness as his father had.

But he walked in the way of the kings of Israel, yea, and made his son to pass through the fire, according to the abominations of the heathen, whom the LORD cast out from before the children of Israel. And he sacrificed and burnt incense in the high places, and on the hills, and under every green tree. (2 Kings 16:3–4)

Judah was attacked by the armies of Syria who retook Elath, occupied the surrounding area, and brought many people captive to Damascus. At the same time, the Northern Kingdom mounted a great slaughter throughout Judah. One hundred twenty thousand valiant warriors were killed in one day because they had abandoned the Lord. A son of Ahaz was slain, as were two of his most important palace administrators.

Two hundred thousand Judeans were taken captive and being carried off to Samaria along with a vast amount of plunder. But the prophet Oded confronted the army of Northern Israel on its return march. He explained that Israel had been victorious over the Judeans because the Lord was angry with the apostasy of the Southern Kingdom, but "ye have slain them in a rage that reacheth up unto heaven" (2 Chronicles 28:9). He criticized the Northern soldiers for seeking to enslave their captives and ordered them to return the Judeans. If they refused, the anger of the Lord would be directed against the Northern Kingdom. A group of generals concurred that Israel had already brought enough trouble upon itself with its continuous violations of the word of the Lord. It would be a great mistake to violate God's Law even further. The army clothed the naked prisoners, anointed them, gave them sandals, fed them with the food they had seized, and returned them to Jericho.

Weakened by the dual assault from Syria and Northern Israel, Ahaz sought relief. He petitioned Tiglath-pileser III (r. 745–727 BCE), king of Assyria. "I am thy servant and thy son: come up, and save me out of the hand of the king of Syria, and out of the hand of the king of Israel, which rise up against me" (2 Kings 16:7). Ahaz removed great store of silver and gold from the Temple of Solomon and the royal palace and sent them to Assyria. Tiglath-pileser invaded Damascus and slew Rezin, king of Syria.

Two Chronicles 28:16 points out that Ahaz sent to Assyria for help because the Edomites were also invading Judah and had taken captives. In addition, the Philistines were attacking Judean cities. "For the LORD brought Judah low because of Ahaz king of Israel [Judah]; for he made Judah naked, and transgressed sore against the LORD" (2 Chronicles 28:19). The Chronicles account of Ahaz's call for help to Tiglath-pileser differs from that given in Kings. In Chronicles, the Assyrian king oppressed rather than helped Ahaz, even after the latter had raided the Temple of Solomon for gold and silver to offer in tribute.

Regardless of which biblical record is used, Ahaz had chosen not to turn toward the Lord in his distress, seeking instead the protection of neighbors. Furthermore, he compounded his heresy:

For he sacrificed unto the gods of Damascus, which smote him: and he said, "Because the gods of the kings of Syria help them, therefore will I sacrifice to them, that they may help me." But they were the ruin of him, and of all Israel [Judah]. Ahaz gathered together the vessels of the house of God, and cut in pieces the vessels of the house of God, and shut up the doors of the house of the LORD, and he made him altars in every corner of Jerusalem. And in every several city of Judah he made high places to burn incense unto other gods, and provoked to anger the LORD God of his fathers. (2 Chronicles 28:23–25)

Ahaz went to Damascus to meet Tiglath-pileser. While there, he saw an altar that he described in detail in a letter to the high priest Urijah, who then built it according to the king's description. When Ahaz returned to Jerusalem, he offered sacrifice on the altar. Furthermore, Ahaz took the brass altar from in front of the Temple of Solomon and placed it to the north of the new altar. He instructed Urijah that he was now to use the new altar for all sacrifices, while the brazen altar would be used by Ahaz for purposes of divination. He cut off the bases from the sacramental lavers, and removed the great sea from the brazen oxen.[17] In deference to the king of Assyria, he took down the covered portal from the king's palace that was used for gatherings on the Sabbath. Then Ahaz died and was succeeded by his son Hezekiah, who would work fervently to restore the Temple of Solomon to its previous splendor as will be discussed at length in chapter 16.

---

17 See image on page 176.

Chapter Fifteen

The Loss of the Kingdom of Israel

Therefore the Lord was very angry with Israel, and removed them out of His sight: there was none left but the tribe of Judah only. (2 Kings 17:18)

With the death of Jeroboam II in 747 BCE, the Kingdom of Northern Israel became even more unstable. Political unrest was thoroughly entwined with religious apostasy. Within twenty-five years, Northern Israel would fall to the Assyrians.

The Reign of Zachariah in Israel (747 BCE)

Zachariah, the son of Jeroboam II, succeeded his father. He reigned for only six months. He was of the fourth generation of Jehu as had been promised by the Lord. He did that which was evil and was overthrown in a conspiracy.

The Reign of Shalum (747 BCE)

The conspiracy that killed Zachariah was led by Shalum, son of Jabesh. He reigned in his stead but one month.

The Reign of Menahem (747–737 BCE)

Shalum was overthrown by Menahem who reigned for ten years. He invaded Tiphsah on the Euphrates River. He too did evil in the sight of the Lord. Then Israel was invaded by Tiglath-pileser (Pul), king of Assyria.[18] Menahem paid him tribute to cease his attacks.

The Reign of Pekahiah (737–735 BCE)

Menahem's son Pekahiah succeeded his father and reigned for two years. He continued in the evil ways of most of the kings of Northern Israel.

---

18 Pul is identified as an alternate title of Tiglath-pileser III in NOAB Chronological Table of Rulers, page 530, Essays.

*King Shalmaneser V, the Assyrian conqueror who was
victorious over the Kingdom of Northern Israel*

THE REIGN OF PEKAH (735–732 BCE)

Pekahiah was overthrown in a coup d'état led
by his captain Pekah. Throughout his reign,
Pekah followed in the ways of wickedness of
his predecessors.[19] Israel was invaded again by
King Tiglath-pileser, who captured much ter-
ritory and carried off many of the Israelites to
Assyria. Pekah was slain by Hoshea, the son of
Elah.

THE REIGN OF HOSHEA (732–722 BCE)

After Hoshea slew Pekah, he reigned as king of
Israel for nine years, also doing evil. He spent
much of his kingship in an Assyrian prison for
his treacherous double-dealings. He had made

---

19 The Hebrew text of 2 Kings 15:27 reports that Pekah
reigned for twenty years instead of three. See NOAB
commentary, page 557, for a discussion of this dating
problem. The JSB acknowledges the problem in its commentary and also dates Pekah's reign to 735–732 BCE.

an alliance with Shalmaneser V (r. 727–722 BCE), the successor of Tiglath-pileser. Hoshea provided Shalmaneser with royal gifts and vows of fealty. But he also made overtures to the pharaoh of Egypt. When Hoshea ceased paying tribute to the Assyrians, Shalmaneser imprisoned him and besieged the kingdom of Israel, defeating the armies and carrying off the citizenry into exile.

The end of the Northern Kingdom occurred in 722 BCE. A litany of reasons for God's punishment of Israel is given in 2 Kings 17:7–17. These have all been highlighted throughout our story but make for an impressive list of the failings of the community to live up to the requirements that were laid upon the Chosen People.

Shalmaneser V began to repopulate Samaria and Northern Israel with Assyrians, Babylonians, and others. The Lord sent lions among them, who killed many of the new settlers. The Assyrians tried to solve this problem by bringing a Jewish priest back to instruct the people in the proper worship of the Lord. But they also kept to their own gods, each from the regions from which they had come. "So these nations feared the Lord, and served their graven images, both their children, and their children's children: as did their fathers, so do they unto this day" (2 Kings 17:41).

This lion stands outside the Church of Saint Gerasimos near Jericho. The church marks the resting place of the family of Joseph, Mary, and Jesus as they fled to Egypt to escape the persecution of Herod the Great.

Chapter Sixteen

The Loss of the Kingdom of Judah

Now it is in mine heart to make a covenant with the Lord *God of Israel,*
that His fierce wrath may turn away from us. (2 Chronicles 29:10)

The Reign of Hezekiah in Judah (727/715–698/687 bce)

Hezekiah, the son of Ahaz, became king at the age of twenty-five and reigned in Judah for twenty-nine years. He was the ideal Hebrew king in the tradition of David and Solomon. He mounted an iconoclastic campaign against the pagan worship. He removed the high places, broke the altars, destroyed the idols, and tore down the groves. He even "brake in pieces the brazen serpent that Moses had made: for unto those days the children of Israel did burn incense to it" (2 Kings 18:4). Hezekiah also revolted against the rule of the Assyrians and asserted the independence of Judah. He made war against the Philistines, reclaiming lost territory all the way to Gaza. It was in the fourth year of Hezekiah's reign that Shalmaneser invaded Northern Israel and three years later that the Assyrian king took Samaria and carried off the people of the North into exile. If there was a problem with Hezekiah, it is that his adherence to the ways of the Lord was the exception rather than the rule among the kings of the Promised Land.

Hezekiah Restores the Temple of Solomon

The account of Hezekiah in Chronicles states that during the first month of his reign, he opened the doors of the Temple of Solomon and undertook repairs. He assembled the Levites and commanded them to sanctify themselves and the Temple.

> For our fathers have trespassed, and done that which was evil in the eyes of the Lord our God, and have forsaken Him, and have turned away their faces from the habitation of the Lord, and turned their backs. Also they have shut up the doors of the porch, and put out the lamps, and have not burned incense nor offered burnt offerings in the holy place unto the God of Israel. (2 Chronicles 29:6–7)

The Temple atop Mount Moriah viewed from the north

Hezekiah identified such negligence as the source of the Kingdom of Judah's inevitable defeat. And he would right the course of the Jewish state, "Now it is in mine heart to make a covenant with the LORD God of Israel, that His fierce wrath may turn away from us" (2 Chronicles 29:10). Then the Levites and the Kohathites sanctified themselves and purified the Temple, removing the unclean things, throwing them into the Kidron Valley. After sixteen days of continuous work, they reported to the king that all was ready.

OPPOSITE: *Hezekiah, the righteous king. This seventeenth-century painting is by unknown artist. It is in the choir of the medieval Saint Mary Church in Ystad, Sweden. Photo by David Castor.*

Hezekiah oversaw the gathering of the populace at the Temple of Solomon. The priestly lineage of Aaron presided over the making of sin offerings. The musical choirs of Levites gathered in the Temple. The people worshiped while the musicians played, the burnt offerings began, the trumpets sounded. Then Hezekiah commanded the Levites to sing praises of the Lord with hymns written by David and the seer Asaph.[20]

Having completed the sin offerings, Hezekiah called for the bringing of the thank offerings. "And the number of the burnt offerings, which the congregation brought, was threescore and ten bullocks, an hundred rams, and two hundred lambs: all these were for a burnt

20 Asaph was a director of the Levitical choirs in David's time, and a coauthor of Psalms.

offering to the LORD. And the consecrated things were six hundred oxen and three thousand sheep" (2 Chronicles 29:32–33). Thus the service of the Temple of Solomon was properly restored after long neglect. Hezekiah and the people rejoiced.

Hezekiah Celebrates the Passover

Hezekiah sent word throughout what remained of Northern Israel after the Assyrian conquest and exile. He particularly reached out to the tribal regions of Ephraim and Manasseh. "Ye children of Israel, turn again unto the LORD God of Abraham, Isaac, and Israel, and He will return to the remnant of you, that are escaped out of the hand of the kings of Assyria" (2 Chronicles 30:6). He invited people from Beersheba in the south to Dan in the north to come to the Temple for a Passover Feast. The timing of the celebration was not quite correct because of the restoration of the Temple worship, but the Passover had not been properly celebrated in a very long time. The tribes of the north rejected the invitation for the most part, with only few people coming to Jerusalem. But the people of Judah were of one heart. A very large assembly came to Jerusalem. Their first task was to complete the removal and destruction of any pagan altars remaining in the area.

While the technicalities of the Passover celebration may have been flawed because the people were not in the proper state of ritual cleanliness, Hezekiah prayed God for forgiveness. "And the LORD hearkened to Hezekiah, and healed the people" (2 Chronicles 30:20). They celebrated the Feast of Unleavened Bread for seven days, praising the Lord, making sacrificial and thank offerings, and experiencing a communal renewal. Then they agreed to continue the feast for another seven days. King Hezekiah donated a thousand bulls and ten

thousand sheep for the offerings and feast. "So there was great joy in Jerusalem: for since the time of Solomon the son of David king of Israel there was not the like in Jerusalem" (2 Chronicles 30:26). Then the priests and the Levites blessed the people and their prayers were heard by the Lord.

The cleansing of pagan altars and groves continued throughout the wider Judean territory and parts of Northern Israel. Hezekiah resumed the organization of the priestly Temple hierarchy that David had originated and Solomon followed. He donated stores of sacrificial offerings to the Temple from his own wealth and encouraged others to do the same. They responded with enthusiasm, tithing themselves for contributions. The Temple and Levites were well supplied.

Azariah, a descendant of Zadok (high priest during Solomon's reign), was made chief priest of the Temple of Solomon. Storerooms were set up to hold the contributions. Hezekiah's reign prospered from his acts of faithfulness.

The Assyrian Invasion of Judah

Shalmaneser was succeeded as king of Assyria by Sennacherib (r. 705–681 BCE). Sennacherib attacked Judah in the fourteenth year of Hezekiah's reign, some ten years after Shalmaneser's initial invasion of Samaria. In the version of the history written in 2 Kings 18:13–16, Hezekiah sued for peace, apologized for his rebellion, and gave all the gold and silver he could find in the Temple of Solomon and the royal palace in tribute to Sennacherib. The account in 2 Kings adds that Hezekiah even stripped the gold from the doors of the Temple and the doorposts that he had added during the restoration. However, in 2 Chronicles, a far different picture of the Assyrian invasion is recorded. Hezekiah and his generals built a water tunnel system to fortify the

City of David and enable it to withstand a siege. He repaired the wall around Jerusalem where it had fallen into disrepair and built another defensive wall. He engaged in a weapons manufacturing program and encouraged the people and their commanders to rely on God and trust in Him. Chronicles makes no mention of an apology from Hezekiah, nor does it include the story of his removing any gold or silver from the Temple for a payoff.

Sennacherib's ministers confronted Hezekiah's ministers. The Assyrians mocked Hezekiah and the Lord. They asked how he could have had faith in the Egyptian pharaoh (with whom he had recently allied) because the pharaoh was weak and unreliable. They taunted the Hebrew ministers by asking why, if Hezekiah had faith in the Lord, did he take down the high places and pagan altars which were home to the Lord. Further they claimed that God had promised Sennacherib success and was responsible for sending the Assyrians against Judah.

Hezekiah's ministers asked the Assyrian representatives to speak in the language of Syria rather than the local language of Hebrew so that their conversation would not be overheard by the people and create fear and uncertainty. But Sennacherib's ministers taunted them even further, bellowing forth to the people in Hebrew not to trust Hezekiah when he told them to look to the Lord. Rather they should put their faith in Sennacherib. Make alliance with him and they would have peace, each man tilling his own field beside his own vine. He would take them to a land of great fertility.

"Hath any of the gods of the nations delivered at all his land out of the hand of the king of Assyria" (2 Kings 18:33)? "Who was there among all the gods of those nations that my fathers utterly destroyed, that could deliver his people out of mine hand, that your God should be able to deliver you out of mine hand"

(2 Chronicles 32:14)? But the people held their peace and refused to answer, because Hezekiah had commanded them not to respond to the Assyrian challenges.

When Hezekiah's ministers returned to the palace, they rent their clothes. They gave him the messages and Hezekiah also tore his clothes and donned sackcloth in despair. Then he went into the Temple of Solomon and prayed, while dispatching a messenger to Isaiah the prophet seeking his counsel. Isaiah sent word back to Hezekiah.

> Thus saith the LORD, "Be not afraid of the words which thou hast heard, with which the servants of the king of Assyria have blasphemed me. Behold, I will send a blast upon him, and he shall hear a rumour, and shall return to his own land; and I will cause him to fall by the sword in his own land." (2 Kings 19:6–7)

The messengers of Sennacherib returned to Hezekiah's court with renewed threats and boasts. They presented him with a letter directly from their king. Hezekiah entered the Temple of Solomon to lay Sennacherib's letter before the Lord. "And Hezekiah prayed before the LORD, and said, 'O LORD God of Israel, which dwellest between the cherubims, thou art the God, even thou alone, of all the kingdoms of the earth: thou hast made heaven and earth'" (2 Kings 19:15). He continued his prayers, openly expressing his fears. Sennacherib had in fact conquered other nations and tossed their false gods into the fire in his victories.

Then Isaiah sent another message to Hezekiah with the word of the Lord. He had heard Hezekiah's prayers and would defeat the Assyrians as He had promised. The Lord's message for Sennacherib began:

The virgin the daughter of Zion hath despised thee, and laughed thee to scorn; the daughter of Jerusalem hath shaken her head at thee. Whom hast thou reproached and blasphemed? and against whom hast thou exalted thy voice, and lifted up thine eyes on high? even against the Holy One of Israel. (2 Kings 19:21–22)

The message continued, "Because thy rage against me and thy tumult is come up into mine ears, therefore I will put my hook in thy nose, and my bridle in thy lips, and I will turn thee back by the way by which thou camest" (2 Kings 19:28).

God promised Hezekiah that He would protect His city Jerusalem against Sennacherib and his army. And that night the Lord passed through the Assyrian camp and slew 144,500 soldiers. And in the morning Sennacherib departed and returned to Nineveh. Upon his return, as he prayed to his god Nisroch, two of his sons slew him and a third reigned in his stead.

Then Hezekiah fell ill and Isaiah came to him and told him to put his affairs in order because he would not recover. But Hezekiah prayed to be spared, and the Lord healed him and granted him fifteen more years because of his righteousness.[21]

The Babylonian king Merodach-baladan (r. 721–710 BCE) sent ambassadors with gifts to Hezekiah on learning that he was sick. Hezekiah showed the ministers his stores of gold and spices and precious things. Then Isaiah came and asked him who the ministers were and what they had seen. Hezekiah told him. Then Isaiah prophesied.

Behold, the days come, that all that is in thine house, and that which thy fathers have laid up in store unto this day, shall be carried into Babylon: nothing shall be left, saith the LORD. And of thy sons that shall issue from thee, which thou shalt beget, shall they take away; and they shall be eunuchs in the palace of the king of Babylon. (2 Kings 20:17–18)

The Chronicles account does not mention the visit of the Babylonian ministers, nor Hezekiah's apparent impropriety in showing them the royal treasury.[22]

THE REIGN OF MANASSEH (698/687–642 BCE)

Hezekiah died and was succeeded by his wicked son Manasseh who reigned for fifty-five years. He rebuilt the high places and erected altars to Baal. He placed pagan altars in the Temple of Solomon and in the royal palace. He sacrificed his son in the fire to Moloch and dealt with wizards, enchanters, and diviners. And he filled Jerusalem with the innocent blood he spilled. The Lord was angered and compared the wickedness of Israel to that of all the nations He had guided them to conquer since the Exodus. And He swore to bring vengeance upon the land.

Behold, I am bringing such evil upon Jerusalem and Judah, that whosoever heareth of it, both his ears shall tingle. And I will stretch over Jerusalem the line of Samaria, and the plummet of the

---

21 In the version of the story of Hezekiah's illness in 2 Chronicles 32:24–26, there is the extra twist that Hezekiah did not properly open his heart in gratitude to the Lord because of his pride. And that he and Jerusalem and Judah were punished accordingly. But Hezekiah humbled himself, as did the people, and the wrath of the Lord was averted.

22 The story of Isaiah's prophecy, however, reappears in Isaiah 39.

The prophet Isaiah in prayer. Engraving by Gustave Dore, 1865.

Assyrian cherub with the body of a lion, the face of a man, the wings of an eagle.

house of Ahab: and I will wipe Jerusalem as a man wipeth a dish, wiping it, and turning it upside down. (2 Kings 21:12–13)

Regarding Manasseh, Chronicles adds that the Lord had spoken to Manasseh and the people and was ignored. He therefore sent the king of Assyria to take Manasseh captive in shackles to Babylon. In his distress, Manasseh called out to the Lord and humbled himself in prayer. God restored him to Jerusalem and Manasseh changed his ways. He undertook construction projects to fortify the walls of Jerusalem and spread his military officers strategically throughout the realm. He removed the foreign gods from the Temple of Solomon and throughout Jerusalem. He restored the altar of the Lord in the Temple and commanded the people of Judah to serve the Lord. It is fascinating to read that "The people, however, still sacrificed at the high places, but only to the LORD their God" (2 Chronicles 33:17 NRSV). Manasseh is a far

different figure in 2 Chronicles than he is in 2 Kings.[23]

THE REIGN OF AMON IN JUDAH (641–640 BCE)

Manasseh died and was succeeded by his son Amon, who reigned for two years. Amon walked in the ways of wickedness and was slain by the servants of his house. Then the people killed those who had conspired to slay him. Of Amon, we learn in Chronicles that he never experienced his father's repentance.

THE REIGN OF JOSIAH (640–609 BCE)

Josiah succeeded his father Amon and reigned for thirty-one years. He proved to be a righteous leader whose personal religious yearnings began in his teenage years. At age sixteen Josiah undertook an intense religious reformation of the kingdom. He traveled north and south in his quest to purify the land and extend the now-shrunken borders of the Promised Land to their former extent and glory. Josiah raised a great deal of wealth throughout this expanded region in order to properly restore the Temple of Solomon. And he did right in the sight of the Lord.

In the eighteenth year of Josiah's reign, he instructed the high priest Hilkiah that all the money in the treasury of the Temple of Solomon should be given to the workmen who would repair and restore it—quarrying sufficient stones and cutting the necessary timber. During the Temple restoration, Chronicles makes mention of the singing of the choirs of Levites.

---

23 Among the Apocryphal texts is one called The Prayer of Manasseh. (For more on the Apocrypha see chapter 20.) The prayer is a moving ode of repentance in which the anonymous poet hymns the story of Manasseh from 2 Chronicles. Writing in the first person, he praises the Lord for His mercy while grieving over the extent of his personal sins. The poem is dated to the second or first century BCE.

A priest offering a child in sacrifice to Moloch

One can imagine the songs of the psalms and prayers filling the air as the workmen strived to the greater glory of God.

The Discovery of the Book of the Law

During the Temple restoration, Hilkiah found a copy of the Book of the Law. He read it and passed it on to Shaphan, the royal scribe, who read it and brought to the king. "And it came to pass, when the king had heard the words of the book of the law, that he rent his clothes" (2 Kings 22:11). Josiah sent the high priest and other dignitaries to inquire of the Lord. They consulted Huldah the prophetess. She gave them a message for the king that outlined the Lord's decision to punish Israel.

Behold, I will bring evil upon this place, and upon the inhabitants thereof, even all the words of the book which the king of Judah hath read: Because they have forsaken me, and have burned incense unto other gods, that they might provoke me to anger with all the works of their hands; therefore my wrath shall be kindled against this place, and shall not be quenched. (2 Kings 22:16–17)

But God also acknowledged the righteousness of Josiah and sent a personal message to him.

Because thine heart was tender, and thou hast humbled thyself before the LORD, when thou heardest what I spake against this place, and against the inhabitants thereof, that they should become a desolation and a curse, and hast rent thy clothes, and wept before me; I also have heard thee, saith the LORD. Behold therefore, I will gather thee unto thy fathers, and thou shalt be gathered into thy grave in peace; and thine eyes shall not see all the evil which I will bring upon this place. (2 Kings 22:19–20)

Josiah's Renewal of the Covenant

Josiah gathered all the people of Jerusalem, both great and small, in the Temple of Solomon. And he read to them the words of Moses as recorded in the Book of the Law. And the king and the people renewed their covenant with the Lord. And any remaining items in the Temple that had been used in the worship of Baal were removed; the groves of the astrological gods were destroyed; the priests of the high places were removed and slain; the houses of the male temple prostitutes were broken down; the fires of Moloch where the children were sacrificed were defiled; and all other signs of alien worship were eliminated. This is all described at length in 2 Kings 23. Josiah's reforms even included removing the high places that Solomon had built for Ashtoreth on the Mount of Olives. Josiah burned the bones of the pagan priests on their altars, exactly as had been prophesied long before to King Jeroboam.[24] Josiah went throughout the land of Judah and through Samaria as well in his campaign to cleanse the land of the idols of the false gods.

Josiah Celebrates the Passover

Further, Josiah reestablished the celebration of the Passover, as described in Deuteronomy, which had not been practiced since the feast of Hezekiah. Taking place in the eighteenth year of his reign, it was a glorious affair, rivaling the great occasions of past worship. The Bible praises Josiah.

And like unto him was there no king before him, that turned to the LORD with all his heart, and with all his soul, and with all his might, according to all the law of Moses; neither after him arose there any like him. (2 Kings 23:25)

Yet it was too late to turn away the wrath of the Lord after the centuries of betrayals by his Chosen People.

And the LORD said, "I will remove Judah also out of my sight, as I have removed Israel, and will cast off this city Jerusalem which I have chosen, and the house of which I said, 'My name shall be there.'" (2 Kings 23:27)

---

24 1 Kings 13:2, and page 190 of this book.

The Ark of the Covenant

During the Passover feast revived by Josiah, the Bible makes the sole mention of the Ark of the Covenant since the reign of Solomon. The lack of scriptural notice of the Ark for a period of over three hundred years is fascinating considering the amount of attention it previously received. From Exodus and the Mount Sinai revelation, to its travels with Joshua, its ecstatic celebration by David, its housing in the Holy of Holies by Solomon—the Ark of the Covenant had been the central theme of every biblical event from the Tabernacle to the Temple. Here we read but one sentence.

> He [Josiah] said to the Levites who taught all Israel and who were holy to the LORD, "Put the holy ark in the house that Solomon son of David, king of Israel, built; you need no longer carry it on your shoulders." (2 Chronicles 35:3 NRSV)

One can only wonder why it needed to be "put" into the Temple of Solomon, unless it had been removed—either for safekeeping by the faithful against the idolatrous ways of previous kings—or worse yet, removed by the heretics and placed elsewhere in order to undercut the importance of the God of Israel against His pagan rivals.

The good King Josiah was slain in battle after he came to the aid of the king of Assyria against the invasion of the armies of the pharaoh of Egypt.[25] 2 Chronicles observes that the Pharaoh Necho II (r. 610–595 BCE) was acting under the command of God and had warned

---

25 It is unclear exactly what was happening. It has also been suggested that the pharaoh instead may have been attempting to aid Assyria in its battle against Babylon. See commentary JSB pages 774–75.

Josiah not to go against him as he posed no threat to Israel.

> And all Judah and Jerusalem mourned for Josiah. And Jeremiah [the prophet] lamented for Josiah: and all the singing men and the singing women spake of Josiah in their lamentations to this day, and made them an ordinance in Israel: and, behold, they are written in the lamentations. (2 Chronicles 35:24–25)

THE REIGN OF JEHOAZ (609 BCE)

Josiah's son Jehoaz succeeded him and reigned but three months in Jerusalem. In that short time it is said he did evil. He was captured by the pharaoh and taken in chains to Riblah in the north so that he no longer ruled in Jerusalem. Then he was taken to Egypt, where he died.

THE REIGN OF JEHOIAKIM (ELIAKIM) (608–598 BCE)

Pharaoh Necho took Eliakim, another son of Josiah, and made him king in place of his brother. In an additional and unmistakable display of his power, the Egyptian ruler renamed Eliakim to Jehoiakim. King Jehoiakim reigned for eleven years in Jerusalem, but Judah had become a simple tributary to Egypt. Jehoiakim taxed the land to raise the gold and silver that he paid to Egypt.

He too did evil in the sight of the Lord—but by this time it hardly mattered. For Nebuchadnezzar II (r. 605–562 BCE) arose as king of Babylon and he made Jehoiakim his servant. After three years in this position, Jehoiakim rebelled.

> And the LORD sent against him bands of the Chaldees, and bands of the Syrians, and bands of the Moabites, and bands of

the children of Ammon, and sent them against Judah to destroy it, according to the word of the LORD, which He spake by His servants the prophets. (2 Kings 24:2)

Jehoiakim was carried off in chains to Babylon.[26] Nebuchadnezzar also brought some of the vessels of the House of the Lord to his palace in Babylon.

THE REIGN OF JEHOIACHIN (597 BCE)

Jehoiakim was succeeded by his son Jehoiachin. He reigned for only three months, also doing evil. Nebuchadnezzar had defeated the Egyptians so they were no longer a threat to what remained of Judah, but the Babylonian king then laid siege to Jerusalem. And Jehoiachin and his family and court surrendered, and Nebuchadnezzar carried them to Babylon. He removed the remaining treasure from the Temple of Solomon and the royal palace. He cut up all the gold ritual implements of the Temple. He carried off some ten thousand captives to Babylon, leaving only the poorest of the poor in Jerusalem. This all occurred in 597 BCE.

THE REIGN OF ZEDEKIAH (MATTANIAH) (597–586 BCE)

Nebuchadnezzar appointed Jehoiachin's uncle Mattaniah to reign in his place, and changed his name to Zedekiah.[27] He reigned in Jerusalem for eleven years. He did evil in the sight of the Lord. Although he was a servant of Babylon, the anger of the Lord caused him to rebel against Babylon. This would lead to the total

OPPOSITE: *The Ark of the Covenant from the Royal Arch Temple of the George Washington Masonic National Memorial. Photo by Arthur W. Pierson.*

destruction of the Holy City and the Temple of Solomon as had been prophesied.

Two Chronicles 36:12 indicts Zedekiah for refusing to humble himself before the prophet Jeremiah. The Temple was again defiled. "Moreover all the chief of the priests, and the people, transgressed very much after all the abominations of the heathen; and polluted the house of the LORD which He had hallowed in Jerusalem" (2 Chronicles 36:14).

Nebuchadnezzar laid siege to Jerusalem for eighteen months. In 586 BCE, a great famine overtook the city. The Hebrew soldiers fled with Zedekiah and were captured at Jericho. They were brought before the Babylonian king encamped in Riblah. The sons of Zedekiah were slain before his eyes, then he was blinded and carried off to Babylon. And Nebuchadnezzar sent his captain to Jerusalem.

And he burnt the house of the LORD, and the king's house, and all the houses of Jerusalem, and every great man's house burnt he with fire. And all the army of the Chaldees, that were with the captain of the guard, brake down the walls of Jerusalem round about. (2 Kings 25:9–10)

All remaining ritual objects were taken from the ruins of the Temple. Almost everyone, including the priests of the Temple, was taken in captivity; only the very poor remained to till the soil and dress the vines. Officials and soldiers were brought to Riblah where they were killed. Nebuchadnezzar appointed the Hebrew nobleman Gedaliah as governor over the few who

---

26 2 Chronicles 36:6.

27 2 Chronicles 36:10 calls Zedekiah the brother of Jehoiachin.

Exiled from the Promised Land, the Babylonian Captivity begins.

stayed in Jerusalem, but he was slain by some surviving warriors, who then fled to Egypt in fear of Nebuchadnezzar.

The LORD, the God of their ancestors, sent persistently to them by His messengers, because He had compassion on His people and on His dwelling place; but they kept mocking the messengers of God, despising His words, and scoffing at His prophets, until the wrath of the LORD against His people became so great that there was no remedy. (2 Chronicles 36:15–16 NRSV)

CHAPTER SEVENTEEN

ISAIAH, JEREMIAH, THE LAST DAYS
OF THE TEMPLE OF SOLOMON, AND THE EXILE

*And I will gather the remnant of my flock out of all countries whither
I have driven them, and will bring them again to their folds;
and they shall be fruitful and increase. (Jeremiah 23:3)*

The quintessential biblical prophets Isaiah and Jeremiah provided a latter day résumé of the message of God as we have learned it throughout the preceding pages. They worked about a century apart.

In the opening lines of Isaiah, he dates himself to the reigns of Uzziah, Jotham, Ahaz and Hezekiah (between 747 and 687 BCE according to the chronology presented earlier).[28] We have noted his counsel several times, particularly during the reign of Hezekiah. Both Isaiah and Jeremiah railed against the people's corruption and that of their kings and priests. They each gave a contemporary voice to the many instances of criticism echoed throughout the earlier chapters of the Bible. But they also expressed God's love for His people and His desire that they walk in the ways of righteousness.

Isaiah repeatedly emphasized the kingship of the line of David. His words are ever present in the story of Jesus, who claimed the mantle of David. Isaiah's visionary record included extensive mention of the figure of the Messiah, the properly anointed coming ruler of Israel. His prophecies include intimations of the Virgin Birth and the Crucifixion. Furthermore—and most importantly from our point of view—Isaiah prophesied extensively on the centrality of Jerusalem. He preached that the Temple of Solomon would be an integral part of the future salvation of all mankind.

> And it shall come to pass in the last days, that the mountain of the LORD's house shall be established in the top of the mountains, and shall be exalted above the hills; and all nations shall flow unto it. And many people shall go

---

28 Textual indications in the Book of Isaiah, however, suggest that it is the work of more than one individual. Scholars identify the three periods of Isaiah as beginning in 747 BCE and extending through Hezekiah's reign; then responding to the destruction of Solomon's Temple in 586 BCE; and continuing perhaps as late as the return from Exile in 538 BCE. For more on this analysis, see the commentary on Isaiah in the NOAB, pages 974–75.

and say, "Come ye, and let us go up to the mountain of the LORD, to the house of the God of Jacob; and He will teach us of His ways, and we will walk in His paths": for out of Zion shall go forth the law, and the word of the LORD from Jerusalem. (Isaiah 2:2–3)

Both Isaiah and Jeremiah's visions are replete with a sense of anger, despair, desolation, depression, impending doom, horror, threats, betrayal, evil, and hopelessness that beggars description. Their writings are a catalog of all the negativity contained within the earlier books of the Bible, with a lesser proportion of the inspirational messaging than therein contained—but perhaps the sweeter for its rarity.

THE HISTORY OF JERUSALEM AS TOLD BY JEREMIAH

In addition to the extensive sermons of both prophets, the Book of Jeremiah provides a wealth of biographical (or autobiographical) detail. Jeremiah offers a unique look at the remnant of the Jewish community in Jerusalem after the first wave of exiles were removed by Nebuchadnezzar in 597 BCE. Jeremiah dates his call to prophesy to the thirteenth year of the reign of Josiah extending to the Exile, thus from approximately 627 to 586 BCE when the Temple was destroyed.[29]

The Two Decades Preceding the Destruction of the Temple

It will be helpful to first briefly review the chronology of this tumultuous period. At the time of King Josiah (r. 640–609 BCE), Assyria was allied with Egypt. Josiah was slain in battle against the Egyptians after which Judah fell to Egyptian control. Josiah was succeeded as king by his son Jehoaz, who reigned for a mere three months before being imprisoned for unspecified reasons by Pharaoh Necho (r. 610–595 BCE). The pharaoh installed Jehoaz's brother Jehoiakim (r. 608–598 BCE) to the throne.

Meanwhile, between 614 and 609 BCE, the Babylonians had been waging a military campaign against Assyria that was ultimately successful. When the Babylonian monarch Nebuchadnezzar (r. 605–562 BCE) came to power in 605 BCE, he defeated Egypt and took full control of Judah. In 598 BCE, Jehoiakim rebelled against Nebuchadnezzar and was carried off to Babylon. Jehoiakim's son Jehoiachin succeeded him, but surrendered to the Babylonians in 597 BCE after a three-month siege of Jerusalem. He was also taken into exile along with many thousands of others, marking the first stage of the Babylonian exile.

Zedekiah (r. 597–586 BCE), Jehoiachin's uncle or brother, was appointed by Nebuchadnezzar as the puppet ruler of Judah. After eleven years, he too rebelled. This resulted in Nebuchadnezzar mounting an eighteen month siege against Jerusalem, after which he destroyed the city and burned and looted the Temple in 586 BCE.

Jeremiah interacted with all five Hebrew rulers, particularly Jehoiakim and Zedekiah. His narrative opens a window on the chaos and fear of the final decades of Solomon's Temple.[30]

Jeremiah During the Reign of Josiah

Jeremiah's initial series of prophecies took place during the reign of King Josiah.[31] Among them, he briefly mentioned the Ark of the Covenant.

---

29 Jeremiah 1:1–3.

30 The reader will note that the narrative that follows jumps from chapter to chapter of Jeremiah. The goal has been to organize the data as sequentially as possible.

31 Jermemiah 3:6

A view of Jerusalem looking across the Kidron Valley from the Mount of Olives

And it shall come to pass … they shall say no more, "The ark of the covenant of the Lᴏʀᴅ": neither shall it come to mind: neither shall they remember it; neither shall they visit it; neither shall that be done any more. (Jeremiah 3:16)

This prophecy is preceded and followed by an abhorrent litany of the evils and agonies that were soon to befall the city of Jerusalem and its residents.

Jeremiah During the Reign of Jehoiakim

Jeremiah wrote that at the beginning of the reign of King Jehoiakim, son and successor of Josiah, he was ordered by the Lord to stand in front of the gate of the Temple of Solomon to deliver what is known as his Temple sermon.[32]

Jeremiah begged the people to amend their behavior, promising God's allegiance if they would do so and His vengeance if they would not. He then went on to delineate an elaborate series of horrors and curses.

Jeremiah's message was so critical of both the political and religious leadership, and so disheartening to the people, that he was actually struck, arrested, and imprisoned for his preaching by the priest Pashur, chief of security of the Temple.[33] Upon his release the next morning, Jeremiah singled out the priest for divine retribution along with his more generalized catalog of despair.

As he resumed his preaching at the Temple, the priests, false prophets, and people who heard his words seized him again.[34] They laid charges against him before the royal officials,

32 The accounts are given in Jeremiah 7 and 26.

33 Jeremiah 20.

34 Jeremiah 26.

233

who agreed Jeremiah should be sentenced to death for his negative pronouncements. But Jeremiah explained that it was the Lord, not himself, who spoke these words, and that if they killed him innocent blood would be upon their hands. The people and the officials warned the priests and prophets that Jeremiah should not be killed because he spoke from the Lord. He remained safe.

Jeremiah was commanded to write a book so that the Israelites might be prepared to live properly when their fortunes had been restored and they were returned from the Exile.[35] The message of the book is for the most part positive, optimistic and inspiring. "And it shall come to pass, that like as I have watched over them, to pluck up, and to break down, and to throw down, and to destroy, and to afflict; so will I watch over them, to build, and to plant, saith the LORD" (Jeremiah 31:28).

Jeremiah was sent by the Lord to the house of the Recabites.[36] This was the same religious sect with whom King Jehu had earlier formed an alliance against the priests of Baal (see page 207). Jeremiah was commanded to bring them wine, setting the cups and pitchers before them. The Recabites, however, refused the wine as they had sworn an oath against alcohol. The Lord was pleased by this. He contrasted their behavior with that of the Israelites and promised them a long line of descendants and protection during the destruction of Jerusalem.

In the fourth year of King Jehoiakim, Jeremiah was instructed to write the words of the Lord on a scroll.[37] Perhaps this would turn the hearts of the people away from their evil. His student Baruch wrote at Jeremiah's dictation. Baruch read the words of the scroll to

OPPOSITE: *Jeremiah and the scribe Baruch prepare the book as commanded by the Lord. Engraving by Gustave Doré, 1865.*

the people at the Temple because the king had banned Jeremiah from the Temple. A royal spy heard his words and flew to the officials of the court to explain what the prophet was telling the people. The officials sent for Baruch who read the scroll to them. They counseled him to take Jeremiah and hide from the king, then they brought the scroll to Jehoiakim. The king sliced off portions of the scroll as he read it, tossing the pieces into the fire. Neither he nor his ministers were afraid however. The king ordered Jeremiah and Baruch arrested, but the Lord had hidden them. Jeremiah was commanded to have Baruch make another scroll and add an account of God's anger at the king for burning the first scroll and His decision that the corpse of the king would be exposed to the elements after his death.

Jeremiah During the Reign of Zedekiah

Jehoiachin, son of Jehoiakim, succeeded his father. Three months later, he was taken into exile and Zedekiah reigned in his stead.

In the beginning of the reign of King Zedekiah, Jeremiah was commanded by the Lord to make a yoke of straps and bars and wear it on his neck.[38] He was to contact the neighboring kings throughout the region and inform them that God had given the land to Nebuchadnezzar. All who refused to accept the yoke of Nebuchadnezzar would be slain. Those nations who would accept the yoke of Nebuchadnezzar would be spared and allowed to remain in their land. Jeremiah warned Zedekiah and

---

35 Jeremiah 30–31.
36 Jeremiah 35.
37 Jeremiah 36.

---

38 Jeremiah 27.

all the kings to ignore any prophet who said otherwise.

A prophet named Hananiah confronted Jeremiah in the Temple in the presence of the priests. He contradicted Jeremiah's words. He said that the Lord had broken the king of Babylon and within two years all the sacred vessels of the Temple would be returned. Jeremiah replied that he wished this were true but it was not. Hananiah struck the yoke from off Jeremiah's neck proclaiming thus would the Lord break the yoke that Nebuchadnezzar had placed on all the nations. The Lord spoke through Jeremiah saying that Hananiah would die soon after for his false prophecy—and so he did.

King Zedekiah approached Jeremiah in search of counsel.[39] Jeremiah explained that the situation was hopeless, that the Lord had arrayed Himself against Jerusalem, that it would be burnt to the ground, and all who were not killed would be taken captive by King Nebuchadnezzar.

Jeremiah sent a letter to the exiles in Babylon counseling them to live well and pray for the welfare of their new land for they would remain there for the next seventy years.

> When ye shall search for me with all your heart ... I will gather you from all the nations, and from all the places whither I have driven you, saith the LORD; and I will bring you again into the place whence I caused you to be carried away captive. (Jeremiah 29:13–14)

On the other hand, Jeremiah made clear that those who had remained in Jerusalem after the first exile, and who continued to sin under the leadership of the corrupt kings of David's line,

were about to endure much suffering through Nebuchadnezzar.

In the tenth year of Zedekiah's reign, Nebuchadnezzar was besieging Jerusalem.[40] Jeremiah was confined in the court prison by the king's guard for the content of his prophecies—which spoke of the futility of resistance and the inevitability of defeat and exile. Zedekiah asked why he had such terrible things to say. Jeremiah again explained that this was the will of the Lord. But, he added on a more optimistic note that the Lord had directed him to purchase his cousin's land. Jeremiah was to seal the deed in an earthenware jar as a sign that the Jews would return to Jerusalem after the appointed period of their exile had expired, when "this city shall be to me a name of joy, a praise and a glory before all the nations of the earth who shall hear of all the good that I do for them ..." (Jeremiah 33:9 NRSV).

As the Babylonian siege continued, Jeremiah was temporarily freed from his confinement. He was directed to approach Zedekiah and tell the king that he would soon be carried to Babylon, but that he would not be killed, and he would live out the rest of his life in peace.[41] Zedekiah next proclaimed an end to slavery, manumitting all Hebrew slaves in the remaining land he controlled. And the people obeyed. But when the Babylonian siege was temporarily lifted because the Egyptian army had come up to Jerusalem, the Israelites re-enslaved their former servants. The Lord spoke through Jeremiah reminding the people of the covenant in Exodus 21:2. A Hebrew slave must be set free after six years of service. The fact that the people had manumitted their slaves—after ignoring the terms of the covenant for so long—was good.

---

39 Jeremiah 21.

40 Jeremiah 32.

41 Jeremiah 34.

But now they were turning back to their evil ways, and such betrayal would be punished.

Zedekiah sent another messenger to Jeremiah asking him to pray for the safety of the Jews.[42] Jeremiah explained that even though the arrival of the Egyptians had temporarily ended the Babylonian siege, the Egyptians would return to their land, and the Babylonians would reinstitute the siege. Jerusalem would be conquered.

As Jeremiah was walking in the city, he was arrested by a sentinel. He was accused of being a Chaldean spy and of trying to desert the city, charges he vigorously denied. Jeremiah was beaten and imprisoned in a dungeon by court officials. Zedekiah sent for him and inquired again if there was any word from the Lord. Jeremiah repeated that the Lord's plan was for the king to be handed over to the Babylonians. Jeremiah complained about the poor conditions of the dungeon and asked for relief. The king arranged for him to be moved to the royal prison and given a daily loaf of bread.

Another court official, hearing Jeremiah's prophecies, spoke against him. He accused Jeremiah of demoralizing the troops and said that he should be killed.[43] The king washed his hands of the matter. Several of his officials took Jeremiah and lowered him by ropes into the cistern of Malchiah where he sank into the mud. Ebed-melech, an Ethiopian eunuch in the king's court, learned of this and pleaded with the king to release Jeremiah from certain death. The king relented and Ebed-melech freed Jeremiah, who was returned to the palace prison.

Zedekiah implored Jeremiah to speak honestly with him. Jeremiah asked if he would not in fact be killed for speaking truth. The king secretly swore to him that he would be safe. Jeremiah privately told Zedekiah that he could avoid having Jerusalem destroyed. His offspring would be spared and he could live in peace in exile—if he would surrender to Nebuchadnezzar. The consequences of resistance however would be most dire. But Zedekiah feared the Babylonians would hand him over to the Judean traitors in their midst and he would be abused. Jeremiah assured him this would not happen.

Zedekiah begged him not to speak to anyone of their conversation. Then Jeremiah was returned to the palace prison where he remained until Jerusalem fell in the eleventh year of Zedekiah's reign. Zedekiah and his court fled and were pursued and captured near Jericho. Nebuchadnezzar killed the king's children and the nobles of Judah. The high priest and the assistant priest, along with a number of the other Temple officials, were all slain. Zedekiah, as noted on page 228, was blinded and taken to Babylon.

Jeremiah After the Destruction of the Temple

The final verses of the Book of Jeremiah catalog the destruction of the Temple and list the ritual objects taken to Babylon, many cut in pieces. The Temple of Solomon was burned down, as was the king's house and the houses of the people. The walls of the city were broken. Only the poorest remained as all others were carried to Babylon. Nebuchadnezzar, however, gave specific commands regarding Jeremiah. He was to be protected. Ebed-melech also received the Lord's protection for having earlier saved Jeremiah.[44]

Jeremiah was entrusted to the care of the captain of the guard of the Babylonians. He was offered the choice of whether he would follow

---

42 Jeremiah 37.

43 Jeremiah 38.

44 Jeremiah 39.

the people to Babylon or remain in Judah. Jeremiah chose to remain in Judah and was placed under the protection of Gedaliah, the newly appointed governor of the region and Jeremiah's friend.

Some surviving Hebrew officers and troops who had escaped to the country learned that the Babylonians had left, that Gedaliah had been appointed governor, and that a remnant of the poorest Jews remained behind. They approached Gedaliah who counseled them to live in peace with the Babylonians, tending to their vineyards and crops.

Gedaliah was warned by an ally of an assassination plot against him directed by the king of the Ammonites. He chose not to act on the message and was killed.

The remnant of the people approached Jeremiah seeking his counsel. They swore to obey the word of the Lord as he conveyed it. After ten days, the word of the Lord came to him. Jeremiah summoned the leaders of the people and told them the Lord would protect them if they remained in Judah. God was sorry for the destruction He had rained on them and would see to their future well-being. But if they disobeyed and traveled to Egypt for comfort and sustenance, He would destroy them all.

They rejected his counsel and traveled to Egypt. Jeremiah conveyed the Lord's displeasure to them, but they swore their defiance—vowing to continue burning incense and pouring libations to the Queen of Heaven along with other acts of apostasy. The Lord spoke through Jeremiah promising destruction upon Egypt and all the lands in the region; they would fall prey to Babylon. And then one day, Babylon itself would fall.

A Final Word on Jeremiah

The Book of Jeremiah is the record of an enormously depressing period of Jewish history. While we have been exposed to many disturbing prophecies and negative pronouncements throughout the pages of this book, nothing quite matches the condensed fury of Isaiah and Jeremiah.

However, among his more inspiring words, Jeremiah offered a unique prophecy of a future covenant—when the Law of the Lord would be engraved in the hearts of humankind—a future in which people would not be the eternal victims of the cycle of temptation, divine disapproval, and punishment.

> Behold, the days come, saith the Lord, that I will make a new covenant with the house of Israel, and with the house of Judah: Not according to the covenant that I made with their fathers in the day that I took them by the hand to bring them out of the land of Egypt; which my covenant they brake, although I was an husband unto them, saith the Lord: But this shall be the covenant that I will make with the house of Israel; After those days, saith the Lord, *I will put my law in their inward parts, and write it in their hearts;* and will be their God, and they shall be my people. And they shall teach no more every man his neighbour, and every man his brother, saying, "Know the Lord": for they shall all know me, from the least of them unto the greatest of them, saith the Lord; for I will forgive their iniquity, and I will remember their sin no more. [Emphasis added.] (Jeremiah 31:31–34)

A glorious sunset paints the sky of Jerusalem.

THE BABYLONIAN CAPTIVITY

By the rivers of Babylon, there we sat down, yea, we wept, when we remembered Zion. (Psalms 137:1)

As told in 2 Chronicles, the Israelites remained in exile in Babylon for seventy years. Two Kings relates that after thirty-seven years of captivity, Jehoiachin, the penultimate king of Judah, was released from prison by the new king of Babylon, Evil-merodach (r. 562–560 BCE). Jehoiachin was thereafter treated kindly, sitting at the king's table with other royal leaders and sup-ported with a regular allowance for the rest of his life.

KING CYRUS OF PERSIA AND THE RETURN

King Cyrus II (r. 559–530 BCE) arose in Persia and his armies defeated the Babylonians in 539 BCE. In 538 BCE, he decreed an end to the Jewish

239

King Cyrus II of Persia on campaign against the Babylonians

exile from the Holy Land. He allowed for the rebuilding of the Temple which was finally completed in 515 BCE.

> Thus saith Cyrus king of Persia, "All the kingdoms of the earth hath the Lord God of heaven given me; and He hath charged me to build Him an house in Jerusalem, which is in Judah. Who is there among you of all his people? The Lord his God be with him, and let him go up." (2 Chronicles 36:23)

Thus, the story of failure and defeat, and the destruction of the Temple ends, in the second Book of Chronicles, with an affirmation of hope for the future, however dim. Every promise and curse made throughout the Bible had been realized in the story of the building and demolition of Solomon's Temple. The crowning glory of the Jewish people lay in ruins. Let us now learn of its rebuilding.

PART SIX

THE SECOND TEMPLE

(Ezekiel, Ezra, Nehemiah, 1 and 2 Maccabees, Josephus)

ABOVE: *Ezekiel described the Temple as approached by six Gates. This is the Eastern Gate with the Angel standing in the entrance.* MIDDLE: *Living quarters for the priests and assistants, and storage facilities, stood at the north and south of the Temple.* BELOW: *A closeup of the priestly chambers at the north. Drawings by Timothy Otis Paine.*

CHAPTER EIGHTEEN

EZEKIEL'S VISION OF THE TEMPLE

And, behold, the glory of the God of Israel came from the way of the east:
and His voice was like a noise of many waters: and the earth
shined with His glory. (Ezekiel 43:2)

Before we visit the historical Second Temple (to be built a half century later),
let us imagine with Ezekiel a Temple that would rival or surpass the glory of
the First. Ezekiel described a visionary Temple whose resplendent elegance was
untainted by the shortcomings of the worshippers or the limitations of earthly
existence, and whose centrality within the land of Israel would signify God's eternal relation with the Jewish people. Ezekiel's Temple may be conceived as an indication of the mystical Third Temple to be built in the days of the Messiah.

Ezekiel was actively engaged in preaching in Babylon between 593 and 571
BCE.[1] He was among the first group of Israelites exiled in 597 BCE after the revolt of
Jehoiakim and the surrender of his son and successor Jehoiachin to Nebuchadnezzar. Ezekiel dates his vision of the renewed Temple to the twenty-fifth year of the
exile, or 572 BCE.[2]

The Book of Ezekiel is a masterpiece of prophetic imagery, following in the
tradition of his predecessors Isaiah and Jeremiah. Like them, he predicted that the
weight of sin of the people and their leaders would lead to the destruction of God's
city of Jerusalem. But he also brought a message of hope in his prophecy of the
rebuilding of the Temple and the renewal of the covenant with God.

While we will be limiting our discussion to those portions of the Book of Ezekiel that describe his vision of the Temple, a few highlights from earlier parts of
the text may be of interest.[3] Ezekiel's visionary record is the source for the che-
rubic zoomorphs designating the fixed signs of the zodiac and their correspond-
ing elemental symbols—the Man for Aquarius (Air), the Lion for Leo (Fire), the
Ox for Taurus (Earth) and the Eagle for Scorpio (Water)—as well as the heavenly
wheel depicted in the Wheel of Fortune card of the Tarot.[4] Ezekiel chronicled his

---

1 See NOAB, page 972.

2 Ezekiel 40:1. See also JSB, commentary page 1118.

3 Placing the Temple description in context, it begins in chapter 40 and runs through chapter 48, the
end of the book.

4 Ezekiel 1 and 10.

archetypal vision of the anthropomorphic Lord seated upon His throne.[5] He ate a scroll, a powerful image repeated in the Book of Revelation some six centuries later.[6] There are several accounts of his ascent through the heavens,[7] the source of the *Merkavah* tradition of the celestial chariot.[8] Ezekiel observed the seventy elders of Israel performing unholy rites in a Chapel of Abominations hidden deep within Solomon's Temple, secure in the belief that their actions were hidden from the eyes of the Lord.[9] The Book of Ezekiel is also the source of the famous vision of the valley of dry bones.[10] Ezekiel thus holds a place of immense importance in biblical prophecy, visionary art, transpersonal psychology, and the esoteric tradition.

EZEKIEL'S VISION OF THE RECONSTRUCTED TEMPLE

Ezekiel was carried in a spiritual vision from Babylon to the Temple Mount in Jerusalem. Here he met an angel who held a measuring rod and a linen cord to delineate the proportions of the new Temple. Ezekiel's task was to record his angelic experience and report it to the House of Israel.

5 Ezekiel 1.

6 Ezekiel 3.

7 Ezekiel 1, 3, 8, 11, 37, and 40.

8 See Peter Levenda, *Stairway to Heaven,* part 2.

9 Ezekiel 8.

10 Ezekiel 37.

The full Temple and Courtyard complex as described by Ezekiel. The east gate, through which Ezekiel and the Angel entered, is in the foreground. The inner and outer courtyards are clearly visible, as is the outer wall. Drawing by Timothy Otis Paine, colored by Nancy Wasserman.

Entering a long hallway, they came upon six recesses or side rooms, three on each side. These were each 1 rod square separated by partitions 5 cubits wide.

A second threshold, 10 feet wide, led to an inner vestibule with columns decorated with carved palm tree designs and windows for light.

The northern and southern gates were of identical construction with the eastern gate. All three gates measured in full 50 cubits in length and 25 cubits in width. The three gates were approached by climbing seven steps to the elevated Temple platform. There was no western gate as the Temple was set against the western side of the Temple Mount.

The Outer and Inner Courts

Ezekiel was then led into the outer court, which had thirty chambers surrounding it. While the biblical text is less than clear, nineteenth-century biblical scholar Timothy Otis Paine explains in his massive two-volume *Solomon's Temple and Capitol* that the outer court measured 600 cubits square (900 square feet).

The inner court measured 400 cubits square (600 square feet). It was approached by entrances in the northern, southern, and eastern gates. Eight steps led up to the inner court.

The Chambers

Chambers at the gates were used for washing the offerings. Two tables stood on either side of

---

The Outer Wall

The entire outer area of the Temple complex was surrounded by a massive defensive wall 1 rod thick and 1 rod tall (that is, some 10 feet).[11]

The Gates

Ezekiel and the angel entered the sacred area through the main gate, the eastern gate facing the rising sun. They climbed a set of stairs that led up to its entrance. The threshold of the gate measured 1 rod wide. The vestibule at the threshold was also 1 rod wide, expanding to 8 cubits at the inner end.

---

11 Ezekiel's description makes use of the "long cubit," approximately 20⅔ inches in length. The rod held by the angel measured 6 long cubits.

The porch of an Inner Gate as described by Ezekiel. The inner gate is shown in the background with palm trees on either side. The pillars in the foreground have been removed to show the entrance more clearly. Drawing by Timothy Otis Paine.

the vestibule for the slaughter of sin and guilt offerings. Ezekiel observed two more tables on the inside of the vestibule and two on the outside for sacrificial slaying. The four tables for the burnt offerings were blocks of stone 1½ cubits in all dimensions.

Chambers for singers were set along the outside of the inner court at the north and east gates. A chamber at the north gate facing south was designated for the priests in charge of the Temple. A chamber at the east gate facing north was reserved for the priests in charge of the altar. These were descendants of Zadok,

the high priest who ministered in the Temple of Solomon.

The Temple

The Temple itself stood in a courtyard measuring 100 cubits square (150 square feet). At the entrance stood an altar.

The Temple was approached by ten steps leading to a portico, 20 cubits wide and 11 cubits deep, surrounded by columns.[12]

12 Ten steps are given in the Greek version; the Hebrew has simply "steps." The Hebrew gives the measure as 11

246

The interior of a Gate described by Ezekiel. The walls separating the rooms have been removed to show the interior. A flight of steps leads upward, seen in the far rear. Animal sacrifices were prepared on the four squat tables of hewn stone. Pillars in the foreground have also been removed. Drawing by Timothy Otis Paine.

The portico led to the great hall or nave. The entrance to the main hall was 10 cubits wide. The great hall measured 40 cubits in length by 20 in width and led to the Holy of Holies.

The heavily fortified walls of the Temple were 6 cubits thick. They were paneled in wood decorated with palm trees between cherubim and contained windows in recessed frames. The cherubim each had two faces: a human face turned toward one palm tree and a lion's face turned toward the other.

In front of the Holy of Holies stood an altar of wood, 3 cubits high by 2 cubits long and 2 cubits deep, while the Greek gives the width as 12 cubits (Ezekiel 40:49).

wide. The nave and the Holy of Holies both had double doors carved with cherubim and palm tree designs like the drawings of the First Temple shown on pages 172 and 178.

The Holy of Holies

The inner chamber, or Holy of Holies, was 20 cubits by 20 cubits. Ezekiel did not enter the sanctuary as it was reserved for the high priest alone, one day a year on the Day of Atonement. There is no mention of the presence of the Ark of the Covenant, the centerpiece of the First Temple.[13]

13 Ezekiel 41:4.

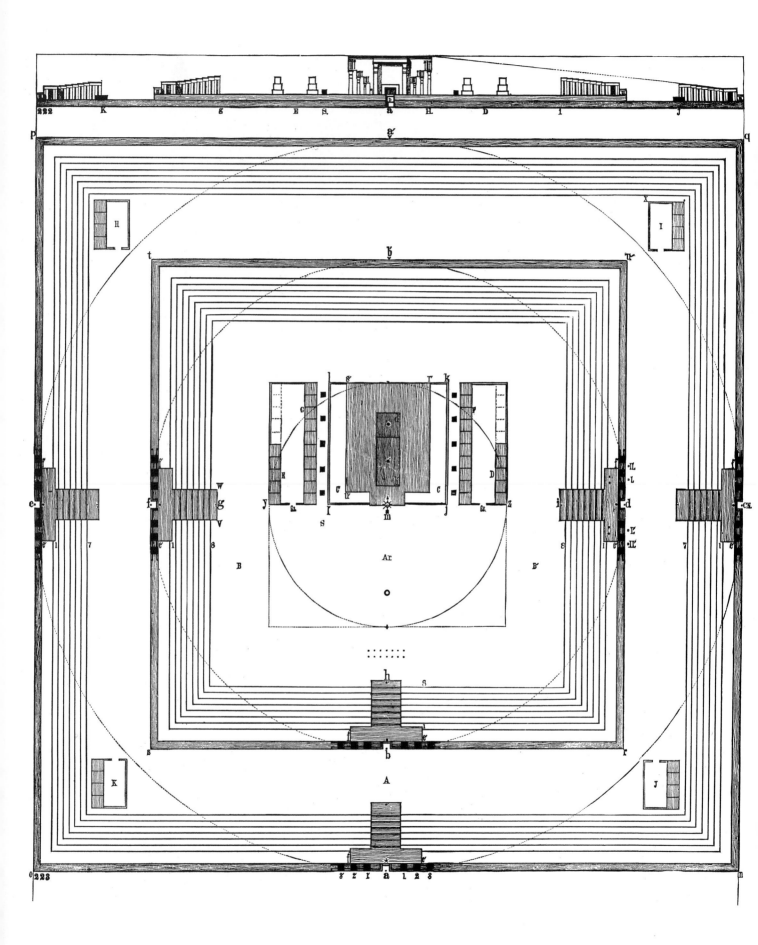

OPPOSITE: *Paine's diagram of the Temple precincts from above as described by Ezekiel. At the top is a horizontal view facing west.*

The Structures around the Temple

Thirty side chambers surrounded the Temple rising in three stories. These ninety chambers were offset from the walls of the Temple, thus independent of support. Each story was progressively wider toward the top. A winding staircase allowed for accessibility.

West of the Temple building stood a large auxiliary building 70 cubits wide and 90 cubits in length.

Running parallel to the north and south sides of the Temple, along the outer court, were complexes rising three stories and measuring 100 cubits long by 50 cubits deep. The Angel explained that these were for the use of the priests—to store and eat the various offerings. The priests were to leave their consecrated vestments inside before crossing the outer court and being seen by the congregants. The two priestly complexes were further separated from the Temple by walls that defined the inner and outer courts.

The total Temple area was a square of 500 cubits (861 feet),[14] "to make a separation between the holy and the common" (Ezekiel 42:20 NRSV).

THE INDWELLING OF THE LORD

Ezekiel was brought to the eastern gate where he beheld, "the glory of the God of Israel ... and His voice was like a noise of many waters: and the earth shined with His glory" (Ezekiel 43:2).

Ezekiel fell upon his face as the spirit of the Lord entered the Temple. Ezekiel was lifted in the spirit and brought into the inner court. Then the angel spoke:

> O mortal, this is the place of My throne and the place for the soles of My feet, where I will dwell in the midst of the people of Israel forever. The House of Israel and their kings must not again defile My holy name by their apostasy … (Ezekiel 43:7, Tanakh)

The angel instructed Ezekiel to describe the magnificence and glory of the Lord's Temple so that the people would be conscious and ashamed of their iniquities. "This is the law of the house; Upon the top of the mountain the whole limit thereof round about shall be most holy. Behold, this is the law of the house" (Ezekiel 43:12).

FURTHER INSTRUCTIONS FOR THE RENEWAL OF THE COMMUNITY

Then the angel commanded Ezekiel to record a series of additional measurements for the altar and gave ordinances for its dedication and consecration. The angel proceeded with instructions for the worship in this new Temple

OVERLEAF: *The contemporary Golden Gate stands at the site of the eastern gate, described by Ezekiel as the entrance of the Lord. In the Gospel of John, Jesus entered the eastern gate on Palm Sunday. Muslims believe the Just will pass through here on Judgement Day and have placed these graves accordingly. Steven Brooke writes in* Views of Jerusalem *that the architecture suggests its construction was by Caliph Abd al-Malik in 685. The entrance has been sealed since the eighth century. Photo by Steven Brooke.*

---

14 As noted in the commentary to Ezekiel 42:15–20 in the JSB, this was an enormous area equivalent to 500 acres or two-thirds the size of Central Park in New York City.

and the laws governing the responsibilities of the people. These rules were clearly based on the reality of the sins that had been committed leading to the destruction of Solomon's Temple.

The eastern gate by which Ezekiel and the angel had earlier entered was henceforth to remain closed, as it was the entrance by which the Lord had returned. Only the prince[15] was allowed to sit there and eat his food before the Lord, entering and leaving only by the outer courtyard. Foreigners were henceforth to be excluded from the Temple precincts.

The Levites, who had been guilty of much dereliction of duty in the past, were to minister to the needs of the Temple despite their earlier behavior. The descendants of Zadok, who had remained faithful to the ways of the Lord, were to administer their sacred duties as Kohathites. God gave directions for the lifestyles and regulations of this group very much in keeping with earlier instructions of the Books of Moses.

A significant portion of the holy city was to be set aside as a holy district. It would measure 25,000 cubits long by 20,000 cubits wide, some 13,000 acres. This area included the Temple complex surrounded by an empty space measuring 50 cubits, an expanse in the south dedicated to houses for the priests, and another section in the north for the Levites. Outside this sacred tract would be lands for the prince and the community of tribes.

Instructions were given for the just conduct of the rulers in their role as leaders of God's people. These included putting away violence and oppression, ceasing the eviction of citizens from their land, and establishing a series of honest weights and measures for the requirements of Temple sacrifice and commerce. Procedures for offerings by the prince and the people were given for the festivals of the year, the new moons and Sabbaths, as well as directions for the celebration of Passover and Sukkot (the Festival of Booths). Further instructions were given for the prince and the people concerning the conduct of Temple worship and regulation of the sacred area—during the year, at festivals, and on the Sabbath. Ezekiel described additional details of priestly activities and the conduct and preparation of sacrifices.

The Angel showed him a river that issued from beneath the throne of God in the Holy of Holies and continued on to the Jordan Valley and Dead Sea. Ezekiel observed that the river deepened as he was transported further along its course during the vision. The Angel explained that its waters brought healing and life, that it was filled with fish, and that trees with fruit and healing herbs flourished along its banks.

The Angel gave instructions for the new national borders of the renewed state of Israel that included an eastern border extending well beyond Damascus. Tribal allotments were delineated for the division of the land. Citizenship for non-Jews was among Ezekiel's instructions. Foreigners were to be allotted a portion of land from the territories of the tribes in which they resided. The city of Jerusalem was to be set up as a normal urban metropolis, except that in the midst of all was the sacred space assigned to the Temple and the maintenance of those who served it. Finally the name of the reborn city of Jerusalem was to be "The LORD Is There," signifying the return of the presence of God among His people.

---

15 The Jewish ruler was now called the "prince" rather than the "king."

Chapter Nineteen

The Return from Exile and the Second Temple

But many of the priests and Levites and chief of the fathers, who were ancient men, that had seen the first house, when the foundation of this house was laid before their eyes, wept with a loud voice. (Ezra 3:12)

The actual Second Temple was considerably less glorious than that described by Ezekiel. In 538 BCE, King Cyrus II of Persia allowed those Jews living in Babylon, who were willing to return to Jerusalem and build a new Temple, to emigrate. He encouraged those who chose to remain in Babylon to donate gold and silver and other requirements to the expenses of its construction. King Cyrus brought forth the immense treasure that the Babylonian king Nebuchadnezzar had seized. Cyrus donated it to the Second Temple to fulfill his charge, "to build [God] an house in Jerusalem …" (2 Chronicles 36:23).

Those who traveled to Jerusalem under the leadership of Sheshbazzar numbered 42,360. An accounting determined that several who claimed to be Kohathites had married outside their tribe and were not included in the official genealogical register of Kohathites. They were therefore to be considered polluted and disqualified from the privileges of the class until they were subjected to the test of a priest bearing the Urim and Thummim.[16] Another 7,337 servants and maids accompanied the Jews on the journey.

They arrived in Jerusalem and immediately made freewill offerings on the site of the Temple. They established a building fund, people contributing according to their means. In the seventh month, Jeshua and Zerubbabel[17] built the altar of the God of Israel and made burnt offerings. While they were in fear of the surrounding tribes, they offered day and night and kept to the festivals of the sacred calendar. They hired Sidonians and Tyrians to bring cedar trees from Lebanon for the Temple's construction.

In the second year after their arrival, Zerubbabel and Jeshua began to organize the Levitical regimens of Temple service. When the builders laid the foundation of the new Temple, the priests and Levites praised the Lord with trumpets and cymbals and the singing of the psalms of David.

---

16 Ezra 2:63. The purpose of the divination was to determine the eligibility of each claimant in the eyes of God.

17 Zerubbabel was a descendant of David as noted in 1 Chronicles 3:19.

But many of the priests and Levites and chief of the fathers, who were ancient men, that had seen the first house, when the foundation of this house was laid before their eyes, wept with a loud voice; and many shouted aloud for joy: So that the people could not discern the noise of the shout of joy from the noise of the weeping of the people: for the people shouted with a loud shout, and the noise was heard afar off. (Ezra 3:12–13)

When their Samaritan enemies learned the Jews had returned to rebuild the Temple, the Samaritans approached Zerubbabel and the heads of the families and offered to help, explaining they too worshipped the God of Israel.[18] But they were refused. Zerubbabel, Jeshua, and the elders proclaimed that they alone would build the Temple, as decreed by King Cyrus, that the Jews might maintain the tribal exclusivity of earlier times. But their enemies prevented them from continuing to build, threatening them with force, bribing officials, and writing to King Cambyses (r. 530–522 BCE), who had succeeded Cyrus. They warned him that the Jews would not pay tribute or recognize the authority of Persia once they had completed the walls of Jerusalem and regained their ability to mount a military defense. The king ordered a halt to the Temple building efforts.[19]

So the construction was suspended until 520 BCE, the second year of the reign of King Darius (r. 522–486 BCE), who had succeeded Cambyses. The Persian governor of the province wrote to King Darius, explaining that the Jews were asking that a search be made of the royal archives for the Temple construction decree of King Cyrus. The decree was found. It proclaimed that the height of the new Temple was to be 60 cubits and its width 60 cubits.[20] Three courses of hewn stone and one course of timber were all to be paid for from the royal treasury. Darius confirmed this order with his own, directing the local officials to cease any opposition to the construction and to pay the costs from royal revenue without delay. Further, he specified that the costs of sacrifices would be borne by royal tribute as well, so that

they may offer sacrifices of sweet savours unto the God of heaven, and pray for the life of the king, and of his sons. Also I have made a decree, that whosoever shall alter this word, let timber be pulled down from his house, and being set up, let him be hanged thereon; and let his house be made a dunghill for this. And the God that hath caused His name to dwell there destroy all kings and people, that shall put to their hand to alter and to destroy this house of God which is at Jerusalem. I Darius have made a decree; let it be done with speed. (Ezra 6:10–12)

All opposition ceased and the building proceeded with great diligence, led by Zerubbabel and Jeshua with the spiritual assistance of the prophet Haggai. The Second Temple was completed in the sixth year of the reign of King Darius, in the spring of 515 BCE. The dedication of

18 These were the descendants of the people who had been brought to Samaria by Shalmaneser, king of Assyria, to repopulate the region after the exile of 722 BCE, as mentioned in 2 Kings 17 (see page 216). They had developed a syncretistic worship that included the rites of the Lord.

19 The text of Ezra 4:7–23 incorrectly identifies this king as Artaxerxes (r. 465–424 BCE), who sent Ezra to Jerusalem in 458 BCE.

20 These measurements are incomplete in the text of Ezra 6:3. No dimension is given for length.

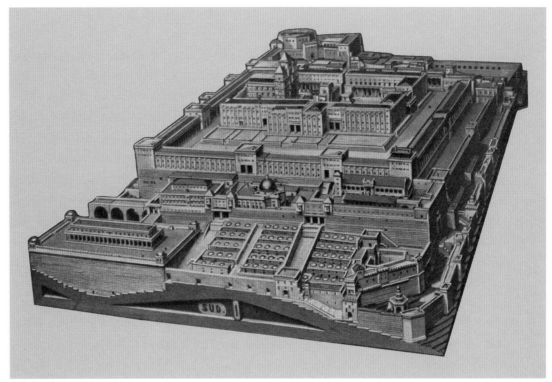

This model of the Second Temple upon Mount Moriah includes the later Herod restoration discussed in chapter 21.

the Temple was celebrated with much joy and many sacrifices. The people kept the Passover as ordained with proper ritual procedure.

EZRA THE PRIEST

In 458 BCE, during the seventh year of the reign of King Artaxerxes of Persia, the priest Ezra traveled from Babylon to Jerusalem as a representative of King Artaxerxes with a group of returning Israelites. Ezra is described as a righteous and learned priest. Artaxerxes gave Ezra much gold and silver as an offering to the Lord and gave him permission to do that which he deemed right when in Jerusalem. He also gave orders to the local officials concerning the extent of their required donations to the Temple. He exempted those entrusted with the service of the Temple from any taxes. Further Artaxerxes authorized Ezra to establish courts of justice to judge the people of Jerusalem in matters of the laws of the God of Israel. Ezra expressed his gratitude for all this.

Blessed be the LORD God of our fathers, which hath put such a thing as this in the king's heart, to beautify the house of the LORD which is in Jerusalem: And hath extended mercy unto me before the king, and his counsellers, and before all the king's mighty princes. (Ezra 7:27–28)

Ezra listed some one thousand five hundred men and their families with whom he traveled to Jerusalem. But when the Israelites established their first encampment, Ezra discovered there were no Levites among them. He arranged for thirty-eight Levites to join the pilgrims so the Temple duties could be properly performed. Two hundred twenty Temple servants came as well. Ezra proclaimed a fast with prayers to prepare the people. Their journey would take them through dangerous territory, and he had been ashamed to ask the king for an armed escort. All the gold and silver and precious ritual equipment was placed in the safekeeping of the Levites and Kohathites. When Ezra and the second wave of emigrants arrived safely in Jerusalem, they offered thanks to the Lord.

Ezra was informed that the Jerusalem community, including its leaders, had intermarried with the neighboring pagan tribes. Tearing his garments, he sat in silence. At the evening sacrifice he prayed. Ezra noted that their ancestors had been handed over to their enemies for the same sins of intermarriage and pagan worship. He acknowledged that now, even while they were forced to live under the domination of foreign kings, the Lord had shown His mercy to this small group of exiles, allowing them to rebuild the Temple and reassemble in the Holy City.

As Ezra prayed at the Temple, a group of people gathered together and wept bitterly. They acknowledged that they had sinned once again. They proposed that they make a new covenant. They promised to send away all their wives and the children they had with them. Then Ezra swore all the people to this plan.

He fasted and mourned that evening while a proclamation was made throughout the land that all Jews assemble in Jerusalem within three days upon the penalty of having their property seized and being cut off from the congregation. They gathered in the rain and Ezra addressed them. It was agreed they would send away their wives and children. The communal decision was accepted by a vote. Although there was some dissent, the majority agreed to the plan. Over the next three months, all the individual cases had been judged and a complete list of those who had taken foreign wives was recorded.[21]

---

21 The canonical Book of Ezra does not state, however, that the wives and children were actually sent away. On the other hand, the apocryphal 1 Esdras reports of those who had been listed in the text of Ezra: "All these had married foreign women, and they put them away together with their children" (1 Esdras 9:36 NRSV).

NEHEMIAH THE GOVERNOR

Written in the first person, the Book of Nehemiah was originally a single text with the Book of Ezra. It begins in 445/444 BCE with a lament. Nehemiah, the cupbearer of King Artaxerxes, greeted a group of travelers from Judah. He learned that the walls of the city of Jerusalem were still in ruins and that the people of the city were thereby defenseless against invasion. He prayed that the Lord would remember His promises—that even after the people were scattered because of their sins, if they turned toward His ways, He would bring them again to the Holy City.

When Nehemiah served the king his wine, Artaxerxes noted his usually cheerful cupbearer was sad and inquired as to the reason. Nehemiah explained about the fallen walls and burned gates of Jerusalem. The king asked how he could help or what Nehemiah wanted to do about the situation. After a prayer, Nehemiah asked that he be allowed to travel to Judah and rebuild the walls. King Artaxerxes granted his request. He also furnished letters to the Judean governor and keeper of the king's forest that Nehemiah be allowed passage and supplies to complete his task.

When he arrived in Judah with his military escort, Nehemiah learned that the governor and other regional officials were not pleased that he would be attending to the welfare of the people of Israel. He surreptitiously inspected the walls by night, telling no one of his activities. He later explained his mission to the Israelites and they were enthusiastic about the rebuilding. But the regional Persian officials mocked and sought to thwart them. Nehemiah was undeterred and the work of repair and restoration of the wall and various gates of Jerusalem proceeded with alacrity. They also repaired the king's pool, garden, and the royal cemetery.

Neighboring officials continued to deride the efforts of the Jews to defend their territory, but Nehemiah tells us the building and repairs of the city walls proceeded. The people offered prayers against those who denigrated the commands of the Lord. Surrounding tribes plotted an attack. The Jews continued to pray and set a guard day and night. They positioned soldiers and armed citizens around the construction site. Nehemiah counseled them not to fear, that the Lord would protect them. Their enemies learned that Nehemiah and the Israelites were aware of their intentions and became frustrated. "From that day on, half of my servants worked on construction, and half held the spears, shields, bows, and body-armor" (Nehemiah 4:16 NRSV). Workers carried their loads with one hand, and their weapons with the other. Each builder was girded with his sword and slept with his clothes on, ever alert to the danger of attack.

A problem arose within the Jewish community itself. The returning exiles had been hit with large expenses for relocating in Judea, as well as the high taxes imposed by the Persian king and the provincial governments. Wealthy Jews lent to their fellows at high interest, eventually taking land and enforcing debt bondage on the less well-off. Nehemiah was enraged. He assembled the higher class and shamed them into returning homes and land and cancelling the interest due on loans. He called the priests to witness the oath of these wealthy lenders.

Nehemiah relates that he served as governor of the region for twelve years, not collecting the food and wine expense allowances so lavishly enjoyed by his predecessors, but, he explained, devoting his sole efforts to the building the wall. "Think upon me, my God, for good, according to all that I have done for this people" (Nehemiah 5:19).

Upon hearing that the wall was nearly complete, the opposition officials tried to lure Nehemiah to a meeting at which they would assassinate him. He refused. They then accused him of intending to rebel and proclaim himself king, and cautioned they would make this report to the king of Persia. Nehemiah scoffed at their lies and continued the work. One day he went to visit a friend who counseled him to enter the Temple to protect himself against his enemies. He understood his friend had become a hired agent of his adversaries, a traitor, seeking to intimidate him and cause him to sin by illegitimately entering the Temple.

Upon the completion of the wall, the neighboring tribes grew afraid. They understood it had been accomplished by the will of the Lord and they had been powerless to stop it despite all their efforts. Seemingly at odds with the sense conveyed by the text of the massive and apparently ongoing nature of the project, Nehemiah says the work took fifty-two days.[22] The speed with which the repair had been completed could only have been a testament to God's help. Even so, there were those among the Jewish aristocracy, financially entwined with foreign neighbors, who resented Nehemiah's accomplishment and the challenge to their own self-importance. He writes that they tried to cause him to fear.

Nehemiah set his brother in charge of Jerusalem and gave him careful instructions regarding entrance to the city and the guarding of the wall. Then God put it in his mind to go through the genealogical tables of those who had first come to Jerusalem a century earlier with Sheshbazzar, Zerubbabel, Jeshua, and Haggai. Nehemiah and the people gathered at the Water Gate, where Ezra, the scribe and priest,

---

22 This period is confirmed in all translations. The NOAB commentary to Nehemiah 6:15 mentions that modern excavations of Nehemiah's wall attest to the haste with which it was built.

Continuous layers of construction by multiple conquerors and regional controllers throughout millennia demand serious archaeological preservation and inquiry. Here is a view of excavation and restoration conducted along the south wall of the Temple Mount with the dome of the al-Aqsa Mosque visible.

brought forth the Book of the Law of Moses and read it aloud for several hours. Ezra stood on a raised platform with people to his left and right in a scene reminiscent of the instructions from Deuteronomy and the ritual performed by Joshua (see pages 101 and 108–9). The people prayed and bowed their heads and worshiped the Lord. Thus the covenant was renewed in the post-exilic, fortified city of Jerusalem at the site of the Second Temple. And the people were instructed to rejoice and eat and drink and send food and wine to those who had none. The next day they began the Festival of Booths which had not been celebrated for a very long time. They celebrated for eight days.

After the Sukkot celebration was concluded,

the people donned sackcloth and put ashes on their heads and made a communal confession of the sins of the Israelites, both their own and those of their ancestors. They read the Book of the Law and prayed and confessed and worshiped. Ezra recited the history of God's choosing the Israelites, the story of Abraham, and the bringing forth of the Jews from Egypt by Moses. He remembered the Exodus, Mount Sinai, and the manna from heaven. Then he spoke of the sins of the Jews in the desert and of the Lord's mercy and forgiveness as they came into the Promised Land. He recited the history of their iniquities and blasphemies, their betrayals of the commandments, and their punishments. He pointed out that in spite of such behavior, the people had been mercifully rescued and forgiven. Ezra prayed that the Lord not forget that the Israelites had suffered greatly from the consequences of their behavior—that they had been severely punished by the destruction of their kingdom and the exile.

> Behold, we are servants this day, and for the land that thou gavest unto our fathers to eat the fruit thereof and the good thereof, behold, we are servants in it: And it yieldeth much increase unto the kings whom thou hast set over us because of our sins: also they have dominion over our bodies, and over our cattle, at their pleasure, and we are in great distress. (Nehemiah 9:36–37)

Then they wrote and sealed a document of the renewal of the covenant bearing the signatures of the Levites and the priests.

All the people pledged themselves to separate from the pagan tribes of the region and to walk in God's law as proclaimed by Moses. They swore to obey the commandments, ordinances, and statutes. They vowed again not to intermarry nor to violate the Sabbath. They vowed to let the fields lie fallow in the seventh year and to forgive debt. They pledged to make contributions to the expenses of maintaining the Temple worship, donating the fruits of the first born and the tithes.

Jerusalem was again a Holy City, pledged to the worship of the Lord and the maintenance of His Temple. One tenth of the Israelite population dwelt in the city while the other ninety percent lived in the surrounding area of Judah.

The people dedicated the city walls with prayers of thanksgiving, singing, and the playing of musical instruments. The priests purified themselves and the people and consecrated the gates of the wall. One half of the people and officials marched along the wall and past the gates with musical instruments led by Ezra. Nehemiah led the other half as they marched in procession in the opposite direction. The two groups met as one at the Temple and offered sacrifice and rejoiced.

They read again from the Books of Moses and took note that contact with the Ammonites and Moabites was forbidden because they did not greet the Israelites with hospitality during the Exodus. Instead they had sent Balaam against the Hebrews with curses, though God turned the curses to blessings. Therefore under Ezra and Nehemiah's guidance the Jews separated those of foreign descent from the community in an attempt to live in harmony with God's statutes.

Plus Ça Change, Plus C'est la Même Chose[23]

Nehemiah recounts that he returned to Persia and King Artaxerxes, having completed his twelve year term as governor. Later, he was given leave to travel back to Jerusalem where he found much that disturbed him. A wealthy nobleman, who had been among Nehemiah's enemies, had been granted a large room within the Second Temple as his personal apartment. This violation had been permitted by a priest, possibly the high priest himself. Nehemiah was enraged and threw out all the man's possessions and arranged to have the chambers cleansed. Then he learned that the portions of sacrificial food that were the due of the Levites and the singers had been withheld. He corrected this as well and prayed that God would remember him for his service.

---

23 "The more things change, the more they remain the same."

He observed violations of the Sabbath taking place and scolded the people and the merchants for their faithlessness. Did they wish to bring upon themselves the destructions that had come to their forebears? He set up a guard of Levites at the gates of the city to prevent traders from entering the gates and engaging in commerce on the Sabbath. He found Jews who had married pagan women and had children who could not even speak Hebrew. And he fought with them and beat some of them, and pulled their hair. Did they not realize that the great Solomon himself—though beloved of God—had fallen because of his sins with foreign women? Further he chased away a Samaritan priest who had not been properly sanctified according to the Mosaic laws.

> Thus cleansed I them from all strangers, and appointed the wards of the priests and the Levites, every one in his business; And for the wood offering, at times appointed, and for the firstfruits. Remember me, O my God, for good. (Nehemiah 13:30–31)

THE SECOND TEMPLE IN THE BIBLE

There is an overall sense of disappointment in the scriptural account of the Second Temple. Observations on the story of Ezra and Nehemiah must include the fact that the exact measurements of the Temple were neither properly recorded in Ezra 6:3, nor corrected in a later part of the text. There are no descriptions of any grandeur, no miraculous cloud or divine fire, no ecstatic frenzy among the Israelites. There is as much or more literary drama and passion in the construction of the wall by Nehemiah as there is in the erection of the Temple by Zerubbabel and the returning exiles.

On top of this apparent lack of textual enthusiasm, Nehemiah ends on a rather depressing note. The Israelites appear to have learned nothing from their seventy-year punishment in Babylon. Extrapolating from the negative consequences we have seen thus far from the failure of the Chosen People to live up to their responsibilities, this does not bode well.

For a sense of the spiritual and emotional importance of the Second Temple to the Jews, we must look beyond the biblical canon. We therefore turn to the Apocryphal writings of the books of Maccabees.

Chapter Twenty

The Second Temple in the Books of Maccabees

A Note on the Apochrypha

The canons[24] of the Hebrew and Protestant Bibles are fairly consistent for the Old Testament, with differences primarily in the ordering of the texts. The Septuagint translation of the Greek Orthodox Church and the Old Latin and Vulgate translations of the Roman Catholic Church include additional books not recognized as canonical by the Jews and Protestants, although they are of Jewish origin. These writings are known as Apocryphal or Deuterocanonical.[25] The books of the Maccabees, while not part of the Hebrew canon proper, are important enough to Judaism to be the source of the universally celebrated holiday of Hanukkah. Our history of the Temple of Solomon has, until now, been carefully limited to the canonical Old Testament. However, Jewish enthusiasm for the Second Temple is better represented in 1 and 2 Maccabees.[26]

The Historical Situation in the Second Century BCE

We recall that between 538 and 515 BCE, the Persian kings, Cyrus and Darius, had allowed for the building of the Second Temple by Zerubbabel, while a third king, Artaxerxes, had sanctioned the rebuilding of the walls of Jerusalem by Nehemiah in 445 BCE. In 331 BCE, Alexander the Great (r. 336–323 BCE) completed his conquest of the Persian Empire. Josephus wrote that Alexander once offered a sacrifice in the Second Temple.[27] When Alexander died, his kingdom plunged into a

---

24 The canon is that selection of texts that constitute the official and accepted version of a religion's scripture.

25 There are eighteen Apocryphal books. Various Christian denominations recognize different ones as canonical. (4 Maccabees is recognized only by the Greek Orthodox Church, in whose Bible it is treated as an appendix.)

26 Four books of the Apocrypha are titled "Maccabees." There is a wonderful account in 3 Maccabees of the Pharaoh Ptolemy IV Philopator aggressively insisting on entering the Second Temple. The priests begged him to desist, explaining that it was a violation of their religion. People prayed in the streets and the priests called upon the Lord. When the Lord heard the sincerity of their petition, the pharaoh was seized with something like an epileptic fit that left him lying helpless on the ground. 4 Maccabees begins by focusing on philosophical themes, and proceeds to a detailed examination of the martyrdom of Eleazar and the seven brothers and their mother, mentioned here on pages 270–71.

27 *The Antiquities of the Jews*, 11, 8, 5, 336.

twenty-year war of succession between his various generals. Among the victors were Ptolemy I, founder of the Ptolemaic dynasty that ruled Egypt, and Seleucus I, founder of the Seleucid dynasty that ruled Syria. Judea was a disputed territory between them. It remained under the dominion of the Ptolemies throughout the third century. In 198 BCE, it fell to Seleucid control, where it remained until the establishment of the Maccabean or Hasmonean dynasty in 142 BCE.

The unique cultural trend of this period is known as Hellenism. It developed as a mixture of Greek and Semitic thought, embracing art, architecture, philosophy, literature, and science. The use of the Greek language became standard throughout the Holy Land. At the same time, the Greek translation of the Old Testament (the Septuagint) allowed Jewish scripture to become more widely influential outside the Hebrew community.[28]

Sharing in such a rich cultural stream, the synthesis of Hellenism led many urban Jews, in particular, far from the strict path of biblical practice to the more relaxed worldliness of the Greeks. As more upper class Jews adopted Hellenistic customs, including even some Kohathites, a growing tension developed with traditionally observant Jews, most often living in the countryside. To further inflame tensions, under Seleucid rule Judaism became a state religion, dependent on tax collection for Temple maintenance and the salaries paid to the priestly class by their Græco-Syrian overlords. Being forced to subsidize the apostasy of

their religious leaders caused even more resentment. Yet, had the Hellenization of the Jewish community been allowed to develop gradually, it may have been effective in eliminating the sharp distinctions between the Jews and other cultures. The books of Maccabees explain why assimilation was not to be the case.

The Books of 1 and 2 Maccabees

One Maccabees presents a detailed history of the years 175–143 BCE. It is thought to have been written sometime between 134 and 63 BCE. Two Maccabees is more narrowly focused on the period from 168 to 164 BCE and was written just after 1 Maccabees. Both tell the story of the Jewish revolt against their Seleucid rulers. Two Maccabees is the more dramatic story, with many miraculous accounts of the Lord's direct intervention.

Two Maccabees begins with two letters from the Jewish religious leaders in Jerusalem to members of the Egyptian Jewish community, encouraging them to adopt the newly declared holiday of Hanukkah, an eight-day festival to celebrate the Maccabean victory over the Seleucids and the restoration and rededication of the Second Temple. The letters serve as a preface to the text, which seeks to establish that the divinely guided Hasmonean victory justifies that this festival be added to the sacred ritual calendar for all Jewry. "Will you therefore please keep these days" (2 Maccabees 2:16 NRSV)?

The second letter also sheds important light on the disposition of the First Temple, the spiritual links between the First and Second Temples, and the history of the Jewish people since. It tells us that the priests of Solomon's Temple took the sacred flame of the eternal light that burned before the Holy of Holies and secretly hid it in the hollow of a dry cistern in an unknown location.

---

28 Legend has it that the Greek translation was begun by seventy (or seventy-two) elders of Jerusalem working in Alexandria during the reign of Ptolemy II Philadelphus (r. 285–246 BCE). They completed the Five Books of Moses in seventy-two days. The original Hebrew manuscript is said to have been written in gold letters. Later biblical manuscripts were translated from Aramaic. "Septuagint" means "seventy" and the Greek translation is sometimes referred to simply as "LXX."

During his rebuilding of the walls of Jerusalem, Nehemiah is declared to have found the flame, which had by then turned into a thick liquid. He ordered the liquid be brought to the altar of the Second Temple where a sacrifice had been prepared. The liquid was sprinkled upon the wood and the offering. When the sun shone down upon the altar, a great fire blazed forth and all marveled.[29] The Persians were most impressed with this and, after investigation, declared the area where the liquid (naphtha) had been uncovered be treated as holy.

The letter also speaks of the actions of Jeremiah in the days of the fall of Jerusalem. We learn that the prophet ordered the people who were going to Babylon to take some of the sacred fire with them. There is also an account of Jeremiah hiding the Ark of the Covenant and the Tent of the Tabernacle in a secret location in Mount Nebo. This portion of the letter is reproduced in full in the afterword.[30]

THE JEWS AND THE SELEUCIDS (198–142 BCE)

At first, the situation in Jerusalem under Seleucid rule was peaceful. When Antiochus III the Great (r. 223–187 BCE) took Judea from the Ptolemies, he issued charters of religious liberties to the Jews, allowing them to live by their own laws, sponsoring Temple expenses, and helping to rebuild Jerusalem. His son and successor, Seleucus IV Philopator (r. 187–175 BCE) continued these policies. The Jewish high priest Onias was described as an upright man.

But Simon, a Jew, had a disagreement with Onias. He went to the governor of the region and made exaggerated reports of the wealth of the Temple treasury, suggesting the money could be appropriated by the king. Seleucus

IV sent Heliodorus as his representative to appraise and confiscate the treasury. Heliodorus spoke to Onias and asked about the funds. Onias explained that the money did not belong to the Temple—that some of it was designated for widows and orphans and some had been left on deposit by a wealthy man for safekeeping.

Heliodorus explained he had been sent to take the money, setting a day to inspect the treasury. This brought distress throughout the city and within the Temple. The priests prayed for the sanctity of the Temple, the high priest showed visible signs of spiritual and emotional anguish. Heliodorus was determined to proceed, even as the people thronged the streets in sackcloth and ashes, bewailing the loss of honor such fiduciary impotence would mean for the Temple.

When Heliodorus approached the treasury, the Lord sent a manifestation of His power. It overwhelmed all who thought to sin against the sanctity of the Temple. A huge spirit horse appeared with a fierce warrior in golden armor astride him and rushed furiously at Heliodorus, striking him with his hooves. Two angels in the form of splendidly attired young men of great beauty also appeared and flogged him. Heliodorus, unconscious, was carried away on a stretcher. Great joy filled the Temple and the city.

Onias offered sacrifice that Heliodorus would survive his wounds lest the Jews be accused of murdering an agent of the king. The two angels appeared to Heliodorus and informed him that since the high priest had prayed for his care, he should be grateful that the Lord had spared his life. Then Heliodorus sacrificed to the Lord and made vows and took his leave. Returning to Syria, he explained to Seleucus what had transpired. The king asked who he should send to Jerusalem to pursue the mission. Heliodorus responded,

---

29 2 Maccabees 1:20–22.
30 2 Maccabees 2:1–8. See page 337 of this book.

If thou hast any enemy or traitor, send him thither, and thou shalt receive him well scourged, if he escape with his life: for in that place, no doubt; there is an especial power of God. For He that dwelleth in heaven hath His eye on that place, and defendeth it; and He beateth and destroyeth them that come to hurt it. (2 Maccabees 3:38–39)

The traitor Simon slandered Onias, claiming it was the priest, not the Lord, who had mistreated Heliodorus—that Onias was the real enemy of the king. Simon sent agents to Jerusalem to murder loyal Jews. He was aided in his vile campaign by the Seleucid royal governor of the region. When Onias realized the true vitriol of the forces arrayed against him, he appealed to the king in hopes of protecting the Jewish community, but Seleucus IV died before he could intervene.

THE WICKED KING ANTIOCHUS AND THE JEWISH CIVIL WAR

Seleucus IV was succeeded by his son Antiochus IV Epiphanes (r. 175–164 BCE). The tension between the Hellenized Jews and those loyal to the Temple teachings escalated. Antiochus, in exchange for a large bribe, appointed Jason, the Hellenized brother of Onias, to replace Onias as high priest. Jason asked permission to establish a Greek style gymnasium in Jerusalem and to have the Jews recognized as citizens of Antioch—in other words, as Græco-Syrians or gentiles.[31] Antiochus built the gymnasium. Because the Greek custom was to exercise naked, men removed the marks of circumci-

sion from their bodies in a further attempt to assimilate.[32]

Antiochus went up against the Egyptians in 170 BCE, doing battle with King Ptolemy VI Philometor (r. 180–145 BCE). He returned by way of Jerusalem. Learning of the strife among the Jews, he entered the city with a strong force. He violated the sanctuary of the Temple and seized much of its wealth before returning to Syria.

Next, Antiochus lifted the special dispensation of his predecessors that had allowed the Jews to practice their religion without interference. He forced them to violate their commandments with the full assent of the evil high priest Jason. Jason and the other priests became more interested in the Greek sporting activities than in their duties of sacrifice. The morally corrupt Temple leadership inevitably plunged into its own series of betrayals. Jason sent Menelaus, the brother of the traitor Simon, to the court of Antiochus in Syria with tribute money and provincial business records. Menelaus used the money to purchase the high priesthood for himself. He was cruel and tyrannical with no qualifications for Temple service. Jason was driven out as a fugitive to Ammon. "For it is not a light thing to do wickedly against the laws of God" (2 Maccabbees 4:17).

Once in power, Menelaus withheld his required tributary payment from Antiochus and was summoned to Syria to explain himself. He put his brother Lysimachus in charge, but before traveling, he arranged to steal golden vessels from the Temple. Some of these he gave to the regional deputy of the king, while selling others for his and his brother's enrichment. When Onias learned of this crime, he publicly exposed Menelaus, Lysimachus, and the Seleu-

---

31 Non-Jews are called "Gentiles" in the NOAB and "Heathens" in the KJV.

32 An uncomfortable procedure called "epispasm." See 1 Maccabees 1:15.

Heliodorus, attacked by the angelic horse and rider and the two Angels who flogged him for invading the Temple precincts. Fresco by Raphael, early sixteenth century.

cid regional deputy. Then Menelaus arranged for the murder of Onias. The Jews were disconsolate. When Antiochus passed through Jerusalem, he too was grieved at heart for the crime against the upright former high priest. He executed his regional deputy in retaliation.

Civil war broke out among the Jews as news of the treachery of Menelaus and his brothers spread more widely. Lysimachus raised an army of three thousand men to put down the rebellion. But the people stoned the soldiers and chaos reigned. Charges were brought against Menelaus. Antiochus came to Tyre to hear the case. Menelaus bribed an official to speak in his favor and the king was persuaded to acquit

him, sentencing to death those who had fought against his thievery and treason. Even the Tyrians were appalled by this injustice, yet Menelaus remained in office.

Antiochus invaded Egypt for a second time in 168 BCE. It is said that angelic armies filled the skies of Jerusalem for forty days. All prayed this was a good omen. But a false rumor spread that Antiochus had been killed in battle. The deposed high priest Jason assembled an army of a thousand men to attack Jerusalem. Menelaus took refuge in the Citadel. Ultimately Jason's assault failed and he fled back to the country of the Ammonites. Universally despised, Jason was exiled and died in isolation.

The Citadel in Jerusalem has a long history as a defensive structure, including having served as the headquarters of the Crusader kings after they moved from the al-Aqsa Mosque in 1128.

Antiochus was informed of the renewed strife in Jerusalem and assumed Israel was in rebellion. He invaded Jerusalem. His forces massacred eighty thousand people in three days. He entered the Temple guided by the traitor Menelaus. He seized all the golden ritual objects and implements including the altar, lampstands, table of the Bread of the Presence, censers, bowls, and anything else of value. He swept away the offerings made by other kings that had enhanced the glory of the Temple. He was so elated in spirit that he did not realize the Lord allowed him this despicable victory because He was so angered by the sins of the Jews.

… that was the reason He was disregarding the holy place. But if it had not happened that they were involved in many sins, this man would have been flogged and turned back from his rash act as soon as he came forward, just as Heliodorus had been, whom King Seleucus sent to inspect the treasury. But the LORD did not choose the nation for the sake of the holy place, but the place for the sake of the nation. Therefore the place itself shared in the misfortunes that befell the nation and afterward participated in its benefits; and what was forsaken in the wrath of the Almighty was restored in all its glory when the great LORD became reconciled. (2 Maccabees 5:17–20 NRSV)

Antiochus carried off eighteen hundred talents of gold from the Temple and returned to Syria, high and mighty in his arrogance. He appointed several corrupt officials to rule over Jerusalem and the land of Israel. He ordered a further assault on the people, killing grown men, and carrying women and boys into slavery. His troops waged their attack on the Sabbath and many were killed.

THE ABOMINATION OF DESOLATION

In 167 BCE, Antiochus issued an edict outlawing the Jewish religion. He seized the Temple, defiling it and consecrating it to the worship of Zeus. He erected a statue, known as the Abomination of Desolation, on the sacred altar of burnt offerings. He filled the Temple with debauchery and instituted the pagan custom of sacred prostitution. Inappropriate sacrifices, forbidden under Jewish law, were offered on the Temple altar. The Sabbath and all regular festivals were forbidden. The Jews were forced to participate in pagan rites. Neighboring communities were ordered to institute these laws on their Jewish populations as well. Death was the penalty for unwillingness to convert. In chapter 6 of 2 Maccabees, however, the author cautions the reader not to despair, but to understand the unique nature of the relationship of God with the Jewish people. God disciplines the Jews regularly to keep them in line with His commandments, while other nations are left to accumulate a large mass of sins for which they are then punished in cataclysms of divine rage.

ENTER THE MACCABEES AND THE HASMONEAN REVOLT

In those days, the priest Mattathias and his five sons moved from Jerusalem to the nearby town of Modein.[33] This fiercely independent family despised the Hellenization of the city dwellers. One of the five brothers was Judas, nicknamed Maccabeus, "the Hammer." When the members of the family of Mattathias learned of the outrages being committed against the Temple in Jerusalem, they tore their clothes, put on sackcloth, and mourned.

As royal troops traveled the land enforcing the religious edicts of Antiochus, a group of soldiers came to Modein. They approached Mattathias as the town dignitary and asked him to be the first to sacrifice to the pagan gods. He and his sons could be an example to the people of the king's new commands. They would be rewarded by being appointed Friends of the king, a special designation for those who received royal favor and largesse, wearing distinctive clothes and insignia to designate their rank. Mattathias did not conceal his contempt for this offer, vowing to continue in the ways of the Jews. After his declaration to the soldiers, a Jew came forward to sacrifice, hoping to gain the soldiers' favor. Mattathias in holy fury killed the Jew and the royal officer, then tore down the sacrifical altar. "Thus he burned with zeal for the law, just as Phineas did …" (1 Maccabees 2:26 NRSV). Mattathias called for the faithful to join him and his sons and they fled into the mountains to build their guerilla army.

_____

33 See 1 Maccabees 2. This family was also known as Hasmoneans (or Asmonean), named after Mattathias' great-grandfather Asamoneous mentioned by Josephus in _Antiquities_, Book 12, 6, 1.

An interesting story is told of the initial battles of the Jewish rebels. The Seleucid forces and their fellow travelers within the Jewish community decided to attack a group of rebel forces on the Sabbath. Rather than surrender or defy the Sabbath laws by fighting, they died. Mattathias mourned their deaths but rejected their strategy, determining that his forces would fight to win. He was joined by a group of Hasidian warriors who lent their strength and valor to his efforts.[34] Mattathias and his army enforced religious doctrine as they traveled through the country, tearing down pagan altars, circumcising Jewish boys, and hunting down traitors.

As Mattathias approached the time of his death, he gathered his sons and the rebels about him. He spoke of the biblical patriarchs and other heroes of antiquity: Abraham, Joseph, Phineas, Joshua, Caleb, David, Elijah, and Daniel. He appointed Judas as military leader and blessed the army.

In the accounts of his early battles, Judas' courage and skill are highlighted. When the commander of the Græco-Syrian army went against him with a much larger force, Judas' faith was an inspiration to his small group of men. He pointed out that with the Lord at their side, their numbers did not matter. What was important was the righteousness of their cause. And when the Jews attacked, the Græco-Syrian army fled. Judas' fame spread throughout the land.

Judas gathered some six thousand men who remained faithful to their religious laws. They prayed for the nation and the Temple. Judas and his army mounted an extensive guerilla campaign against the superior forces of the armies of Antiochus. Because Judas' army functioned under the commands of righteousness, they were undefeatable. Neighboring regional troops were called in as reinforcements, swelling the enemy ranks. Judas fortified his men with stories of the triumph of the Jews in similar situations from older times. The rebels were victorious over the larger army and seized much wealth to continue their campaign. After keeping the Sabbath, they distributed part of the captured booty to those who had suffered from the onslaught of the armies of Antiochus. It became their practice after each victory to distribute part of the spoils to widows and orphans and others who had suffered. They stored the captured weapons of the enemy in scattered depots hidden throughout Israel.

Antiochus meanwhile was suffering defeat in Persia. Attempting to rob a temple in Persepolis, he and his army were put to flight and retreated. When he learned of the defeat of his Jerusalem forces, he traveled to Jerusalem in a rage, vowing revenge. "But the all-seeing LORD, the God of Israel, struck him with an incurable and invisible blow" (2 Maccabees 9:5 NRSV). Seized with intestinal agonies he drove on in his fury until he fell out of chariot and broke the bones of his body. He was now carried in a

---

34 The Hasidians (*Hasidim,* the Pius) were an ultra-observant sect within Judaism who normally would not have been part of the political process. Later in the Maccabee history, after the cleansing of the Temple had taken place, Demetrius I Soter (r. 162–150 BCE) ascended the Seleucid throne. A contingent of renegade, godless Jews approached him led by Alcimus, a descendant of Aaron, who sought to become high priest. Although Alcimus was a known scoundrel, Demetrius appointed him to the office he sought because of his support for the Seleucid rulership and his priestly heritage. Alcimus developed the tactic of approaching the rebel Jewish armies with royal offers of peace. While Judas refused to have any involvement with this deception, the Pietist Hasidians appealed for peace. They had been roused to action by the desecration of the Temple but now felt their victory at the Temple signaled they had gone far enough into the affairs of man. Since God had placed a man of the proper lineage in the position of high priest, even if he were corrupt, they could honorably consider their work done. Unfortunately, as is often the case with political passivity, the moment they laid down their arms, Alcimus seized and killed sixty of them. To further compound the outrage, their bodies remained unburied. See 1 Maccabees 7.

Judas Maccabee leading the Hasmonean army against the wicked Antiochus IV.
Detail from an engraving by Gustave Doré, 1865.

litter, punished for the pride and arrogance of his ungodly ways. Unable to endure the stench of his own body, he cried out, "It is meet to be subject unto God, and that a man that is mortal should not proudly think of himself if he were God" (2 Maccabees 9:12).

In his agony, he had a change of heart. He vowed that Jerusalem would be free and the Jews be made citizens with equal rights to Greeks. He swore to adorn the Temple with fine offerings and holy vessels and to subsidize the Temple worship with his own funds. He even swore to convert to Judaism himself. He sent a royal letter to the Jews, announcing the appointment of his son Antiochus V Eupator (r. 164–162

BCE) as his successor, assuring them of his good will. Then he died.

THE PURIFICATION OF THE TEMPLE

Judas Maccabeus and his followers recovered the Temple. The sight of its defilement caused them great mourning. They tore their clothes, sprinkled themselves with ashes, and fell face down on the ground. Then they arose and began to purify it from its desecration. They took down the altar—carefully disassembling it rather than destroying it, since it had once been the consecrated altar of the Temple. They stored its stones in a convenient place until they could find a prophet to instruct them on what to do with it. They rebuilt a new altar of unhewn stones as the law commands. They repaired and purified the sanctuary. They took down the curtains where the temple prostitutes had lain. They consecrated the courts. They made new ritual vessels including a new lampstand, altar of incense, and table of offering. They hung new curtains. They offered sacrifice for the first time in two years, lighting lamps and setting out the Bread of the Presence. They prayed for the people.

The purification of the Temple took place on the very anniversary of its desecration, two years earlier, on the twenty-fifth day of the month of Kislev (December) in 164 BCE. They celebrated an eight-day festival in honor of the restoration of the Temple and victory over their enemies. "Then Judas and his brothers and all the assembly of Israel" (2 Maccabees 4:59) proclaimed that Jews should henceforth observe this period as the annual festival of Hanukkah. The traditional Hanukkah story of a single day's supply of oil miraculously burning in the Temple lamp for eight days—the time it took to properly prepare a new supply of holy oil—is not found in the books of Maccabees. Rather it comes from the Talmud.[35]

> What is Hanukkah? The rabbis taught: On the twenty-fifth day of Kislev Hanukah commences and lasts eight days, on which lamenting (in commemoration of the dead) and fasting are prohibited. When the Hellenists entered the sanctuary, they defiled all the oil that was found there. When the government of the House of Asmoneans prevailed and conquered them, oil was sought (to feed the holy lamp in the sanctuary) and only one vial was found with the seal of the high priest intact. The vial contained sufficient oil for one day only, but a miracle occurred, and it fed the holy lamp eight days in succession. These eight days were the following year established as days of good cheer, on which psalms of praise and acknowledgment (of God's wonders) were to be recited.[36]

TALES OF COURAGE AND MARTYRDOM

Two important stories are told of the heroism of Jewish civilians during the Maccabean rebellion. They celebrate those who followed the commands of their faith and honored the ways of the Lord at great personal sacrifice.

The first is of Eleazar, an elderly scribe in high position, who was forced to eat swine's flesh.[37] He spit it out and faced torture rather than submit. The soldiers approached him with compassion and quietly suggested he commit a deception to save himself. They offered to let him eat his own food while pretending to eat the swine's flesh. Thus he could be observed by the people apparently following the royal edict while not actually breaching God's law. But Eleazar refused, declaring that he would rather provide an example to the young and thereby demonstrate himself worthy of having lived a righteous life. He died a martyr to the laws of the God of Israel.

A second story is told of seven brothers and their mother.[38] Each brother endures unbelievable tortures in the presence of his mother rather than recant his faith. All die including the

---

35 The "Babylonian Talmud" was first published circa 500 CE.

36 *The Babylonian Talmud, Book 1: Tract Sabbath*, tr. by Michael L. Rodkinson [1903], at sacred-texts.com (www.sacred-texts.com/jud/t01/t0110.htm).

37 2 Maccabees 6.

38 2 Maccabees 7 and elsewhere in 1 and 4 Maccabees.

mother. The second brother, after he watches the first brother die, shouts to the Seleucid officer as he too was dying, "You accursed wretch, you dismiss us from this present life, but the King of the universe will raise us to an everlasting renewal of life, because we have died for His laws" (2 Maccabees 7:9). Each succeeding brother offers similar affirmations of the promise of God's mercy in the afterlife as does their mother, all dying in triumph to the ways of the Lord. Thus the concepts of a righteous reward in the afterlife for proper behavior in earthly trials—and the archetype of martyrdom—were introduced into Jewish scripture. Within two centuries such beliefs would become cornerstones of the Christian faith.

Many more tales of heroism grace the account of the Maccabean campaign, as do stories of miraculous assistance provided to the holy warriors. Their courage and devotion to the military model of holiness inspired Pope Celestine II to refer to the Knights Templar as the "New Maccabees" in his important bull *Milites Templi* of 1144, that awarded special privileges to the Order.

The love and respect the people showed for the Second Temple bears witness to that which we have seen in the stories of the First Temple, especially in the histories of David, Solomon, Hezekiah, and Josiah.

THE ESTABLISHMENT AND SIGNIFICANCE OF THE HASMONEAN DYNASTY

The campaigns of Judas and his brothers continued until they secured victory in 142 BCE. Judas himself had been killed in battle by this time. The surviving Maccabean brothers and their descendants ruled Israel as the Hasmonean dynasty until the Romans conquered the region in 63 BCE. The century of Hasmonean rule represented the first time since the destruction of the First Temple in 586 BCE that Israel had thrived as an independent nation. Such a political condition would not occur again until the re-establishment of the state of Israel in 1948.

CHAPTER TWENTY-ONE

HEROD'S TEMPLE

Herod the Great was one of the ancient world's most prolific builders, "that he might leave monuments of the fineness of his taste, and of his beneficence to future ages."[39] Born ca. 73 BCE, he reigned as King of Judea from 37 BCE until his death in 4 BCE. He was the son of Antipater, the coruler of Judea after the Roman conquest of 63 BCE. His father appointed Herod governor of Galilee when he was only fifteen years old. Proclaimed king by Antony, Octavian, and the Roman Senate at age thirty-six, Herod began a three-year military campaign to put an end to the Hasmonean dynasty and assume his throne. Because he was descended from a family of Idumean (or Edomite) nobles who had been forcibly converted to Judaism by the Maccabees around 140 BCE, and because he was appointed to political office by the Roman overlords of Judea, he was looked upon with distrust by the majority of the population over whom he ruled. It certainly did not help his popularity with the Jews when he instituted Hellenistic games on a five-year cycle to honor Caesar, building large amphitheatres in Jerusalem and elsewhere.

Herod possessed great physical courage, was skilled with the bow and javelin, and was a mighty hunter.[40] He was a man of great contradictions: ferociously ambitious, a talented general, shrewd diplomat, and competent administrator. He was a generous but ruthless ruler, devious, manipulative, and prone to periods of mental instability. He killed several members of his family including two brothers-in-law, the first and most beloved of his ten wives, and three of his sons. Historian Will Durant points out that Herod's extensive construction projects were out of all proportion to the national wealth of Judea and caused him to overtax the people.[41] At times he could be an absolute despot, depriving his subjects of the right to congregate, setting a network of spies to entrap people into uttering harsh assessments of the government, then punishing critics with imprisonment, torture, even murder. The New Testament story of the "Massacre of the Innocents"—Herod's attempt to stop the rise of Jesus as told in Matthew 2:16—has long darkened his name. On the other hand, during a famine he cut up the gold and silver furniture of his palace to buy food for the people, not only of Judea but neighboring lands as

---

39 Josephus, *Antiquities of the Jews,* 15, 8, 5, 298.

40 Josephus, *Wars of the Jews,* 1, 21, 13, 429–30.

41 Will Durant, *Caesar and Christ,* page 532.

TOP OF PAGE: *An idealized portrait of Herod's Temple from the Citadel Museum in Jerusalem. Photo by Vere Chappell.*
ABOVE: *The Robinson Arch, discovered in 1838 by Edward Robinson, is the first part of the archaeological evidence for the giant staircase at the southwest of the Temple Mount shown in the portrait. The excavations of Professor Benjamin Mazar from 1968–1978 uncovered the bottom of that staircase.*

well.[42] He was favorably disposed to the Essenes, exempting them from a state loyalty oath because of a childhood experience with an Essene master who predicted Herod would become king.[43]

While Herod's massive expansion and rebuilding of the Second Temple was his most important accomplishment, it was just one among countless architectural feats. He built the shrine of Machpelah in Hebron, a breathtaking edifice that stands to this day; the fortress and vacation palace at Masada; the magnificent fountains, baths and colonnaded quadrangles in Ascalon; his seaside city of Caesara with a temple of white marble dedicated to Augustus

---

42 Josephus, *Antiquities*, 15, 9, 1–2.
43 Josephus compared the Essenes to the Pythagoreans, *Antiquities*, 15, 10, 4, 371.

A street level view of the excavations of the Herodian street at the
southwest of the Temple Mount. On the left are the remains of shops
that served the needs of ancient visitors to the Temple.

and a large amphitheatre; a massive fortress, palace complex, and burial ground south of Jerusalem known as the Herodian; and his magnificent Jerusalem palace west of the Temple Mount, fortified by three great towers. He also built structures in neighboring countries including Syria and Greece.

The primary source for the description of Herod's Temple is the historian Josephus writing toward the end of the first century CE. Josephus is another controversial figure. A Jewish general from a priestly family, he fought against the Romans in Galilee during the Jewish Revolt of 66–70 CE. The emperor Nero sent Vespasian, his trusted general (later to become emperor), to put down the rebellion. Josephus was defeated in an early battle with Vespasian and surrendered. He later accompanied Vespasian to Rome. He returned to Judea with Vespasian's son Titus, who led the siege of Jerusalem. Josephus tried to convince the Jewish rebels to

surrender in the face of the overwhelming military superiority of the Roman army but they refused. Titus conquered the city and destroyed the Temple. After returning to Rome with Titus, Josephus wrote his timeless history *The Wars of the Jews*, followed sixteen years later by *The Antiquities of the Jews*. Josephus' historical descriptions are known to be factual because he was writing for people who had actually seen the Temple.

There are also early accounts of the Second Temple in the *Mishnah*, the earliest collection of rabbinic law compiled circa 200 CE. The *Middot* and *Tamid* are two early tracts of the *Mishnah* that discuss the Temple. The *Middot* focuses on a description of the building, while the *Tamid* discusses the rules governing daily sacrifice. The New Testament is another contemporary source about the Temple of Herod in the four gospels and the Acts of the Apostles, as are the Roman records of the conquest of Jerusalem.

Herod's extension of the eastern wall of the Temple Mount is best seen at the southeast corner. (Note arrow shown in photo above.) Herod added 106 feet to the south of the existing Hasmonean wall. Elie Ben-Meir points to the seam in closeup at right.

RIGHT: *These Herodian ashlars show the distinctive rectangular border and tightly fitted construction characteristic of Herod's stonemasons. Their well-preserved condition is explained by the fact that they were covered by a tremendous layer of rubble and debris after the destruction of the Temple Mount by the Romans. Prior to the archaeological excavations of the late Professor Benjamin Mazar in the late 1960s and early '70s, they had not been exposed to the elements for nearly fifteen hundred years. The retaining wall ashlars weigh on average two and a half tons. The two largest ashlars, excavated in the Western Wall Tunnel, weigh five hundred eighty tons.*

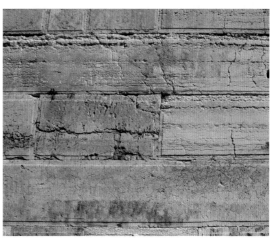

The Walls of the Temple Mount

Herod's first task was to extend the walls of Mount Moriah so he could begin construction on a suitably stable foundation. Herod enlarged the retaining walls of the Temple Mount to double their previous size, then filled and leveled the area with soil for the new building. Historian Herschel Shanks describes the walls around the Temple Mount: "The massive retaining wall of the Temple Mount encloses the largest platform of its kind in the ancient world. The area enclosed is nearly thirty-six acres, large enough to hold about twenty-four football fields."[44] Josephus called it, "the most prodigious work that was ever heard of by man."[45]

The eastern wall bordering the Kidron Valley could not be expanded further eastward so it was extended at the north and south ends. The photos above show the southeast corner, where Herod added another 106 feet to the

---

44 Hershel Shanks, *Jerusalem's Temple Mount*, page 71.
45 Josephus, *Antiquities*, 15, 11, 3, 346.

Hasmonean wall. He built new walls in the south, west and north. The Western Wall or Wailing Wall is part of the Herodian retaining wall of the Temple Mount.

Because of the abrupt drop off at the southeast portion of the Temple Mount leading down to the City of David, Herod reinforced the area by building massive vaulting east of the modern al-Aqsa Mosque. This underground space is known as Solomon's Stables because the Knights Templars kept their horses there. In 1999, the Muslim Waqf began construction of a new entrance to Solomon's Stables, which they converted to the Marwani Mosque, dumping thousands of tons of archaeologically rich material, concealing evidence dating as far back as the First Temple period.[46]

THE TEMPLE ON THE MOUNT

Herod undertook his work in the eighteenth year of his reign, circa 20 BCE. He first needed to demolish Zerubbabel's Second Temple and build a new foundation before being able to erect his building.[47] Because people were fearful that he would be interrupted and unable to finish after he tore down the Second Temple, he agreed to assemble the entire construction apparatus in advance. He gathered together a thousand carts to carry the stones and ten thousand skilled workmen. He arranged for one thousand priestly garments to be fashioned and for members of priestly families to be trained in stonemasonry and carpentry that the work might be properly performed by consecrated Kohathites. The Temple was completed in a year and six months, although related construction on the Temple Mount continued for decades.

A magnificent structure known as the Royal Stoa or Portico ran along the southern end of the Temple Mount. Called Solomon's Porch in the New Testament, it had 162 huge columns running in four rows that formed three aisles. The central structure covered the middle aisle. Because Herod was not of priestly birth, and thus forbidden from entering the Temple, the Royal Stoa allowed him the kingly grandeur he would have expected while visiting the Mount.

An outer court, known as the Court of the Gentiles, opened between the Royal Stoa and the Temple. It hosted the moneychangers and sellers of the sacrificial animals to be brought to the Temple. People gathered here as in a public square and visitors of all faiths were welcomed.

Jews alone were able to approach the Temple compound itself, entering through the eastern gate (called the Beautiful Gate in Acts, 3:2) by mounting a set of fourteen steps. Signs announced that non-Jews were forbidden to enter under pain of death. Inside the gate was the first walled enclosure known as the Court of the Women. It measured two hundred twenty-two feet square and can be seen opposite.[48] Men and their wives passed here to sacrifice after they had been purified in the mikvah baths outside the south wall of the Temple Mount.

Continuing west, men came to a flight of fifteen semicircular steps that led up to the Nica

---

46 Shanks, page 79. In 2004, a private archaeological effort was permitted to sift through the discarded soil. It has uncovered pottery and other objects from the First Temple period along with other important artifacts.

47 Traditionally, Herod's Temple is viewed as a restoration of the Second Temple rather than being designated the Third. My descriptions of the Temple are based on the accounts of Josephus in *Wars*, 5, 5, *Antiquities*, 15, 11; Herschel Shanks, *Jerusalem's Temple Mount*; George Farrah, *The Temples at Jerusalem and Their Masonic Connections*; William J. Hamblin and David Rolph Seely, *Solomon's Temple: Myth and History*; and Benjamin Mazar, *The Mountain of the Lord*. The measurements in these books vary somewhat so I have noted the source of the data I give.

---

48 Mazar, page 117.

The gold-plated Temple with its white limestone and marble construction. The Eastern and Nicanor gates are visible as is the Court of the Women. At left is a portion of the Royal Stoa and the Court of the Gentiles. Photo by permission of Israel Museum.

nor Gate.[49] This gate opened to the Court of the Israelites, a long narrow area, 19 feet deep by 222 feet long,[50] where people could stand and watch the priests make offerings in the Court of the Priests.

The Court of the Priests was directly in front of the Temple. Only consecrated priests were allowed in this area. It measured 313 feet by 227 feet.[51] A large altar for burnt offerings, 40 feet square by 15 feet high,[52] stood in the midst. It

was approached by a ramp. North of the altar was the Place of the Slaughtering where the sacrificial animals were killed and prepared. In front of the Temple toward the south was a large laver for the priests to wash before entering the Temple.

The Temple itself was also open only to priests. It was approached by a stairway of twelve steps. These led to the first room of the Temple, an enclosed Porch, the *Ulam*. It was tall and wide but narrow in depth. Its wings extended beyond the width of the inner two rooms. It was 100 cubits wide and 100 tall[53] (150 feet). Josephus says it had no doors or

49 Josephus explains that women were not allowed to proceed past the Court of the Women. (*Antiquities*, 15, 11, 5, 419 and *Wars*, 5, 5, 2, 199).

50 Mazar, page 116.

51 Ibid.

52 Hamblin and Seely, page 45.

53 Josephus, *Wars*, 5, 5, 4, 207.

curtain blocking its view because it represented the universal visibility of heaven that cannot be excluded from any place.[54] The large open entranceway measured 60 feet high by 30 feet wide.[55]

The next room was the *Hechal* or Holy Place. It was approached through a set of gigantic bronze doors decorated with golden vines and adorned with embroidered purple veils. It contained the seven-branched Candlestick, Altar of Incense, and Table of Offering with the Bread of the Presence. Josephus writes that the seven lamps signified the seven planets; the twelve loaves of the Bread of the Presence symbolized the circle of the Zodiac; and the thirteen sweet-smelling spices of the incense proclaimed that God is the possessor of all things.[56] The Main Hall measured 30 feet wide by 60 feet long by 60 feet high.[57] Its walls and ceiling were covered with plates of beaten gold. It was the center of activity for the priests.

The third room of the Temple was the *Debir* or Holy of Holies. It was separated from the Main Hall by an embroidered curtain of blue, purple, scarlet, and fine linen. This curtain will later be torn in two when Jesus is crucified (as mentioned in Matthew 27:51 and Mark 15:38). Josephus assigns mystical significance to the colors: scarlet symbolizes fire, the fine linen earth, blue the air, and purple the sea.[58] Josephus adds that the curtain was embroidered with mystic symbols. The Holy of Holies was fashioned in the shape of a cube of thirty feet[59]

as it was in Solomon's Temple. It was elevated and approached by a ramp or steps.[60] The room was empty as it no longer held the Ark of the Covenant. It was entered once a year by the high priest on the Day of Atonement. Its walls and ceiling were also covered with plates of gold. Rabbinic tradition states that the floor of the Holy of Holies was the bedrock of the Foundation Stone of the World that "stood three fingers higher than the ground."[61] The high priest would sprinkle sacrificial blood on the Stone during the annual Day of Atonement ceremony.[62] The location of the Holy of Holies on the Foundation Stone was shared by the Temples of Solomon, Zerubbabel, and Herod.[63]

The Temple was built entirely of polished white limestone with marble and plated in gold. "At the first rising of the sun, [it] reflected back a very fiery splendor, and made those who forced themselves to look upon it to turn their eyes away, just as they would have done at the sun's own rays. But this temple appeared to strangers, when they were at a distance, like a mountain covered with snow."[64] Limited to the biblical dimensions of Solomon's Temple, Herod's Temple was smaller in scale than his usual massive construction projects.

A series of thirty-eight small storage chambers ran along three sides of the Temple in three stories. Herod later added large cloisters outside the Temple as well. This additional construction lasted eight years. At the north of the Temple Mount, he built a tower called the Antonia Tower in remembrance of his friend Marc

54 Josephus, *Wars*, 5, 5, 4, 208.

55 Farrah, page 135.

56 Josephus, *Wars*, 5, 5, 4, 217–18

57 Farrah, page 135.

58 Josephus, *Wars*, 5, 5, 4, 213. George Farrah explains that purple was appropriate for the sea because dye of that color was obtained from a certain seashell. *The Temples at Jerusalem and Their Masonic Connections*, page 136.

59 Farrah, page 136.

60 Mazar, page 114.

61 Mazar, page 113, quoting the *Mishna, Yoma* 5.2.

62 William J. Hamblin and David Rolph Seely, *Solomon's Temple: Myth and History*, page 48, quoting the *Mishnah Yoma* 5:1 and *Tosefta Yoma* 4.6.

63 Benjamin Mazar discusses this concept in *The Mountain of the Lord*, pages 20, 99, and 113.

64 Josephus, *Wars*, 5, 5, 6, 222–23.

A large model of Jerusalem stands on the grounds of the Israel Museum in Jerusalem. It depicts the city in 66 CE just before the Jewish Revolt. Built under the supervision of scholar Michael Avi-Yonah between 1962 and 1966, it was moved to the Israel Museum grounds in 2006. The model covers nearly an acre and is at a scale of 50:1. This photo shows the elevated Temple Mount rising above the city. It would have served as the central focus of attention for the entire community. Photo by permission of the Israel Museum.

Antony, defeated in earlier Roman internecine conflicts. It served as a defensive garrison for soldiers against attacks from the north, as well as an asset for crowd control of those on the Mount. Herod also constructed a hidden underground tunnel leading from the Temple to the Antonia fortress to protect himself in the event of sedition.

Upon completion of the Temple, circa 18 BCE, the people were overjoyed. They were apprecia-tive of Herod's commitment and the speed with which he accomplished the task. There was a great feast and Herod sacrificed three hundred oxen. Everyone joined him in offering sacrifice, each contributing according to his means. The celebration of the completion of the Temple fell on the anniversary of the beginning of Herod's reign, "which coincidence of them both made the festival more illustrious."[65]

65 Josephus, *Antiquities*, 15, 11, 6, 423.

PART SEVEN

THE CHRISTIAN REVELATION

(MATTHEW, MARK, LUKE, JOHN, REVELATION)

*Madonna and Child atop the Church of Our
Lady of the Ark of the Covenant at Kiriath-
jearim. The church was built in memory
of the presence of the Ark prior to King
David's moving it to Jerusalem. The Womb
of the Virgin is here identified as the Ark
of the New Covenant. The Christ child is
considered the Divine Law within the Ark.*

Chapter Twenty-two

The Temple in the Story of Jesus

In the beginning was the Word, and the Word was with God, and the Word was God…. And the Word was made flesh, and dwelt among us. (John 1:1 and 14)

Let us now explore the link between Jesus, the New Testament, and the Temple. As the Church of Our Lady in Kiriath-jearim dramatically asserts, the womb of the Virgin was the Ark of the New Covenant and the Christ child the New Law within. The Gospels thus seamlessly identify Jesus with his Old Testament precedents, especially Moses and David. We will also seek after some of the ancient prophecies he fulfilled. The overview of the life of Jesus presented in this chapter is limited to understanding his role in relation to the Temple.

In the ordering of the Protestant canon, the last 25 percent of the Old Testament is the writings of the Prophets. For the most part, as shown in chapter 17, this group of texts is filled with dark and violent images. A harsh but reasonably accurate characterization of the overall sense of the Prophets could read as follows: The tone is generally heavy-handed and joyless, conveyed by a series of accusations and threats, accompanied by a litany of sins and punishments. There is some real comedy in the Book of Jonah and the story of Daniel is truly inspiring—but the Protestant Old Testament ends with a sense of hopelessness. The Jewish canon arranges the texts in a different order. The Prophets are placed toward the middle of the collection. However, the Jewish Bible ends with the fatalistic finale of 2 Chronicles—the destruction of the Temple and beginning of the Babylonian exile.

Thus, from a purely literary point of view, if nothing else, the Gospels provide an altogether refreshing and optimistic uplifting of the spirit. While it does not take long for the New Testament to plunge into similarly negative territory, especially after the introduction of Saint Paul, the story of Jesus is in a class by itself.

Jesus referred to his teaching as the "good news" or "gospel." While little from the pen of humanity has ever reached the literary quality of such Old Testament writings as Psalms, Proverbs, and the Song of Solomon, the Gospels of Jesus are among them. Like a breath of fresh air, Jesus spoke of hope and religious creativity.

OPPOSITE: *The Virgin Mary and Saint Elizabeth with the babies Jesus and John the Baptist, by Bachiacca (Francesco d'Ubertino Verdi), ca. 1545.*

The Archangel Gabriel visits the Virgin Mary and explains that she will bear the Christ child.
The Annunciation, *by Lorenzo di Credi (detail), ca. 1480–1485.*

The overly stylized and rigid laws of contemporary Judaism were to be relaxed in favor of the inner spirit of God's message.

The Birth of Jesus

Jesus is presented in the first Gospel, that of Matthew, in his most Jewish light—obviously intended to convince his own people that the long-promised Messiah[1] had arrived and should be recognized by those most familiar with the scriptural references to his coming. Matthew's argument also seems to imply that accepting his

divine mission would allow the Jews to retain their status as the Chosen People. Matthew begins with an account of the genealogy of Jesus that places him squarely in the Davidic line and as a descendant of Abraham. His ancestors include the Patriarchs, along with Boaz, Ruth, David, Solomon, and their royal descendants. His heritage continues through the Babylonian Exile and the return to Jerusalem. He is identified as a descendant of Zerubbabel and, thus, tied by blood to the builders of both the First and Second Temples. It is noted by Matthew that fourteen generations preceded David from Abraham, fourteen generations followed from David to the Babylonian Exile, and another fourteen followed from the Exile to Jesus.

---

1 "Messiah" is Hebrew for "Anointed." In Greek, it is "Christos."

Matthew explains that Jesus was fathered by the Holy Spirit while Mary was engaged to be married to Joseph, but before they lived together. Joseph was unaware of the miracle and was embarrassed by Mary's pregnancy, assuming she was not a virgin. He decided to quietly dismiss her. But an angel of the Lord appeared to him in a dream and explained that Mary was indeed pure, and that he should marry her as planned. The child, to be named Jesus, would save his people from their sins.

Matthew quotes Isaiah so that we may understand why all this should be happening. "Look, the virgin shall conceive and bear a son and they shall call him Emmanuel"[2] (Matthew 1:23, quoting Isaiah 7:14). The seamless interaction between the life of Jesus and his Old Testament antecedents permeates the Gospels. Event is added to event in which Jesus fulfills a prophecy or a teaching as the long awaited scriptural messiah.

In the Gospel of Luke, we learn additional details of the birth of both Jesus and his cousin John the Baptist. Zechariah the priest and his wife Elizabeth lived righteous lives but were childless. When Zechariah was chosen to offer incense in the Temple, the angel Gabriel appeared in the Sanctuary and told him a son would be born to them, to be named John, who must never drink wine or strong liquor and who would be filled with the Holy Spirit even while in the womb.

> And many of the children of Israel shall he turn to the Lord their God. And he shall go before him in the spirit and power of Elias, to turn the hearts of the fathers to the children, and the disobedient to the wisdom of the just; to make ready a people prepared for the Lord. (Luke 1:16–17)

Six months later, Gabriel was sent to Nazareth in the Galilee region to present himself to Mary. Gabriel explained that she would bear a son fathered by the Holy Spirit who "shall be great, and shall be called the Son of the Highest: and the Lord God shall give unto him the throne of his father David: And he shall reign over the house of Jacob for ever; and of his kingdom there shall be no end" (Luke 1:32–33). Gabriel told Mary of the pregnancy of Elizabeth and she set off to visit Elizabeth. When Mary entered the house, the baby John leapt in his mother's womb. Elizabeth was filled with the Holy Spirit and proclaimed to Mary, "Blessed art thou among women, and blessed is the fruit of thy womb" (Luke 1:42).

JESUS' CHILDHOOD

Jesus is presented as the new Moses, come to lead God's people on the next stage of their sacred journey. For example, after his birth in Bethlehem, wise men from the East, following a star, came to Jerusalem to pay him homage.[3] They asked King Herod the Great (r. 37–4 BCE) where the royal-born child could be found. The king was frightened and emulated pharaoh's behavior in trying to cheat fate and retain power. After Herod unsuccessfully tried to locate the baby, he ordered the mass slaying of all male children under two years of age. The wailing of their mothers, the daughters of Rachel, had been prophesied in Jeremiah.[4] The flight of Jesus' family from the threat posed by the king placed him in Egypt. When an angel announced Herod's death, they returned to

---

2 "God is with us."

3 Matthew 2.
4 Jeremiah 31:15.

The flight of the Holy Family to Egypt was forced upon them by the persecution launched by Herod the Great. As mentioned in the caption on page 216, their first resting place was the Church of Saint Gerasimos just outside Jericho. DeLisle Psalter, 1308–1310.

Israel in fulfillment of the prophecy of Hosea, "out of Egypt I called my son" (Hosea 11:1).

There are variations of the story in the different Gospels. Luke does not include the flight to Egypt but places Jesus in Jerusalem, soon after his circumcision, that he may be sanctified in the firstborn ritual at the Second Temple according to the law of Moses.[5] Joseph and Mary offered

the traditional sacrifice. While they were in the Temple, a devout and righteous man named Simeon, who had been promised he would not die before he had seen the Lord's Messiah, was guided by the Spirit to the Temple. He held the baby in his arms and praised God. "Lord, now lettest thou thy servant depart in peace, according to thy word: For mine eyes have seen thy salvation, Which thou hast prepared before the face of all people; A light to lighten the Gentiles, and the glory of thy people Israel" (Luke 2:29–32). An elderly prophetess named Anna lived

---

5 "Sanctify unto me all the firstborn, whatsoever openeth the womb among the children of Israel, both of man and of beast: it is mine" (Exodus 13:2).

Mary and Joseph present the infant Jesus at the Second Temple in accord with the laws of Moses regarding the special sanctity of, and obligations attendant upon, the firstborn among people, animals, and crops. DeLisle Psalter, 1308–1310.

at the Temple. She worshipped continually with prayer and fasting, night and day. When she saw the child, she too began to praise God and speak about the child to all who sought the redemption of Jerusalem.

After their obligations were fulfilled at the Temple, Jesus' family returned to their home in Nazareth. Each year they returned to Jerusalem for the annual Passover festival. The year Jesus turned twelve, he remained behind at the Tem-

ple without telling his parents. They assumed he was visiting with other pilgrims in their group as they traveled home. When they realized he was missing, they returned to Jerusalem looking for him. They found him in the Temple in discussion with the learned rabbis—who were astonished at the wisdom of the youth. Needless to say, Joseph and Mary were quite upset. Mary said, "'Son, why hast thou thus dealt with us? behold, thy father and I have sought thee sorrowing.' And he said unto them, 'How is it that ye sought me? wist ye not that I must be about my Father's business?' And they understood not the saying which he spake unto them" (Luke 2:48–50). After this incident, his behavior proved to be that of a model son.

BAPTISM BY JOHN

John the Baptist, the cousin of Jesus, reenters the story in the fifteenth year of the reign of Roman Emperor Tiberius (r. 14–37).[6] All four Gospels quote Isaiah, characterizing John as the preparer of the way for the Messiah. "Behold, I send my messenger before thy face, which shall prepare thy way before thee. The voice of one crying in the wilderness, 'Prepare ye the way of the LORD, make his paths straight'" (Mark 1:3, quoting Isaiah 40:3). John was conducting large-scale baptisms at the Jordan River that would eventually include Jesus himself. In the Gospel of John, when the Baptist saw Jesus coming he proclaimed, "Behold the Lamb of God, which taketh away the sin of the world" (John 1:29). After Jesus rose from the water, "the heavens were opened unto him, and he saw the Spirit of God descending like a dove, and lighting upon him. And lo a voice from heaven, saying, 'This is my beloved Son, in whom I am well pleased'"[7] (Matthew 3:17). In Mark, the baptism offered by John the Baptist is called one of repentance, and the people are described as confessing their sins.[8]

Many wondered if the Baptist was the Messiah. He answered by explaining that another baptism would be offered by the one to follow him. It would be even more powerful. "I indeed baptize you with water unto repentance: but he that cometh after me is mightier than I, whose shoes I am not worthy to bear: he shall baptize you with the Holy Ghost, and with fire"[9] (Matthew 3:11).

The concept of baptism, the spiritual cleansing and rebirth through full water immersion, is one of the distinguishing characteristics of the New Testament. Old Testament parallels to baptism include the cleansing and renewal of the Earth in the Flood. The Tabernacle and Temple both had basins for the priests to cleanse themselves, along with lavers and instructions for the ritual washing of sacrifices. There were various levels of washing specified in the hygienic laws, both for the cleansing of sins and the healing of skin disease. At the Second Temple, an extensive area outside the south wall was reserved for the *mikvah*, the ceremonial pools where men and women pilgrims would separately bathe before entering the Temple gates to make their offerings. But the New Testament style baptisms, as performed by John, do not have a direct Old Testament antecedent.

THE DEVIL'S TEMPTATION

Matthew, Mark, and Luke again identify Jesus with Moses by recounting his forty-day fast in the wilderness and later on the mountain—reminiscent of the Mount Sinai revelation.[10] Jesus' temptation by the Devil is described as a battle of Old Testament scriptural references in which the devil is bested by his more pure-hearted and worthy opponent.[11] After his triumph,

---

6 Luke 3:1.

7 Here is the origin of countless variations of later Grail symbolism.

8 Mark 1:4-5.

9 This was a concept later taken to heart by the Cathars. See *The Templars and Assassins: The Militia of Heaven*, chapter 19.

10 Matthew 4:1–11, Luke 4:1–13, Mark 1:12–13.

11 Their confrontation was the inspiration for the famous line in Shakespeare about the Devil citing scripture in *The Merchant of Venice*, Act I, Scene III, vv. 98–103.

The dramatic confrontation between Jesus and Satan took place on the mountain shown in this magnificent image. It is just outside the city of Jericho. Two Greek Orthodox monasteries and several hermit caves commemorate the spiritual battle. Photo by Steven Brooke.

Jesus began to choose his disciples, preach with greater authority, and conduct numerous exorcisms and healings.[12] He also performed signs and wonders that people might believe. At a wedding feast in Cana of Galilee, he turned water into wine, called by John the first of his signs.[13]

THE SERMON ON THE MOUNT

Jesus delivered his well-known Sermon on the Mount standing on a mountain near the Sea of Galilee, reminiscent of Moses giving the Ten Commandments from Mount Sinai. The Beatitudes (Matthew 5) propound a series of moral teachings with many levels of interpretation that go well beyond the subservience themes by which they are sometimes characterized in modern circles. Among the practical spiritual instructions to be found in the Sermon is one of universal application for meditation. "The light of the body is the eye: if therefore thine eye be single, thy whole body shall be full of light" (Matthew 6:22). Jesus' overall moral guideposts given in Matthew chapter 7 may be worth reexamining by any who have been over-quick to dismiss them.

12 See Mark 1:16-33.
13 John 2:11.

A hillside near the Sea of Galilee where Jesus preached the Sermon on the Mount. Photo by Vere Chappell.

Jesus added in the Sermon, "Think not that I am come to destroy the law, or the prophets: I am not come to destroy, but to fulfil" (Matthew 5:17). The importance of this is evident as we contemplate his connection to the Temple—equally central to the New Testament as in the Old. The rectification of Jewish law undertaken by Jesus was bold. And he would pay dearly for it. Yet, when he healed a leper, he counseled his patient to offer the gift that Moses commanded, i.e. a sacrifice at the Temple.[14]

MISSION TO THE GENTILES

We gradually observe the spiritual teaching of Jesus spread beyond the Jews as the scope of his message becomes incrementally more universal.[15] For example, the quality of faith expressed by a Roman centurion amazed Jesus. He thereby performed the requested healing for the centurion's servant. Later, Jesus would come upon a Canaanite woman in distress. She begged him to heal her daughter, possessed by a demon. Jesus tried to explain that his mission was to the Jews alone, but like the Roman centurion, the intensity of her faith and humility caused him to reach beyond even his own understanding of his task, and he healed the child.[16]

Luke adds more detail to a story, also told by Matthew and Mark, of Jesus visiting the

---

14 Matthew 8.

15 We recall the words of Isaiah on the universal nature of the Temple quoted on pages 231–32.

16 Matthew 8 and 15.

The White Synagogue in Capernaum was the scene of several sermons, healings, and exorcisms performed by Jesus. Photo by Vere Chappell.

synagogue in Nazareth. He read passages from Isaiah during the service, in which the prophet spoke of the healing and comfort that would come to the oppressed. He sensed the wonderment of his neighbors that one of themselves could speak with such authority. He made his famous statement, "No prophet is accepted in his own country" (Luke 4:24). Then—as if from irritation—he added that Elijah the prophet was sent to the widow at Zarephath in Sidon, a Gentile, during a bitter famine.[17] Elisha healed the Syrian general Naaman of his leprosy.[18] Jesus warned them that God was willing to extend His mercies to more deserving people should

the Jews not prove worthy to receive them. The people in the synagogue were furious and chased after him to hurl him off a cliff. "But he passing through the midst of them went his way" (Luke 4:30).

THE RADICALISM OF HIS TEACHING

Jesus was criticized by the Pharisees for associating with tax collectors and sinners. Why did he not limit his association to the righteous? "But when Jesus heard that, he said unto them, 'They that be whole need not a physician, but they that are sick'" (Matthew 9:12). He then made an extraordinary statement, "But go ye and learn what that meaneth, I will have mercy, and not sacrifice" (Matthew 9:13). Imagine the effect of

17 1 Kings 17:8–16, and page 194 of this book.
18 2 Kings 5:1–14, and page 203 of this book.

291

such words upon those religious authorities who lacked spiritual vitality, yet whose knowledge of scripture would have made them aware that Jesus was paraphrasing the prophet Hosea, "For I desired mercy, and not sacrifice; and the knowledge of God more than burnt offerings" (Hosea 6:6).

Jesus was advocating a new awareness of the old Jewish law. "Neither do men put new wine into old bottles: else the bottles break, and the wine runneth out, and the bottles perish: but they put new wine into new bottles, and both are preserved" (Matthew 9:17). Jesus did not mince words about the radical nature of his reformation. "Think not that I am come to send peace on earth: I came not to send peace, but a sword" (Matthew 10:32).

One can almost feel the tension building as he quoted the prophet Malachi in support of the mission of John the Baptist—currently imprisoned by Herod Antipas. Jesus identified John with Elijah the prophet, precursor of the Messiah, "Behold, I will send my messenger, and he shall prepare the way before me: and the LORD, whom ye seek, shall suddenly come to this temple" (Malachi 3:1). The conflict escalated when he responded to the Pharisees criticizing his disciples for plucking grain on the Sabbath.[19] He reminded them of David fleeing Saul—when the priest Ahimelech fed David and his soldiers with the Bread of the Presence.[20] Citing Elijah and David as predicates of his behavior drove the political and religious establishment into a fury because of the provocation such comparison implied.

The overall threat Jesus presented was further highlighted when he was publicly addressed as "Son of David."[21] Such an appellation made clear his connection with the royal bloodline of the ancient Jewish monarchy as mentioned in his genealogy. He thus represented a challenge to the Roman overlords and the Jewish ethnarch Herod Antipas,[22] as well as to the religious establishment of the Jews.

The Gospel of Mark repeatedly mentions the enormous crowds that came to receive Jesus' teachings—so large that much of his preaching was done from a boat so that he would not be crushed by the people. His popularity could only have been perceived as a problem by the power structure.

THE TEMPLE IN JOHN'S GOSPEL IN THE EARLY PERIOD

The gospels of Matthew, Mark, and Luke are called the Synoptic Gospels (i.e., "viewed together") because they tend to agree in chronology. John's account of Jesus' preaching and travel differs from the others. For example, he has Jesus traveling to Jerusalem several times as an adult, while the others paint his one visit to Jerusalem as the climax of the story (except Luke who includes him visiting the Temple as a child with his family). We will present some of John's account here because these events occur in the early part of Jesus' mission.

John records a fascinating discussion concerning the Temple that took place in Samaria. There are several accounts of Samaria in the Gospels because it bordered the Galilee region on the way to Judea. We recall that it had been the capital of the Northern Kingdom of Israel since the ninth century BCE. After it was conquered and repopulated by the Assyrians in the eighth century BCE, the Samaritans had devel-

---

19 Matthew 12.
20 Samuel 21:1–6, and page 143 of this book.
21 Matthew 9:27.

22 Herod Antipas (r. 4 BCE–39 CE) was the son and successor of Herod the Great. He served as the leader of the Jews (ethnarch) in Galilee under the authority of Rome. His brother, Herod Archelaus, was ethnarch of Judea.

Mount Gerazim is regarded by the Samaritans as the true sacred mountain of the Bible. Photo by Steven Broooke.

oped a heterogeneous worship that included pagan and Jewish rites. Their doctrine specifies that Mount Gerizim, near Shechem, is the true Mountain of the Lord rather than the Temple Mount in Jerusalem. A Temple built on that mountain in the fifth century BCE was destroyed by the Maccabees in 128 BCE. The Samaritans also have their own version of the Five Books of Moses, that differs from the Jewish version. There are very few surviving Samaritans today.

During biblical times, there was much hostility between the Jews and the Samaritans. Returning to Galilee from a visit to Judea, Jesus stopped at a well and had a conversation with a local Samaritan woman. He convinced her that he spoke with spiritual authority. The fol-

lowing conversation is recorded, after which he revealed to her that he was the Messiah. She said, "Our fathers worshipped in this mountain; and ye say, that in Jerusalem is the place where men ought to worship." He replied:

Woman, believe me, the hour cometh, when ye shall neither in this mountain, nor yet at Jerusalem, worship the Father. Ye worship ye know not what: we know what we worship: for salvation is of the Jews. But the hour cometh, and now is, when the true worshippers shall worship the Father in spirit and in truth: for the Father seeketh such to worship him. (John 4:20–24)

The Early Temple Teachings in John

Jesus went to Jerusalem for Sukkot, the Festival of Booths. He went incognito at first because of the growing number of threats against him. But once he arrived at the Temple, he revealed himself and preached. The Temple hierarchy was astounded at the extent of his knowledge. But people asked how he could be the Messiah if he came from Galilee. The prophet Micah had specified the Messiah would be born in Bethlehem, birthplace of David.[23]

The next day at the Temple, the scribes and Pharisees brought a woman taken in adultery and asked him to judge her case. They did this as a test in an attempt to trip him up. They quoted Moses, saying the penalty for adultery was stoning.[24] Jesus answered their challenge by saying, "He that is without sin among you, let him first cast a stone at her" (John 8:7). Silenced and ashamed, they left the Temple one by one. Jesus was alone with the woman. "'Woman, where are those thine accusers? hath no man condemned thee?' She said, 'No man, Lord.' And Jesus said unto her, 'Neither do I condemn thee: go, and sin no more'" (John 8:10–11).

In another of Jesus' early Temple teachings, he told the Pharisees, "I am the light of the world: he that followeth me shall not walk in darkness, but shall have the light of life" (John 8:12). They argued with him but did not arrest him, "for his hour was not yet come" (John 8:29). They were baffled and disturbed by his repeated statements of identity with God the Father. Jesus railed against them for wanting to kill him because he spoke truth. He accused them of being children of the Devil, whom he described as, "a murderer from the beginning … because there is no truth in him … he is a liar, and the father of [lies]" (John 8:44). As they began to pick up stones to throw at him, he hid himself and left the Temple.

THE CONTINUING MISSION IN THE FOUR GOSPELS

Jesus continued healing the sick, performing signs and wonders, and disputing with the religious establishment for the legitimacy of the reforms he was pursuing. His spiritual pronouncements and open contempt for the ruling elite continued to inflame the situation.

He conducted healings on the Sabbath and justified his behavior by explaining the preciousness of human life to the very God who had sanctified the Sabbath. In Mark, Jesus is depicted as angry and grieved at the hardness of heart of those who were unable to grasp why this was self-evident.[25] Who could argue against healing even if it appeared to violate artificial rules ossified through long use and dwindling spiritual awareness?

One of the numerous exorcisms Jesus performed is given a frightening new detail in Mark. A demoniac was famously possessed in the town of Gadara (or Gerasa). Jesus battled the evil spirit and demanded its name. "And he answered, saying, 'My name is Legion: for we are many'" (Mark 5:9). Jesus cast the demon into a herd of two thousand swine who flung themselves off a cliff, plunging to their death in the sea.

In Luke, Jesus was in the town of Nain in Galilee and met a funeral procession in which the only son of a widow was being carried to his burial. He had compassion for her and touched the bier and the dead son arose and began to speak. Fear seized the people and they glorified God.[26]

---

23 Michah 5:2.
24 Leviticus 20:10 and Deuteronomy 22:23–24.

25 Mark 3:5.
26 Luke 7:11–17.

The Sea of Galilee played a central role in the preaching of Jesus. Photo by Vere Chappell.

A friend named Lazarus fell ill, and his sisters sent an urgent message asking Jesus to come and help. While he loved the family deeply, he knew this was an opportunity to demonstrate his mission to the greater glory of God. He delayed his coming and Lazarus died and was entombed. Jesus told the disciples they must travel to Bethany, near Jerusalem, to heal Lazarus, but they were nervous because of the increasing death threats. When they arrived and were confronted with news of Lazarus' death, Jesus comforted the sisters. He told Martha, "I am the resurrection, and the life: he that believeth in me, though he were dead, yet shall he live: And whosoever liveth and believeth in me shall never die" (John 11:25–26). Then he called forth the dead man from the tomb.

Herod Antipas, learning of the growing fame of Jesus, feared that he was John the Baptist risen from the dead. For Herod had arrested

and beheaded John.[27] When Jesus heard of the Baptist's death, he withdrew by himself. Yet the crowds continued to come to him and Jesus resumed his healings out of compassion for their suffering. Then he miraculously fed those who had joined him, some five thousand people. We have seen precedents for this in Exodus when God fed the Israelites with manna, and in 2 Kings when Elisha fed the people of Gilgal during the famine.[28]

After feeding the crowds, the Gospel of John recounts Jesus walking on water to meet the disciples who were sailing across the Sea of Galilee, a miracle mentioned in the other gospels. But in John's account, the people noticed that Jesus had mysteriously appeared on the other shore. They questioned him about how he

---

27 Matthew 14:2–11, Mark 6:14–16, Luke 9:7–9.
28 2 Kings 4:38–44, and page 203 of this book.

had gotten there. He ignored their direct query and spoke of the food he had given them. But he spoke in images strange to all, telling them, "I am the bread of life: he that cometh to me shall never hunger; and he that believeth on me shall never thirst" (John 6:35). He added, "And this is the will of Him that sent me, that every one which seeth the Son, and believeth on him, may have everlasting life: and I will raise him up at the last day" (John 6:40). Many of the disciples were puzzled and disturbed by this language, and questioned him about the meaning of these astounding assertions.

A Word on the Disciples

We should take a moment to understand that there was an inner corps of twelve disciples, originally chosen to spread the teachings. Mark lists them by name and adds that Jesus gave them the power and authority to cast out demons.[29] Jesus promised they would sit on twelve thrones in the kingdom of Heaven judging the twelve tribes of Israel.[30]

But there were many other disciples as well. For example, Luke mentions Jesus appointing seventy followers to go out and preach and heal. They went off two by two. Jesus commented, "I send you forth as lambs among wolves" (Luke 10:3). Luke tells us later they returned with joy, saying, "Lord, even the devils are subject unto us through thy name" (Luke 10:17).

After Jesus made the statements recorded above by John, people, including disciples, began to question what they heard. What did he mean by saying he was the bread of life or that those who believed in him would experience eternal life? He noted their discomfort.

"But there are some of you that believe not." For Jesus knew from the beginning who they were that believed not, and who should betray him.... From that time many of his disciples went back, and walked no more with him. (John 6:64–66)

The fact that some disciples left the group may have been part of the natural sorting-out process that occurs within all spiritual groups.

At one point, Jesus asked the original twelve disciples who people thought he really was. Various answers were put forward. Then he asked, "'But whom say ye that I am?' And Simon Peter answered and said, 'Thou art the Christ, the Son of the living God'" (Matthew, 16:15–16). Jesus acknowledged the truth of this answer and designated Peter as the rock upon which his Church would be established.

The Female Disciples

Jesus also had a number of female disciples. While this was controversial in Jewish culture, it is one of the more significant aspects of his reformation. These women were among his most loyal followers. According to Luke,[31] while in the Galilee region, Jesus was invited to dine at the home of a Pharisee named Simon. The dinner occurred after Jesus had healed the Roman centurion's servant in Capernaum and raised the widow's son in nearby Nain. While at Simon's table, a mysterious woman entered the house carrying an alabaster jar. She knelt behind Jesus and began to wash his feet with her tears, and dry them with her hair, and kissed them, and anointed them with ointment. The Pharisee was silently outraged because the woman was a known sinner. Jesus pointed out that

---

29 Mark 3:14–19.
30 Matthew 19:28.

31 Luke 7:36–50.

*Known as the Madonna of the Sacred Coat, this image may be
perceived as an iconic representation of those female
disciples who flocked to the teachings of Jesus.*

sinners have the most gratitude when they are forgiven. While Simon may have been a righteous man, he did not offer the hospitality of the foot washing to Jesus. The woman's realization that she had been forgiven her many sins caused her to feel even greater love. And Jesus forgave her because of her great love.[32] People at the table murmured about who he thought he was that he could forgive sins.

While at the home of Martha and Mary, Mary sat near Jesus and listened to his teachings while Martha performed the many tasks of housekeeper and host. Martha complained about Mary and asked Jesus to tell her to help with the chores. But he replied, "Martha, Martha, thou art careful and troubled about many things: But one thing is needful: and Mary hath chosen that good part, which shall not be taken away from her" (Luke 10:41–42).

THE FINAL JOURNEY TO JERUSALEM

The all-important visit to Jerusalem of the Synoptic Gospels was fast approaching. Jesus began to explain to the disciples that he would undergo great suffering there at the hands of the Jewish religious establishment. He told them he would be killed and raised on the third day. When Peter begged him to avoid this agony, "he turned, and said unto Peter, 'Get thee behind me, Satan: thou art an offence unto me: for thou savourest not the things that be of God, but those that be of men'" (Matthew 16:23). Jesus was fully aware that the next part of his story must be his own sacrifice.

He took three disciples—Peter, James, and John—high up Mount Tabor where he was transfigured, his face shining like the sun, his clothes of dazzling white.[33] We recall Moses needing to wear a veil after his ascent of Mount Sinai so the people could bear his presence. In fact, Moses and Elijah appeared on the mountain and stood with Jesus in sight of the three disciples.

When Jesus came down the mountain to the larger group of disciples, he continued to emphasize that his life would soon be taken. He instructed the disciples on the conduct he expected them to manifest as they went forward. Since they would be on their own, they would need to work within the spiritual framework he was laying out. In conversation with some Pharisees who challenged him, Jesus pointed out that certain tenets of the Mosaic law, such as divorce, were spelled out because Moses realized the hard-heartedness of the Jews to whom he spoke. Jesus demanded more. The disciples then asked which of the commandments was most important. He listed the prohibitions against murder, adultery, stealing, and bearing false witness. He added the importance of honoring mother and father, and commanded them that they should love their neighbors as themselves.[34]

After making a most interesting defense of private property, Jesus began the final leg of his journey to Jerusalem.[35] At Bethphage, on the east side of the Mount of Olives, he instructed the disciples to bring a donkey and a colt they would find tied in the village.

All this was done, that it might be fulfilled which was spoken by the prophet,

---

32 Tradition, reaching back at least to the sermon of Pope Gregory the Great in 591, identifies the sinful woman who performed this anointing as Mary Magdalene. However, there is uncertainty about the identity of Mary Magdalene. Dan Burstein and Arne de Keijzer's collection of essays in *The Secrets of Mary Magdalene* provides evidence of the historical and religious controversies surrounding Mary.

---

33 Matthew 17:2, Mark 9:3, Luke 9:29.
34 Matthew 19:18–20. Jesus was quoting Leviticus 19:18.
35 Matthew 20:15.

Mount Tabor was the scene of the Transfiguration of Jesus before the three disciples,
similar to that of Moses described in Exodus. Photo by Steven Brooke.

saying, "Tell ye the daughter of Sion, Behold, thy King cometh unto thee, meek, and sitting upon an ass, and a colt the foal of an ass." And the disciples went, and did as Jesus commanded them. (Matthew 21:4–6, quoting Zechariah 9:9)

Jesus rode toward the city accordingly, while people laid their cloaks on the road before him and spread palm cuttings along his path.[36] Luke writes that as they approached closer, his followers burst into song. Some Pharisees told Jesus to quiet them. He replied, "I tell you that, if these should hold their peace, the stones would immediately cry out" (Luke 19:40).

John tells us that some Greeks approached the disciples to ask if they could speak with Jesus. When word of this was conveyed to him, he seemed to have taken it as an important sign and immediately stated, "The hour has come for the Son of Man to be glorified. Very truly, I tell you, unless a grain of wheat falls into the earth and dies, it remains just a single grain; but if it dies, it bears much fruit" (John 12:23–24 NRSV).

As they continued down the path of the Mount of Olives, they were overlooking Jerusalem and the Temple Mount. Jesus wept at the coming destruction of the city and the Temple. "Indeed, the days will come upon you, when your enemies … will crush you to the ground … and they will not leave within you one stone upon another; because you did not recognize the time of your visitation from God" (Luke 19:43–44). The Church of Dominus Flevit ("the Lord wept") commemorates the spot where Jesus and the disciples stood.

---

36 This is the origin of the Palm Sunday remembrance a week before Easter.

299

*The Church of Dominus Flevit (the Lord Wept) stands on the Mount of Olives.
It is built in the shape of a teardrop. Photo by Steven Brooke.*

JESUS AT THE TEMPLE

Jesus went directly to the Temple. When he arrived, he confronted the moneychangers. They were an old and necessary part of the Temple worship. An obligatory annual tithe of produce and livestock was to be donated at the Temple. Moses wrote in Deuteronomy that those who would have to travel long distances to the spiritual center of God's choosing would be allowed to sell the first fruits of their crops and herds and bring money instead.[37] When they arrived, they could purchase food and wine and the required animal and grain sac-

rifices. But since there were so many different local currencies and variations in the types of things one might bring for trade (such as jewelry, pottery, and the like), the institution of the financial exchange had developed. The problem that Jesus addressed was that rather than serving the religious needs of the community as designed, the vendors and currency brokers had become corrupt and were exploiting their franchise for profit inside the walls of the Temple.

And Jesus went into the temple of God, and cast out all them that sold and bought in the temple, and overthrew the tables of the moneychangers, and

---

37 See Deuteronomy 14:24–26, and page 101 of this book.

the seats of them that sold doves, And said unto them, "It is written, 'My house shall be called the house of prayer'; but ye have made it a den of thieves."[38] (Matthew 21:12–13)

John points out that the anger of Jesus was in fulfillment of scripture. "And his disciples remembered that it was written, 'The zeal of thine house hath eaten me up'" (John 2:17). This was a reference to King David, who described his own personal emotional identification with the sanctity and even the reputation of the Temple. "For the zeal of thine house hath eaten me up; and the reproaches of them that reproached thee are fallen upon me" (Psalm 69:9).

John adds a dialog between Jesus and some Jews in the Temple that displays their misunderstanding of his often repeated statement that he would raise the Temple in three days. Like David above, Jesus had personalized the archetype.

"What sign shewest thou unto us, seeing that thou doest these things?" Jesus answered and said unto them, "Destroy this temple, and in three days I will raise it up." Then said the Jews, "Forty and six years was this temple in building, and wilt thou rear it up in three days?" But he spake of the temple of his body. (John 2:18–21)

In conversation with a sympathetic Pharisee named Nicodemus, Jesus described his destiny with a fascinating allusion. "And as Moses lifted up the serpent in the wilderness, even so must the Son of man be lifted up: That

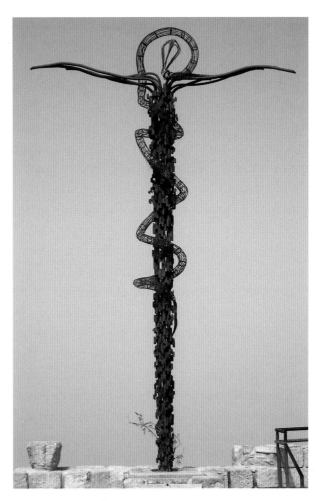

The Brazen Serpent at the Franciscan Monastery atop Mount Nebo. Photo by Vere Chappell.

whosoever believeth in him should not perish, but have eternal life"[39] (John 3:14–15). What makes this especially tantalizing is the identity between the numerical values of the Hebrew name of the serpent in Genesis, *Nachash*, NHSh (נחש = 358) and the Hebrew word for *Messiah*, MShYH (משיח = 358).[40]

The next day, Jesus returned to the Temple. Confronted by the elders and chief priests, he expressed his disdain for their betrayal of the

---

38 The overturning of the tables of the moneychangers happens much earlier in John during one of the Passover pilgrimages of Jesus. John 2:13–22.

39 See the story of the Brazen Serpent in Numbers 21:9, and page 90 of this book.

40 Nachash, NHSh (ש = 300 + ח = 8 + נ = 50 = 358); Messiah, MShYH (ח = 8 + י = 10 + ש = 300 + מ = 40 = 358).

spirit of the Lord and their responsibilities as religious leaders. In one exchange, he recited a parable that served as a prophecy for the destruction that would come to the Temple and the city, and suggested that the status of Chosen People would be transferred to those who accepted the new teaching: "He will miserably destroy those wicked men, and will let out his vineyard unto other husbandmen.... The kingdom of God shall be taken from you, and given to a nation bringing forth the fruits thereof" (Matthew 21:41 and 43). The priests and Pharisees at the Temple wanted to arrest him but feared his popularity with the people. They plotted among themselves and reached out to the Herodians—members of the political party that supported the dynasty, despite the fact that the Herods were not native Jews but converts.

Later, Mark and Luke record a tender incident during the Temple teaching. Jesus observed several wealthy people making large donations to the shrine. A poor woman, by contrast, gave some pennies. He understood how precious her donation was because of her poverty, and gently explained her self-sacrifice to the disciples.[41]

Jesus on the Commandments

His discourses at the Temple included a series of answers to questions posed by the Pharisees and Sadducees. These were designed to either expose his radical political agenda or religious heresy so he could be arrested. But they all failed. In fact, Jesus summarized his entire teaching by quoting two verses of the Hebrew scripture.

> Then one of them, which was a lawyer, asked him a question, tempting him, and saying, "Master, which is the great commandment in the law?" Jesus said unto him, "Thou shalt love the LORD thy God with all thy heart, and with all thy soul, and with all thy mind.[42] This is the first and great commandment. And the second is like unto it, 'Thou shalt love thy neighbour as thyself.'[43] On these two commandments hang all the law and the prophets." (Matthew 22:36–40)

A PROPHECY ON THE TEMPLE

He then began a long denunciation of the corrupt religious hierarchy of the Jews that ended with these chilling words:

> O Jerusalem, Jerusalem, thou that killest the prophets, and stonest them which are sent unto thee, how often would I have gathered thy children together, even as a hen gathereth her chickens under her wings, and ye would not! Behold, your house is left unto you desolate. For I say unto you, "Ye shall not see me henceforth, till ye shall say, Blessed is he that cometh in the name of the Lord." (Matthew 23:37–39)

While walking away from the Temple, the disciples began to point out different buildings in the Temple complex, admiring its beauty. But Jesus said to them, "See ye not all these things? verily I say unto you, There shall not be left here one stone upon another, that shall not be thrown down" (Matthew 24:2).

---

41 Mark 12:41–44.

42 This is the *Shema* from Deuteronomy 6:4–5 (see page 97). Mark renders this as, "Hear, O Israel; The LORD our God is one LORD: And thou shalt love the LORD thy God with all thy heart, and with all thy soul, and with all thy mind, and with all thy strength" (Mark 12:29–30).

43 Leviticus 19:18.

Jesus and the disciples would have looked upon Herod's Temple when they stood on the Mount of Olives and gazed at the Temple Mount.

THE END TIMES

As the disciples sat with him on the Mount of Olives, gazing down on the Temple, they asked him about their future, the signs of his return, and the end of the age. Jesus spoke of the tribulation they would endure in his name and encouraged them to persevere, for "he that shall endure unto the end, the same shall be saved" (Matthew 24:13). He warned that great suffering was coming to the world. He added that when they saw the "Abomination of Desolation, spoken of by Daniel the prophet, stand in the holy place ..." (Matthew 24:15), it would be the sign that they should flee with all haste.[44] For the end of times would be upon them and the coming of the Son of Man. The timing of this apocalyptic event was known only to the Lord. Like the flood of Noah, most people would be caught unawares, engaged in their normal activities; while the chosen of Jesus would heed his summons because they would be watchful and awake.

44 See also Mark 13:14. The Abomination of Desolation is mentioned in the Book of Daniel in verses 9:27, 11:31, and 12:11

303

The Dinner in Bethany before the Passover

It was almost time for the Passover feast. Jesus explained that he would soon be arrested and crucified. The high priest of the Temple, Caiaphas, was conspiring with the chief priests and elders against him. In Bethany, Jesus sat at dinner with his disciples.[45] An unnamed woman came forth, carrying an alabaster jar filled with costly oil and anointed Jesus as he sat at the table. (In John, the woman performing the anointing is identified as Mary, sister of Lazarus and Martha.[46]) The disciples were critical. They complained she was wasting precious oil which could be sold and the proceeds used to feed the poor. But Jesus pointed out that she was actually preparing him for his burial, and that her

---

45 The Gospels of Matthew (26:6–13) and Mark (14:3–9) agree that this dinner took place two days before the Passover at the home of Simon the Leper. John (12:1–11) has it six days before the Passover at the home of Lazarus.

46 John 11:2. This is all rather confusing. Matthew, Mark, and John agree that this anointing took place in Bethany days before the Last Supper. In Matthew and Mark, the woman is mentioned as anointing the head of Jesus. In John, she washed the feet of Jesus with her hair. The anointing described by Luke (see pages 296–98) takes place in the Galilee region much earlier in the story. Luke's mysterious woman is the only one described as sinful, and she washes the feet of Jesus with both her hair and her tears. See notes 32 and 56.

Detail from The Last Supper, *by Leonardo Da Vinci, 1495–1498. Photo by Rusfuture.*

Last Supper. During the meal, Jesus performed the Eucharist ritual, or ceremony of Communion, with bread and wine—identifying the bread as his flesh given for them, and the wine as his blood poured out for the new covenant.

John recounts that during the supper, Jesus stood up and took off his outer robe and tied a towel around himself. He poured water into a basin and began to bathe the feet of his disciples and wipe them with the towel. He commanded them to follow his example.[49]

He knew that he had been betrayed. "The Son of man goeth as it is written of him: but woe unto that man by whom the Son of man is betrayed! it had been good for that man if he had not been born" (Matthew 26:24). Then Judas went to the priests and collected the thirty pieces of silver to betray his master. Luke writes that Satan entered into him.[50] In John, Jesus sent Judas on his way after bathing his feet with the others.[51]

After the meal, Jesus and the eleven disciples walked to the Mount of Olives and then down to the Garden of Gethsemane. He asked his three closest disciples—Peter, James, and John—to pray with him in this hour of peril. He walked on slightly ahead. When he returned, he found them asleep. This happened two more times as his isolation and suffering increased.

act would be long remembered.[47] (In the Gospel of John, the disciple who objected loudest was Judas, who was in charge of the finances of the group. John called Judas a thief and accused him of embezzlement.[48])

THE LAST SUPPER IN JERUSALEM

"Then came the day of Unleavened Bread, on which the Passover lamb had to be sacrificed" (Luke 22:7 NRSV). Jesus and the disciples went into Jerusalem to celebrate the Passover dinner, the ritual *sedar* that would become known as the

---

47 Matthew 26:6–13.

48 John 12:6.

---

49 The Rule of the Knights Templar required the Master of the Order to wash the feet of thirteen paupers on Maundy Thursday in commemoration of Christ's humility in washing the feet of his disciples. See *The Templars and the Assassins*, page 161. Maundy Thursday, the day before Good Friday, memorializes the Last Supper and the betrayal and arrest in the Garden.

50 Luke 22:3.

51 John 13:27.

The Agony in the Garden. *Jesus alone, confronting the imminent reality of his own death, prays, while his disciples have fallen asleep, by Andrea Mantegna, ca. 1460.*

THE BETRAYAL AND ARREST

Then Judas approached and identified Jesus with a kiss. Members of the Temple police started to arrest him. One of his supporters swung his sword and cut off the ear of a servant of the high priest. But Jesus told him to sheathe his sword, then he healed the injured man. He spoke:

"Thinkest thou that I cannot now pray to my Father, and he shall presently give me more than twelve legions of angels? But how then shall the scriptures be fulfilled, that thus it must be?" In that same hour said Jesus to the multitudes, "Are ye come out as against a thief with swords and staves for to take me? I sat daily with you teaching in the temple, and ye laid no hold on me." (Matthew 26:53–55)

THE INTERROGATIONS

Taken before the high priest Caiaphas, two false witnesses accused him of having said, "I am able to destroy the temple of God, and to build it in three days" (Matthew 26:61). In Mark, Jesus was asked directly by the priest, "Art thou the Christ, the Son of the Blessed?"

> And Jesus said, "I am: and ye shall see the Son of man sitting on the right hand of power, and coming in the clouds of heaven." Then the high priest rent his clothes, and saith, "What need we any further witnesses? Ye have heard the blasphemy: what think ye?" And they all condemned him to be guilty of death. (Mark 14:61–64)

Jesus was struck, spat upon, and slapped. The next day, he was taken before Pontius Pilate, the Roman governor of the region. (Judas meanwhile repented of his actions and hanged himself.) Pilate was reluctant to proceed against Jesus as he realized he was innocent and the priests were acting from jealousy. He offered to pardon him as part of the annual Passover pardoning ceremony. But the people—urged on by the corrupt Temple leadership—demanded Pilate pardon the notorious rebel Barabbas instead. He was identified as having committed a murder during a recent insurrection.[52]

Pilate ceremonially washed his hands of the affair, declaring himself innocent of the shedding of the blood of Jesus. The people shouted that his blood would be upon them and their children.[53] So Barabbas was released, and Jesus was flogged and handed over for crucifixion. The Roman soldiers dressed him in royal purple, made a crown of thorns, placed it on his head, and mocked him.

THE CRUCIFIXION

They took him to Golgotha (the Place of the Skull) and crucified him. They placed a sign over his head that read, "This is Jesus, the King of the Jews." Two thieves were crucified beside him and they derided him for claiming he could destroy and rebuild the Temple in three days.[54] The priests, scribes, and elders also taunted him. If he were the legitimate son of God, let him prove it by saving himself.

Jesus was crucified at nine o'clock in the morning. The soldiers cast lots for his garments as written by David in Psalms, "They part my garments among them, and cast lots upon my vesture" (Psalm 22:18). At noon, the sky darkened over all the land for three hours. Jesus cried out, "Father, into thy hands I commend my spirit"[55] (Luke 23:46). He was ridiculed again by those present, then breathed his last. "At that moment the curtain of the temple was torn in two, from top to bottom" (Matthew 27:51 NRSV). This refers to the tearing asunder of the curtain that separated the Holy of Holies from the Great Hall and reinforces the identification of Jesus with the Temple.

---

52 Mark 15:7.

53 Matthew 27:25.

54 Luke differs. He writes that one of the thieves chastised the other for mocking Jesus, saying they were being crucified for their crimes while Jesus was innocent. He asked Jesus to remember him in the kingdom and Jesus promised him a place in Paradise (Luke 23:39–43).

55 Matthew records the cry as "'Eli, Eli, lama sabachthani?' that is to say, 'My God, my God, why hast thou forsaken me'" (Matthew 27:46)? Mark agrees in 15:34. John has Jesus state simply, "It is finished" (John 19:30).

The Lamentation of Christ after he is taken down from the Cross,
by Giotto di Bondone, ca. 1305.

And the earth did quake, and the rocks rent; And the graves were opened; and many bodies of the saints which slept arose, And came out of the graves after his resurrection, and went into the holy city, and appeared unto many. Now when the centurion, and they that were with him, watching Jesus, saw the earthquake, and those things that were done, they feared greatly, saying, "Truly this was the Son of God." (Matthew 27:51–54)

THE RESURRECTION

A group of loyal women disciples who had served Jesus stood at a distance ready to help. Among them were Mary Magdalene,[56] his mother Mary, and Mary the mother of the dis-

---

56 See note 32. The names of the three women vary slightly in the three Gospels where they are identified, but Mary Magdalene is the constant in all. Luke does not mention the women by name. Earlier he writes that Mary Magdalene was healed of seven demons (Luke 8:2), as does Mark in 16:9.

*The Church of the Ascension on the Mount of Olives includes the Dome
of the Ascension from which Jesus is said to have risen to Heaven.
Photo by Steven Brooke.*

ciples James and John. Joseph of Arimathea went to Pilate to ask for Jesus' body, to which Pilate agreed. Joseph arranged for the body to be wrapped in a clean cloth and laid in a tomb. The chief priests and Pharisees approached Pilate and expressed their fear that Jesus' body would be secretly removed by those seeking to trick the credulous into believing he had in fact risen after three days. So Pilate allowed them to set a guard over the tomb.

In the end of the sabbath, as it began to dawn toward the first day of the week, came Mary Magdalene and the other

Mary to see the sepulchre. And, behold, there was a great earthquake: for the angel of the Lord descended from heaven, and came and rolled back the stone from the door, and sat upon it. His countenance was like lightning, and his raiment white as snow: And for fear of him the keepers did shake, and became as dead men. And the angel answered and said unto the women, "Fear not ye: for I know that ye seek Jesus, which was crucified. He is not here: for he is risen, as he said. Come, see the place where the Lord lay. And go quickly, and tell his disciples that he is risen from the dead; and, behold, he goeth before you into Galilee; there shall ye see him: lo, I have told you." And they departed quickly from the sepulchre with fear and great joy; and did run to bring his disciples word. (Matthew 28:1–8)

The priests bribed the soldiers to keep silent about what had happened. Mark writes that Jesus appeared first to Mary Magdalene.[57] In Luke, after the angels informed the women of his resurrection, he appeared to Cleophas and an unnamed disciple, but they were kept from recognizing him for a time. Then he came to the eleven disciples as they sat at a table in Galilee and upbraided them for their lack of faith. Luke continues that he interpreted Moses for them, and the Prophets, and all the scriptures that referred to his mission, that he opened their minds to the scripture.[58] He told them to go forth and preach the good news through all the world, swearing to remain with them always until the end of the age. He described the signs by which they would recognize those who had faith. By using his name, the faithful would cast out demons, speak in new tongues, handle snakes with their hands, drink poisons without danger, and heal the sick by the laying on of hands.[59]

So then after the Lord had spoken unto them, he was received up into heaven, and sat on the right hand of God. And they went forth, and preached everywhere, the Lord working with them, and confirming the word with signs following. (Mark 16:19–20)

And [the disciples] were continually in the temple, praising and blessing God. (Luke 24:53)

---

57 Mark 16:9. In John, Jesus also appeared first to Mary Magdalene (John 20:14–17). Matthew writes that Jesus appeared to Mary Magdalene and "the other Mary" mentioned above (Matthew 28:9). Luke explained that two angels appeared to Mary Magdalene and several other women and told them of his resurrection. The women then informed the other disciples who were initially skeptical (Luke 24:4–11).

58 Luke 24:27 and 45.

59 Mark 16:9–18.

Chapter Twenty-three

The New Jerusalem

And I saw no temple therein: for the Lord God Almighty and
the Lamb are the temple of it. (Revelation 21:22)

We have at last arrived at the end of this long biblical journey. It began in the Garden of Eden, as we walked with God—enjoying His presence in peace and harmony, an underlying sense of unity at the root of a natural state of being. We needed no rules, no curses, no promises, no threats. One action only was forbidden: the eating of the fruit of the Tree of the Knowledge of Good and Evil. Natural curiosity and the internal streak of independence with which our species has been endowed at its core—and the Serpent's promise that we should be as gods—won out over even this simple restriction.

As readers, we have since been subjected to the painful and sweeping history of the consequences of such behavior: from banishment out of the Garden, to the need to earn our sustenance with the sweat of our brows. We have endured slavery in Egypt and been forced to wander in the desert for forty years. We were given an ever-growing and rigid set of rules whose very oppressiveness caused endless rebellion. When we arrived at last in the Promised Land, we were attacked by countless raids and suffered military losses associated with such disobedience.

Ultimately, we were compelled to witness the destruction of the one real success we had achieved since being banished from the Garden. For the Temple of Solomon stood high and proud above the sacred city, a central focal point for all the world, symbolizing the intersection of divine and human. As the meeting ground of Heaven and Earth, its splendid opulence and exquisite workmanship hymned the return to Eden. Yet it too would be taken away, falling victim to the war between the demands of our inner natures and the responsibilities of three-dimensional incarnation. The Word made flesh is indeed limited by boundaries it does not experience in the world of the Spirit.

Too soon after that magnificent Temple had been completed, consecrated, and indwelt by the Lord of Israel, a devastating series of setbacks began to mount, one after the other, as we continued to violate His laws. We, who had once danced half-naked in ecstasy before the Ark of the Covenant with David, now sat trembling with Jeremiah in the cold and darkness of his dungeon. Finally, we were cast forth from the land of promise. We sat down and wept by the rivers of Babylon.

The eventual return never felt right. The rebuilt Temple was inadequate and our political power sorely diminished. Buffeted by fate and fortune, ever at the will of foreign rulers, we struggled against powerlessness and a sense of futility.

Then a light appeared. A leader emerged who embodied within himself the unity of God and Man. In fact he called himself at one moment the Son of Man, and at the next the Son of God. He spoke of a more natural unity between Creator and Created. He sought the spirit of the law within its letter and appeared to have been able to reach a compromise within himself that satisfied both his instinctual needs and the demands of the Heavenly Father in whose kingdom he strode. He demonstrated his acceptance of God's Will by successfully internalizing it as his own Will. He who allowed himself to be sacrificed in a painful and demeaning manner, remained ever aligned with his spiritual destiny even in the worst moments. His example embodied that promise given in Jeremiah of a New Covenant—when the law of God would be written in our hearts and flowing in our blood. Christians believe Jesus' self-sacrifice opened the way for the salvation of humanity. I, who vigorously reject the principle of vicarious atonement, appreciate and admire the example he provided.

Now we shall be given new details of the promise made so long ago by our true Creator—that Great Mystery which placed within us even the seeds of our disobedience when He brought forth Heaven and Earth from the Void of Eternity.

Let There Be Light

We see a manifestation of that Light in the words of the penultimate chapter of the Book of Revelation. This mysterious and controversial text is filled with images that have inspired, confused, and terrified innumerable people for two thousand years and counting. Written in the first century by one who identified himself as John, he may or may not have been the author of the fourth Gospel. He was intimately familiar with the scriptures, the Temple, and Jerusalem. Composed while he was in exile on the small island of Patmos in the Aegean Sea, the Book of Revelation records a series of visions so powerful they established the broad term "apocalyptic" for an entire class of spiritual literature. Derived from the root word apocalypse ("disclosure"), such writings are characterized by a sense of intensity and drama with themes that include great wars between the forces of Good and Evil aligned with magical beings of enormous power. Such visionary literature speaks of supreme horrors, unimaginable loss, untold destruction, along with great victory, infinite beauty, and at last, perhaps, redemption—all wrapped in the impenetrable shroud of mystery.

John's vision of the New Jerusalem, however, is simple, direct, eloquent, and inspiring. It is beautifully written and translated. His uninterrupted words from chapter 21 of the Book of Revelation are the perfect conclusion to the story of the Temple in the Bible. The physical Temple will become the spiritual Temple.

Saint John on the island of Patmos, ca. 1416

CHAPTER 21 OF THE BOOK OF REVELATION

[1]And I saw a new heaven and a new earth: for the first heaven and the first earth were passed away; and there was no more sea. [2]And I John saw the holy city, new Jerusalem, coming down from God out of heaven, prepared as a bride adorned for her husband. [3]And I heard a great voice out of heaven saying,

Behold, the tabernacle of God is with men, and he will dwell with them, and they shall be his people, and God himself shall be with them, and be their God. [4]And God shall wipe away all tears from their eyes; and there shall be no more death, neither sorrow, nor crying, neither shall there be any more pain: for the former things are passed away.

[5]And he that sat upon the throne said, "Behold, I make all things new." And he said unto me, "Write: for these words are true and faithful." [6]And he said unto me,

It is done. I am Alpha and Omega, the beginning and the end. I will give unto him that is athirst of the fountain of the water of life freely. ⁷He that overcometh shall inherit all things; and I will be his God, and he shall be my son. ⁸But the fearful, and unbelieving, and the abominable, and murderers, and whoremongers, and sorcerers, and idolaters, and all liars, shall have their part in the lake which burneth with fire and brimstone: which is the second death.

⁹And there came unto me one of the seven angels which had the seven vials full of the seven last plagues, and talked with me, saying, "Come hither, I will shew thee the bride, the Lamb's wife."

¹⁰And he carried me away in the spirit to a great and high mountain, and shewed me that great city, the holy Jerusalem, descending out of heaven from God, ¹¹Having the glory of God: and her light was like unto a stone most precious, even like a jasper stone, clear as crystal; ¹²And had a wall great and high, and had twelve gates, and at the gates twelve angels, and names written thereon, which are the names of the twelve tribes of the children of Israel: ¹³On the east three gates; on the north three gates; on the south three gates; and on the west three gates.

¹⁴And the wall of the city had twelve foundations, and in them the names of the twelve apostles of the Lamb.

¹⁵And he that talked with me had a golden reed to measure the city, and the gates thereof, and the wall thereof. ¹⁶And the city lieth foursquare, and the length is as large as the breadth: and he measured the city with the reed, twelve thousand furlongs. The length and the breadth and the height of it are equal. ¹⁷And he measured the wall thereof, an hundred and forty and four cubits, according to the measure of a man, that is, of the angel.

¹⁸And the building of the wall of it was of jasper: and the city was pure gold, like unto clear glass. ¹⁹And the foundations of the wall of the city were garnished with all manner of precious stones. The first foundation was jasper; the second, sapphire; the third, a chalcedony; the fourth, an emerald; ²⁰The fifth, sardonyx; the sixth, sardius; the seventh, chrysolite; the eighth, beryl; the ninth, a topaz; the tenth, a chrysoprasus; the eleventh, a jacinth; the twelfth, an amethyst. ²¹And the twelve gates were twelve pearls; every several gate was of one pearl: and the street of the city was pure gold, as it were transparent glass.

²²And I saw no temple therein: for the Lord God Almighty and the Lamb are the temple of it. ²³And the city had no need of the sun, neither of the moon, to shine in it: for the glory of God did lighten it, and the Lamb is the light thereof.

²⁴And the nations of them which are saved shall walk in the light of it: and the kings of the earth do bring their glory and honour into it. ²⁵And the gates of it shall not be shut at all by day: for there shall be no night there.

²⁶And they shall bring the glory and honour of the nations into it. ²⁷And there shall in no wise enter into it any thing that defileth, neither whatsoever worketh abomination, or maketh a lie: but they which are written in the Lamb's book of life.

OPPOSITE: *This powerful etching by Gustave Doré is the finest image of the visit of Saint John and the Angel to the Mount of Olives that they might overlook the New Jerusalem. 1865.*

This Masonic Apron depicts the Temple of Solomon framed between the Masonic compasses and the Pillars of Jachin and Boaz. Various tools of the Craft, discussed on pages 332–34, are shown in the foreground. Eighteenth century.

PART EIGHT

THE TEMPLE IN THE ESOTERIC TRADITION

The Templar Seal shows two knights riding on one horse illustrating the monastic Vow of Poverty taken by the members of the Order. Twelfth century.

Chapter Twenty-four

The Knights of the Temple

The Knights Templar have become a primary component in the myths of nearly all Western esoteric secret societies, many of whom claim descent from the medieval Order. There are three critical and indisputable historical facts in the story of the Templars that have helped to make them so attractive to people with an interest in the occult. The first is that the Order was intimately related to the Temple of Solomon since the day of its founding. The second is that the Knights Templar were a spiritual brotherhood of holy warriors. The third is that the Templar story is laced with heresy. These three themes more than any other offer a delicious opportunity for myth making, imagination, and speculation based on both the historical reality of the Templars and the individual psychology of the investigator.

To the historical Knight Templar, however, the meaning and reality of the Order would have been considerably different. His concerns were undobtedly far more mundane and immediate: desert heat and blinding sunshine; unquenchable thirst; the irritation of endless quantities of sand rubbing against leather, metal and skin; fear as the arrows of the enemy rained from the sky and the crush of horses, swords, and lances enveloped his position—the air filled with the screams of battle; his loneliness for home and the yearning for the familiar that soldiers have ever endured in alien and hostile cultures.

The Crusades

The Crusades were launched in 1095 after the Muslim threat to Constantinople led the Byzantine emperor Alexius Comnenus to send representatives begging the help of the Roman pope. The Catholic Church had been divided between Eastern and Western churches since the fourth century, when the Roman emperor Constantine moved his capital to the ancient city of Byzantium—later Constantinople and later still Istanbul—after declaring Christianity the official religion of Rome. The political division of the Empire between Rome and Constantinople had lasting religious consequences. Escalating conflicts between the Roman Catholic pope and the Eastern Orthodox patriarch ultimately led each to excommunicate the other in the late ninth century. While this particular breakdown was healed soon after the death of both leaders, the Great Schism of 1054 renewed the crisis. The pope and patriarch once again cut each other off from the true faith.

Emperor Alexius perceived his kingdom to be in mortal peril from the onslaught of the Muslim enemy. Nothing short of the need to survive would have allowed him to overcome the intensity of resentment between the rival branches of Christianity.

Like any important and transformative event in history, the Crusades had a medley of complex causes. However, in my opinion, self defense was the most important. The armies of Islam had been coming after Europe for three hundred years. By the mid-seventh century, Islam had conquered the Arabian Peninsula and continued through the Mideast, taking Antioch in 636 and Jerusalem in 638. In Egypt, Alexandria fell in 641. The subsequent centuries of Arab/European miltary activity are summarized in the accompanying table. The defeat of the armies of the Byzantine Empire, the Eastern Roman Empire, by the Seljuk Turks in 1071 at the Battle of Manzikert severely weakened Christendom. When Alexius Comnenus ascended the Byzantine throne in 1081, he faced a dire situation. The economy was in a shambles from the debts of war and the tribute demanded by the Seljuks; civil unrest and political intrigue plagued the country; and some 30,000 square miles of territory had been surrendered.

Pope Urban II responded to the Byzantine plea for help and worked tirelessly to encourage European support for military action against the Muslim invaders. The Crusades began in 1095, the start of a two-hundred-year effort whose consequences continue to this day. In 1099, the Crusaders took Jerusalem. Contemporary accounts describe the streets as running with blood from the wrath of the Christian armies against the Muslims and Jews who inhabited the holy city. The leader of the army that took Jerusalem was Godfrey de Bouillon.

MUSLIM INVASIONS OF EUROPE
652–1071

638	Jerusalem conquered by Caliph Omar.
652	Cyprus conquered by Arab naval forces in the Mediterranean.
655	Rhodes conquered.
711	Spain conquered.
732	Arab army defeated by Charles Martel, the Hammer, as they attempt to cross the Pyrhenees into France.
735	Second Arab invasion of France captures Arles and Avignon. They remained in the Lanquedoc for forty years.
759	Pepin the Short expels Muslims from France.
809	Corsica conquered.
810	Sardinia conquered.
823	Crete conquered.
827	Sicily conquered. By 970, there were some three hundred mosques in Sicily.
831	Palermo conquered.
843	Messina conquered.
870	Malta conquered.
878	Syracuse conquered.
846	Eleven hundred Muslims marched on Rome and plundered the churches of St. Peter and St. Paul.
849	Pope Leo IV turned back a second Muslim invasion of Italy.
879	Rome begins paying an annual tribute to Arabs for a non-aggression pact.
1010	Fatimid caliph, al-Hakim, destroyed the Church of the Holy Sepulcher, arousing great emotion in Europe.
1071	Byzantine army defeated by the Seljuk Turks at the Battle of Manzikert.
1095	First Crusade launched.
1099	Crusaders take Jerusalem.

The entrance to the al-Aqsa Mosque showing the vaulted arches of Crusader architecture.
The Crusaders mistakenly believed it to be the Temple described in the New Testament.
It served as the administrative palace of the Crusader kings until 1128 when they
moved to the Citadel, and it was the headquarters of the Knights Templar
from 1118 or 1119 until the fall of Jerusalem to Saladin in 1187.

He deferred from accepting the title of King of Jerusalem, reserving that for Jesus Christ, and called himself the Protector of the city and the region. He did establish his headquarters on the Temple Mount, which he knew from the Bible to be the Second Temple, the scene of so many of the events in the life of the Savior. He established his palace in the al-Aqsa Mosque, which the Crusaders believed was the Temple of Solomon. They referred to the Dome of the Rock as the Temple of the Lord and placed a large Crucifix above it.

Godfrey's brother succeeded him in 1100 and had no scruples about calling himself Baldwin I, king of Jerusalem, the Crusader capital of the Holy Land. The weakness of the Crusader state however was painfully evident. While the European armies controlled the Mediterranean coastal cities, being able to resupply and reinforce their troops from the sea, their hegemony in the interior was far less secure. As later events would demonstrate, Jerusalem was a priority for its symbolic importance rather than its tactical soundness. Surrounded by hostile Muslim armies and the many brigands who lined the road from Jaffa to Jerusalem, the Crusader's grip on Jerusalem was tenuous at best.

On the other hand, the launching of the Crusades had much religious and ideological stimulation from the rage fanned by the pope against the travesty of the birthplace of Jesus being controlled by the Infidel. Israel had long been a magnet for religious pilgrims, and the ostensible victory of the First Crusade encouraged an influx of religious visitors from Europe. In 1118, Baldwin I died and was succeeded by his cousin, who called himself Baldwin II. King Baldwin II and the Patriarch of Jerusalem, Warmund of Picquigny, were acutely aware of the limitations and vulnerability of the city. They needed to offer both economic incentives to encourage people to settle there and physical protection for religious tourists and other visitors from Europe.

ENTER THE KNIGHTS TEMPLAR

A group of knights led by Hughes de Payens helped provide an answer. These men were moving in the direction of the spiritual life. Hughes was a widower, fifty years old, who had served during the First Crusade and remained in the region since that campaign. In 1118 or 1119, he approached Patriarch Warmund with the idea that he and some fellow knights take vows of holy obedience, poverty, and chastity, becoming religious mendicants. Either Hughes offered or Warmund suggested that they use their martial skills to protect pilgrims who were seeking spiritual inspiration and solace while visiting the Holy Land. The timing was crucial: recently a massacre of some three hundred pilgrims by Arab brigands had scandalized and caused great fear among Christians throughout Europe and the Holy Land.

Hughes and his men (either nine knights, or thirty as another near-contemporary account relates) agreed to accept this task. They were provided with lodging at the Temple of Solomon (the al-Aqsa Mosque) and began their work. They were called Knights Templar, or Poor Knights of the Temple of Solomon, the Poor Fellow Soldiers of Jesus Christ. Originally little is known about their activities. They lived

off the donations of the faithful. The Templar seal (see page 318) shows two knights sharing one horse in testament to their poverty. In time, as nobles would come to visit the region and become aware of this small contingent of knights—whose weapons were dedicated to the service of God rather than that of kings or personal honor—their fame would spread.

They soon came to the attention of the French abbot Bernard of Clairvaux (later canonized). Bernard had grown up with a profound interest in becoming a knight and was fascinated by martial culture. However ill health prevented him from realizing this ambition. He underwent a profound series of religious experiences, taking monastic vows and joining the Cistercian order in 1112. He was gifted with managerial and administrative skills and helped the Cistercians to grow from a relatively insignificant order when he joined to a powerful monastic brotherhood.[1] He also developed the reputation for extreme piety and wisdom and became an influential leader in Europe.

In 1126, Bernard's uncle André de Montbard, one of the original Knights of the Temple, traveled to Europe with letters from Patriarch Warmund and King Baldwin II seeking Bernard's support to present the Knights Templar with a Rule of Conduct (the spiritual instructions by which they should live), and to have them recognized as an official monastic order within the Catholic Church. Bernard was captivated by the idea of the warrior/monk, the righteous man of God carrying the weapons of spiritual warfare and defending the Holy Kingdom of the Lord. He had little trouble tracing this concept back from Moses to Joshua to King David, all of whom conducted vast military

---

1 The Cistercians grew from seven monasteries in 1118 to 328 by 1152.

campaigns and provided religious leadership for God's People.

Bernard's prestige and advocacy thrust the ideal of the Holy Warrior into European consciousness. The Templars were recognized as an official order of the Catholic Church at the Council of Troyes, convened in 1128. They were awarded their distinctive dress, a plain white robe to which was affixed the red cross of martyrdom in 1147. Bernard indeed provided a rule of conduct based on the Benedictine rule but updated for the needs of a fighting force. In 1135, he wrote an inspiring letter that was widely publicized, *Liber ad milites Templi: De laude novae militae* ("The Book of the Knights of the Temple: In Praise of the New Knighthood"[2]). This letter fanned the flames of interest in the Templar cause to a conflagration. Nobles throughout Europe either joined the Order or contributed financially to its well-being. From this point on the Templars became an increasingly growing fixture of medieval life, expanding to become a major fighting force of the Crusader period.

They were deeply involved in building a supply network throughout Europe for practical survival and were involved in farming, ship building, horse raising, castle construction, weapons manufacture, and accounting. They eventually developed their own clergy and were rewarded with papal privileges that extended far into the realm of politics and warfare. They became a force of their own right, the pope's private army, free of external allegiance to European kings and the Palestinian baronage. The Order grew extremely wealthy as well, functioning ultimately as bankers for those who traveled the dangerous route from Europe to the Holy Land and sought to protect their wealth by depositing it in trust in European Templar

The Templar dress and insignia accurately re-created by artist Richard Scollins.

strongholds. The Templars thus developed the modern practice of checking accounts. A pilgrim would place funds in Europe and receive a signed certificate of deposit. As he traveled and when he arrived in the Holy Land, he could draw cash from Templar strongholds to meet his needs. On return to Europe, funds could be reclaimed less the amount taken during travel. Thus the Templars became international bankers, fluent with various languages, currencies, and exchange rates. In time, the Templar order accumulated vast holdings of land in Europe donated by wealthy aristocrats who sought the spiritual benefits of charitable giving.

---

2 For a modern translation by Lisa Coffin, see *The Templars and the Assassins,* pages 277–86.

The Knights Templar also received land grants in the Holy Land to meet the defensive needs of the various territories they would control. Local barons began to donate castles and territories for more practical reasons as they faced the enormous costs of castle defense. They learned it was cheaper to give excess property to a military order more capable of maintaining it. The Templars became expert in castle construction, fortification, and restoration. They learned how to defend against Muslim military engineers who were able to undermine castle integrity by digging beneath the walls.

THE DESTRUCTION OF THE ORDER

Over the two centuries of their existence (1118–1312), the Templars had become such a powerful force that they attracted the malignant attention of the French King Philip IV, who was deeply in debt and sought to grasp the political and financial advantages of a takeover of the Order. He trumped up a series of charges of the vilest of heresies against these men, including, among others, the following accusations: that the Templars were guilty of denying Christ and trampling and/or spitting upon the Crucifix at their initiation; teaching that Jesus was a false prophet who had not died on the Cross; worshipping a cat and/or a hideous pagan idol; engaging in treasonous alliance with the Muslims; denying the sacraments; insisting on homosexual behavior between members and practicing a series of obscene kisses during their ceremonies. Philip sent his henchmen to round up and arrest some five thousand members of the Order throughout France on Friday, October 13, 1307.

Templars were systematically interrogated, tortured, and killed during the next seven years by the combined forces of many European monarchs acting under direct orders from Philip's puppet, Pope Clement V. Their property and wealth were confiscated by state and church. The Order was officially disbanded by the pope in 1312.

The last Grand Master of the Order, Jacques de Molay, having endured seven years of trial and torture, was burnt at the stake on March 18, 1314, along with Geoffroi de Charney another high-ranking officer of the Temple. On a small island in the Seine, loudly proclaiming their innocence, the two men joined the ranks of those holy martyrs across the millennia who chose death rather than blaspheme the Truth. De Molay uttered a curse against the French King and the Pope, and both were dead within eight months.

VARIOUS TEMPLAR THEORIES

What might be called a cottage industry has grown up around the idea that the original Knights Templar made a startling and important discovery of some kind in the earliest years of the Order's existence. Most of the speculation attaches to the decade between their founding and 1128—when they came to the attention of Saint Bernard and lost whatever early anonymity they may have enjoyed. The theory is that the earliest members of the Order conducted intensive archaeological excavations beneath what they believed to be the Temple of Solomon: either the al-Aqsa Mosque, the Dome of the Rock, or both.

Those who suppose the Templars discovered a treasure during their explorations differ as to what they may have found. Some assert the Templars discovered the Ark of the Covenant hidden by Jeremiah. (Many traditions reckon that the Ark was secreted below the Foundation Stone beneath the Well of Souls.) Other schools hold that the Templars found the Holy Grail— the Cup that collected Christ's blood during the

Crucifixion—and/or the Lance or Spear of Destiny that pierced the Savior's side. It has been suggested these sacred relics were the magical source of Templar power and prominence. Some of the highest ranking Nazi leaders were firm believers in this concept.

Certain proponents of the hidden treasure theory—on whom Dan Brown's *The DaVinci Code* draws heavily—believe the Templars found secret documents describing a hidden history of the life of Jesus. They postulate the records proved that Jesus and Mary Magdalene were married and had children and that Jesus survived the Crucifixion and served as a Master of Wisdom for many more years. Some even attach a sexual teaching to this material and affirm this gave rise to later charges of heresy made against the Templars. Certain proponents of this view suppose the Order blackmailed the Church into extending the privileges and autonomy with which the Templars were imbued by successive popes in return for their silence.

On an even more mundane level than blackmail is the notion that the Templars discovered a literal treasure of gold, a portion of the fabulous wealth of Solomon's Temple mentioned throughout these pages. While we have seen that the Temple treasure was often taken by force or squandered by excess, there are theories that suggest enough was left behind to fuel the vast climb to wealth so long associated with the Order.

Regarding the charges of heresy made against the Order, various writers have speculated that the Templars really were a group of heretics and devil worshippers who were found out by the French king and duly reported and disciplined by the pope. They note that the knights and sergeants initially confessed, including some of the Order's highest leaders, even initially Jacques de Molay himself. Such writers point to the Templar acquisition of wealth and the corrupting influence of power as proof of the Order's heretical ways, given the Templar vows of charity and poverty. The similarity between the charges leveled against the Templars and the antinomian practices ascribed to dualist/gnostic and tantric sects has been observed. In contrast is the view that the Templars were innocent of all charges and martyred to the cupidity and lust for power of European political leaders. The evidence for this is the sanctity of the Order's founding and the continued support of the Church. Despite normal human character flaws, the Templars as a whole were in fact obedient servants of their faith and accusations of heresy have blasphemed their purity. Esoteric thinkers assert that the Templars were great spiritual luminaries who lit the heavens of the Middle Ages with an initiated Gnostic radiance that blossomed into the occult renaissance that has continued ever since. Finally, there are the academics who dismiss the whole idea of either heresy or spiritual purity, viewing the Templars as a medieval phenomena, an interesting curiosity, which can shed light on the period, is well worth studying, but has little influence in the world of today.

* * * *

I suggest that the early Templar knights were quite busy building their living quarters in the al-Aqsa Mosque. They undoubtedly spent a great deal of time on their primary mission—that of offering protective services in the Holy Land. While they were already trained and experienced warriors, they would have been involved in acquiring weapons and drilling in individual and small group combat tactics, rather than the more formal military tactics they had been able to employ while among the larger Crusader armies. They would need to establish regimens of patrolling, develop communication protocols, and work out scheduling of visiting travelers. Creating an intelligence network would have necessitated developing assets among Europeans and sympathetic indigenes, including Muslims, along the dangerous pilgrim route from Jaffa to Jerusalem. There would be supply considerations to be worked out, and discussions and negotiations with King Baldwin II to further their mission by acquiring food, maintaining horses, and the myriad of other requirements of a military force.

I think the fabulous wealth ascribed to the Templars is an exaggeration based on the vast amount of money that did indeed pass through their hands. But I look at the enormous expenses associated with their conducting a two-hundred-year military campaign and am amazed they were able to so skillfully finance such efforts. Between supplying soldiers with food, clothing, shelter, weapons, transportation, and medical care, there would have been unbelievable costs. Add to that the expense of castle construction and restoration, maintenance of the vast number of horses, and caring for and feeding the extensive support personnel who outnumbered the knights by at least ten times. There were costs associated with ransom, bribery, tribute, and of course loans to kings and nobles that were often not repaid, let alone treasure seized by the enemy. The mind boggles at the extent of the operation they ran: their supply network of farms, granaries, and mills; their accounting departments charged with recording and distinguishing between donations to the Order and the loans, deposits, and other financial services they offered. All these expenses must have drained their legendary wealth only too well.

I suggest the fabled Templar treasure is contained within the heresy of which they were accused. Imagine these fledgling warrior/

monks experimenting with the monastic practices their newly acquired religious roles had brought them. They would have first sought religious guidance from Patriarch Warmund. It is quite likely the awakened spiritual aspirations of at least some of the knights encouraged them to reach beyond even their own religion, to seek understanding of the spiritual life from people of other faiths with whom they would have been in regular contact. The Holy Land was a crossroads for culture and commerce. It provided opportunities for interaction with Hindus and Buddhists from India; Zoroastrians from Persia; Egyptian, Jewish, and Christian Gnostics; and Qabalists, anchorites, and others who pursued beliefs and practices far wider than whatever the knights may have encountered in medieval Europe. There is especially a considerable historical record of contacts between the Templars and the Syrian Assassins. These heretical Muslims practiced a Sufi/Gnostic tradition that took them far afield of orthodox Islam. Their particular organization and goals were similar to the Templars, blending militancy and religion.[3]

It is likely that an inner corps of more spiritually aware Templars developed over time within the Order. This inner corps would have learned and disseminated a wide variety of Gnostic doctrines and practices among themselves. Yet, they would have been forced to observe the utmost secrecy—as other members of the Order would have been far less educated and broad-minded. These others would be uninterested in such "nonsense," let alone prepared to countenance religious treason. My screenplay *Divine Warriors: The Birth of Heresy* posits an inner order of warrior/adepts devel-

---

3 For more on their beliefs and interaction, see *The Templars and the Assassins: The Militia of Heaven* and *An Illustrated History of the Knights Templar.*

oping from contact with Assassin/Sufi and Gnostic spirituality. It is based on the reductionist principles of Occam's Razor, historical facts, and active imagination.

* * * *

Whatever one believes the Templar treasure to have been, the Order has become an inseparable part of the Western Mystery Tradition. Esoteric knowledge taught by surviving Templars is widely held to have influenced the development of the Grail literature, the Hermetic resurgence during the Renaissance, the Rosicrucian movement that flourished in the seventeenth century, and most important, the founding of Freemasonry.

While the fury of King Philip IV's hatred allowed for few French Templars to escape his well-crafted net, most of those arrested survived their imprisonment. By contrast, English Templars had a sympathetic monarch and at least six months warning of the papal arrest decrees. A contingent of fugitive English Templars could easily have escaped to Scotland. They would have been welcomed as allies by King Robert the Bruce in his efforts to declare independence from England. The mysteries of the Battle of Bannockburn on June 24, 1314, just three months after the execution of the Templar Grand Master Jacques de Molay, force us consider the possibility of Templar involvement. To begin with, Robert's excommunication in 1306 placed him well outside the range of papal authority. How was the skilled English army defeated at the hands of the much smaller Scottish force? Is the legend of a contingent of mounted reinforcements who turned the tide of the battle historically accurate? We do know that Scotland soon after played a major role in

the earliest development of Freemasonry. Templars in Spain, Germany, Italy and other European sections of the Order were also alerted by what happened in France. While the Order was disbanded, many members suffered techniques of torture whose descriptions would turn the reader's stomach, and hundreds more died in the flames of infamy, most Templars lived to see another day.

So what did survivors do? Some were allowed to join other Orders. Others were permitted to live out their lives on property formerly owned by the Templars. Others still must have quietly returned to civilian life or become monks or anchorites living in seclusion and contemplation. On the assumption that an infinitely small number of the knights actually were the spiritual luminaries legend has insisted they were—and common sense indicates they well may have been—I believe they would have spread themselves throughout Europe and quietly continued to teach and practice the secret knowledge that had been accumulated within their elite subgroup for two hundred years. This would clearly involve principles of meditation, visualization, ritual, and the other tools of spiritual development that circulated so widely in the Middle East. The special significance of sacred architecture, particularly centered on the Temple of Solomon, would be a self-evident aspect of this secret tradition. Do we have proof? Of course not. The hard lessons learned by the fires in which their fellow warriors burned had established beyond doubt the necessity for caution about behavior or beliefs that would arouse the attention of bigots whose political and religious power were indisputable. Yet this knowledge was passed on and survives in many esoteric traditons, the best known of which is Freemasonry.

Chapter Twenty-five

The Freemasons and the Temple

Freemasonry may be considered the crown jewel of the esoteric tradition. Its teachings have influenced untold numbers of people in all walks of life. Its ideals triumphed so profoundly in the political realm, especially during the eighteenth century, that Freemasons played an integral role in the American Revolution and the founding of the American Republic.

While it is impossible to find a consensus on the historical origin of Freemasonry, we do know that from the twelfth through the sixteenth centuries, an ambitious series of construction projects of cathedral, castle, and public building was undertaken throughout Europe. Well over two hundred examples survive today in some twenty-five countries. The overwhelming majority are churches. The work was performed by a unique group of people—the Stonemasons and Architects of the Gothic style. These skilled craftsmen, geometricians, and designers formed a class of medieval worker outside the restrictions of the feudal system. They were extended the right to travel to various worksites as required. They were considered free of any town or estate. They were known as Freemasons.

Operative Masons were allowed to elect their own officers and establish and enforce guild practices and standards; construct and occupy their own worksite living quarters often in isolated areas for long periods of time; and organize themselves to create charitable, health, and death-benefit programs. Concerns for safety and efficiency would require them to find ways to recognize and impart various levels of technical skill among strangers, even those of different languages. Errors made by a Mason could result in the collapse of a building. They needed to protect workers during construction and to ensure the safety of those for whom they built. They had to be able to identify a stranger's ability and training to assign his rate of pay and degree of responsibility. It was essential to be able to detect fraudulent claims by those who sought to trick their way into positions for which they were unqualified. Developing signs of recognition—including secret handshakes, passwords, and ritualized answers to seemingly innocent questions—was an excellent practical means of safeguarding knowledge and protecting against deceit. Freemasons developed the lodge system to properly transfer knowledge from Master to Apprentice, to test one another in their various levels of competence, and to meet their social needs while traveling and living far from home.

EARLY FREEMASONRY

In the annals of Freemasonry is a collection of some one hundred documents of English origin, known as the "Old Charges," the oldest of which dates back to 1390, while the latest extends through the first quarter of the eighteenth century. The Old Charges present the traditional history, legends, and rules of Freemasonry and are believed to have served as constitutions for the old Operative lodges. The best known is that compiled by Dr. James Anderson and published in 1723, known popularly as "Anderson's Constitutions."[4] Authorized by the British Grand Lodge, founded just six years earlier, *The Constitutions* presents a mythical history of Freemasonry that—as this book does—places the first Temple in the Garden of Eden. Here God infused the knowledge of Geometry into the hearts of His human offspring. After the Fall such knowledge developed into the Mechanical Arts and specifically Architecture. Adam and his sons formed the first Freemasonic Lodge in which Adam taught the principles of Architecture, the knowledge of which allowed humankind to escape the beastly fate of living in caves, arbors, tree branches, and mud huts. Anderson's legendary account identifies Noah and his three sons as the "four Grand Officers [from whom] the whole present Race of Mankind are descended."[5]

As the Fraternity continued its construction activity, it made the error of overreach in building the Tower of Babel. Suitably chastened, Masons spread throughout the world, using their talents in the making of even Pagan Temples such as those erected to Baal. They developed signs and tokens by which they could recognize each other despite the confusion of tongues that had developed among them. They built the Pyramids in Egypt, the great Labyrinths, Palaces and Temples of the Greeks, spreading throughout Europe, the Americas, Chaldea, Asia, China, and Japan.

Abram conveyed the knowledge to the Canaanites who honored him as their prince. His great grandson Joseph became Grand Master of the Egyptian Masons and constructed the royal granaries and store houses by which Egypt and the surrounding territories survived the great seven-year famine.

Moses however excelled all the Grand Masters who had preceded him, building the Tabernacle in which resided the Holy Ark, "the Symbole of God's Presence, which, though not of Stone or Brick, was framed by Geometry, a most beautiful Piece of true symmetrical Architecture, according to the Pattern that God discover'd to Moses on Mount Sinai, and it was afterwards the Model of Solomon's Temple."[6] Moses convened the Grand Lodge at the Tabernacle during the Passover Week and gave them the charges and regulations passed down since by Oral Tradition.

The subsequent history of the Jews continued with Joshua, who set the Tabernacle at Shiloh. When the Jews fell into servitude through their sins, the Judges revived the Mosaic Laws. Despite the exceptional skill of the Phoenicians and Canaanites in sacred Architecture with Stone, the Tabernacle at Shiloh exceeded all the works of all nations in its Wisdom and Beauty, if not its Strength and Dimensions. Still, great

---

4 Anderson's 1723 edition was reprinted in Philadelphia by Benjamin Franklin in 1734. Though scoffed at by modern Masonic scholars as a collection of fabulous legends of Freemasonry, it is the first major publication officially authorized by the founding brothers.

5 James Anderson D.D., *The New Book of Constitutions of the Antient and Honourable Fraternity of Free and Accepted Masons,* page 4.

6 Anderson, page 9.

Temples were also built in Troy, Libya, Tyre, and Gaza.

But of all the magnificent structures of antiquity, none was comparable to the Temple in Jerusalem, "built by that wisest mere Man and most glorious King of Israel, Solomon … the Prince of Peace and Architecture, the Grand Master Mason of his Day, who performed all by divine Direction, and without the Noise of Tools …"[7]

BUILDING THE TEMPLE OF SOLOMON

Freemasonry is inextricably bound to the Temple of Solomon. In 1420, the Cooke Manuscript attributed the founding of Freemasonry to King David and Solomon who charged members of the order to build the Temple to the Lord. The scriptural account presented in the books of Kings and Chronicles mentions Hiram Abiff as the skilled craftsman sent by King Hiram of Tyre to construct the brass implements for the Temple. In 2 Chronicles 2:7, Hiram is further described as a man "cunning to work in gold, and in silver, and in brass, and in iron, and in purple, and crimson, and blue …" In a long footnote on Hiram Abiff, Anderson's *Constitutions* points out that in 1 Kings 7:14, Hiram Abiff is described as "a widow's son of the tribe of Napthali, and his father was a man of Tyre." Thus Hiram was Jewish because of the law of matrilineal descent. Anderson further points out that the mention of Hiram's father as "a man of Tyre," may refer to his domicile rather than non-Jewish heritage.[8]

Freemasons add a legendary history of Hiram Abiff to the brief scriptural accounts of Kings and Chronicles. Solomon, King Hiram of Tyre, and Hiram Abiff were said to be the three Grand Masters of the Lodge of Jerusalem. The renowned twentieth century occultist Manly P. Hall writes that Hiram Abiff served as the Deputy Grand Master in Solomon's absence, and the Senior Grand Warden in his presence.[9] Hiram, as the Master of the Builders, divided his workmen into three groups based on their level of skill. He termed the entry level workers Entered Apprentices, the second level with greater ability and knowledge as Fellow Craftsmen, and the most highly skilled as Master Masons. To each group, he gave certain secret signs and passwords. However, three evil-minded Fellow Craftsmen were angry and jealous at the division, resenting that they were not entitled to the respect and more generous wages they could enjoy as Master Masons. Rather than work to develop the level of education and skill needed to qualify for more advanced status, they developed an insidious plot.

They knew that it was Hiram Abiff's custom to enter the unfinished Holy of Holies at noon each day to pray to the God of Creation. They plotted among themselves, deciding to wait at the three gates of the Temple to accost Hiram and demand the Master Mason's Word by force. When Hiram had finished his prayers, he rose to leave by the south gate where he was confronted by one of the armed ruffians and threatened with the twenty-four inch Ruler. He refused to divulge the Word and was struck in the throat. The wounded Master ran to the west where the second ruffian, armed with the Square, demanded the Word. Hiram again refused and was struck in the breast. He staggered to the east gate where he was accosted by the third ruffian who again demanded the communication of the Word. Bleeding from

---

7 Anderson, page 11.

8 Anderson page 12. In 2 Chronicles 2:14, Hiram Abiff is described as a son of a woman of tribe of Dan, likewise Jewish, whether his father was of pagan birth or a Jewish man living in Tyre.

---

9 Manly P. Hall, *The Secret Teachings of All Ages*, page lxxvii.

his wounds, the Master again refused and was struck between the eyes with the Mallet. He fell dead to the ground. The murderers buried him on Mount Moriah and placed a sprig of acacia wood on his grave. They attempted to flee but were captured, admitted their guilt, and were executed for their crime. King Solomon sent out several groups of three men each to seek after the Master's body. One of the groups located his newly-dug grave. The Entered Apprentice tried to raise him by vibrating the Word of the Entered Apprentice. It failed. The Fellow Craftsman tried to raise him with the Word of the Fellow Craft and was similarly unsuccessful. When the Master Mason made use of the Word of the Master Mason and the secret Lion's Paw Grip of the Tribe of Judah, Hiram was raised from the grave and embraced with the Five Points of Fellowship.

HIRAM ABIFF AND THE CODE OF MASONRY

The mythic story of Solomon and Hiram Abiff informs the progress of those who seek to explore this brotherhood. The willing martyrdom of Hiram in service to the secrets of the fraternity forms a central pillar of the behavior expected of the brothers. Integrity was at the root of Hiram's behavior. Each Mason is expected to live out the personal values of the story he is told during his initiations, much as the self-sacrifice of Jesus is an inspirational goal for mystical Christians. Hiram represents the archetype of the dying god, widespread through the Mystery Traditions. He is Orpheus slain by the Bacchanates, Socrates forced to drink the hemlock, Osiris murdered by his wicked brother Set, Adonis slain by the Bull, and the innumerable savior gods whose death and resurrection hymns the eternal promise of the immortality of the soul. Jacques de Molay, final Grand Master of the Knights Templars,

was martyred while proclaiming the innocence of the Templar Order.

The Temple of Solomon, the spiritual heart of the Bible, is also the unambiguous spiritual heart of Freemasonry and the touchstone of all progress through the first three degrees of Entered Apprentice, Fellow Craftsman, and Master Mason. Masonic writer W. Kirk MacNulty writes that Solomon's Temple represents the psyche. He describes the Temple as a three story building.[10] On the Ground Floor, the Entered Apprentice degree is conferred. The Middle Chamber is the scene of the Fellow Craft initiation. And the degree of Master Mason is reserved for the Holy of Holies. In the first degree, the unconscious mind is prepared to receive higher truth; in the second, the soul is informed and uplifted; and the third degree brings the spirit of the candidate into universal consciousness.

Manly P. Hall notes that the thirty-three degrees of Freemasonry correspond to the thirty-three years that the Temple of Solomon stood unmolested before the invasion of Jerusalem by the Egyptian pharaoh Shishak during the reign of Solomon's son Rehoboam. Thirty-three years is the length of time David reigned in Jerusalem. The human spinal column is divided into thirty-three segments. And Jesus was crucified at the age of thirty-three.[11]

SPECULATIVE MASONRY

Freemasonry underwent an important and mysterious transformation during the seventeenth century. In 1646, Sir Elias Ashmole recorded in his diary that he had been admitted to a Masonic Lodge in England. Ashmole

---

10 W. Kirk MacNulty, *Freemasonry: A Journey Through Ritual and Symbol*, page 16.
11 Manly Hall, *The Secret Teachings of All Ages*, page lxxviii.

was a member of the Royal Society, an intellectual, scholar, librarian, nobleman, alchemist, and occultist. What possible relation could he have had with the rough hewn leather aprons and tools of the builder's Craft? This is the first recorded evidence that the idea of Freemasonry had begun to spread outside the confines of builder, architect, laborer, and artisan. The Mason's skills were believed to include universal secrets of Sacred Geometry and the Holy Mysteries of Hidden Wisdom. The expansion of Freemasonry beyond the confines of a society of builders is known as Speculative Masonry.

Speculative Masonic spirituality entwined itself seamlessly with the secular rationality of the Enlightenment that infused Europe during the seventeenth and eighteenth centuries. Enlightenment thinkers shared a recognition of the mind as the means for exploring reality. They looked to the scientific method to understand nature. They rejected superstition and the role of religion in establishing scientific truth. They also rejected the concept of the flawed nature of human beings and the hopelessness of earlier Catholic thought. Instead, they espoused respect for humanity and were optimistic, believing man has a natural and rightful place in creation. They promulgated the political ideal of consent of the governed. They sought after justice and liberty. But some Enlightenment writers plunged into atheism and agnosticism, denying the craving of the human soul for religion, spirituality, and a oneness with God. Divine consciousness is the highest form of human attainment—the goal of art, philosophy, and love. Masonry promoted the unity of heart and mind, soul and spirit, that Enlightenment writers such as Voltaire neglected and Rousseau blasphemed.

Freemasonry offered to reveal to the seeker of knowledge the secrets of the Universe. The aspirant could turn to Masonry for answers to pressing questions without leaving his intellect or self-respect at the door of the dark confessional. In well-lit Lodge rooms, men could discuss ideas of liberty, philosophy, science, and commerce while surrounded by sacred symbols. They found themselves in the presence of a Higher Power that both sustained the Universe and looked kindly on their quest for Truth.

THE TOOLS OF FREEMASONRY

Speculative Masons developed ritual themes in which the tools of the bricklayer and builder became the symbolic tools of self development.

The most important of these are known as the THREE GREAT LIGHTS OF MASONRY: the Square, the Compasses, and the Volume of the Sacred Law.

The VOLUME OF THE SACRED LAW is generally the Bible in the West, but in Masonic Lodges elsewhere in the world may be the Torah, the Koran, the Vedas, or the Zend-Avesta.

The SQUARE allows for coherence, the making of ordered life choices within the seemingly random universe of nature—the defining of straight lines, intersections, and measurement of angles. It establishes the relationship between Justice and Mercy—the two pillars of the Temple—and represents honesty, integrity, and fair dealing

The COMPASSES represent truth and loyalty. They circumscribe one's action, symbolizing self-discipline, the ruling of the passions, and the making of correct choices.

The LEVEL measures the horizontal plane, allows for straight lines, and thus becomes a symbol of straight dealing and an ordered personality. It represents Justice and Judgment.

The TRIANGLE defines the two dimensional plane and is the basis of coherence, integrity, and completion.

The TROWEL is that aspect of the human char-

This statue of Archimedes at Union Square Station in Washington, D.C., depicts the ancient Greek mathematician as a Master Mason holding Compasses and Gavel. It is the work of renowned sculptor and designer Louis Saint-Gaudens, 1908.

acter that carefully builds—slowly, patiently, with forethought, smoothing over differences, layer by layer—to create the greater structure with the cement of universal brotherhood.

The GAUGE or RULER of twenty-four inches represents the hours of the day, the value of the proper use of one's time, and allows for the precision of definition in which reality may be measured and communicated.

The PLUMB LINE defines verticality. It is the divine measure completely consistent with all laws of gravity that allows the builder or the seeker to align his aspiration with the highest, eschewing distraction and uncertainty by forming a direct line with the highest. It represents Mercy.

The GAVEL or HAMMER represents force. But it is ordered force that allows one to chip away at the corners of the Rough Ashlar, the unfinished stone that must be smoothed and fitted to become the Perfect Ashlar, from which vice and inharmony are removed, so that it may be included in the Temple.

The CHISEL represents the power of analysis, carefully directed intention, and the judicious use of force.

The SKIRRET or CHALKLINE is used to mark out the area of a new building. It thus symbolizes the establishment of conscious individuality in the construction of the higher personality.

The PENCIL allows for the creative process to be applied to conceptual projects of greater and greater complexity.

The tools of the Mason allow for the building of a personal space within the mind and heart of the Brother that separates him from his fellows, unites him with his deity, and allows him to join in respectful interaction as a sovereign being with his similarly pledged brothers. This is exactly what we saw in the biblical separation of space that accompanied the building of Solomon's Temple. While the Garden of Eden represented an unfettered world of simple choices with few boundaries, the establishment of Altars represented the drawing of distinctions between sacred and profane.

* * * *

Freemasonry surfaced after the Templars were destroyed. The Templars had built or restored the mighty castles and fortresses throughout Europe and the Holy Land such as Jacob's Ford, Castle Pilgrim, Tortosa, and Safed. Is it possible that surviving Templars were able to pass on their building techniques and teachings about the relationship between modern churches and the spiritual edifices of biblical times? It does not require a fevered imagination or a personality prone to delusional thinking to posit that such teachings were passed on. Various commentators and historians have pointed out that the Masonic oaths of secrecy and protection of fellow members in need hearken to potential links with fleeing Templars. The prohibition against discussing politics in the Lodge could well be a carryover from the period when the Templars were bitterly betrayed by the kings of Europe. Finally the idea that a belief in God is required of all members—but that belief is not to be questioned or pursued in detail by others—well fits in with the idea of people forced from the arms of religion by papal corruption and subservience to political masters. All but the most radical dualistic beliefs humbly recognize God at the center of the Universe.

The lofty goals of the society envisioned by Freemasonry include the concepts of universal education, universal democracy, and universal brotherhood. Masonry attempts to achieve this by making good men better. It is the refinement of the philosophy of the Enlightenment—in which rationality is placed in service to the attainment of tolerance, and the battle is fought against the three great enemies of Truth: superstition (the church), tyranny (the state), and ignorance (the mob). *It is the quest for Universal Beauty, the precious longing of the human soul for the sacred symmetry of Eternity.* On the Tree of Life, Beauty is represented by Tiphareth, the home of the resurrected savior gods, the sacrifice of the lower self to the higher goal of Divinity. Beauty in the soul is nobility; in the mind it is intelligence; in the body it is health. The arts of music, poetry, literature, and painting may partake of and hymn the beauty of creation, as science may measure and understand it.

The Temple of Solomon—symbolic or in its historical reality—manifests them all.

Masons at work on the Temple of Solomon by Jean Fouquet, fifteenth century

REFLECTIONS ON THE TEMPLE

One finds in the records that the prophet Jeremiah . . . having received an oracle, ordered that the tent and the ark should follow with him, and that he went out to the mountain where Moses had gone up [Mt. Nebo] and had seen the inheritance of God. Jeremiah came and found a cave-dwelling, and he brought there the tent and the ark and the altar of incense: then he sealed up the entrance.

Some of those who followed him came up intending to mark the way, but could not find it. When Jeremiah learned of it, he rebuked them and declared: "The place shall remain unknown until God gathers His people together again and shows His mercy. Then the Lord will disclose these things, and the glory of the Lord and the cloud will appear, as they were shown in the case of Moses, and as Solomon asked that the place should be specially consecrated." (2 Maccabees 2:4–8 NRSV)

The interaction between humanity and the divine—on earth—is the central theme of the Temple of Solomon and of this book. We must turn our bodies, minds, and hearts into the essence of the true Temple of Solomon that the Lord may indwell His sacred habitation.

I struggled mightily throughout the research and writing of this book with the concept of the loss of the Ark by the Jews. I reached a personal understanding of the true meaning of the Ark during my visit to Israel and Mount Sinai in October and November of 2009.

I had been invited to Israel to do an interview on the Knights Templar at the Temple Mount. The trip was a gift that seemed to confirm many of the difficult decisions I had made concerning the text presented here. Yet my trip was fraught with anxiety. In addition to being something of a Cancerian home body, the politics of the region were at a particularly high state of tension, with riots

Mount Nebo, the final resting place of Moses, where Jeremiah hid the Ark. Photo by Vere Chappell.

OPPOSITE: Moses and the Burning Bush, *by William Blake, early nineteenth century.*

ABOVE LEFT: *The Jewish side of the Shrine of Machpelah.* **LEFT**: *The construction on the Muslim side.* **ABOVE**: *The entrance to the mosque at Machpelah.*

taking place on the Temple Mount in the weeks preceding my flight. Israel is a country at war. The conflict between Muslims and Jews dominates everything.

I extended my stay in Israel to work on this book. I traveled with an official Israeli guide in Jerusalem and the surrounding areas to maximize my time. Elie Ben-Meir became a good friend in the process. He arranged for a Palestinian cab driver/guide named Abu Isa, with whom I also developed a deep affinity. We traveled through places most Westerners dare not go at this time.

I was determined to get to Hebron, one of the most dangerous cities in Israel. I wanted to visit the shrine of Machpelah, regarded by both

Muslims and Jews as the sacred burial place of Abraham, Isaac, Jacob, Sarah, Rebecca, and Leah. What an interesting place. The building is divided in two; one half is a mosque, one half is a synagogue. The caves of the actual burial sites are now safely sealed, thanks to terrorist attempts to destroy them, however, there are visible tomb representations, cenotaphs, on both sides. Muslims and Jews share each other's side for ten days each year. The Muslim half is currently being extensively renovated on the outside; the Jewish half is more finished on the outside. However I found the interior more attractive on the Muslim side, as it is regularly used for community prayer—spacious with beautiful rugs. I found the Jewish interior a bit

At left is an entrance to the Crusader Church of Our Lady of Mount Zion, home of both the Cenotaph of King David and the Coenaculum, the room where the Last Supper was celebrated, shown at right. Photo of the Coenaculum by Steven Brooke.

cramped and oddly laid out, yet it is considered the second most holy site of Judaism after the Temple Mount. I heartily agree.

I was allowed in the mosque, but Abu Isa was not allowed in the synagogue. A symbolic ray of hope occurred nevertheless. It is customary to wash one's hands upon leaving a Jewish cemetery. I had forgotten to do so when leaving the Jewish side, but saw a setup for washing on the Muslim side and requested permission to use it. Universal religious dignity here we come.

David's Tomb on Mount Zion had an incredible spiritual energy for me. David is a figure I greatly admire: a courageous warrior, a lover of the Lord, a man of great passion, a capable ruler and diplomat, and a deeply flawed human being. A poet and a musician, his ecstatic dancing accompanying the Ark from the house of Obedom to Jerusalem is the biblical scene with which I most identify. I found myself experiencing gratitude to Judaism for establishing him as a role model: David was a very practical fellow

who didn't wear his religion on his sleeve; he was man of firmly held beliefs, for which he was willing to both kill and die. The traditional site of the Last Supper is, strangely enough, upstairs in the same building as David's Tomb—the twelfth-century Crusader Church of Our Lady of Mount Zion. Jerusalem is indeed the crossroads of many faiths.

I had been deeply troubled about going to the Western Wall as I have long regarded it as a symbol of pathos and failure. Being there in person, however, I found such a powerful vortex of swirling magical energy that I was forced to reexamine my feelings and take a longer view. There is dignity. Perhaps it really is a symbol of hope, patience, and faith. In the Western Wall tunnel that runs along the length of Temple Mount I took a photo that was out of character for me. I had scrupulously avoided any photos of people praying. But there was a woman seated facing the wall at the exact spot that archaeologists believe faces the location of

Station XII of the traditional Stations of the Cross, mapping the path of Jesus during the Crucifixion, is located in the Church of the Holy Sepulcher. It is the spot where the Cross was inserted in the rock of Golgotha. Photo by Steven Brooke. Detail above by Vere Chappell.

the Holy of Holies to the north of the Dome of the Rock. I was compelled to take this shot and, to my surprise, found her clothing scintillating with energy patterns not present elsewhere in the photo. I am hardly a proponent of "spirit photography." The unretouched photo shown on the opposite page captured something I did not expect.

My visit to the Church of the Holy Sepulcher was breathtaking. I was overcome with reverence during my time there. The Church has been the central site of the religious aspirations of millions of Christians since the fourth century. Whether it is or is not the scene of the Crucifixion is irrelevant to the spiritual energy generated by those who believe it is—there is no evidence that it is not. I visited the shrine where the Cross is said to have been inserted into the bedrock of Golgotha and entered the cave where the body of Jesus was laid to rest

OPPOSITE ABOVE LEFT: *The Western Wall.*
ABOVE RIGHT: *The sign announcing the location of the Holy of Holies in the Western Wall Tunnel.*
BOTTOM: *Woman seated in prayer in front of the Holy of Holies.*

afterward. A fragment of the stone that was found rolled away from the entrance to his tomb is displayed there. I saw the room where Saint Helena discovered the True Cross. The church is an architectural masterpiece of intense beauty and piety.

I was able to enter the Dome of the Rock and touch the Sacred Rock because of permissions acquired by the documentary film crew hosting my travel. The Rock is the Foundation Stone of the world, the Kether of Malkuth, the point from which material existence proceeded. Feeling the Stone with my hand was one of the more profound experiences of my life, perhaps the most archetypically rich experience possible for an incarnate human being. It may be described as touching Eternity.

I was also admitted to the al-Aqsa Mosque, home of the Templars during the Crusades. It is so spacious and beautifully apportioned inside. I could feel the Templar presence in the midst of the very enemy who had defeated them—when the knights were not engaged in their own self destruction.

We were led around the Temple Mount by a Palestinian guide hired by the film crew.

He was at great pains to avoid any mention of either the Temples of Solomon or Herod that preceded the Dome. He was also persistent in uttering a continuous series of prayers for the destruction of Israel.

Anticipating Mount Sinai as the spiritual centerpiece of my trip was indeed an accurate intuition. I rode a camel up to the area where people dismounted from the camels and began the long walk up to the top of the mountain. The drivers and camels stay in a staging area to await the return of their passengers. I had arranged with my driver to walk back to Saint Katherine's by myself, rather than have him wait for me. I continued climbing alone. The walking path is much steeper and more treacherous than the camel path. There are seven hundred fifty "steps" going up to the top of the Mount. I was having a difficult time. Part of it

ABOVE LEFT: *The Well of Souls in the Dome of the Rock is a cave beneath the Foundation Stone.* ABOVE RIGHT: *A view of the beauty of the Dome's ceiling and columns.* BELOW LEFT: *Another view of the interior grandeur of the Dome.* ABOVE: *The Minbar, or pulpit, in the al-Aqsa Mosque is a restoration of that built by Saladin.*

Some of the seven hundred fifty "steps" leading to the top of Mount Sinai

The Greek Orthodox Chapel at the top of Mount Sinai

was the steep angle of ascent and the roughness of the terrain. I believe part of it was the thinness of the air. I considered quitting. I had been reading Rudyard Kipling's "If" virtually every morning and evening of my trip. His description of pushing past the point of muscle and sinew quitting, with only the will to sustain them remaining intact, was much in my mind.

At last, I reached the top. Where was the Jewish Star? I had alloted an hour for myself on the summit. Miraculously I was able to be completely alone for a full hour and a quarter. Then I had to leave so that I could reach Saint Katherine's Monastery before dark.

During my time alone on the mountain, I took some pictures and began to rest a bit for the first time since I had left for Israel a week and a half before. I scooped some dirt from the very highest point to take home, removed my gear, stretched out on a rock, and relaxed. I did the Noon Adoration in Egypt precisely at noon (if Sinai is Egypt).

I realized after some time at rest that the only things I had been thinking about during the strenuous climb and solitary time at the summit were my family, my friends, my faith, and my God. I was free of all of the accretion of other beliefs that had so characterized my experience in Jerusalem—the heart of Judaism, Christianity, and Islam. I had tried (and succeeded) in personalizing each of them that I might experience the universal spirituality of the Holy Land. Here on the Holy Mountain, they were at last put back where they belonged—in context as not my own.

I was at the top of Mount Sinai, the legendary sacred ground where God delivered the Law to the world. Was this the "real" mountain? It did not matter. It had become my personal shrine. The place where the reality of tradition may matter, but historicity does not. The place where I was able to fully experience the Gnosis that is my life.

I resolved my aforementioned struggle with this book. God engraved the Ten Commandments on the Tablets of Moses and they were put in the Ark, and eventually lost to the Jews. What did the loss of the Ark mean to Judaism? The answer that I found on Mount Sinai is that I do not know the answer to that question.

What I came to understand is that God has written His Commandments in each of our hearts, the home of the true Tablets of the Law. The Ark is the body that encloses and enshrines that Law. If we are living a correct life, the Pillar of Cloud and Fire of the Lord will indeed guide us through the desert—telling us where to stop, telling us when and where to go forth. That is all that matters to me as an initiate. One day, the Ark of my body will also be lost. So be it. The Law shall live eternally.

Through the writing of this book, I have come to accept that perhaps Jeremiah really did sequester the Ark in a hidden and safe location near Mount Nebo. Perhaps there is an unbroken lineage from the sixth century BCE among certain Jews still aware of its location. Perhaps it awaits the day when it may be placed in the Holy of Holies in the rebuilt Temple on Mount Moriah where it belongs.

Whether this happens or not, my goal is to keep the Tablets of the Law alive in my own heart. I can wish no more precious gift for the reader than to be able to do the same.

Pslam XXIII
A Psalm of David

The Lord is my shepherd; I shall not want.

He maketh me to lie down in green pastures: He leadeth me beside the still waters.

He restoreth my soul: He leadeth me in the paths of righteousness for His Name's sake.

Yea, though I walk through the valley of the shadow of death, I will fear no evil: for thou art with me; thy rod and thy staff they comfort me.

Thou preparest a table before me in the presence of mine enemies: thou anointest my head with oil; my cup runneth over.

Surely goodness and mercy shall follow me all the days of my life: and I will dwell in the House of the Lord for ever.

APPENDIX I

A Brief History of Jerusalem and the Promised Land

The following is an account of Jerusalem from the destruction of the Second Temple (or Temple of Herod) in 70 CE. We will touch lightly on the various conquerors of the Holy City, including the Romans, Byzantines, Early Muslims, Fatimids, Crusaders, Ayubbids, Mamelukes, and Ottomans. I also include a brief summary of the modern history of Jerusalem from Napoleon to the birth of Israel in 1948.

The Bible first mentions Jerusalem in Genesis 14:18 in the person of Melchize-dek, "king of Salem" and priest of the most high God, who blessed Abram. History becomes aware of the existence of Jerusalem during the early Bronze Age (3200–2200 BCE) as a Canaanite settlement. Its first literary mention is in a 20th century BCE Egyptian curse (perhaps that explains it). Jerusalem was fortified as a city state during the Late Bronze Age (1550–1200 BCE) and is referenced in the Egyptian el-Amarna letters, an archive of cuneiform clay tablets from the fourteenth century BCE. Joshua conquered the region circa 1200 BCE but was unable to retain control of the city. This task would remain for King David to complete in 1000 BCE, as extensively discussed in part 4.

The Destruction of Herod's Temple

In chapter 21 we learned of King Herod the Great and his magnificent restoration and rebuilding of the Second Temple. Upon Herod's death in 4 BCE, the Romans took a far more active role in the region. Judea was formally annexed to the Roman Empire in 6 CE. The excesses of direct Roman rule resulted in a Jewish uprising led by a revolutionary group known as Zealots in 66 CE. Four years later, in the year 70, six thousand Jewish rebels battled to their deaths on the Temple Mount against the army of the Roman general Titus. After his victory, Titus oversaw the dismantlement and destruction of the Temple. Surviving Zealots fled to Masada, a fortress built by Herod near the Dead Sea, where they held out against a Roman siege for three years.

Bar Kochba's Revolt

The Roman emperor Hadrian visited Jerusalem in 130 and decided to turn it into a Roman colony, renaming it Aelia Capitolina. When he placed a statue of Jupiter on the Temple Mount, the Bar Kochba revolt of 132 began. The revolt was supported by Rabbi Akivah, the most prominent religious figure of his day. The rebels enjoyed a brief period of success during which they captured Jerusalem. The Bar Kochba rebels attempted to gain the alliance of newly converted Christians. They even

345

The Arch of Triumph in Rome shows the sacking of the Second Temple and the carrying away of the Temple Lampstand by the troops of Titus. Photo by בית השלום.

minted coins depicting the Temple entrance.[1] The Jews erected a provisional Temple on the Mount before they were defeated in 135.

The Romans engaged in massive retaliation after the rebellion, banning all religious practices associated with political freedom—such as Passover (the escape from bondage) and Hanukkah (the reclaiming of the Second Temple from the Seleucids). They changed the name of the region from Judea to Syria-Palestina, Palestina for short, "the Land of the Philistines," a deliberate insult to the Jews. Hadrian recognized Jerusalem as a symbol of Jewish aspiration and banned Jews from the city. The ban was temporarily lifted during the Day of Mourning for the destruction of the Temple on the ninth day of the month of *Av* (July/August), the Jewish holy day of *Tisha b'Av*.

Obverse of a coin minted by the Bar Kochba rebels during their short-lived victory against the Roman occupation. Photo by David Hendin.

---

1 The object between the four pillars was long thought by numismatists and historians to be the Ark of the Covenant. However, according to research discussed by David Hendin, it is more likely an image of the Table of Offering of the Bread of the Presence. See Hendin, *Guide to Biblical Coins*, 5th edition, chapter 10.

Since the time of the expulsion of Jews from Jerusalem after the destruction of the Second Temple and the failure of the Bar Kochba revolt, Jewish synagogues in the Diaspora ("separation from the homeland") have been oriented so that the direction of worship faces Jerusalem. Jewish

*The Herodian fortress of Masada where the Zealots fought to their
deaths against the invincible Roman legions*

prayers, recited three times a day throughout the world, include invocations for the return to and rebuilding of Jerusalem.

Jerusalem and Christianity

The story of Jesus is deeply entwined with Jerusalem and the Temple as discussed in detail in part 7. Rome officially adopted Christianity as the state religion in 325 during the reign of Emperor Constantine. Yet as Christianity spread in later centuries, the connection with Jerusalem and the Jewish roots of Christianity were less emphasized. The "heavenly Jerusalem" became more important than the historical city. Christ replaced the Temple as the embodiment of the Divine on earth.

The Byzantine Christians of the Eastern Roman Empire were actually hostile to the Temple Mount and waged a campaign against the memory of the Second Temple. Their opposition was rooted in the Gospels.

And Jesus went out, and departed from the temple … And Jesus said unto them, "See ye not all these things? verily I say unto you, There shall not be left here one stone upon another, that shall not be thrown down." (Mark 24:1–2)

Constantine was influenced by the theologian Eusebius, who held strong views against the importance of Jerusalem—he was much concerned with distinguishing Christianity from Judaism and with spreading its teaching beyond the Israeli region. The complicity of the Jewish religious establishment in the death of Jesus created a conflict between Judaism and Christianity that continues to surface.

Yet Constantine maintained a deep interest in Jerusalem as the historical home of the Christian religion. His mother, later canonized as St. Helena, traveled to the city in 326. She is said to have found the True Cross on which Jesus was crucified and the crypt where he had been interred. A Roman temple to Venus stood on the spot. Constantine ordered it destroyed and built the Church of the Holy Sepulcher, the holiest place in Christendom. It stands on the hill of Golgotha, the site of the Crucifixion and

LEFT: *The Dream of Constantine on the eve of his battle to win the emperorship of Rome. He was shown the Cross as his path to victory. He later built both the Church of the Holy Sepulcher in Jerusalem (CENTER) and the Church of the Nativity in Bethlehem (RIGHT).*

added a new luster to Jerusalem for Christianity. However, the Temple Mount itself remained a shambles, used by the Byzantines as a dumping ground.

In 361, Julian the Apostate became the sole emperor of Rome. He rejected Christianity and longed to reestablish Pagan worship in the Empire. He formed a brief alliance with the Jews of Judea. He allowed them to return to Jerusalem and offered to help finance the construction of a Third Temple. Contemporary historians wrote that fires and earthquakes regularly interrupted their efforts.[2] Julian's reign was cut short

by his death in 363 in a battle against the Persian forces of King Shapur II (r. 309–379).

Julian's Christian successors resumed Constantine's massive architectural agenda for religious shrines while continuing to neglect the Temple Mount. They reactivated Hadrian's ban on Jews in the city, although Jews remained the majority population in the Palestine region.

The Persians under King Khosrow II briefly conquered Jerusalem in 614 with the help of the Jews. The Persians allowed Jews to retain the Temple Mount from 614 to 617 but subsequently returned it to Christian control. The Byzantine emperor Heraclius reconquered Jerusalem in 629—carrying the True Cross in

---

2 Fourth-century historian Ammianus Marcellinus wrote in *The Roman History of Ammianus Marcellinus*, Book 23, 1, 2–3: "[Julian] proposed to rebuild at a vast expense the once magnificent temple of Jerusalem, which after many deadly contests was with difficulty taken by Vespasian and Titus … He assigned the task to Alypius of Antioch … But though Alypius applied himself vigorously to the work, and though the governor of the province co-operated

with him, fearful balls of fire burst forth with continual eruptions close to the foundations, burning several of the workmen and making the spot altogether inaccessible. And thus the very elements, as if by some fate, repelling the attempt, it was laid aside."

his triumphant entry into the city. He renewed hostilities against the Jews.

JERUSALEM AND ISLAM

The Muslim conquest of Jerusalem by Caliph Omar (r. 634–644) in 638 opened a new chapter in the history of the city. Almost immediately, the Muslims began to clean up the Temple Mount, believing it to be the sacred site of Solomon's Temple. The Koran had acknowledged David and his son as allies of Allah. "And We verily gave knowledge unto David and Solomon, and they said: 'Praise be to Allah, Who hath preferred us above many of His believing slaves!'" Solomon served Allah when he helped turn the Queen of Sheba from her worship of the Sun. Sheba became illuminated upon entering a hall made smooth as glass in Solomon's palace and proclaimed, "My Lord! Lo! I have wronged myself, and I surrender with Solomon unto Allah, the Lord of the Worlds."[3]

Omar was the second of the four Rightly Guided Caliphs (those who had personally served with Muhammad). Omar allowed a small group of Jews to move back to Jerusalem and authorized them to serve on the advisory council overseeing the reclamation of the Temple Mount. The earliest known Jerusalem synagogue unearthed thus far dates to the reign of Omar.[4] It was located at the southwest corner of the Temple Mount. The main Jerusalem synagogue, also built around this time, is nearby at the north end of the Western Wall close to the Holy of Holies. Known as "the Cave," it still stands today.[5]

The Dome of Solomon commemorates Muslim respect for this Jewish monarch, which has been de-emphasized in recent times for political reasons. Photo by Steven Brooke.

UMAYYADS. In 660, Mu'awiya (r. 661–680) chose Jerusalem as the place to have himself proclaimed as the first of the Umayyad caliphs. Yet, he established his dynastic capital in Damascus.

The Dome of the Rock was completed in 692 by the Umayyad caliph Abd-al-Malik (r. 685–705). While the tradition of the Temple Mount as the place from which Muhammad ascended to heaven (as part of his Night Journey) was not yet fully established, the Dome's prominence was clearly designed to overshadow the Church of the Holy Sepulcher as the center of the Holy City.

Political motivations may also have been at play in Abd al-Malik's decision to build the magnificent Dome. A rival caliphate was established in Mecca from 683 to 692. Abd al-Malik had ample reason to increase the importance of Jerusalem in the eyes of Islam. The Dome is an exquisite example of Muslim architecture. Abd

---

3 Koran, Surah 27 verses 14 and 44. *The Meaning of the Glorious Koran,* translated by Marmaduke Pickthall. Solomon is mentioned repeatedly in the Koran.

4 Eilat Mazar, *The Complete Guide to the Temple Mount Excavations,* pages 94–96.

5 Dore Gold, *The Fight for Jerusalem,* page 99.

Persian painting of the Night Journey of Muhammad. He rides his heavenly steed Burak and is guided by the archangel Gabriel, sixteenth century.

The Cave of Muhammad within the Dome of the Rock where the Prophet is said to have rested during the Night Journey

al-Malik may have correctly reasoned it would become an important pilgrimage site.

The al-Aqsa Mosque was constructed soon after by Abd al-Malik's son and successor Caliph al-Walid (r. 705–715). A wooden mosque had been built on the site by Caliph Omar, that could hold three thousand worshippers. Al Walid's splendid mosque was subsequently identified in Muslim tradition as the extreme (*aqsa*) end of the Night Journey. Al-Walid also converted a number of Christian churches to mosques.

The beautiful Dome of the Rock has stood on the Temple Mount since the late seventh century.

ABBASIDS. The Umayyads were conquered by the Abbasids in 750. They were harsh rulers who laid heavy taxes on Christians and Jews and banned Jews from the Temple Mount. The Abbasid capital was established in Baghdad, even farther from Jerusalem. The Abbasids seem to have had little interest in Jerusalem. For example, the second Abbasid caliph, al-Mansur (r. 754–775) refused to fund local Muslims to help rebuild the al-Aqsa mosque after it had been severely damaged in an earthquake. During the ninth century, Jerusalem was depleted of Muslim population by famine, peasant revolts, and Abbasid neglect.

SALAFIYYA. Political instability increasingly weakened Islam during the ninth and tenth centuries. This led some to seek a religious renewal to regain Muslim power. The *Salafiyya*, or community of True Believers, looked for inspiration from the first three generations of Muslims (the *salaf* or "forerunners," the pious ancestors who followed Muhammad). Islamic orthodoxy may be traced back to Ahmad ibn Hanbal (780–855). He was the leader of the strictest of the four schools of Islamic jurisprudence and compiled

OPPOSITE: *The al-Aqsa Mosque was built in the very beginning of the eighth century soon after the Dome of the Rock. During the Crusades, it served as the palace of the king of Jerusalem and the headquarters of the Knights Templar. Photo by Steven Brooke.*

the Traditions of the Prophet. He was persecuted by the Abbasid caliph after he refused to accede to a secular, rationalist interpretation of the Koran. His courageous martyrdom at the hands of his persecutors has earned him the undying respect of religious Muslims for over a millennium.

FATIMIDS. The Fatimid caliphate arose in Egypt in 909 as a Shiite rival to the Sunni Abassid caliphs. The early Fatimids were initially tolerant of both Christians and Jews. But when the psychologically unstable Caliph al-Hakim (r. 996–1021) took power, he opened a campaign against Christians and Jews, destroying the Church of the Holy Sepulcher in 1009, dismantling it down to the very stones, and destroying the Jewish synagogue in Jerusalem.

Jerusalem During the Crusades

In 1099, the Crusader armies took Jerusalem as discussed in chapter 24. The Roman Catholic Crusaders had an altogether different religious perception of the sanctity of the Temple Mount than the Byzantines. They immediately seized the Mount and established their headquarters there. Jerusalem was established as the capital city of the Crusader Kingdom. Extensive Crusader building projects took place throughout the Holy Land, but especially in Jerusalem. Crusader intolerance of Jews and Muslims led both groups to form a natural alliance with each other. Each was forbidden to live in Jerusalem.

The reconquest of Jerusalem by Saladin in 1187 led to another Islamic restoration. The legendarily chivalrous Saladin had founded the

Ayyubid dynasty after he defeated the Fatimids in 1174. He allowed Eastern Christians to manage the Church of the Holy Sepulcher and permitted a small contingent of Knights Hospitaller to remain and operate their hospital for one year. All other Christians were expelled from the city. Saladin reclaimed the Dome of the Rock. The Great Cross that had been placed above the Dome was paraded through the streets in a two-day procession during which it was continuously whipped. Saladin allowed Jews to resettle in Jerusalem. Among Saladin's advisors was the famous Jewish philosopher Moses Maimonides. Saladin's treaty with Richard the Lionhearted allowed Christian pilgrims to visit the holy city.

Saladin's nephew and one of his two successors, al-Muazzam, sultan of Damascus, made a strategic decision in 1219 indicative of the psychology of Islam toward Jerusalem at this time. The Crusaders were gathering for another invasion after the success of the Fifth Crusade in Egypt. Al-Muazzam realized Jerusalem would be indefensible, so he took down the walls encircling the city, deciding that they would give advantage to the Christians once the city was taken. Jerusalem remained unfortified for the next three hundred years, constantly attacked by Bedouin tribes.

In 1229, the Ayyubid Sultan al-Kamil of Cairo (the rival of Damascus) signed a ten-year truce with the Holy Roman Emperor Frederick II. Al-Kamil returned Jerusalem to Christian rule on condition that the Muslims maintain religious control of the Temple Mount. Christians were allowed to pray on the Mount. Frederick, however, again forbade both Muslims and Jews from living in the city.

The End of the Crusades

The Mameluke dynasty had arisen in Egypt in 1230, superceding the Ayyubids. In 1292, the Mameluke general Baybars drove the Crusaders out of the Holy Land. The Mamelukes ruled Jerusalem for the next two hundred fifty years. They repaired the Dome of the Rock and engaged in various other construction projects. However, they never rebuilt the city walls and left the management of the city to low-level officials.

Ibn Taymiyya, Jerusalem, and Islamic Purity

An important trend developed within Islam at this time that hearkened back to the ninth century Salafiyya reform—a call to return to doctrinal purity and the original unblemished religion of Muhammad. The most prominent leader of this movement was Ibn Taymiyya (1263–1328), who remains an inspiration to both orthodox Muslims and militant Islamists. Ibn Taymiyah was a member of the Pietist school, founded by Ibn Hanbal. He endured imprisonment and persecution by secular Muslim leaders because he refused to bend from his traditionalist, orthodox view of the Koran as the inspired word of God. He died in prison.

Ibn Taymiyya decried the attachment of religious significance to Jerusalem. He accused the Umayyads of having built the Dome of the Rock to distract from the centrality of Mecca. He spoke out against the rituals that had grown around the Dome, including the custom of circumambulating it and offering animal sacrifices. These practices, he insisted, were exclusive to Mecca. While Jerusalem was once the direction of Muslim prayer, the first *quibla*, it had been replaced on direct orders of the Prophet once he had conquered Mecca and cleansed the Kaaba of its pagan tarnish.

The launching of the Crusades in 1095 was a European-wide phenomenon that captured the popular imagination.

Jerusalem under Ottoman Rule

The Ottoman Turks took Constantinople from the decrepit Christian Byzantine Empire in 1453 and ruled until the end of World War I in 1917. In 1516, the Turks entered Jerusalem unopposed where they reigned for the next four hundred years. In 1517, they defeated the Mamelukes in Egypt.

Suleiman the Magnificent (r. 1520–1566) undertook a series of massive construction projects in Jerusalem including the rebuilding of the city walls. He also did extensive repairs and restoration on the Temple Mount and built the Prophet's Oratory.

Jews were welcomed back during this period, particularly refugees from the Spanish Inquisition, and permitted to build a synagogue. Suleiman allowed Jews a place to pray at the Western Wall. He welcomed Christians in the city but construction of churches was restricted. The population of Jerusalem tripled by the mid-sixteenth century under Ottoman tolerance. Suleiman restored the Church of the Holy Sepulcher in 1555, and various Christian sects laid claim to their own sections of the church.

After Suleiman, however, Jerusalem entered another period of decline. It was repeatedly attacked by Bedouins in the late sixteenth century. By the seventeenth century, it was no longer a center of either trade or industry.

Jerusalem in the Modern Era

European involvement in the affairs of the Mideast may be said to begin with Napoleon, the first European leader to call for the establishment of a Jewish state in Palestine in 1798.

In 1831, the Ottomans in the Holy Land were briefly conquered by Egypt. The Egyptians modernized the politics of Jerusalem, granting equality to all citizens. Both Christians and Jews were allowed to engage in restoration and construction projects. European interests grew in the city as Byzantine and Roman Church officials moved to Jerusalem. Protestant missionary activity was widespread. A British consulate opened in 1838.

The Ottomans reconquered Jerusalem in 1840 with European backing. However, they were unable to roll back the Egyptian reforms. Estimates by the Prussian consulate show Jews to be about half the population of Jerusalem in 1845. The British consulate confirmed that estimate in 1864.[6]

In 1852, the Ottoman Empire, under European prodding, published an edict acknowledging Christian rights to five holy places. This was incorporated into the Treaty of Paris in 1856 and the Treaty of Berlin in 1878. The Treaty of Berlin also recognized an ethnic national right to a territorial homeland as part of international law. In 1891, this treaty was cited as precedent for recognizing Jewish claims to Palestine by Christian Zionist William Blackstone in a petition to U.S. president Benjamin Harrison. President William McKinley supported Israel as a Jewish homeland, as did prominent members of Congress, chief justice of the Supreme Court Melville Fuller, and financiers like J. P. Morgan and John D. Rockefeller. Those who supported Zionist claims took the position that the Jews had been driven from their ancestral home by force rather than choice.

The Fall of the Ottoman Caliphate and the Rise of the Mideast Nation States

The alliance of the Ottoman Turks with the Germans in World War I struck the deathblow to their dynasty. The Turks were soundly defeated by the allied forces of Britain, France, and the United States. The Turks surrendered Jerusalem to British General Edward Allenby in 1917.

For centuries after the coming of the Prophet, Islam had been a unified cultural/religious/political entity that knew no national boundaries, besides those of various clans or tribes who reigned over specific regions. For nearly thirteen hundred years, Islam was ruled by a caliphate, a form of government that blended religious and political authority. Numerous dynasties claimed the caliphate. Since the death of Muhammad in 632, we have seen it change hands from the Four Rightly Guided Caliphs to the Ummayads, Abbasids, Fatimids, Ayyubids, and Ottomans.

The division of the people of the Middle East into modern nation states dates to the fall of the Ottoman Empire in 1920. The process of creating these states was neither evolutionary nor organic. On the contrary, it was a construction imposed by European imperialists, primarily French and British, who drew maps and insisted their drawings were reality. This is a useful perspective with which to begin to understand the chaos we see in that region today.

Jerusalem under the British

Among the maps establishing Syria, Jordan, Iraq, Iran, and Lebanon was the state of Israel. Answering the two-thousand-year longings of the Jews, the British Balfour Declaration of 1917 called for the establishment of a Jewish state in Palestine as the national homeland of the Jewish people. It was the result of decades of work by both Jewish and Christian Zionists, and sympathetic politicians. Chaim Weitzmann, who became the first president of Israel, represented the Jewish Zionists. U.S. President Woodrow Wilson expressed his support for the Balfour Declaration, although rather tepidly, as the issue of a Jewish homeland was not high on his long list of priorities.

The Paris Peace Conference of 1919 was convened to end World War I with the signing of the Treaty of Versailles. It also established the League of Nations, the predecessor organization to the United Nations. The League of Nations recognized the right of the Jewish

---

6 Gold, *The Fight for Jerusalem*, page 120. Ambassador Gold adds that in 1914, the total population of Jerusalem was sixty-five thousand people, of whom Jews numbered forty-five thousand.

people to their national homeland in Israel. Although U.S. membership in the League was rejected by the Senate, Woodrow Wilson and members of his administration were obsessed with the effort to establish a supra-national government and were intimately involved with the details of the Treaty of Versailles.

The Ottoman Empire formally relinquished control over all its provincial territories outside the boundaries of Turkey in 1920 in the Treaty of Sèvres. The Republic of Turkey (that replaced the Ottoman Empire in 1923) affirmed the Ottoman position in the Treaty of Lausanne in 1923.

The League of Nations Palestine Mandate of 1922 confirmed British rule of the region and Jerusalem as the capital of Palestine.[7] The Mandate acknowledged the pre-existing rights of the Jews to Palestine as their national homeland. President Wilson expressed his general support for the British plan, but Winston Churchill was far more passionate about Israel. Churchill favored the idea of helping to populate the land with massive immigration of any European Jews who suffered from poverty and/or persecution. The British Mandate, or Palestine Mandate, divided a large territory on both sides of the Jordan River into Arab and Jewish areas. The Jewish territory extended from the Mediterranean Sea to the Jordan River, the natural boundaries of Israel then and now. The Mandate sought to secure the holy places for the free exercise of religion by Jews, Christians, and Muslims. In 1937 the British released their Palestine Royal Report, further stating the British understanding of Palestine as the unique Jewish homeland. The Report discounted Arab territorial claims to Israel as more applicable to traditional Arab lands such as Syria and Iraq.

The Great Game and Its Lasting Consequences

The British supported the Hashemite King Hussein of the Hijaz region (modern Saudi Arabia) whose family was the traditional custodian of Mecca and Medina. The Hashemites are believed to be descended from the Prophet. Hussein needed British backing against the Wahhabi resistance allied with the House of Saud (that eventually defeated him). Hussein's goal was to rebuild the caliphate under the Hashemites. His son, Emir Faisal, later king of the British-created states of first Syria and then Iraq, represented the Arabs at the 1919 Paris Peace Conference. Faisal was a popular figure because of his leadership during the Arab Revolt against the Ottomans. Faisal sought international recognition at the conference for the twenty-two Arab nations that emerged from the dissolution of the Ottoman caliphate.

Emir Faisal supported the idea of a Jewish homeland in Palestine and signed an agreement to that end with Chaim Weitzmann at the conference. The Weitzmann-Faisal agreement was dated January 3, 1919. In it, Faisal expressed his willingness to recognize a future Jewish state and his support for encouraging large-scale Jewish immigration to Israel. His only concern was that the British and French might undermine these efforts, so he wrote a handwritten caveat that the agreement was conditional upon acceptance by Europe of the entire plan.[8] Because he envisioned a Hashemite caliphate controlling a vast Muslim region, he could be gracious to his Jewish neighbors. Faisal wrote to future Supreme Court Justice Felix Frankfurter on March 3, 1919 that Zionist demands for land were quite "moderate and proper." In the same letter, Emir Faisal promised, "we will wish the Jews a most hearty welcome home."[9]

---

7 The Jewish Agency, an office that served as a quasi-government for the Jewish community, established its headquarters in Jerusalem in 1922 with League of Nations support.

---

8 Dore Gold, *The Fight for Jerusalem,* page 126.

9 Letter from Emir Faisal to then dean of the Harvard

Faisal's concerns about being undermined by European power brokers were well-placed. France rejected Hashemite rulership in its sphere of influence in Syria. Although there was majority support for the creation of a large Arab state under Hashemite kingship, the Arabs were betrayed by secret negotiations between England and France. It is fascinating to consider that European manipulation of the remains of the Ottoman Empire undermined the nascent cooperation between Arabs and Jews at this critical early stage in the formation of the state of Israel.

Of course, some Arab nationalists disputed such cooperation and demanded Arab control of the entire region. Thus, while Jewish immigration increased during the period and Jerusalem regained its economic and cultural vitality, conflicts with Muslims became increasingly violent. Arab resentment against an Israeli state was fueled by its anger and impotence against the influence of the European imperialists.

ARAB NATIONALISM AND THE RISE OF ANTI-JEWISH DOCTRINES

During the nineteenth century, a series of anti-colonial protests fanned throughout much of the Arab world. Their common rallying cry was a rejection of the increased secularization taking place through Islam's post-Crusade contact with Europeans and a lament for the overall sense of failure of Muslims in the modern world. They attributed this condition to the abandonment of the tenets of their faith.

The 1920s and 1930s gave birth to two influential political/religious movements whose doctrines were designed to negate the possibility of meaningful cooperation between Islam and the West.[10] Both are flourishing in full force today and each has been responsible for a great deal of suffering among Muslims, Christians, and Jews. The Palestinian Arab resistance was initiated in the 1920s by the Grand Mufti of Jerusalem. The Muslim Brotherhood, founded in 1931 in Egypt, has become one of the most successful ideological and revolutionary groups of all time.

Arab Resistance and the Grand Mufti of Jerusalem

A seminal figure in the genesis of the unhappy situation we face today was Hajj Amin al-Husseini (1895–1974). He was born to a wealthy and influential family in Jerusalem. Both al-Husseini's grandfather and half-brother had served in the position of Grand Mufti of Jerusalem.[11] Al-Husseini became exposed to militant Islam while a student at the prestigious al-Azhar University in Cairo. In 1919, he established a paramilitary group called *al-Nadi al-Arabi* (The Arab Club). Members violently attacked a group of Jews praying at the Western Wall in 1920. A coordinated campaign of attacks followed in which forty-seven Jews were killed and another one hundred forty wounded. Al-Husseini was arrested by the British, released on bail, fled to Syria, was convicted in absentia, and sentenced to ten years in prison.

(con't. from p. 355) law school Felix Frankfurter, quoted in full at http://hetebliksem.blogspot.com/2007/06/history-faisal-frankfurter.html.

10 "There is no orthodox sect or school of Islam that teaches that Muslims must coexist peacefully as equals with non-Muslims on an indefinite basis." Robert Spencer, *Stealth Jihad,* page 5. Sufism, the mystical Gnostic tradition of Islam, is not considered an "orthodox sect or school."

11 The term "grand mufti" denotes both religious and civil authority as is the general practice in Islamic culture. He may issue legal opinions and edicts (*fatwas*) on Muslim law (*sharia*). His opinions help define the practical application of the law and make binding precedents in civil jurisprudence. In criminal courts, his recommendations are not binding. The grand mufti may be considered the titular head of the Muslim community in which he resides.

Al-Husseini was pardoned by the British civil government in an effort to calm the situation.[12] In 1922, the British appointed him as the Grand Mufti of Jerusalem, despite his having been rejected by fellow Muslims as insufficiently educated in Islamic doctrine to have achieved the status of *sheikh*, a requirement for the position of grand mufti. Later, al-Husseini was made the head of the Supreme Muslim Council of Jerusalem—set up by the British to provide political representation for the Palestinian Arabs. Thus, for most of the thirty years of British rule, al-Husseini managed to be an effective enemy to Jews as well as moderate Arabs.

In 1929, al-Husseini preached a sermon at the al-Aqsa Mosque accusing Jews of defiling mosques. Sixty-seven Jews were murdered in Hebron the next day. In total, 133 Jews were murdered throughout the region and over 300 wounded in response to his inflammatory sermon. The British responded to the Hebron massacre by evicting all Jews from that city so that militant Arabs would be less irritated.

British refusal to protect Jews against the escalating violence of the Palestinian Arabs led to the establishment of the *Haganah* (The Defense), a civilian Jewish militia. Active from 1920 to 1948, it grew into the Israel Defense Forces, the national army. By 1931, as Arab violence and British passivity simultaneously escalated, a number of Haganah leaders rejected the doctrine of defensive restraint that had been the founding ideology of their militia. They formed the *Irgun Zvai Leumi* (National Military Organization), adopting a more aggressive paramilitary stance. While the Irgun always remained a smaller more radical force, they shared intelligence and cooperated with the Haganah. In addition to their military activities against the Arabs, the Irgun became increasingly involved in anti-British resistance.[13]

In 1933, Adolph Hitler was elected chancellor of Germany. Al-Husseini was part of an enthusiastic Arab response to Hitler's widely pronounced anti-Semitic views. In 1937, Adolph Eichmann traveled to Palestine and recruited al-Husseini as an agent of the Nazi regime. He was deported soon after Eichmann's visit for his role in the 1936 Great Arab Revolt. He traveled to Lebanon, then moved on to Iraq. In 1941, al-Husseini traveled to Germany where he remained until the end of the war. On arrival in Berlin, he met with Hitler, who received him as a state dignitary.[14] Al-Husseini was a close friend of both Eichmann and Heinrich Himmler. He toured Auschwitz with Eichmann. He recruited and trained a Nazi brigade of Bosnian Muslims, the SS Hanzar division, which he called the Arab Liberation Force. Some one hundred thousand Muslim fighters filled its ranks. He made radio broadcasts that were transmitted from Berlin to the Middle East and used his extensive contacts in the Mideast for

---

12 The reader might contemplate some of the absurdities of America's modern Mideast policies in seeking to understand the extent of British ineptness in the early to mid-twentieth century.

13 From 1943 to 1948, the Irgun was led by future Israeli Prime Minister Menachem Begin. When the British launched a nationwide military operation against the Jewish resistance movement in 1946, they discovered a cache of documents linking members of the Jewish Agency to the resistance. The papers were taken to the central offices of the British Mandatory authority at the King David Hotel in Jerusalem. Soon after, the Irgun launched a terrorist bombing that resulted in the deaths of at least ninety-one people, with forty-six more sustaining injuries. At the formation of the state of Israel in 1948, the Irgun was classified a terrorist group.

14 The official minutes of their meeting, along with extracts from al-Husseini's diary, are included as appendices in *The Nazi Connection to Islamic Terrorism* by Chuck Morse. Both leaders recognized the unity of purpose between the Nazis and the Arabs, including an overriding ambition to crush worldwide Jewry and prevent the formation of a Jewish state. Hitler pledged his full support for the elevation of al-Husseini as supreme leader of the allied Arabs after the Nazi victory.

espionage and intelligence operations in support of the Nazis.

A majority of Arabs were enthusiastic about the Nazis. They showed high regard for Hitler, assigning him Muslim names and titles.[15] Paramilitary groups used variations of the Nazi salute and held Nazi-style torchlight parades. The future Egyptian ruler, Gamel Abdel Nasser, was a member of the Young Egyptian Green Shirts, a paramilitary organization modeled after Hitler's Brown Shirts. Nasser's successor as president of Egypt, Anwar Sadat, was also a member, arrested as a Nazi collaborator by the British. (Sadat became more moderate in later years, for which he was assassinated in 1981 by Islamist radicals associated with the Muslim Brotherhood.)

After Hitler's defeat, al-Husseini fled Berlin for Cairo, where he remained for the rest of his life, working tirelessly against Israel. He was involved with the Odessa efforts to smuggle Nazis out of Germany and into the Middle East. With much hard wealth in the form of confiscated gold and other funds, Nazi survivors willing to convert to Islam were welcomed as ideological allies, particularly in Egypt and Syria, where they assumed Arabic names, and were accepted into the highest level of intelligence circles and other influential positions.[16] (During my tour of the al-Aqsa Mosque, I was enthusiastically informed that Mussolini donated the vast marble columns shown on page 351.)

Al-Husseini trained terrorists during the Cairo years including Yasser Arafat, who worked with him in 1946. Nasser also collaborated with al-Husseini.

Hajj Amin al-Husseini's contribution to the combustible modern situation was to internationalize Arab resistance to the Jewish presence in Israel. He elevated the models of identity politics and grievance ideology to a new plateau. A political struggle had become an epic battle of religious dimensions, and it remains so today for both sides. Al-Husseini set the stage for Yasser Arafats's propaganda campaign that took the grand mufti's strategy to the next level.

The Muslim Brotherhood

The Muslim Brotherhood (*Ikhwan al-Muslimun*) is the fundamentalist movement that was founded in Egypt in 1931 by Hassan al-Banna (1906–1949). Along with al-Husseini, he was among the first modern Muslims to introduce "… a corrosive hatred of the Jews, which he seemed to have adopted from Nazism."[17] The Brotherhood is one of the most successful subversive movements of all time—a true Muslim Illuminati. Its program reaches far and wide through a vast worldwide network of dependent organizations, all camouflaged to obscure their radical origins.[18]

The goal of the Muslim Brotherhood is the reestablishment of the caliphate, a pan-Islamic government spanning all countries in which Muslims reside. Militant Islam is both a revolutionary political movement and a fundamentalist religious revival. Language barriers and national identities recede before its declared unity of faith and sense of destined mission. Like the secular Internationalist's vision of global

---

15 Hitler was called Muhammad Haidar in Egypt and Abu Ali elsewhere.

16 For example, Alois Brunner served as an advisor to the Syrian general staff and Otto Skorzeny was employed by Nassar. Escaped Nazi Louis Heidan (Louis al-Hadj) translated Hitler's *Mein Kampf* into Arabic. Morse, *The Nazi Connection to Islamic Terrorism*, pages 110–19.

17 Steven Schwartz, *The Two Faces of Islam*, Doubleday, New York, 2002, page 129.

18 See among many others, *The Grand Jihad* by Andrew C. McCarthey, *American Jihad* by Steven Emerson, and *Stealth Jihad* by Robert Spencer.

government superseding national sovereignty, the Jihadist seeks the dissolution of national boundaries and the erection of a Muslim super state—a world in which all nations and all peoples live under *Sharia*, the Muslim rules of religious, social, and political governance.[19]

Israel sits like a stone in the shoe of the Jihadist. As we have seen, such irritability contradicts many historical precedents of mutual tolerance between Muslims and Jews.

THE ESTABLISHMENT OF THE STATE OF ISRAEL

The post World War II diplomatic climate included a larger role for international governing bodies. The United States, which had rejected membership in the League of Nations, joined its successor organization the United Nations, formed in 1945. Awareness of the Nazi genocide created an international climate sympathetic to the establishment of a Jewish state. The UN Charter specifically recognized the rights of Jews to Palestine in Article 80, which confirmed the League of Nations Palestine Mandate of 1922.

In 1947, the United Nations partitioned the region into Jewish and Arab states, envisioning Jerusalem under international rule. The area was in a literal state of warfare with attacks against the British and between Arabs and Jews.

A third, even more radical Jewish paramilitary group, had splintered off from the Irgun in 1940. Known as the *Lehi* (Fighters for the Freedom of Israel), they were also called the Stern Gang after their founder Avraham Stern. The avowed purpose of this group was evicting

the British by force and establishing the state of Israel. The Nazi Holocaust ratcheted up the intensity of Jewish resistance to any attempts by the British to appease Arab sentiments. Radicals perceived the British as co-equal enemies of Israel.[20] The ever-escalating Jewish guerilla war from 1945 to 1947 encouraged the British to give up their thirty year Mideast misadventure.

The 1948 Arab-Israeli War

The British Mandate to the rulership of Palestine expired May 14, 1948. The state of Israel was officially born on May 15, 1948. On that very day, Israel was invaded by Egypt, followed by Jordan, Syria, Iran, Iraq, Saudi Arabia, Yemen, and members of the Muslim Brotherhood. The success of the grand mufti's decades-long propaganda campaign may be measured by the near unanimity of Muslim rejection of the Jewish state. For the Jews, the unexpected consequences of their success in evicting the British and winning nationhood was that they were no longer protected by the British military.

The UN Secretary General characterized the Arab invasion as the first act of international aggression since the end of WWII. However, the UN made absolutely no attempt to protect Jerusalem, abandoning the day-old state to its own defenses. After a month of fierce fighting, an initial cease-fire was declared in June of 1948. Fighting resumed and continued through December. Six thousand Jews died in the war—fully one percent of the entire regional Jewish population at this time—fifteen hundred in Jerusalem alone.[21]

---

19 The meaning of *Jihad* is struggle. For the moderate Muslim, Jihad means combatting personal spiritual weakness to become a better person. But it is also the term by which fundamentalist political activists, hardline Islamists, designate their efforts to establish worldwide Islamic supremacy under *Sharia*.

20 After two high-profile assassinations, the Lehi were banned as a terrorist group by the newly established government of Israel in 1948, but members were granted a general amnesty. Yitzhak Shamir, a future prime minister of Israel, was one of the group's leaders.

21 By way of comparison, one percent of America today is three million people.

The results of the fecklessness of the UN during the First Arab-Israeli War resulted in the official Jewish renunciation of Jerusalem as an international city on December 5, 1949. On December 13, 1949, Israel pledged herself to the protection of the holy sites of all three religions, but repeated that Jerusalem would remain under Jewish control.

In 1949, an armistice was signed with Jordan, Syria and Egypt. It was based on the tentative and temporary military borders that included the West Bank territories and portions of East Jerusalem that the Arabs had conquered. In 1950, Jordan announced it intended to annex these territories west of the Jordan River, a position Israel flatly rejected.

A new era of reclamation and restoration of the holy places in Jerusalem ensued with renewed archeological activity. The nation of Israel paid for the rebuilding of Christian sites that had been damaged by Arab mortars and explosives.

The 1956 Suez War

Arab nationalists, disappointed with Hitler's defeat, found solace in the arms of the Soviet Union. During the 1950s, countries with Soviet backing that adopted socialist governments, included Egypt, Algeria, Libya, Yemen, Syria, and Iraq. Despite its embrace of atheism, the socialist/communist model of governance shares the ideology of collectivism with Sharia law. Recognizing the strategic geographical position and abundant natural resources of their Arab clients, the Soviets took this opportunity to expand their sphere of influence, spread the communist gospel to the undeveloped and seething societies of the Middle East, and poke a geo-political stick in the eye of America.

Gamel Abdel Nasser became president of Egypt in 1954. In 1956, he seized the Suez Canal and closed it to Israeli shipping. He also launched cross-border terror strikes against Israel from Gaza and Sinai. The Israeli army, aided by France and England, took the Gaza Strip and the Sinai Peninsula and demilitarized both zones, while British and French forces occupied the Suez Canal. However, American and Soviet pressure resulted weeks later in an Israeli pullout from the Sinai and the British and French leaving the canal zone. Nasser turned his loss into a face-saving victory in the eyes of his public. In 1958, he encouraged Syria to join Egypt in the United Arab Republic. He set up a puppet regime in Yemen.

The 1967 Six Day War

Rising military tension between Israel and Syria allowed the Soviets to convince Nasser that Israel was preparing to attack. Nasser massed eighty thousand troops along the Sinai/Negev border; demanded the UN security forces that had been deployed there for a decade withdraw; and declared a naval blockade of the Israeli port of Eilat, considered an act of war. On May 26, 1967, he announced his intention to destroy Israel. Jordan joined the coalition of Arab states, placing its military forces under the command of Egypt and allowing Iraqi troops to march through its territory and join the assault. Two hundred fifty thousand enemy troops stood along Israel's borders.

On June 5, the shooting war began when Israel preemptively took out most of the Egyptian air force as it sat on the ground. After three days, the Israeli army beat back the assembled Arab armies and recaptured the Old City of Jerusalem and the West Bank territories. Jerusalem was reunited for the first time since the founding of Israel. A cease fire agreement was negotiated with the Arab League. The Jewish Parliament (Knesset) vowed to protect the holy sites of all three Abrahamic religions. Israel left the Temple Mount under the administration of the Jordanian *Waqf*,[22] however it insisted that Jews who wished to visit the Temple Mount be allowed to do so.

The post-victory borders of the united Israel have been a source of discontent ever since.

The 1973 Yom Kippur War

The Yom Kippur attack by the Arabs is reminiscent of the assaults against the Maccabees timed for the Sabbath. The holiest day of the Jewish year was the date of an invasion that took Israel by surprise. Their rapid success during the Six Day War led many Israeli leaders to have an exaggerated sense of their own military capacity and a lack of respect for the enemy. The Egyptian forces had, by 1973, received Soviet surface-to-air missiles, which they placed along the Suez Canal. Anwar Sadat succeeded Nasser and had taken steps to modernize and improve the Egyptian army, introducing superior training programs for his soldiers. Political infighting within the civilian government of Israel's Prime Minister Golda Meir had weakened the military.

An Egyptian force of eighty thousand men launched a carefully planned surprise attack along the Suez Canal. Israeli tactics that had succeeded in 1948, 1956, and 1967 failed miserably as Egyptian forces had learned from their mistakes.

With the Soviets aligned with regional Muslim states all the way to Pakistan, the United States provided critical resupply to the Israelis. Ariel Sharon's leadership, and the much-needed supplies, turned the tide in favor of Israel. With four times the casualties of the 1967 War, the 1973 War caused all parties to rethink the regional situation. Political compromises and treaties were the order of the day for everyone. Israel returned the Sinai Peninsula in 1981. Neither Egypt nor Syria has launched an attack since.

The Palestine Liberation Organization (PLO)

The Palestine Liberation Organization (PLO) was founded in 1963. Controlled in its early period by Egypt, the PLO rejected Jewish claims to Israel and the validity of the League of Nations mandate that had led to the establishment of the Jewish state by the UN. While the PLO paid lip service to Islam, it originated as a Marxist, Soviet-funded and trained, revolutionary organization based on the ideology of nationalism and the tactics of terror—a political protest decorated with the bangles of religion.

Yasser Arafat took over leadership of the PLO in 1968. He had earlier founded the terror group Fatah which he folded into the PLO. Arafat was born in Cairo in 1929. He was distantly related to Hajj Amin al-Husseini through tribal lineages. And he certainly assumed the mantle of leadership that al-Husseini had worn.

Arafat's greatest accomplishment was in the realm of nomenclature. He identified the Israeli Arabs as "Palestinians." This term had been used since the period of the British Mandate to describe regional Jews. After 1948, Jews began to refer to themselves as "Israelis."

Since the early 1990s, the PLO has assumed a more respectable veneer as the legal government of the Israeli Arabs. Hamas and Hezballah have taken up the regional terrorist mantle, while al-Qaeda and allied organizations work along international lines, and the Muslim Brotherhood network conducts its transnational cultural campaigns.

---

22 The Waqf is the name of the Muslim authority in charge of the Temple Mount. In one form or another, the Waqf has been in control of the Mount since the reconquest of Jerusalem by Saladin in 1187.

Is There a Solution?

The pathos of the current situation, in which worldwide Jewry prays at the remains of the Western Wall in Jerusalem, was foretold with painful accuracy in 2 Chronicles 7:20–22, where the means of redemption is also suggested. These verses are quoted in full on page 179.

Numbers 34:1–12 describes the natural borders of Israel: with the Mediterranean at the west; the Jordan River at the east; the southernmost reaches of the Great Salt Sea running in a descending arc to ancient Karnesh-barnea as the southern border; and the area beginning south of Tyre and extending east to modern Tel-Dan, north of the Sea of Galilee, as its northern border. (See map on page 372.)

The biblical importance of Jerusalem as the religious and political capital of the land of Israel for three thousand years seems to be lost on diplomats who insist on a partition of both Israel and Jerusalem in the interests of "fairness." Their fantasies of peace will continue to fail unless and until they acknowledge Jerusalem's non-negotiable place in Jewish religious and national life—as the home of the Temple, the center of the Promised Land.

The amount of territory in the Muslim dominated region is enormous, as the accompanying table shows. Yet, we hear no end of further diminishing Israel with a "two-state solution" (which might be more honestly characterized as "the final solution"). Israel is the easternmost outpost of Judeo-Christian civilization. Unlike Saudi Arabia, a strict Muslim theocracy in which non-Muslims are forbidden entry to Mecca, people of all faiths are welcome in Jewish Israel, and their holy places are respected.

Jews are not ready to take the Temple Mount to build the Third Temple. The position of the most religious Jews—since at least the time of the British Mandate—is that those who even walk on the Temple Mount risk standing on the location of the Holy of Holies. This is forbidden to all but the High Priest, who may only do so one day a year. The building of a Third Temple brings more responsibility than most modern Jews are willing to accept. However, the Temple Mount needs adult supervision. Israel should have political charge of the Mount and delegate religious administration to the Waqf. All construction and archaeological investigation must require complete transparency.

Jews will remember that Isaiah 56:7 describes the Temple as "a house of prayer for all people." Judaism, Christianity, and Islam share a common descent from our father Abraham. The baseline for Jerusalem must take into account its centrality for all three faiths. The number one priority must be free and open access for the worshippers, and especially the protection of those ancient sites through proper maintenance, adherence to strict archaeological and scientific protocols, and the open flow of information between all interested parties. As my friend Peter Levenda quips, a three-faith solution is more important than a two-state solution.

With the holy sites protected and mutually accessible, we will have come a long way toward settling the rancorous millennia-old issues of the region. Tolerance and mutual respect are the keys to much else in life, and certainly offer the best solution to the political issues facing Jerusalem, the axis of the world.

> Jerusalem has always sat on an inter-civilizational fault line between the East and the West. It is where civilizations can collide or learn to coexist. In this sense, Jerusalem is more than the center of spirituality for millions of believers; it is also one of the keys to world peace.[23]

23 Dore Gold, *The Fight for Jerusalem*, page 31.

Comparative Landmass of the Middle East

(Territory of Israel represents 0.001495 of the total area)

Country	Area in Square Miles
ISRAEL	**Total Landmass 8,015**

Muslim Countries	
AFGHANISTAN	251,773
ALGERIA	919,355
BAHRAIN	225
EGYPT	386,095
IRAN	636,130
IRAQ	169,235
JORDAN	35,000
KUWAIT	9,370
LEBANON	4,015
LIBYA	679,180
MOROCCO	274,414
OMAN	104,970
PAKISTAN	310,320
QATAR	4,415
SAUDI ARABIA	926,745
SYRIA	71,675
TUNISIA	63,378
TURKEY	300,870
UNITED ARAB EMIRATE	29,010
YEMEN	73,280
YEMEN SOUTH	111,045
MUSLIM COUNTRIES	**Total Landmass 5,360,500**

Source: *Times Family Atlas of the World*. Topsfield, MA: Salem House Publishers, 1988.

A Suggestive Chronology
of the Temple and Jerusalem

Timeline in Pre-History (All dates are bce)

3760 BCE   Beginning of the Jewish Calendar.

2000   Approximate period of the birth of Abraham and the beginning of the era of the Patriarchs.

1300   Approximate time of the Exodus from Egypt.

1200   Approximate time of Joshua's conquest of Canaan.

1150   Approximate time of the beginning of the period of the Judges.

Timeline in More Historical Times (All dates are bce)

1025 BCE   Saul (r. 1025–1005 BCE) is anointed by Samuel as king of Israel, the first ruler of the United Monarchy.

1005   David (r. 1005–965 BCE) succeeds Saul after the king is slain in battle against the Philistines.

1000   Approximate date of David's conquest of Jerusalem, where he establishes his capital.

968   Solomon (r. 968–928 BCE) succeeds his father David.

964   **Solomon begins work on the Temple.**

957   **The Temple is completed in eleventh year of Solomon's reign.**

928   Beginning of the Divided Monarchy with the reign of Rehoboam (r. 928–911 BCE) in the Southern Kingdom of Judah, and Jeroboam (r. 928–907 BCE) in the Northern Kingdom of Israel. Jeroboam establishes his capital in Shechem.

925   Egyptian invasion of Jerusalem by Pharaoh Shishak I (r. 945–924 BCE) who carries off treasure from the Temple of Solomon.

ca. 900   Ethiopian invasion of Judah by Zerah who is defeated by King Asa (r. 908–867 BCE).

ca. 875   King Omni of Israel (r. 882–871 BCE) builds the city of Samaria as the capital of the Northern Kingdom.

853   The Battle of Qarqar between the united forces of King Ahab of Israel (r. 873–852 BCE), King Hadadezer of Damascus (who may have been the biblical Benhadad II), and ten other kings, against Shalmanessar III (r. 858–824 BCE). This battle is not recorded in the Bible, but is inscribed on the ancient Assyrian Kurkh stela.

842   The deaths of Ahaziah of Judah (r. 843–842 BCE) and Jehoram of Israel (r. 851–842 BCE) at the hand of Jehu temporarily ends the Davidic line. Jehu becomes king of the Northern Israel (r. 842–814 BCE).

836   The crowning of Joash (Jehoash) (r. 836–798 BCE) restores the Davidic monarchy. He did extensive repairs on the Temple of Solomon.

ca. 739   Assyrian dominance of Judah by Tiglath-Pileser III (r. 745–727 BCE) who was given much tribute from the Temple of Solomon by King Ahaz (r. 743/735–727/715 BCE).

727/715	**Hezekiah (r. 727/715–698/687 BCE) begins his reign in Jerusalem. He restored the Temple and celebrated the Passover.**
722	The end of the Northern Kingdom of Israel at the hand of Shalmaneser V (r. 727–722 BCE), king of Assyria. He repopulated Samaria with pagan citizens from Assyria and Babylon. These people developed a syncretistic religion that included strong Jewish elements.
ca. 700	Assyrian invasion of Judah by Senacherib (r. 705–681 BCE) who was defeated by Hezekiah.
640	**Beginning of the reign of Josiah who restored the Temple, celebrated the Passover, recovered the Book of the Law, and returned the Ark to the Holy of Holies.**
612	Babylonian conquest of the Assyrian capital of Nineveh.
609	Egyptian invasion of Judah by Pharaoh Necho (r. 610–595 BCE).
605	Babylonian conquest of Egypt by Nebuchadnezzar II (r. 605–562 BCE).
597	Babylonian invasion of Judah by Nebuchadnezzar, and the first part of the Babylonian Exile.
586	**Destruction of Jerusalem, including the burning and dismantling of the Temple of Solomon by Nebuchadnezzar. This is the second and final stage of the Babylonian Exile.**
580	Birth of Pythagoras (ca. 580–500 BCE).
539	Cyrus II, king of Persia (r. 559–530 BCE) conquers Babylon.
538	**Cyrus allows the Jews to return to Jerusalem and authorizes them to rebuild the Temple under the leadership of Sheshbazaar.**
530	Cyrus' son and successor Cambyses (r. 530–522 BCE) halts the rebuilding of Second Temple because of local complaints and accusations of treason.
520	**Darius I (r. 522–486 BCE) allows construction of Temple to be resumed under the leadership of Zerrubabel, Jeshua, and the prophet Haggai.**
515	**The Second Temple is completed and dedicated**
458	Artaxerxes I of Persia (r. 465–424 BCE) allows for the second wave of emigrants to return to Jerusalem led by Ezra.
445	Artaxerxes authorizes the rebuilding of the walls of Jerusalem by Nehemiah, whom he appoints as governor of Jerusalem.
331	Alexander the Great (r. 336–323 BCE) conquers the Persian Empire.
323	Upon his deathbed, Alexander the Great divides his kingdom among his generals, including Ptolemy who took Egypt and Seleucas who took Syria. Both founded successful dynasties.
301	The Ptolemies expand their rule to Judea.
ca. 250	The beginning of the translation of the Bible into Greek encourages the growth of Hellenism, the union of Greek and Semitic cultures.
198	Judea falls to the Seleucids.
167	Mattathias establishes the Hasmonean dynasty when he leads the Maccabean revolt. It began in response to the Seleucid king Antiochus IV (r. 175–164 BCE) plundering the Temple and outlawing Jewish religious practices.
166	Judas Maccabeus, "the Hammer," succeeds his father as king of the Hasmoneans.
164	**The success of the Maccabean campaign allows for the rededication of the Temple. This is the origin of the Jewish festival of Hanukah.**

63	Roman conquest of Judea by Pompey ends Hasmonean rule.
37	Herod the Great (r. 37–4 BCE) assumes the throne of Judea, under the authority of Rome.

20 Herod begins his restoration and expansion of the Temple, and pursues ambitious construction projects throughout Jerusalem and Judea.

ca. 18 Herod's Temple completed.

ca. 4	Approximate date of the birth of Jesus which took place during the reign of Herod the Great. Herod tried to kill Jesus, perceiving him as a potential rival when he learned of his birth from the Wise Men.
4	Death of Herod
4	Herod Archelaus (r. 4 BCE–6 CE) becomes Tetrarch of Judea under Rome.
4	Herod Antipas (r. 4 BCE–39 CE) becomes Tetrarch of Galilee and Perea under Rome.

THE FOLLOWING DATES ARE ALL CE (COMMON ERA)

6 CE	The Roman Empire annexes Judea.
14	Tiberius (r. 14–37) becomes emperor of Rome.
26	Pontius Pilate (r. 26–36) is appointed Roman governor of Judea.
ca. 30	Jesus is crucified by the Romans.
41	Caligula demands a golden statue of himself be erected in the Temple, however his assasination nullifies his demands.
66	Revolt of the Jewish Zealots against Rome.

70 Titus defeats the Zealots on the Temple Mount and destroys Herod's Temple.

74	The remaining Zealots at Masada fall to the Romans.
117	Hadrian (r. 117–138) becomes the Roman emperor.
130	Hadrian decides to rebuild Jerusalem (still in ruins after the campaign by Titus) and rename it Aelia Capitolina, forbidding Jews to live there.

132 Bar Kochba revolt begins against Rome in response to Hadrian's placing a statue of Jupiter on the Temple Mount. The rebels began construction of a provisional Third Temple.

135	Bar Kochba revolt defeated and the Jews were again banned from Jerusalem. This represents the beginning of the Diaspora.
325	The Roman Empire officially embraces Christianity as the state religion under Emperor Constantine.
326	Helena, later canonized, the mother of Constantine, visits Jerusalem and finds the True Cross, setting in motion Constantine's construction of the Church of the Holy Sepulcher.

361 The reign of Julian the Apostate begins. He was a fierce adversary of Christianity and sought to return Rome to the Pagan worship. He made alliance with the Jews and authorized them to begin construction of the Third Temple. The efforts were said to be interrupted by a series of flames and earthquakes.

363	The death of Julian in battle against the Persians.
455	In the attack on Rome, the Vandal leader Gaiseric seized the gold table and candlesticks taken by Titus and the Romans in 70 CE.
570	Birth of Muhammad (570–632).

614	Persian conquest of Jerusalem by Khosrow II.
629	Roman Emperor Heraclius and the Byzantine army re-conquer Jerusalem.
630	Muhammad conquers Mecca.
638	Caliph Omar leads the Muslim armies to conquer Jerusalem.
692	The Dome of the Rock is completed by Caliph Abd al-Malik.
ca. 710	The al-Aqsa Mosque is completed by Caliph al-Walid.
1010	Caliph al-Hakim razes the Church of the Holy Sepulcher.
1054	The Great Schism divides Eastern Orthodox and Western Roman Christianity.
1095	The Crusades are launched in Europe.
1099	The Crusaders take Jerusalem.
1118	Knights Templar founded in Jerusalem and are headquartered at the al-Aqsa Mosque.
1128	Crusader kings move their headquarters to the Citadel.
1187	Saladin takes Jerusalem.
1244	The Khwarizmians take Jerusalem.
1258	The Mongols conquer Baghdad.
1260	The Mameluks under Baybars defeat the Mongols at the Battle of Ain Jalut.
1292	Baybars expels Crusaders from the Holy Land and takes control of Jerusalem.
1307	The Knights Templars are arrested in France on Friday the 13th of October.
1312	The Knights Templar Order is officially dissolved by Pope Clement V.
1314	Jacques de Molay and Geffroi de Charney are burned at the stake on March 18, proclaiming the innocence of the Knights Templar.
1390	Oldest document of the "Old Charges" collection of Masonic documents.
1420	The Cooke Manuscript attributes the founding of Freemasonry to David and Solomon.
1453	The Ottoman Turks take Constantinople.
1516	The Ottomans take Jerusalem.
1646	Elias Ashmole records joining a Masonic lodge in his diary, making him history's first known "speculative" Mason to be initiated.
1717	British Grand Lodge of Freemasonry is announced in London.
1732	Anderson's Constitutions published in London.
1734	Benjamin Franklin prints Anderson's Constitutions in Philadelphia.
1798	Napoleon conquers Egypt.
1838	The British establish a consulate office in Jerusalem.
1917	The Ottomans, allied with Germany, surrender Jerusalem to the British after their defeat in Word War I.
1948	The modern state of Israel is founded.

The Temple Holidays

The Jews have an active holiday schedule throughout the course of the year. Here we are specifically concerned with those holidays that are derived from the Five Books of Moses, the Spring and Fall festivals. Two other Temple-related holidays will also be mentioned.

In the days of Moses, there were three major Jewish festivals in which all adult males were required to travel to the Sanctuary to take part in the communal worship. Instructions for these gatherings are given in Exodus 23:14, 34:23–24; and Deuteronomy 16:16. People were first required to join together at the Tabernacle while they wandered through the desert; later all Israel would travel to the Temple of Solomon after God had chosen Jerusalem as the spiritual center of the nation. Instructions for the Temple worship are given in Deuteronomy 16:2, 16:5–6, and 16:11. The tradition of the community festivals obviously refers to the time before the Exile (in the case of gathering at the Temple), and the Diaspora (in the case of gathering together as a united people). The three great communal festivals were Passover (including the Feast of Unleavened Bread), the Festival of Weeks or Pentecost, and the Festival of Tabernacles or Booths.

The Temple-related holidays of Moses begin in the Spring with Passover, the New Year in the older tradition. They include Passover, the Feast of Unleavened Bread, and the Feast of Weeks. In the Fall, we have the Feast of Trumpets, the Day of Atonement, the Feast of Tabernacles, and the Feast of the Eighth Day of Assembly.

(March/April) **The Feast of the Passover** and the **Feast of Unleavened Bread** (*Pesach*) (Passover begins on the evening of the fourteenth day of the first month of *Nisan*. The Feast of Unleavened Bread technically begins on the fifteenth day of Nisan.) These are two parts of one holiday. Passover itself commemorates the night the Angel slew the firstborn of Egypt but passed over the Hebrew households because they had identified themselves by smearing the blood of a lamb on the doorposts of their houses. It begins in the first month of the Priestly ritual year—the first full moon after the Vernal Equinox, adjusting as needed for the lunar calendar. The Feast of Unleavened Bread continues for seven days, and marks the beginning of the Exodus, when the Hebrews left Egypt so quickly they had no time to add yeast to their dough for baking. This is the first of the great communal festivals.

(Exodus 12:2–20, 12:34, 12:43–49, 34:18, 34:25; Leviticus 23:5-8; Numbers 9:1–14, 28:16–25; Deuteronomy 16:1–8; see also Ezekiel, 45:21–25.)

(May/June) **The Feast of Weeks** (*Shavuot*) (The sixth day of the third month of *Sivan*) This celebrates the summer harvest festival. It is also called Pentecost (a Greek word meaning fifty days), because it begins seven weeks or fifty days from the second day of Passover. It marks the end of the first harvest of the wheat crop and the offering of the first fruits to the Lord. The Feast of Weeks is a day of rest and was observed after the children of Israel settled in the Promised Land. This is the second of the communal festivals.

(Exodus 23:16, 34:22; Leviticus 23:15-21; Numbers 28:26-31; Deuteronomy 16:9–12.)

After the early and late Spring Festivals above, the next series of Mosaic holidays begins in the Fall in the seventh month of Nisan. It is a busy period. The first ten days are the most solemn of the Jewish year. Five days later, on the fifteenth of the month, this solemnity is balanced with a joyful eight-day celebratory harvest festival.

(September/October) **The Feast of Trumpets** (*Yom Teruah*, now called *Rosh Hashanah*) (The first day of the seventh month of *Tishri*) This is the day of the blowing of the ram's horn, the *shofar*, to call the people to prepare for the Day of Atonement. It replaced the Spring festival as the beginning of the New Year in later Jewish tradition.

(Leviticus 23:23-25; Numbers 29:1-6.)

(September/October) **The Day of Atonement** (*Yom Kippur*) (The tenth day of *Tishri*) This is the most solemn day of the Jewish year. In the time of the Tabernacle and the Temple, the High Priest sacrificed sin offerings to atone for the community. This was the one day of the year when the High Priest alone was authorized to enter the Holy of Holies in his white linen robe and offer prayers. It remains a day of fasting, repentance, and rest.

(Exodus 29:10–16; Leviticus 16:1–34, and 23:27–32; Numbers 29:7–11.)

The ten-day period from the Feast of Trumpets to the Day of Atonement is known in modern Judaism as the "Days of Awe" (*Yamim Noraim*). During this period, people search their hearts and examine their lives. It is believed that at this time God writes names in, or removes them from, the Book of Life for the coming year.

(September/October) **The Feast of Tabernacles or Booths** (*Sukkot*) (The fifteenth day of *Tishri*) This is a seven-day feast (see the next entry for its eighth day conclusion.) It is also called the Festival of the Ingathering and celebrates the fall harvest, the final harvest of the year when the fruit, grapes, and olives are ripened and collected. It also commemorates the Exodus when the people lived in tents for forty years. It is a feast of rejoicing. Jews erect tents, or booths, as they had done in the wilderness. This is the third of the great communal festivals. It is mentioned twice in Exodus in the same sentence as the Feast of Weeks.

(Exodus 23:16, 34:22; Leviticus 23:33-43; Numbers 29:12-40; Deuteronomy 16:13-15.)

(September/October) **The Feast of the Last Great Day, or the Eighth Day of Assembly** (*Shemini Atzeret*) This marks the conclusion of the festival year and is actually the eighth day of the seven-day Feast of Sukkot. The people gather a final time at the Tabernacle and offer sacrifices before returning to their homes. It is a day of rest, as if a day of nostalgia at the end of a long period of religious activity that began with *Rosh Hashanah*.

(Leviticus 23:36, 23:39; Numbers 29:35–38.)

There are two holidays not mentioned in the Torah that are specifically related to the Temple. The earlier of these is Hanukkah, established in the second century BCE; Tisha b'Av developed after the destruction of the Temple in 70 CE.

(December) **The Festival of Lights** (*Hanukkah*) (The twenty-fifth day of the ninth month of *Kislev*) This commemorates the second century BCE rededication of the Second Temple after its desecration by the Greeks. The eight-day consecration of the Temple was modeled on Judas Maccabees' understanding of 1 Kings, 8:66, which states that Solomon sent the people home after the eighth day of his consecration of the Temple.

(July/August) **Ninth of Av** (*Tisha b'Av*) (The fifth month) This is an annual mourning period, including one to three days of fasting, over three weeks. It commemorates the destruction of the Second Temple by the Roman general, later emperor, Titus in 70 CE, as well as the destruction of the First Temple in 586 BCE. The Book of Lamentations of Jeremiah and the Vision of Isaiah are read in synagogues throughout the world. A tradition asserts that the Jewish Messiah will be born on this day, turning it from a day of mourning to one of celebration.

The **Purim** festival on the fourteenth day of the twelfth month of *Adar* (February/March) celebrates events in the Book of Esther that have not been discussed here. They concern the fifth century BCE Jewish community that remained in Persia/Babylon after other Jews had returned to Jerusalem.

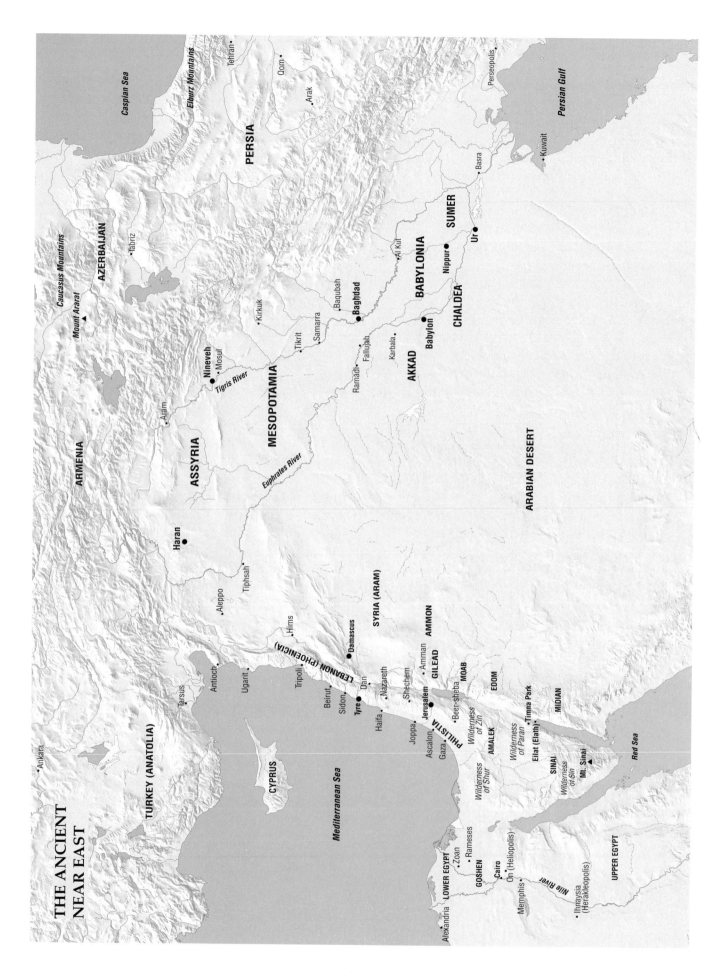

THE ANCIENT NEAR EAST

TURKEY (ANATOLIA)

ARMENIA

AZERBAIJAN

PERSIA

ASSYRIA

MESOPOTAMIA

BABYLONIA

AKKAD

CHALDEA

SUMER

ARABIAN DESERT

SYRIA (ARAM)

LEBANON (PHOENICIA)

AMMON

GILEAD

MOAB

EDOM

MIDIAN

AMALEK

PHILISTIA

SINAI

LOWER EGYPT

GOSHEN

UPPER EGYPT

Caspian Sea

Elburz Mountains

Caucasus Mountains

Mount Ararat

Persian Gulf

Mediterranean Sea

Red Sea

Tigris River

Euphrates River

Nile River

CYPRUS

Wilderness of Shur

Wilderness of Zin

Wilderness of Paran

Wilderness of Sin

Mt. Sinai

Timna Park

Tehran
Qom
Arak
Perseopolis
Kuwait
Basra
Tabriz
Al Kut
Nippur
Ur
Baqubah
Baghdad
Babylon
Kirkuk
Samarra
Tikrit
Fallujah
Karbala
Ramadi
Nineveh
Mosul
Aram
Haran
Tiphsah
Aleppo
Hims
Damascus
Antioch
Tarsus
Ankara
Ugarit
Tripoli
Beirut
Sidon
Tyre
Dan
Haifa
Nazareth
Shechem
Jerusalem
Joppa
Ascalon
Gaza
Beer-sheba
Amman
Eilat (Elath)
Alexandria
Zoan
Rameses
Cairo
On (Heliopolis)
Memphis
Ihnasya (Herakleopolis)

370

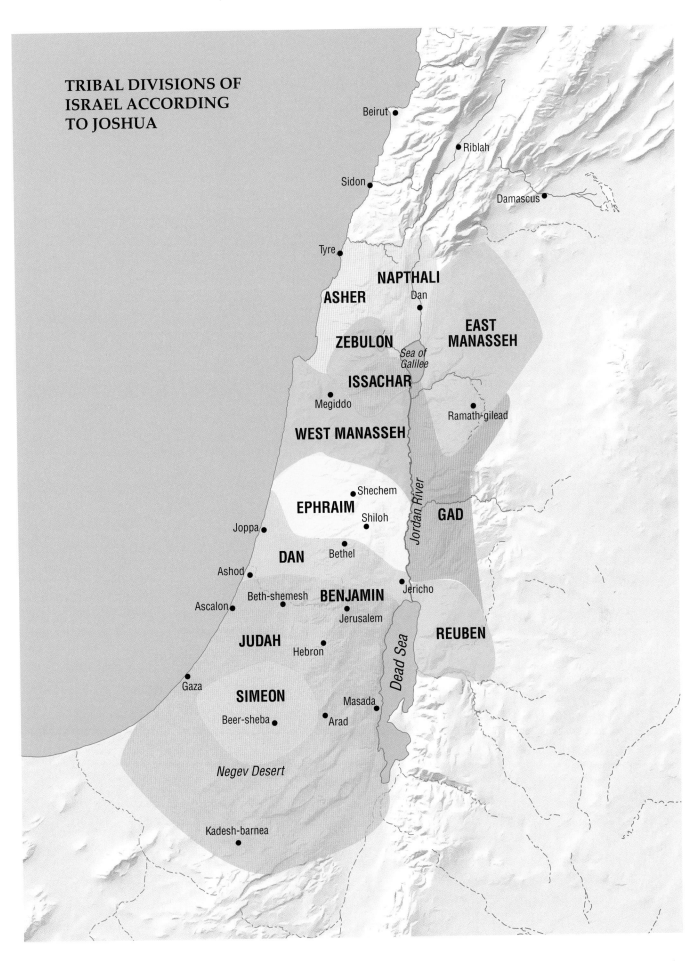

TRIBAL DIVISIONS OF
ISRAEL ACCORDING
TO JOSHUA

Beirut

Riblah

Sidon

Damascus

Tyre

NAPTHALI

ASHER

Dan

EAST
MANASSEH

ZEBULON

Sea of
Galilee

ISSACHAR

Megiddo

Ramath-gilead

WEST MANASSEH

Shechem

EPHRAIM

Shiloh

GAD

Joppa

DAN

Bethel

Jordan River

Ashod

Beth-shemesh

BENJAMIN

Jericho

Ascalon

Jerusalem

REUBEN

JUDAH

Hebron

Dead Sea

Gaza

SIMEON

Masada

Beer-sheba

Arad

Negev Desert

Kadesh-barnea

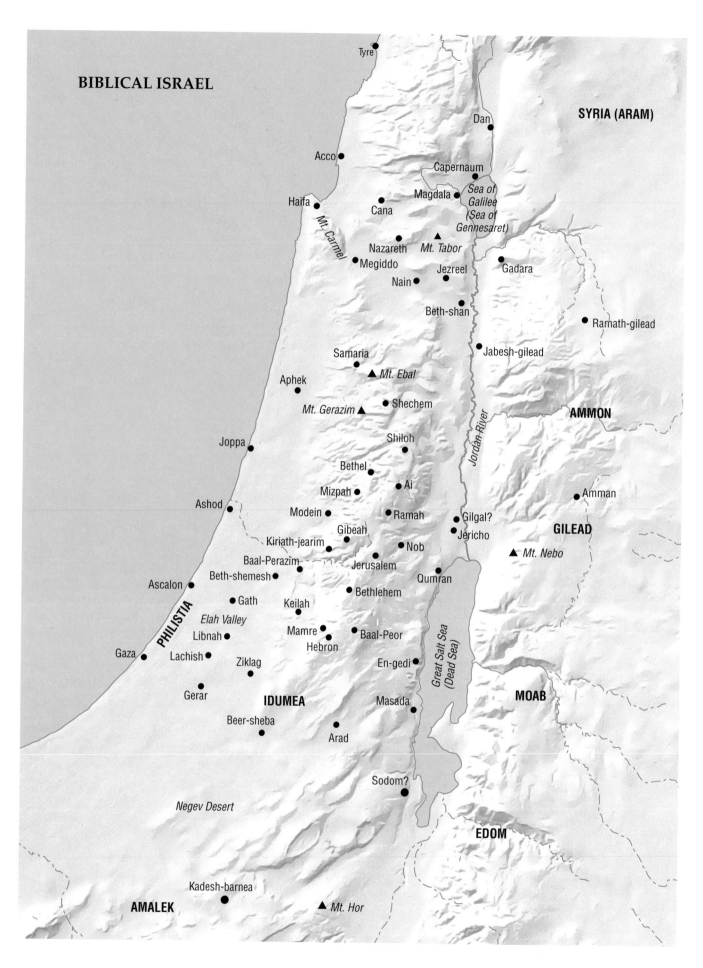

BIBLICAL ISRAEL

SYRIA (ARAM)

Tyre

Dan

Acco

Capernaum

Haifa

Magdala

Sea of Galilee (Sea of Gennesaret)

Cana

Nazareth

Mt. Tabor

Megiddo

Jezreel

Gadara

Nain

Beth-shan

Ramath-gilead

Samaria

Jabesh-gilead

Mt. Ebal

Aphek

Mt. Gerazim

Shechem

AMMON

Shiloh

Joppa

Jordan River

Bethel

Ai

Mizpah

Ashod

Modein

Ramah

Gilgal?

Amman

Gibeah

Jericho

GILEAD

Kiriath-jearim

Nob

Baal-Perazim

Jerusalem

Mt. Nebo

Beth-shemesh

Ascalon

Bethlehem

Qumran

Gath

Keilah

PHILISTIA

Elah Valley

Baal-Peor

Libnah

Mamre

Great Salt Sea (Dead Sea)

Gaza

Lachish

Hebron

Ziklag

En-gedi

Gerar

IDUMEA

Masada

MOAB

Beer-sheba

Arad

Sodom?

Negev Desert

EDOM

Kadesh-barnea

AMALEK

Mt. Hor

372

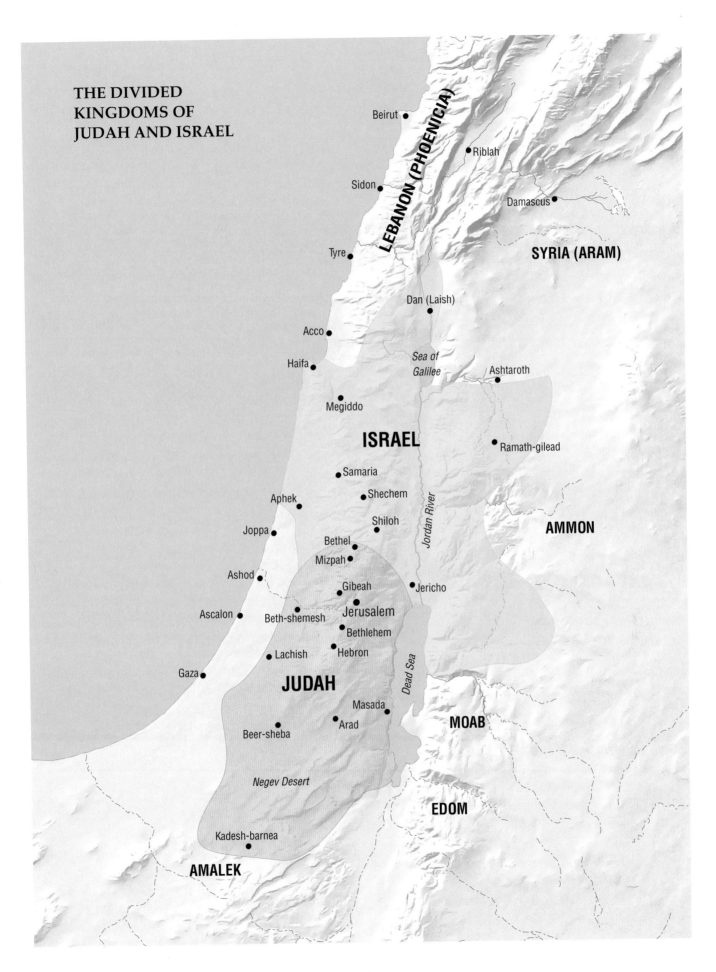

THE DIVIDED
KINGDOMS OF
JUDAH AND ISRAEL

Beirut

LEBANON (PHOENICIA)

Riblah

Sidon

Damascus

SYRIA (ARAM)

Tyre

Dan (Laish)

Acco

Sea of
Galilee

Ashtaroth

Haifa

Megiddo

ISRAEL

Samaria

Shechem

Ramath-gilead

Aphek

Jordan River

Joppa

Shiloh

AMMON

Bethel

Mizpah

Ashod

Gibeah

Jericho

Ascalon

Beth-shemesh

Jerusalem

Bethlehem

Lachish

Hebron

Gaza

JUDAH

Dead Sea

Masada

MOAB

Arad

Beer-sheba

Negev Desert

EDOM

Kadesh-barnea

AMALEK

BIBLIOGRAPHY

BIBLES CONSULTED

KJV *Holy Bible: King James Version*. Holman Bible Publishers.

NRSV *Holy Bible: New Revised Standard Version with Apocrypha*. New York: Oxford University Press, 1962, rev. 1977.

JSB Berlin, Adele, and Marc Zvi Brettler, eds. *The Jewish Study Bible: Featuring the Jewish Publication Society Tanakh Translation*. New York: Oxford University Press, 2004.

NOAB Coogan, Michael D., ed. *The New Oxford Annotated Bible: Augmented Third Edition, with the Apocryphal/Deuterocanonical Books. New Revised Standard Version*. New York, Oxford: Oxford University Press, 2007.

Holy Bible: The New Standard Reference Bible. Chicago: The John A. Hertel Co., 1963.

Holy Scriptures According to the Masoretic Text. Philadelphia: Jewish Publication Society of America, 1917, 1955.

The Septuagint Bible. Thomson, Charles, trans., and C. A. Muses, ed. Indian Hills, CO: The Falcon's Wing Press, 1954.

Anderson, James, and W. J. Hughan. *The New Book of Constitutions of the Antient and Honourable Fraternity of Free and Accepted Masons*. London, 1738. Reprinted, Kessinger Publishing, n.p., n.d.

Ariel, Rav Yisrael, and Rav Menachem Makover, eds. *The Light of the Temple: Art, History, Service*. Jerusalem: The Temple Institute, 1998.

Baigent, Michael, and Richard Leigh. *The Temple and the Lodge*. New York: Arcade Publishing, 1989.

Barnes, Ian. *The Historical Atlas of the Bible*. New York: Chartwell Books, 2010.

Beitzel, Barry J., ed. *Biblica: The Bible Atlas*. Hauppague, NY: Barron's Educational Series, 2006.

The Book of the Law, Liber AL vel Legis. New York: Samuel Weiser, 1976.

Brooke, Steven. *Sacred Journey: A Pilgrimage to the Stations of the Cross in Jerusalem*. Lake Worth, FL: Nicolas Hays, 2010.

———. *Views of Jerusalem and the Holy Land*. New York: Rizzoli, 1998.

Burstein, Dan, and Arne J. DeKeijzer, eds. *Secrets of Mary Magdalene: The Untold Story of History's Most Misunderstood Woman*. New York: CDS Books, 2006.

Cantor, Norman F. *The Sacred Chain: History of the Jews*. New York: HarperCollins, 1994.

Capt, E. Raymond. *King Solomon's Temple: A Study of Symbolism*. Muskogee, OK: Hoffman Printing, 1996.

———. *Petra*. Thousand Oaks, CA: Artisan Sales, 1987.

Chappell, Vere. *Sexual Outlaw, Erotic Mystic: The Essential Ida Craddock*. San Francisco, CA/Newburyport, MA: Weiser Books, 2010.

Charles, R. H. (trans.) *The Apocrypha and Pseudepigrapha of the Old Testament*. Oxford: Clarendon Press, 1913. Available at http://wesley.nnu.edu/biblical_studies/noncanon/ot/pseudo/jubilee.htm.

———. (trans.) *The Book of Enoch the Prophet*. San Francisco, CA/Newburyport, MA: Weiser Books, 2003.

Dobbins, Frank Stockton. *Error's Chains: How Forged and Broken*. New York: Standard Publishing House, 1883.

Durant, Will. *The Age of Faith*. New York: Simon and Schuster, 1950.

———. *Caesar and Christ*. New York: Simon and Schuster, 1944.

Edersheim, Alfred. *The Temple: Its Mysteries and Services As They Were at the Time of Jesus Christ*. Grand Rapids, MI: Wm. B. Eerdmans Publishing Company, 1990.

Emerson, Steven. *American Jihad: The Terrorists Living Among Us*. New York: The Free Press, 2002.

Farrah, George. *The Temples at Jerusalem and their Masonic Connections*. Hinckley, Leics, England: Central Regalia Limited, 2003.

Frazer, Sir James G. *The Golden Bough: A Study in Magic and Religion,* abridged edition. London: Macmillan and Co. Limited, 1929.

Gardener, Joseph L., ed. *Atlas of the Bible*. Pleasantville, NY: The Reader's Digest Association, 1981.

Goelet, Ogden, ed. *The Egyptian Book of the Dead: The Book of Going Forth by Day*. San Francisco: Chronicle Books, 1994, rev. 1998.

Gold, Dore. *The Fight for Jerusalem: Radical Islam, the West, and the Future of the Holy City*. Washington, D.C.: Regnery Publishing, 2007.

Grabar, Oleg, and Benjamin Z. Kedar, eds. *Where Heaven and Earth Meet: Jerusalem's Sacred Esplanade*. Austin: University of Texas Press, and Jerusalem: Yad Ben-Zvi Press: 2009.

Grafton, Carol Belanger, ed. *120 Great Paintings*. Mineola, NY: Dover Publications, Inc., 2006.

———, ed. *120 Great Paintings from Medieval Illuminated Books*. Mineola, NY: Dover Publications, Inc., 2008.

———, ed. *120 Italian Renaissance Paintings*. Mineola, NY: Dover Publications, Inc., 2007.

Graves, Robert, and Raphael Patai. *Hebrew Myths: The Book of Genesis*. New York: Doubleday & Company, 1963-1964.

Green, David, trans. The *History of Herodotus*. Chicago: The University of Chicago Press, 1987.

Greenburg, Irving. *The Jewish Way: Living the Holidays*. New York: Touchstone, 1988.

Harwood, Jeremy. *The Secret History of Freemasonry*. London: Lorenz Books, 2006.

Hendin, David. *Guide to Biblical Coins*. 5th edition. Nyack, NY: Amphora, 2010.

Hodgson, Godfrey. *Woodrow Wilson's Right Hand: The Life of Colonel Edward M. House*. New Haven and London: Yale University Press, 2006

Horne, Alex. *King Solomon's Temple in the Masonic Tradition*. Wellingborough, Northampshire, UK: The Aquarian Press, 1972.

James, E. O. *The Ancient Gods: The History and Diffusion of Religion in the Ancient Near East and Eastern Mediterranean*. New York: G. P. Putnam's Sons, 1960.

Kazantzakis, Nikos. trans. P. A. Bien. *The Last Temptation of Christ*. New York: Simon and Schuster, 1960.

Koestler, Arthur. *The Thirteenth Tribe*. New York: Random House, 1976.

Lacroix, Paul. *Military and Religious Life in the Middle Ages and the Period of the Renaissance*. London: Chapman and Hall, 1874.

Larkin, Clarence. *Dispensational Truth or God's Plan and Purpose in the Ages*. Glenside, PA: Rev. Clarence Larkin Estate, 1918, rev. 1920.

Levenda, Peter. *The Secret Temple: Masons, Mysteries, and the Founding of America*. New York: Continuum International, 2009.

———. *Stairway to Heaven: Chinese Alchemists, Jewish Kabbalists, and the Art of Spiritual Transformation*. New York: Continuum International, 2008.

Levin, Daniel. *The Last Ember*. New York: Riverhead Books, 2009.

Lewis, Bernard. *The Crisis of Islam: Holy War and Unholy Terror*. New York: Modern Library: 2003.

———. *What Went Wrong? Western Impact and Middle East Response*. New York: Oxford University Press, 2002.

Mackey, Albert G. *The History of Freemasonry*. 7 volumes. New York and London: The Masonic History Company, 1920.

Mackey, Albert G., and Charles T. McClenachan. *Encyclopedia of Freemasonry*. 2 volumes. New York: The Masonic History Company, 1920.

MacNulty, W. Kirk. *Freemasonry: A Journey Through Ritual and Symbol*. New York: Thomas & Hudson, 1991.

Man, John. *Attila: The Barbarian King who Challenged Rome*. New York: Thomas Dunne Books, an imprint of St. Martin's Press, 2005.

Marcellinus, Ammianus. *The Roman History of Ammianus Marcellinus*. www.gutenberg.org/catalog/world/read file?pageno=1&fk_files=1234342.

Mazar, Benjamin. *The Mountain of the Lord: Excavating in Jerusalem*. New York: Doubleday & Company, 1975.

Mazar, Eilat. *The Complete Guide to the Temple Mount Excavations*. Jerusalem: Shoham Academic Research and Publication, 2002.

McCarthy, Andrew C. *The Grand Jihad: How Islam and the Left Sabotage America*. New York: Encounter Books, 2010.

Morse, Chuck. *The Nazi Connection to Islamic Terrorism: Adolph Hitler and Haj Amin Al-Husseini*. Washington, D.C.: World Net Daily, 2010.

Murphy-O'Connor, Jerome. *The Holy Land: An Oxford Archeological Guide*. New York: Oxford University Press, 2008.

Nerval, Gerard de, trans. by Norman Glass. *Journey to the Orient*. London: Peter Owen Publishers, 2001 (orginally published in French in 1851, *Voyage en Orient*).

Nicholson, Helen. *The Knights Templar: A New History*. Gloucestershire, U.K.: Sutton Publishing, Ltd., 2001.

Paine, Timothy Otis. *Solomon's Temple and Capitol, Ark of the Flood and Tabernacle, or the Holy Houses of the Hebrew, Chaldee, Syraic, Samaritan, Septuagint, Coptic, and Itala Scriptures: Josephus, Talmud, and Rabbis*, 2 volumes. Boston and New York: Houghton, Mifflin and Company, 1886.

Patai, Raphael. *The Hebrew Goddess*. KTAV Publishing House: 1967.

Peloubet F. N., ed. *Peloubet's Bible Dictionary*. Grand Rapids, MI: Zondervan Publishing House, 1967.

Pickthall, Marmaduke, trans. *The Meaning of the Glorious Koran*. New York: Alfred A. Knopf, 3rd edition 1992.

Pineda, Daniel. *The Book of Secrets: Esoteric Societies and Holy Orders*. San Francisco, CA/Newburyport, MA: Weiser Books, 2011.

Qutb, Sayyid. *Social Justice in Islam.* New York: Islamic Publications International, 2000.

Ralls, Karen. *Knights Templar Encyclopedia: The Essential Guide to the People, Places, Events, and Symbols of the Order of the Temple.* Franklin Lakes, NJ: New Page Books, 2007.

Ralls, Karen. *The Templars and the Grail.* Wheaton, IL: Quest Books, 2003.

Ridpath, John Clark. *History of the World.* 10 volumes. Cincinnati: The Ridpath Historical Society, 1921.

Roberts, J. M. *The New History of the World.* New York: Oxford University Press: 2003.

Robinson, James M. *The Nag Hammadi Library.* San Francisco: Harper & Row, 1988.

Robinson, John J. *Born in Blood: The Lost Secrets of Freemasonry.* New York: M. Evans & Company, 1989.

Romer, John. *Testament: The Bible and History.* Old Saybrook, CT: Konecky & Konecky, 1988.

Sachar, Abram Leon. *A History of the Jews.* New York: Alfred A. Knopf, 1930, rev. 1953.

Scholem, Gershom G. *Major Trends in Jewish Mysticism.* New York: Shocken Books, 1941.

Schwartz, Stephen. *The Two Faces of Islam: The House of Sa'ud from Tradition to Terror.* New York: Doubleday, 2002.

Shanks, Hershel. *Jerusalem's Temple Mount: From Solomon to the Golden Dome.* New York: Continuum International, 2007.

Shehadeh, Fawzia D., Essa Al-Masu, trans. *Jericho Cultural Studies.* 2008.

Sieff, Martin. *The Politically Incorrect Guide to the Middle East.* Washington, D.C.: Regnery Publishing, 2008.

Silberman, Neil Asher. *Digging for God and Country: Exploration, Archeology, and the Secret Struggle for the Holy Land, 1799–1917.* New York: Alfred A, Knopf, 1982.

Spencer, Robert. *Stealth Jihad: How Radical Islam is Subverting America without Guns or Bombs.* Washington, D.C.: Regnery Publishing Inc., 2008.

Stanley, Thomas. *Pythagoras: His Life and Teachings.* Lake Worth FL: Ibis Press, 2010.

Vagi, David L. *Coinage and History of the Roman Empire.* 2 volumes. Sidney, OH: Amos Press, 1999, rev. 2000.

Van Der Toorn, Karel, Bob Becking, and Pieter W. Van Der Horst, eds. *Dictionary of Deities and Demons in the Bible—DDD.* Leiden, The Netherlands: Brill Academic Publishers, and Grand Rapids, MI and Cambridge: Wm. B. Eerdmans Publishing Company, 1995, rev. 1999.

Vermes, Geza, trans. *The Complete Dead Sea Scrolls in English.* London: Penguin Books, 2004.

Villars, Abbé N. de Montfaucon de. *Comte de Gabalis.* London: The Brothers, 1913.

Wasserman, James. *The Mystery Traditions: Secret Symbols and Sacred Art.* Rochester, VT: Inner Traditions International, 2005.

———. *The Secrets of Masonic Washington: A Guidebook to Signs, Symbols, and Ceremonies at the Origin of America's Capital.* Rochester, VT: Inner Traditions International, 2008.

———. *The Slaves Shall Serve: Meditations on Liberty.* New York: Sekmet Books, 2004.

———. *The Templars and the Assassins: The Militia of Heaven.* Rochester, VT: Inner Traditions International, 2001.

Weller, Andrew, ed. *120 Visions of Heaven & Hell.* Mineola, NY: Dover Publications, Inc., 2010.

Whiston, William, trans. *The Works of Josephus.* Peabody, Mass, Hendrickson Publishers, 1987.

Wise, Michael, Martin Abegg Jr., and Edward Cook, translators. *The Dead Sea Scrolls.* New York: HarperOne, 1996, rev. 2005.

Wise, Terence, and Richard Scollins. *The Knights of Christ.* Men at Arms Series #155. London: Osprey Military, 1984.

Wright, Lawrence. *The Looming Tower: Al-Qaeda and the Road to 9/11.* New York: Alfred A. Knopf, 2006.

Primary Internet Resources:

http://en.wikipedia.org has been an invaluable and trustworthy research resource when a topic is lacking in controversy. Their Creative Commons efforts are greatly appreciated. The true copyright status of individual works of art, however, must be analysed with caution.

http://quod.lib.umich.edu/k/kjv has been an excellent online source for quotations and search tools in the King James translation of the Bible.

www.sacred-texts.com is an electronic archive for out of print and scarce religious texts from myriad religious and spiritual traditions.

www.gutenberg.org is another online resource for ancient texts.

PERMISSIONS

Chapter and part opening decorations: From the Church of Our Lady of the Ark of the Covenant at Kiriath Jearim.

Frontispiece: *Solomon Dedicates the Temple at Jerusalem*, ca. 1896–1902. Tissot, James Jacques Joseph (1836-1902) and Followers. Photo by John Parnell. Location: The Jewish Museum, New York, NY, U.S.A. Photo Credit: The Jewish Museum, NY/Art Resource, NY.

Page 6: The Temple of Solomon. Photo: René-Gabriel Ojéda. Location: Musée Condé, Chantilly, France. Photo Credit: Réunion des Musées Nationaux/Art Resource, NY.

Page 16: Templar Seal Reverse. Photo by Antiqua, Inc. Woodland Hills, CA.

Page 19: Masons at work in the tenth century, from Albert Mackey, *Illustrated History of Freemasonry*.

Page 28: God Creating the World from the Bible, Moralisée, 1120–1230. *120 Great Paintings from Medieval Illuminated Books*, Dover Publications.

Page 30: Tree of Good and Evil, by Berthold Furtmeyer, ca. 1478. *120 Great Paintings from Medieval Illuminated Books*, Dover Publications.

Page 32: *The Creation of Adam*, by Michelangelo in the Sistine Chapel, 1508–1512. *120 Visions of Heaven & Hell*, Dover Publications.

Page 33: Eve tempted by the serpent, by William Blake (1757–1827), late eighteenth century. Location: Victoria and Albert Museum, London, Great Britain. Photo Credit: V&A Images, London/Art Resource, NY.

Page 34: *The Creation of the World and Expulsion from Paradise*, by Giovanni di Paolo, ca. 1445. *120 Visions of Heaven & Hell*, Dover Publications.

Page 35: The body of Abel found by Adam and Eve, ca. 1826, by William Blake (1757–1827). Location: Tate Gallery, London, Great Britain. Photo Credit: Tate, London/Art Resource, NY.

Page 37: Tower of Babel, by the Bedford Master, The Bedford Hours, ca. 1423–1430. *120 Great Paintings from Medieval Illuminated Books*, Dover Publications.

Page 39: Abraham Traveling from Haran to Canaan (1850), by Molnár, József (1821–1899). Scanned and uploaded to Wiki Creative Commons by Csanády. http://en.wikipedia.org.

Page 40: *Hagar and Ishmael in the Wilderness*, by Giovanni Baptista Tiepolo, ca. 1732. *120 Great Paintings*, Dover Publications.

Page 44: Altar, Beer-sheba, Israelite period. Photo copyright © The Israel Museum, Jerusalem, reproduced by permission.

Page 45: *Jacob's Ladder*, by William Blake, 1800. *120 Visions of Heaven & Hell*, Dover Publications.

Page 49: Burial scenes from *The Egyptian Book of the Dead, The Book of Going Forth by Day*, details from plates 5 and 6. Copyright © James Wasserman 1994, 1998, Chronicle Books.

Page 50: Moses, by Michelangelo (1475–1564), the San Pietro in Vincoli Church in Rome (1513–1515). Photo by Jean-Christophe Benoist. http://en.wikipedia.org.

Page 52: The Pharoah's Daughter finding the Infant Moses in the Nile River, ca. 239 CE. Location: Synagogue, Dura Europos, Syria. Photo Credit : Art Resource, NY.

Page 59: Osiris and Isis from *The Egyptian Book of the Dead, The Book of Going Forth by Day*, detail from plate 19. Copyright © James Wasserman 1994, 1998, Chronicle Books.

Page 61: *Crossing of the Red Sea*, by Belbello da Pavia (ca. 1430–1473). Location: Biblioteca Nazionale, Florence, Italy. Photo Credit: Scala/Art Resource, NY.

Page 91: *The Brazen Serpent*, ca. 1896–1902, by Tissot, James Jacques Joseph (1836–1902). Photo: John Parnell. Location: The Jewish Museum, New York, NY, U.S.A. Photo Credit: The Jewish Museum, NY/Art Resource, NY.

Page 95: Dividing up the Promised Land, by Licherie de Beurie, Louis (1629–1687). Photo: René-Gabriel Ojéda. Location: Musee Magnin, Dijon, France. Photo Credit: Réunion des Musées Nationaux/Art Resource, NY.

Page 103: Moses in the Book of Deuteronomy from the Bible of San Paolo, ca. 870–875. *120 Great Paintings from Medieval Illuminated Books*, Dover Publications.

Pages 110–11: Joshua's Victory over the Amorites, 1624; by Poussin, Nicolas (1594–1665). Location: Pushkin Museum of Fine Arts, Moscow, Russia. Photo Credit: Erich Lessing/Art Resource, NY.

Page 115: Mosaic of Yael at the Dormition Church on Mount Zion in Jerusalem, by Radbod Commandeur (1890–1955). Photo by Deror avi. http://commons.wikimedia.org.

Page 119: *The Sorrow of Jepthah*, by Giovanni Antonio Pellegrini, ca 1700–1725. http://en.wikipedia.org. Current location: Sammlung Denis Mah-on. Source/Photographer: The Yorck Project.

Page 122–23: Samson and Delilah (1628–1630), by Anthony van Dyck (1599–1641). http://commons.wikimedia.org. Current location: Kunsthistorisches Museum. Source/Photographer: The Yorck Project.

Page 128: Naomi entreating Ruth and Orpah to return to the Land of Moab, 1795, by William Blake (1757–1827). Location: Victoria and Albert Museum, London, Great Britain. Photo Credit: V&A Images, London/Art Resource, NY.

Page 136: Samuel anointing Saul, from John Clark Ridpath, *History of the World*.

Page 141: "How all mortal sins deserve death": David killing Goliath. From "Le Livre de bonnes moeurs," by Jacques Legrand, ca. 1490. Photo: René-Gabriel Ojéda. Location: Musée Condé, Chantilly, France. Photo Credit: Réunion des Musées Nationaux/Art Resource, NY.

Page 142: David plays the harp as Saul raises his javelin, by Heinrich Suso, ca. 1455–1460. *120 Great Paintings from Medieval Illuminated Books*, Dover Publications.

Page 142: David claiming the hand of Michal from Saul, ca. 1250. *120 Great Paintings from Medieval Illuminated Books*, Dover Publications.

Page 147: David at war against the Philistines, ca. 1250. *120 Great Paintings from Medieval Illuminated Books*, Dover Publications.

Page 151: The Israelites carrying the Ark to Jerusalem, from Albert Mackey, *Illustrated History of Freemasonry*.

Page 152–53: An aerial view from the south of the Temple Mount (July 1997). Albatross Aerial Photography, Israel.

Page 157: Bathsheba at her Bath (1859), by Francesco Hayez (1791–1882). http://commons.wikimedia.org. Source/Photographer: The Yorck Project.

Page 169: *The Judgment of Solomon,* by Raphael (Raffaello Sanzio) (1483–1520). Location: Logge, Vatican Palace, Vatican State. Photo Credit: Scala/Art Resource, NY.

Page 170: The Plans for the Temple, by Allyn Cox. Copyright the George Washington Masonic National Memorial Association. All rights reserved. Photography by Arthur W. Pierson, Falls, Church Virginia.

Page 173: The Holy of Holies. Copyright the George Washington Masonic National Memorial Association. All rights reserved. Photography by Arthur W. Pierson, Falls, Church Virginia.

Page 175: Hiram at Prayer, by Allyn Cox. Copyright the George Washington Masonic National Memorial Association. All rights reserved. Photography by Arthur W. Pierson, Falls, Church Virginia.

Page 181: *The Queen of Sheba,* by Nancy Wasserman, photo by Illia Tulloch.

Page 195: The God Baal of the thunderstorm. 2nd–1st millennia BCE. Location: Louvre, Paris, France. Photo Credit: Erich Lessing/Art Resource, NY.

Page 207: Medallion with Jehu destroying the god Baal, by Michelangelo Buonarroti (1475–1564). Location: Sistine Chapel, Vatican Palace, Vatican State. Photo Credit: Scala/Art Resource, NY.

Page 215: Shalmaneser V on his throne, from John Clark Ridpath, *History of the World.*

Page 218: King Hezekiah on a 17th-century painting by unknown artist in the choir of Sankta Maria kyrka. Photo by David Castor. http://en.wikipedia.org.

Page 219: The Temple of Solomon on Mount Moriah, from John Clark Ridpath, *History of the World.*

Page 224: Assyrian cherub, from Albert Mackey, *The History of Freemasonry.*

Page 225: Sacrifice to Moloch, from Frank Stockton Dobbins, *Error's Chains: How Forged and Broken.*

Page 229: The Ark of the Covenant. Copyright the George Washington Masonic National Memorial Association. All rights reserved. Photography by Arthur W. Pierson, Falls, Church Virginia.

Page 230: The Babylonian Captivity, from John Clark Ridpath, *History of the World.*

Page 233: View of Jerusalem, from John Clark Ridpath, *History of the World.*

Page 240: King Cyrus II on campaign, from John Clark Ridpath, *History of the World.*

Page 255: Model of the Second Temple, from Albert Mackey, *Illustrated History of Freemasonry.*

Page 265: Heliodorus being driven out of the temple, by Raphael (Raffaello Sanzio) (1483–1520). Location: Stanze di Raffaello, Vatican Palace, Vatican State. Photo Credit: Scala/Art Resource, NY.

Page 277: Photo of the model of Herod's Temple on the Temple Mount in Jerusalem in 66 CE. Copyright © Israel Museum. Reproduced by permission.

Page 279: Photo of the model of Jerusalem in 66 CE. Copyright © Israel Museum. Reproduced by permission.

Page 282: The Virgin and Child with Saint Elizabeth and John the Baptist, by Bachiacca, ca. 1545. *120 Italian Renaissance Paintings,* Dover Publications.

Page 284: *The Annunciation,* by Lorenzo di Credi (detail), ca. 1480–1485. *120 Great Paintings,* Dover Publications.

Page 286: The flight of the Holy Family, from the De Lisle Psalter, 1308–1310. *120 Great Paintings from Medieval Illuminated Books,* Dover Publications.

Page 287: The presentation of the baby Jesus at the Temple, from the De Lisle Psalter, 1308–1310. *120 Great Paintings from Medieval Illuminated Books,* Dover Publications.

Page 297: *Madonna of the Sacred Coat,* by C. B. Chambers, ca. 1890.

Pages 304–5: *The Last Supper,* by Leonardo da Vinci, 1495–1498. Photo by Rusfuture. http://en.wikipedia.org.

Page 306: *The Agony in the Garden,* by Andrea Mantegna, ca. 1460. *120 Italian Renaissance Paintings,* Dover Publications.

Page 308: The Lamentation of Christ, by Giotto, ca 1305. *120 Great Paintings,* Dover Publications.

Page 313: Saint John on the island of Patmos, by the Limbourg Brothers, ca. 1416. *120 Visions of Heaven & Hell,* Dover Publications.

Page 316: Freemason's apron, silk, gold embroidery. 18th CE. Location: Private Collection, Vienna, Austria. Photo Credit: Erich Lessing/Art Resource, NY.

Page 318: Templar Seal Obverse. Photo by Antiqua, Inc. Woodland Hills, CA.

Page 323: Templar Uniform, by Richard Scollins. The Knights of Christ, Terence Wise and Richard Scollins, Men at Arms Series #155, Osprey Military.

Page 335: Construction of the temple of Jerusalem under the order of Solomon. Jean Fouquet (ca.1415/20–1481). Location: Bibliotheque Nationale, Paris, France. Photo Credit: Bridgeman-Giraudon/Art Resource, NY.

Page 336: *Moses and the Burning Bush,* William Blake (1757–1827), early 19th century. Location: Victoria and Albert Museum, London, Great Britain. Photo Credit: Victoria & Albert Museum, London/Art Resource, NY.

Page 346: Roman Triumphal arch panel showing spoils of Jerusalem temple. http://commons.wikimedia.org. Source: Hebrew Wikipedia. Photo by בית השלום. User: Yonidebest.

Page 348: The Dream of Constantine, from Albert Mackey, *Illustrated History of Freemasonry.*

Page 350: The Night Journey of Muhammad on the winged steed al-Buraq, unknown artist, 15th century. *120 Visions of Heaven & Hell, Dover Publications.*

Page 353: Crusaders preparing to depart for the Holy Land, from Paul Lacroix, *Military and Religious Life in the Middle Ages and the Period of the Renaissance.*

Pages 371–74: The four maps of the Ancient Near East and Israel are copyright © XNR Productions. Reproduced (with modifications by the author) by permission.

INDEX

At Mount Sinai, November 2009

JAMES WASSERMAN is a student of religion and spiritual development. A book designer and producer by trade, he founded Studio 31 in 1977. He is a passionate advocate of individual liberty and an admirer of the teachings of Aleister Crowley. He has played a key role in numerous seminal publications of the Crowley corpus and been an active member of Ordo Templi Orientis since 1976.

His writings and editorial efforts focus on spirituality, creative mythology, secret societies, history, religion, and politics. They include the following:

Aleister Crowley and the Practice of the Magical Diary
The Egyptian Book of the Dead: The Book of Going Forth by Day
An Illustrated History of the Knights Templar
The Mystery Traditions: Secret Symbols & Sacred Art
Pythagoras: His Life and Teachings (by Thomas Stanley, with Manly P. Hall, and J. Daniel Gunther)
The Secrets of Masonic Washington: A Guidebook to Signs, Symbols, and Ceremonies at the Origin of America's Capital
Secret Societies: Illuminati, Freemasons, and the French Revolution (by Una Birch)
The Slaves Shall Serve: Meditations on Liberty
The Templars and the Assassins: The Militia of Heaven
To Perfect This Feast: A Performance Commentary on the Gnostic Mass (with Nancy Wasserman)
The Weiser Concise Guide Series (as editor)

For more information, please visit
www.jameswassermanbooks.com